井上雄彦

Takehiko Inoue

THE JAPANESE BASKETBALL TEAM DIDN'T
QUALIFY FOR THE '92 BARCELONA OLYMPICS. IT
SEEMS WE'RE STILL LAGGING BEHIND CHINA, THE
ASIAN CHAMPS. WILL JAPANESE BASKETBALL
EVER CATCH UP?!

I'D LOVE IT IF JAPAN COULD ONE DAY DEFEAT
OUR RIVALS—CHINA AND KOREA—TO REPRESENT
ASIA AT THE OLYMPICS! GO TEAM JAPAN!!

Takehiko Inoue's *Slam Dunk* is one of the most
popular manga of all time, having sold over 100
million copies worldwide. He followed that series
up with two titles lauded by critics and fans
alike—*Vagabond*, a fictional account of the life
of Miyamoto Musashi, and *Real*, a manga about
wheelchair basketball.

SLAM DUNK
Vol. 5: Rebound

SHONEN JUMP Manga Edition

STORY AND ART BY TAKEHIKO INOUE

English Adaptation/Kelly Sue DeConnick
Translation/Joe Yamazaki
Touch-up Art & Lettering/James Gaubatz
Cover & Graphic Design/Sean Lee
Editor/Kit Fox

© 1990 - 2009 Takehiko Inoue and I.T. Planning, Inc.
Originally published in Japan in 1991 by Shueisha
Inc., Tokyo. English translation rights
arranged with I.T. Planning, Inc. All rights reserved.

The SLAM DUNK U.S. trademark is used with
permission from NBA Properties, Inc.

Some scenes have been modified from the original
Japanese edition.

The stories, characters and incidents mentioned in
this publication are entirely fictional.

Printed in the U.S.A.

Published by VIZ Media, LLC
P.O. Box 77010
San Francisco, CA 94107

10 9 8 7 6 5 4 3
First printing, August 2009
Third printing, June 2017

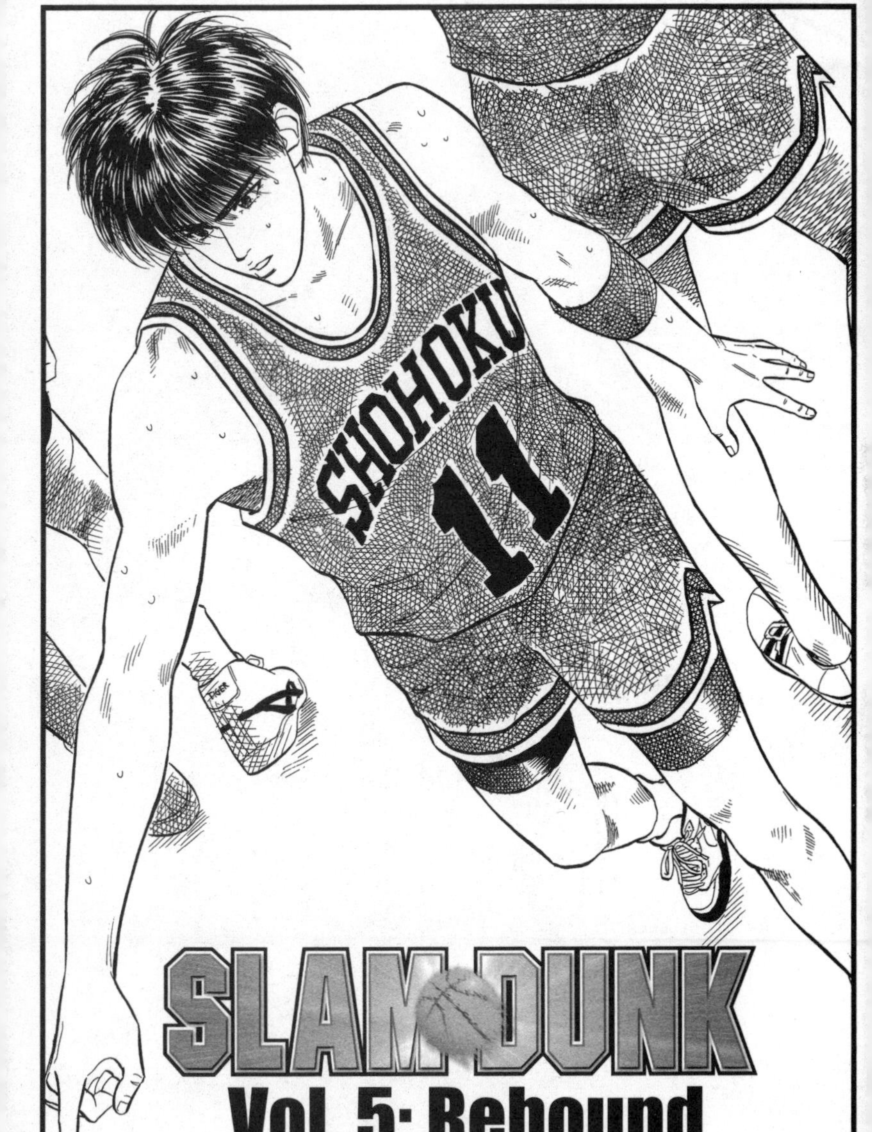
SHOHOKU
11

SLAM DUNK

Vol. 5: Rebound

STORY AND ART BY

TAKEHIKO INOUE

Character Introduction

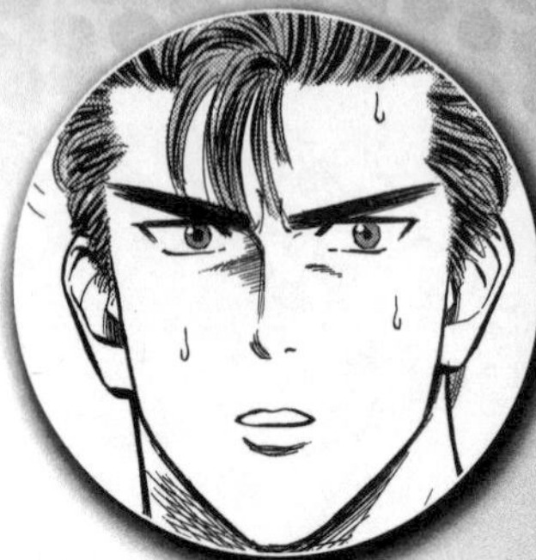

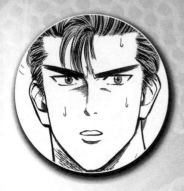

Hanamichi Sakuragi
A first-year at Shohoku High School, Sakuragi is in love with Haruko Akagi.

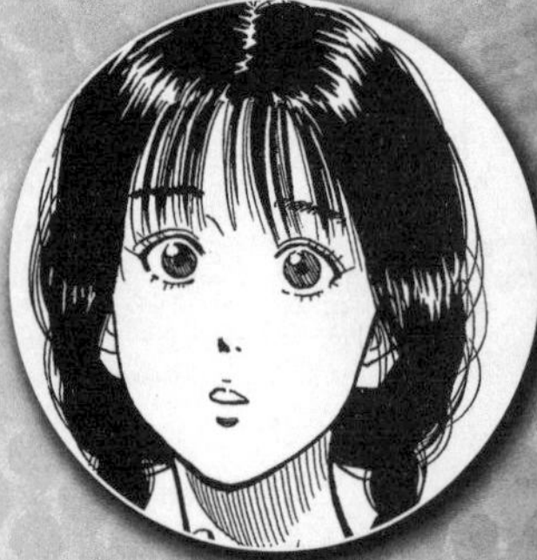

Haruko Akagi
Also a first-year at Shohoku, Takenori Akagi's little sister has a crush on Kaede Rukawa.

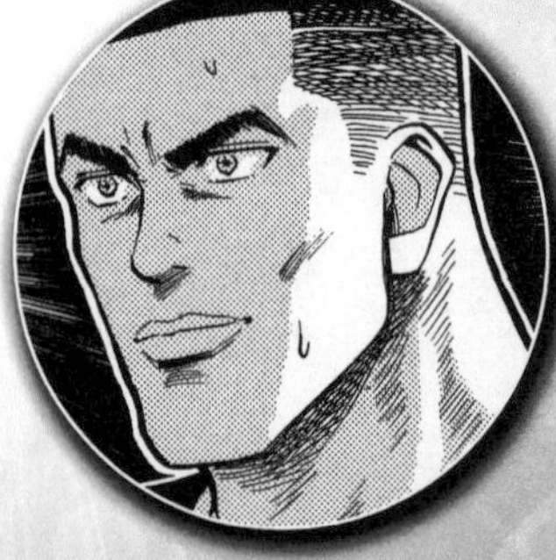

Takenori Akagi
A third-year and the basketball team's captain, Akagi has an intense passion for his sport.

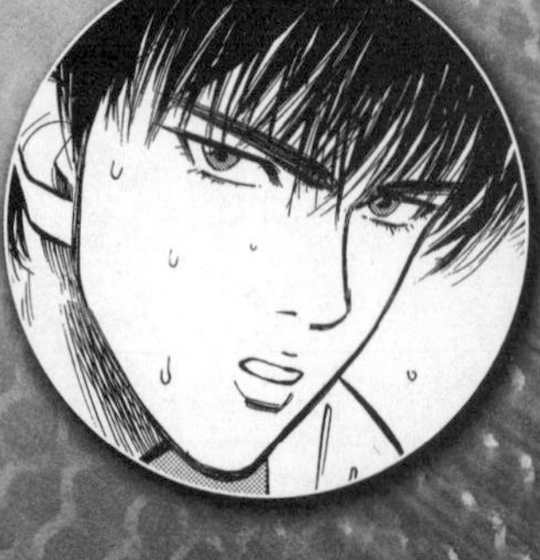

Kaede Rukawa
The object of Haruko's affection (and that of many of Shohoku's female students!), this first-year has been a star player since junior high.

Sakuragi's Friends
Ohkusu Mito Takamiya Noma

BRING IT ON.

Ayako
Basketball Team Manager

Our Story Thus Far

Hanamichi Sakuragi is rejected by close to 50 girls during his three years in junior high. He finally becomes a high school student, but the 50th girl he asks out tells him that her heart belongs to Oda from the basketball team. Hanamichi is still trying to overcome the shock when he meets Haruko Akagi. Haruko approaches him in the hallway and asks, "By any chance, do you like basketball?"

In the exhibition game against rival Ryonan, Sakuragi is not in the starting lineup. Shohoku struggles to score against Ryonan's captain, Uozumi, and their phenom, Sendoh. When Akagi is injured, Sakuragi gets his chance to play. He's nervous at first, but a kick from Rukawa shifts him into gear, and now he's ready to take on Uozumi and Sendoh…

Vol. 5: Rebound

Table of Contents

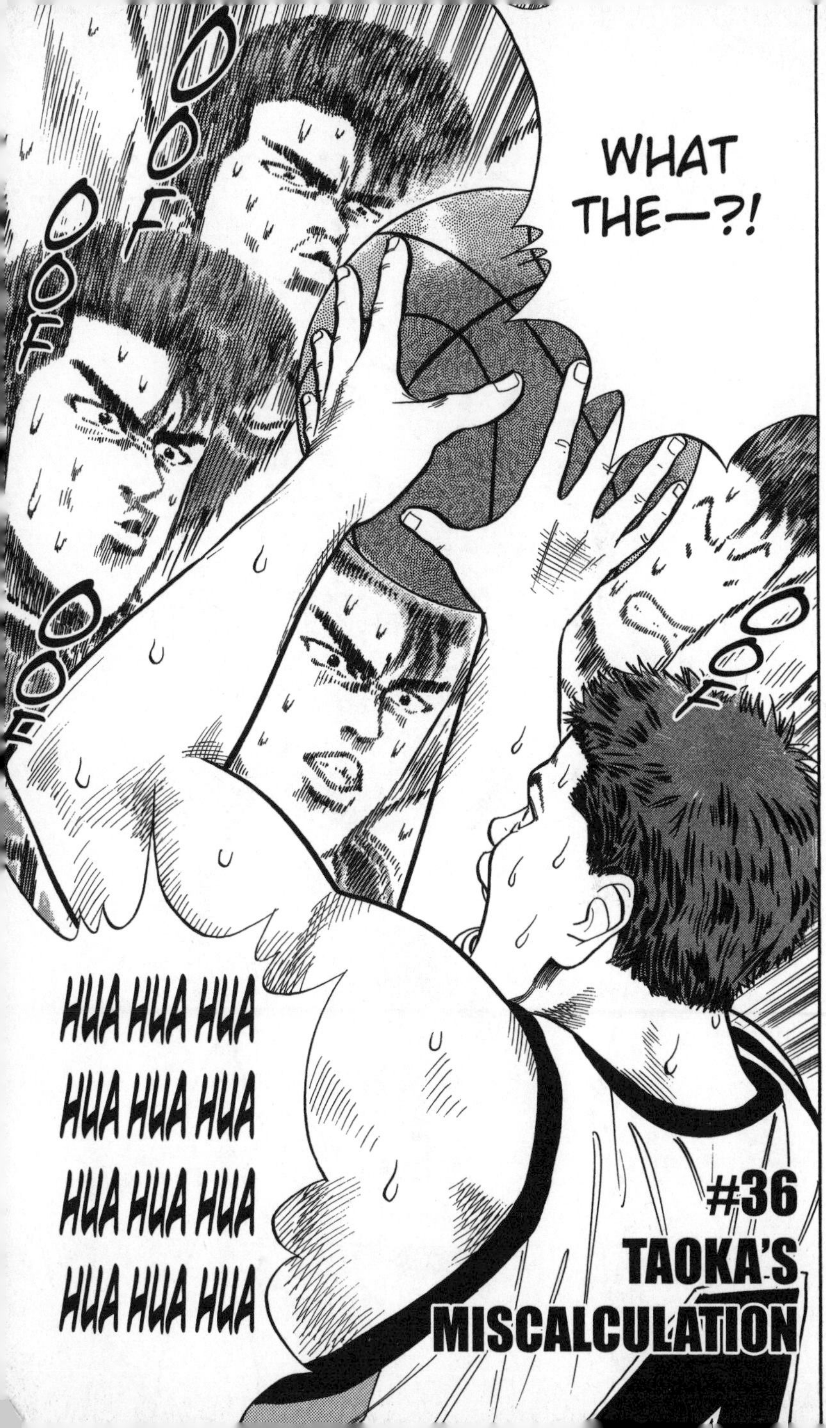
WHAT THE—?!
OOOF
OOOF
OOOF
OOOF
HUA HUA HUA
HUA HUA HUA
HUA HUA HUA
HUA HUA HUA
#36
TAOKA'S
MISCALCULATION

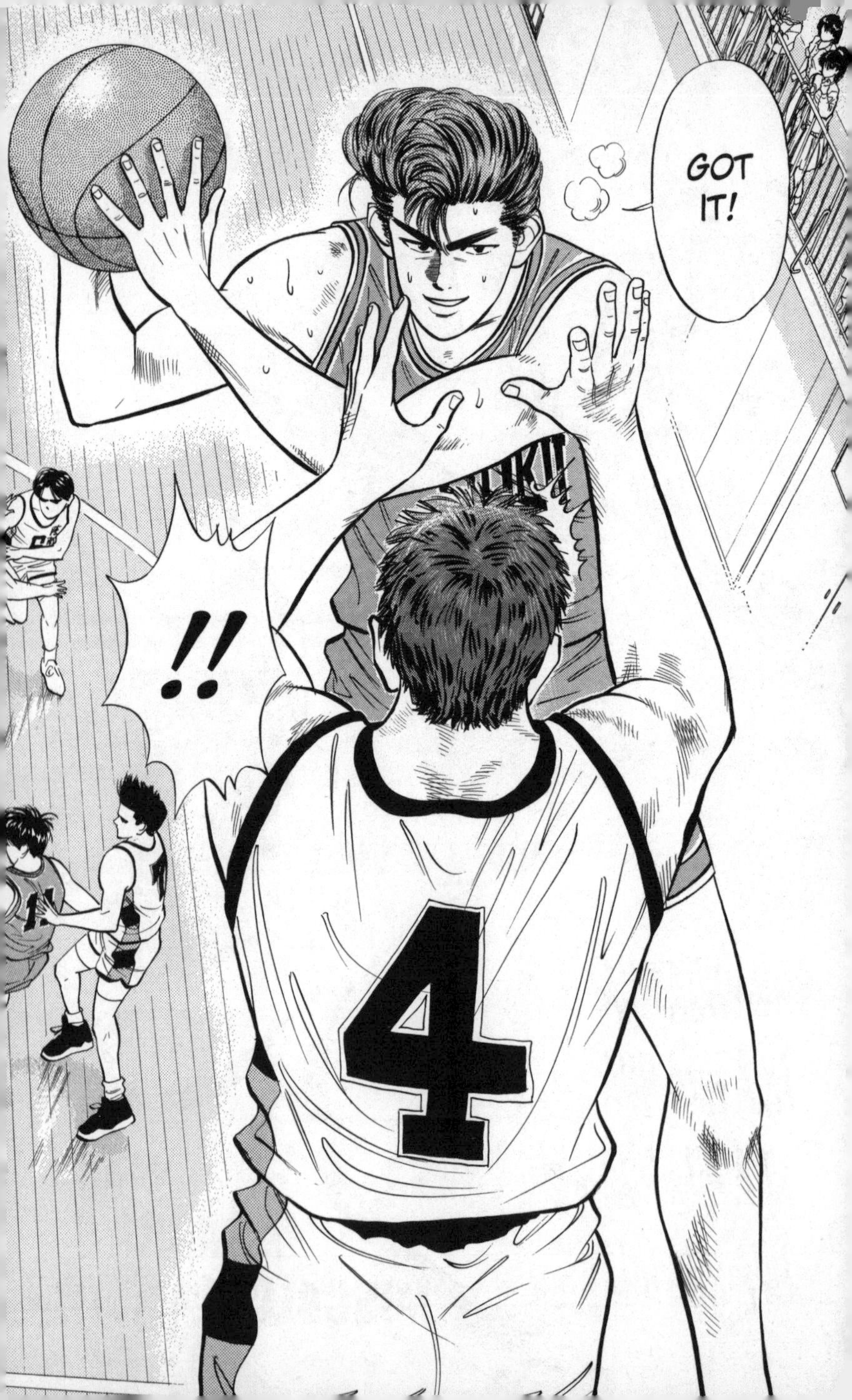
GOT IT!
!!

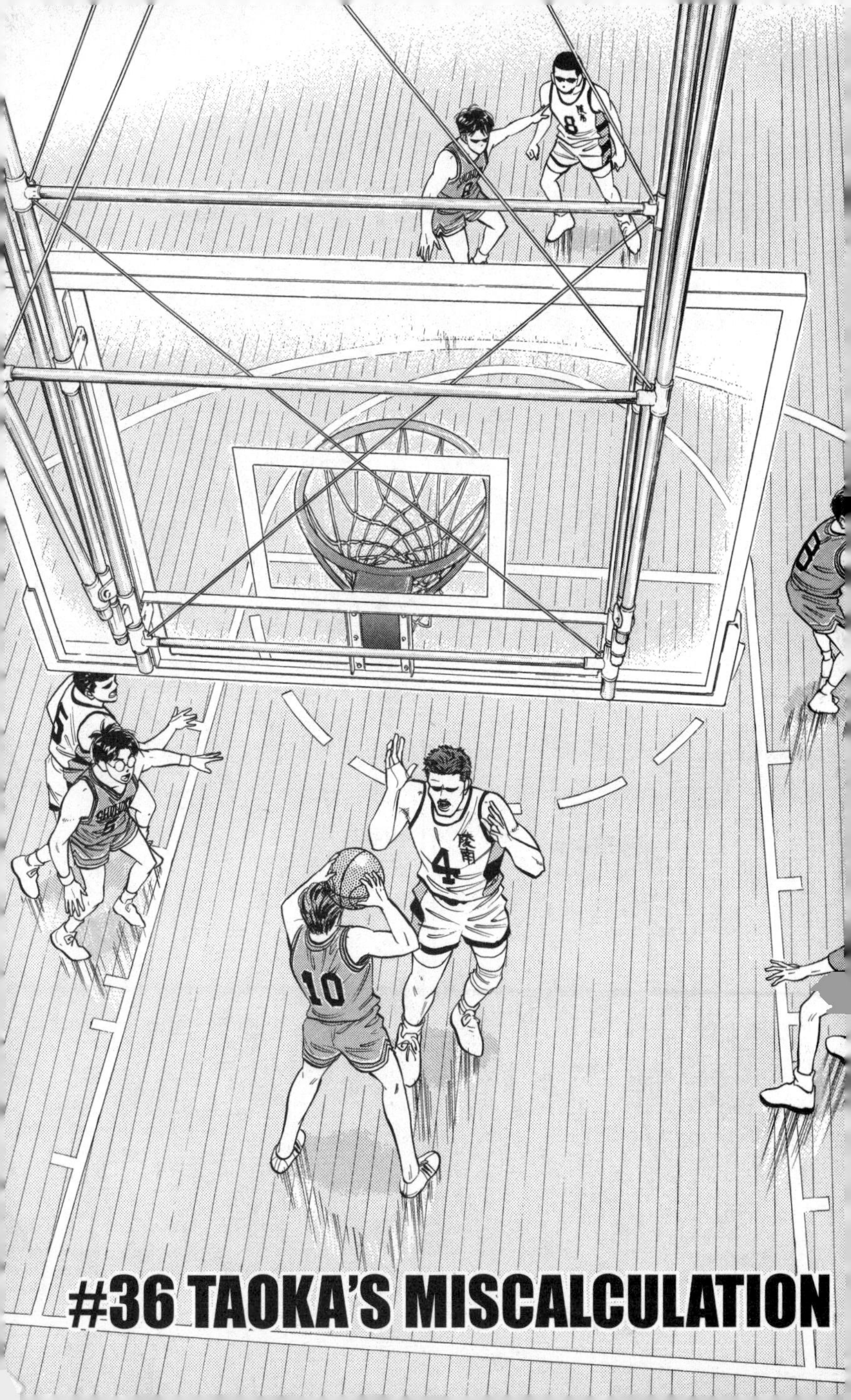

#36 TAOKA'S MISCALCULATION

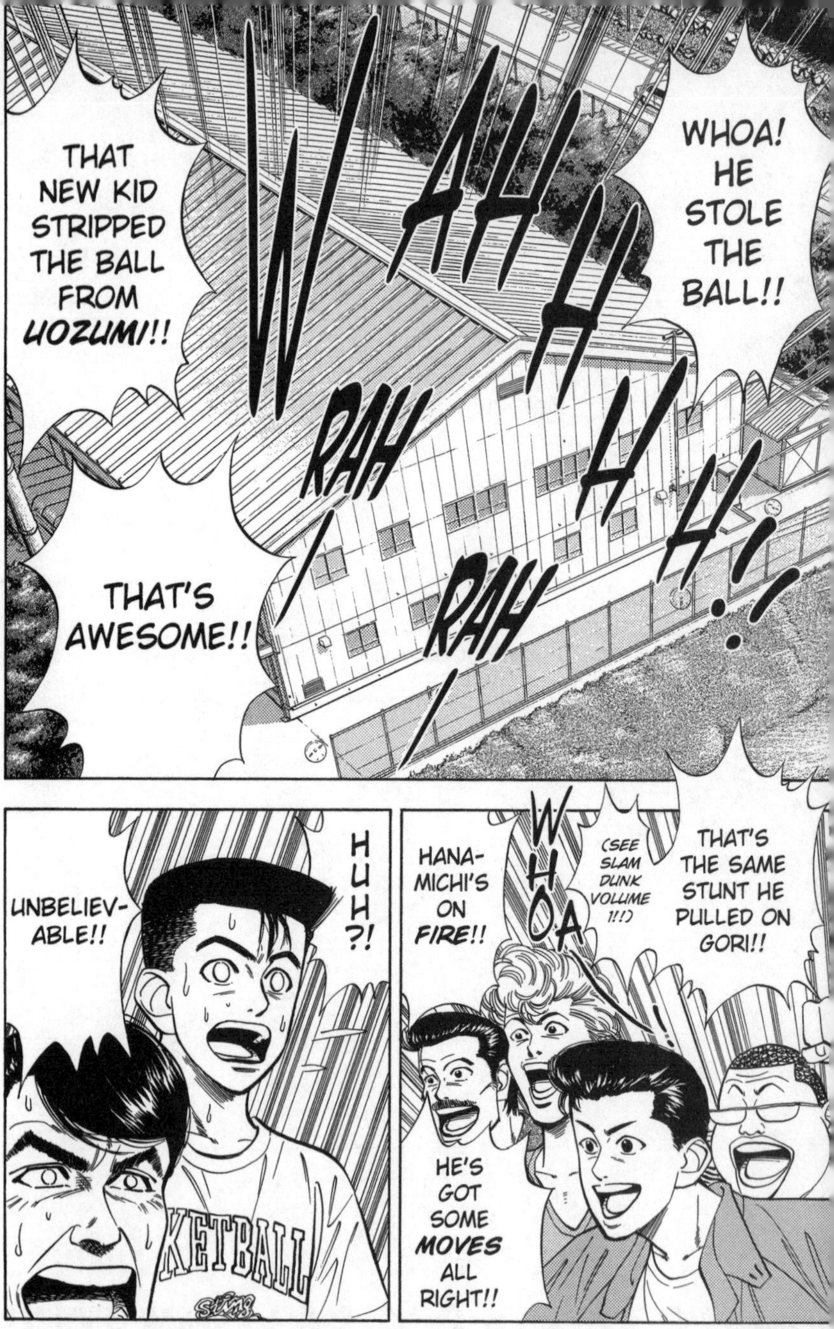
WHOA! HE STOLE THE BALL!!
WAHHHHH!!
RAH RAH
RAH RAH
THAT NEW KID STRIPPED THE BALL FROM UOZUMI!!
THAT'S AWESOME!!
THAT'S THE SAME STUNT HE PULLED ON GORI!!
(SEE SLAM DUNK VOLUME 1!!)
WHOA...!!
HANA-MICHI'S ON FIRE!!
HE'S GOT SOME MOVES ALL RIGHT!!
HUH?!
UNBELIEV-ABLE!!
KETBALL

READ THIS WAY

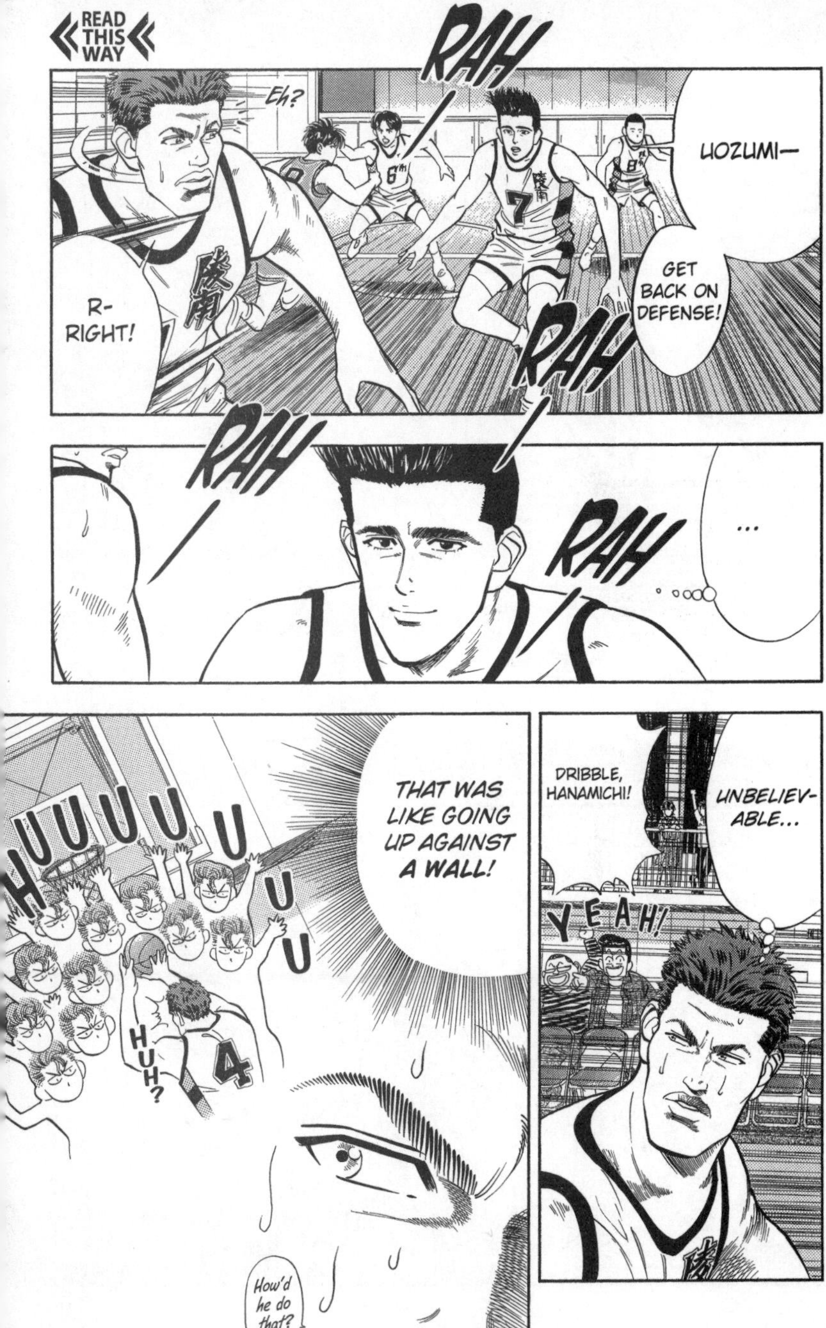
RAH
UOZUMI—
GET BACK ON DEFENSE!
Eh?
RAH
R- RIGHT!
...
RAH
RAH
UNBELIEV-ABLE...
DRIBBLE, HANAMICHI!
YEAH!
THAT WAS LIKE GOING UP AGAINST A WALL!
HUUUUUUUUUU
HUH?
How'd he do that?

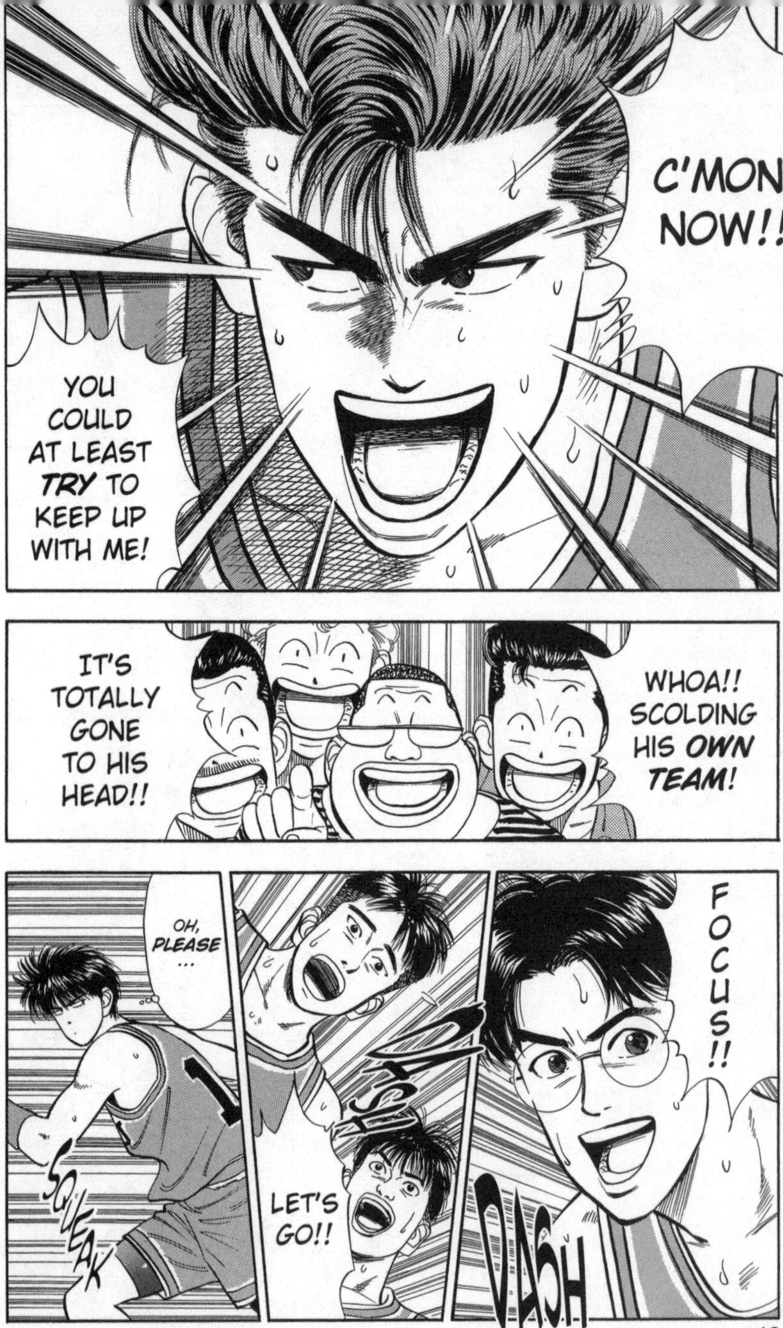
C'MON, NOW!!
YOU COULD AT LEAST TRY TO KEEP UP WITH ME!
WHOA!! SCOLDING HIS OWN TEAM!
IT'S TOTALLY GONE TO HIS HEAD!!
FOCUS!!
DASH
LET'S GO!!
DASH
OH, PLEASE ...
SQUEAK

READ THIS WAY

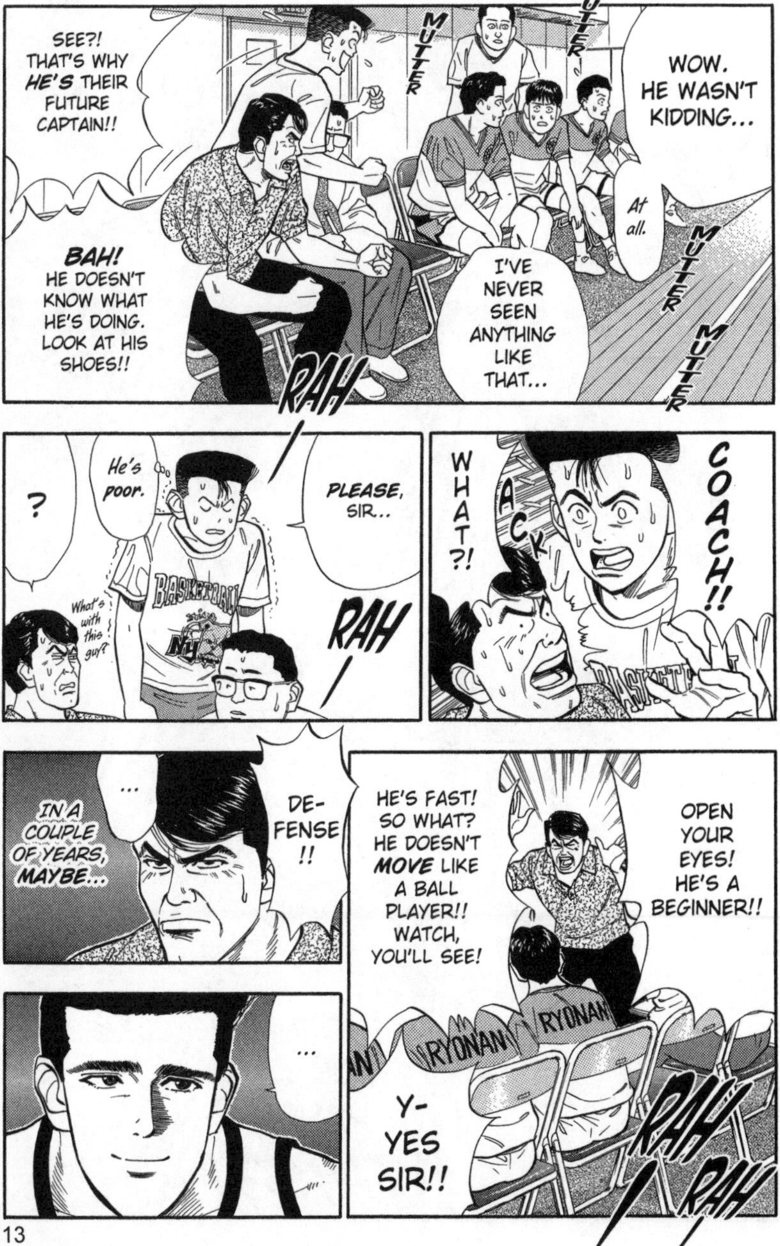
MUTTER
WOW. HE WASN'T KIDDING...
MUTTER
At all.
SEE?! THAT'S WHY *HE'S* THEIR FUTURE CAPTAIN!!
I'VE NEVER SEEN ANYTHING LIKE THAT...
MUTTER
MUTTER
BAH! HE DOESN'T KNOW WHAT HE'S DOING. LOOK AT HIS SHOES!!
RAH
COACH!!
WHAT?!
ACK
PLEASE, SIR...
RAH
He's poor.
?
What's with this guy?
OPEN YOUR EYES! HE'S A BEGINNER!!
HE'S FAST! SO WHAT? HE DOESN'T ***MOVE*** LIKE A BALL PLAYER!! WATCH, YOU'LL SEE!
RYONAN
RYONAN
RAH
RAH
RAH
Y- YES SIR!!
DE- FENSE !!
...
IN A COUPLE OF YEARS, ***MAYBE...***
...

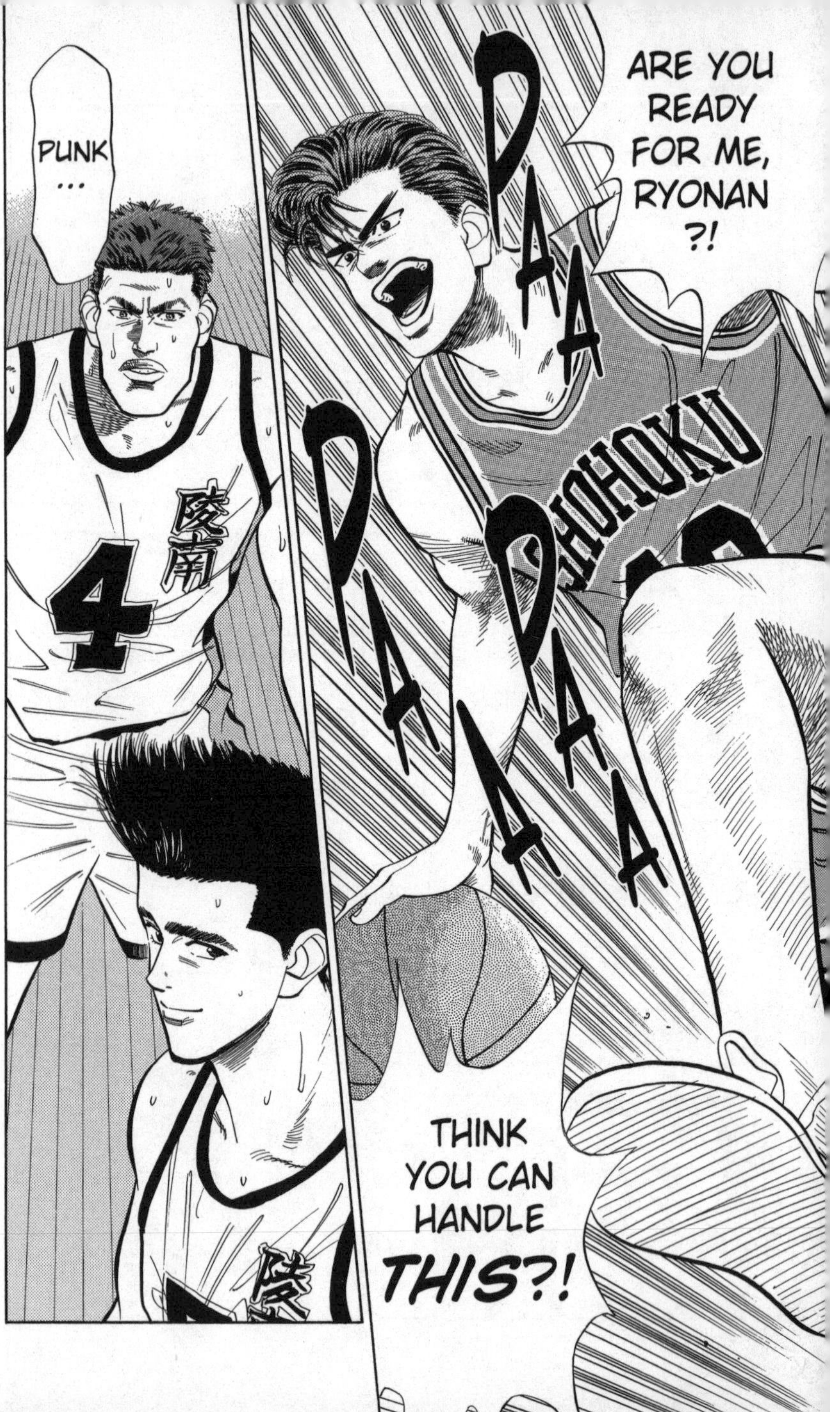
ARE YOU READY FOR ME, RYONAN ?!
PAA
PAA
PAAA
THINK YOU CAN HANDLE THIS?!
PUNK ...

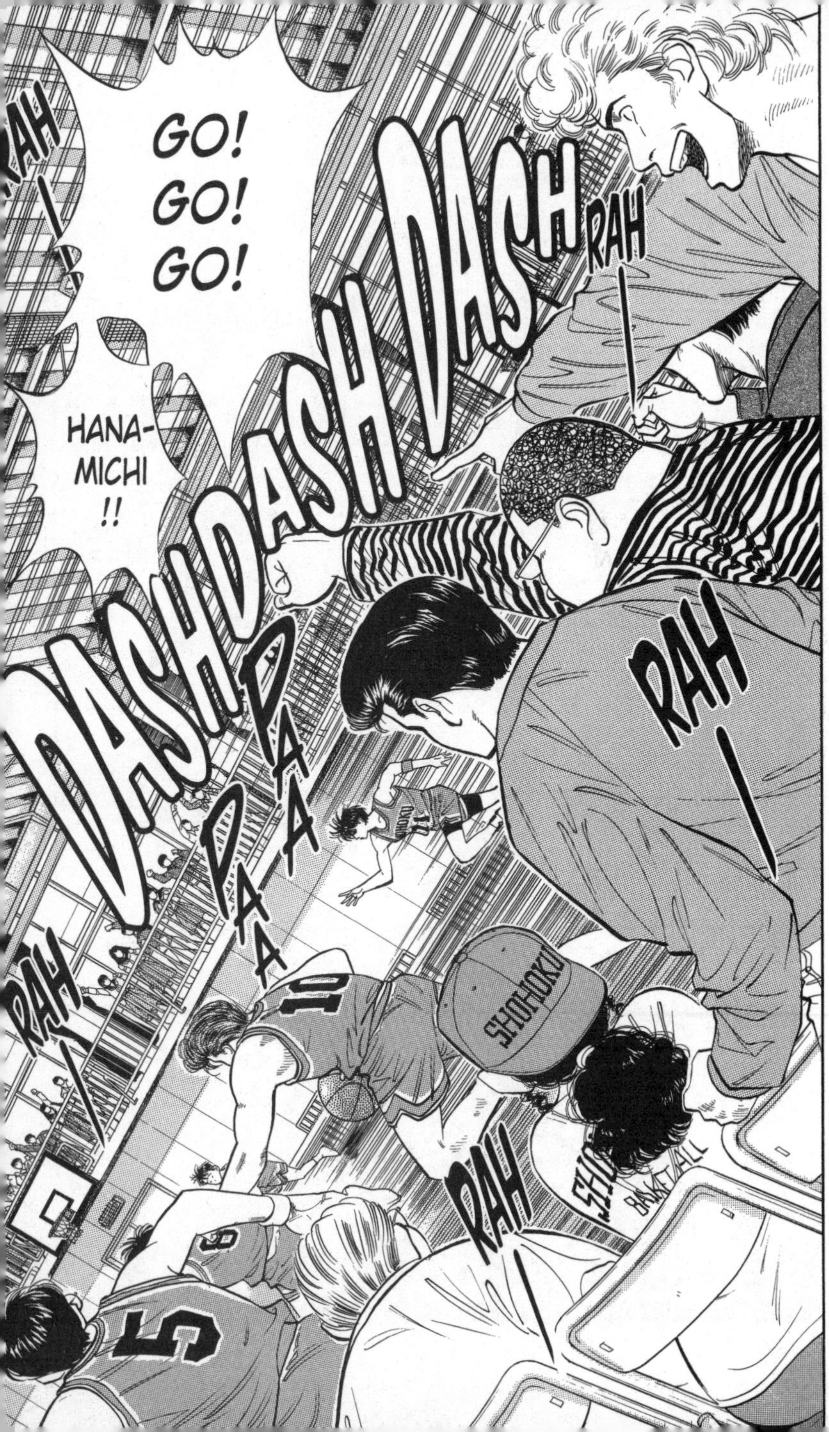
RAH
GO! GO! GO!
RAH
HANA-MICHI !!
DASH DASH DASH
RAH
PA PA PA
RAH
RAH
RAH
SHOHOKU
SHOHOKU

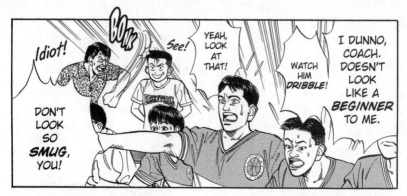

I DUNNO, COACH. DOESN'T LOOK LIKE A BEGINNER TO ME.
WATCH HIM DRIBBLE!
YEAH, LOOK AT THAT!
See!
BONK
Idiot!
DON'T LOOK SO SMUG, YOU!
HM...
Sorry!
ALL THOSE DRILLS I DID WITH HIM ARE PAYING OFF.
HEE HEE HEE!
Yowza!
RYONAN IS GOING ONE-ON-ONE WITH SAKURAGI STARTING AT HALF COURT.
SQUEAK
PAAA
UOZUMI CONTINUES TO DEFEND SAKURAGI, AKAGI'S REPLACEMENT.
PAAA
SQUEAK

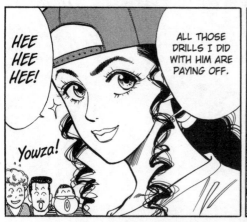

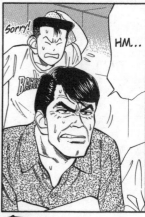

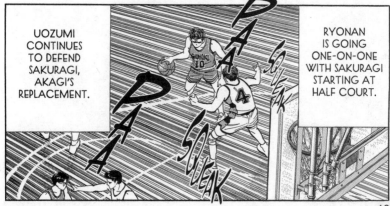

READ THIS WAY

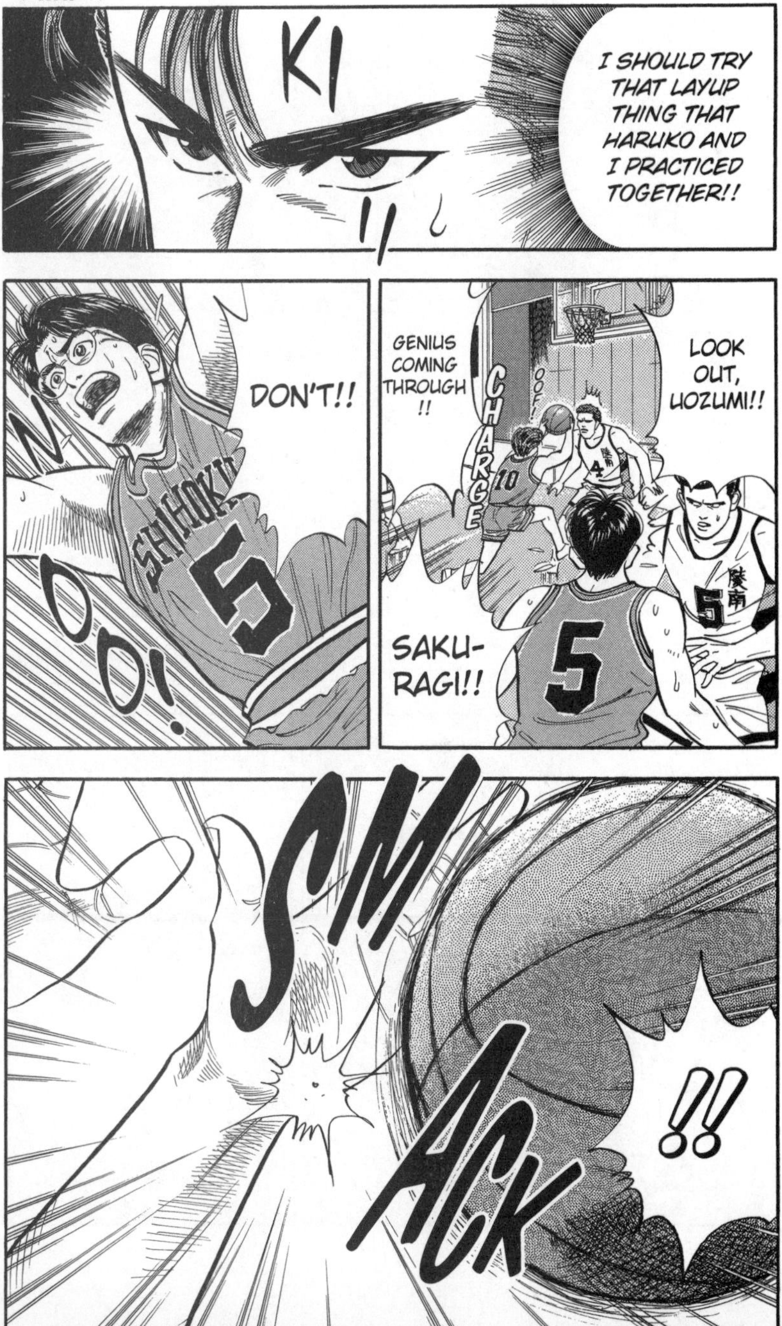

KI
I SHOULD TRY THAT LAYUP THING THAT HARUKO AND I PRACTICED TOGETHER!!
LOOK OUT, UOZUMI!!
GENIUS COMING THROUGH!!
CHARGE
OOF
SAKU-RAGI!!
DON'T!!
NOOO!
SMACK
!!

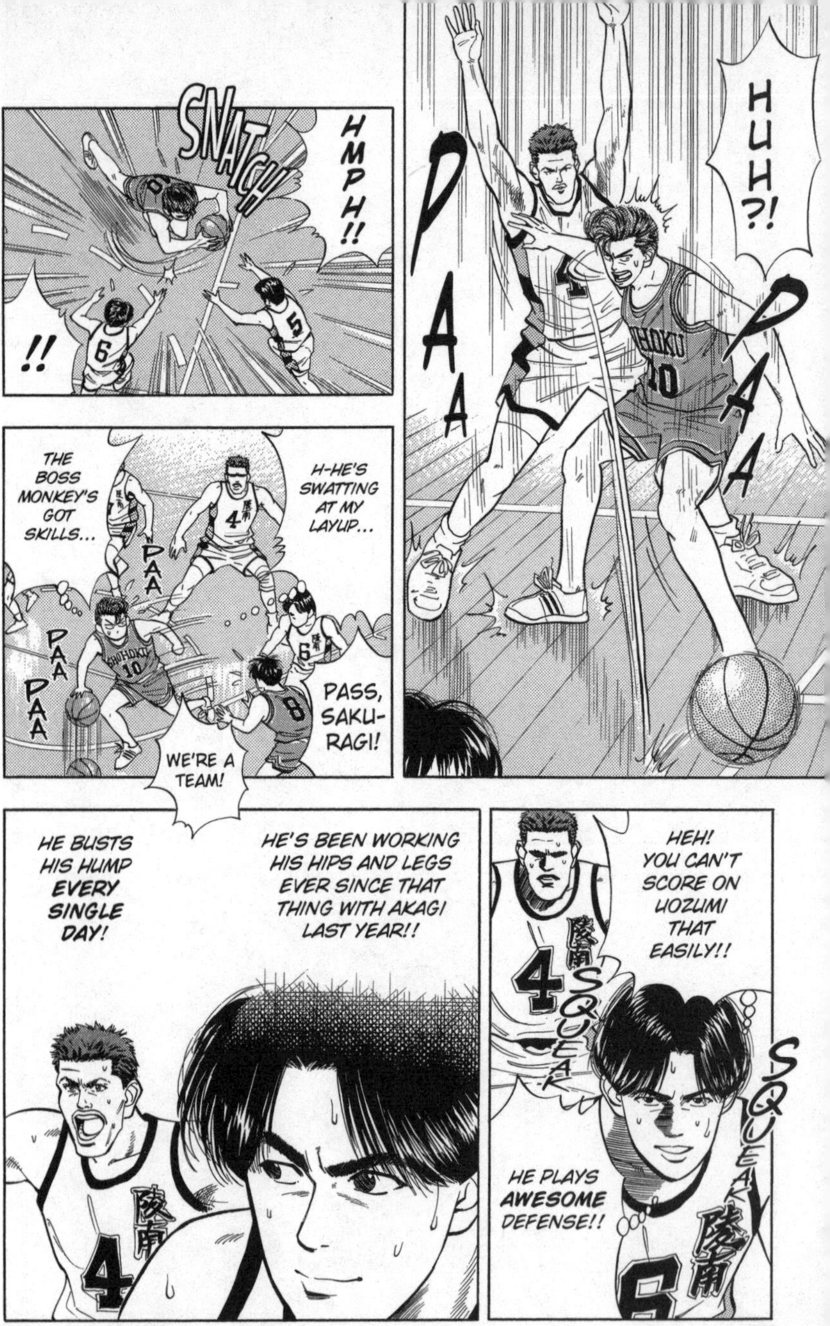
HUH?!
PAA
PAA
HMPH!!
SNATCH
!!
H-HE'S SWATTING AT MY LAYUP...
THE BOSS MONKEY'S GOT SKILLS...
PAA
PASS, SAKURAGI!
WE'RE A TEAM!
PAA PAA
HEH! YOU CAN'T SCORE ON UOZUMI THAT EASILY!!
SQUEAK
SQUEAK
HE PLAYS AWESOME DEFENSE!!
HE'S BEEN WORKING HIS HIPS AND LEGS EVER SINCE THAT THING WITH AKAGI LAST YEAR!!
HE BUSTS HIS HUMP EVERY SINGLE DAY!

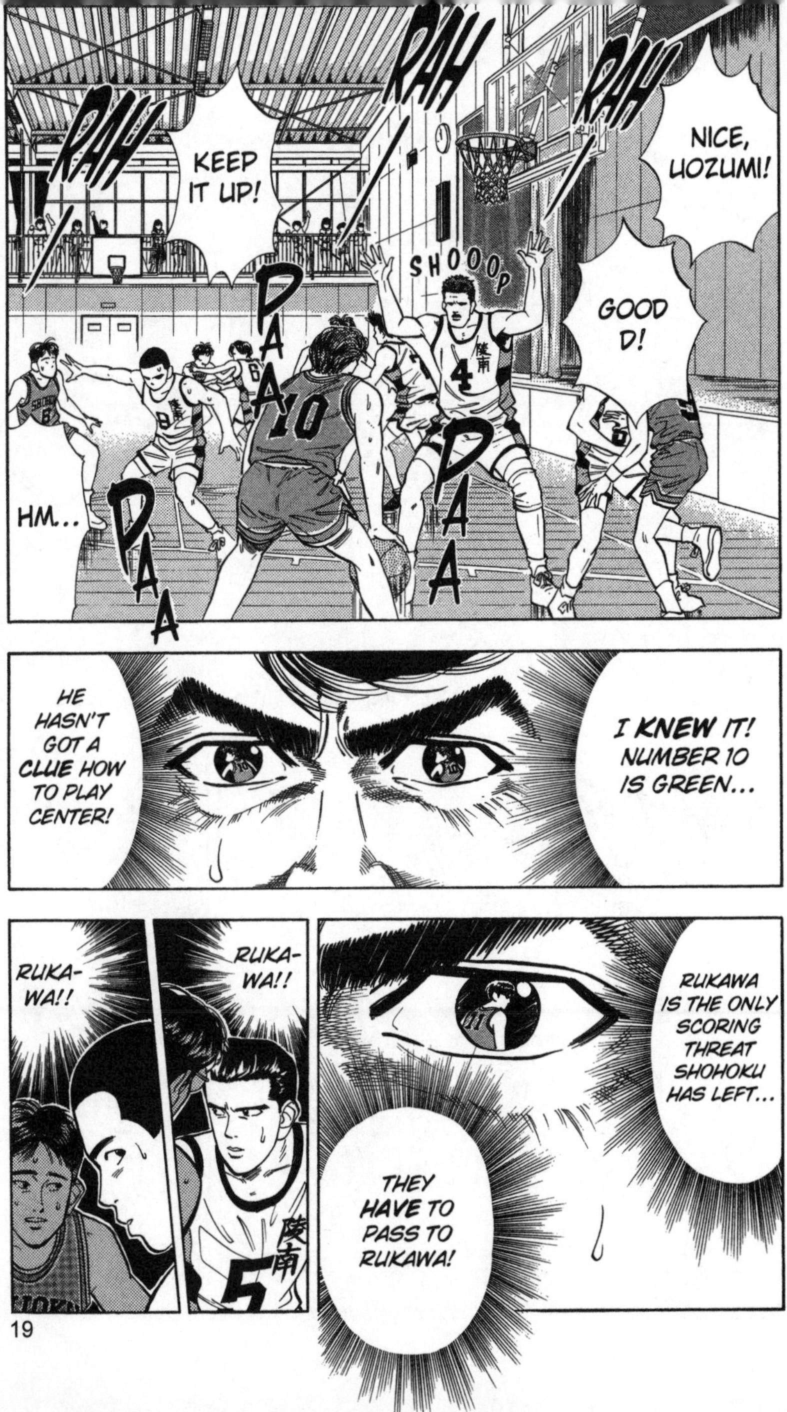
NICE, UOZUMI!
RAH
GOOD D!
RAH
SHOOOP
KEEP IT UP!
RAH
DAA
DAA
PAA
HM...
I KNEW IT! NUMBER 10 IS GREEN...
HE HASN'T GOT A CLUE HOW TO PLAY CENTER!
RUKAWA IS THE ONLY SCORING THREAT SHOHOKU HAS LEFT...
THEY HAVE TO PASS TO RUKAWA!
RUKA-WA!!
RUKA-WA!!

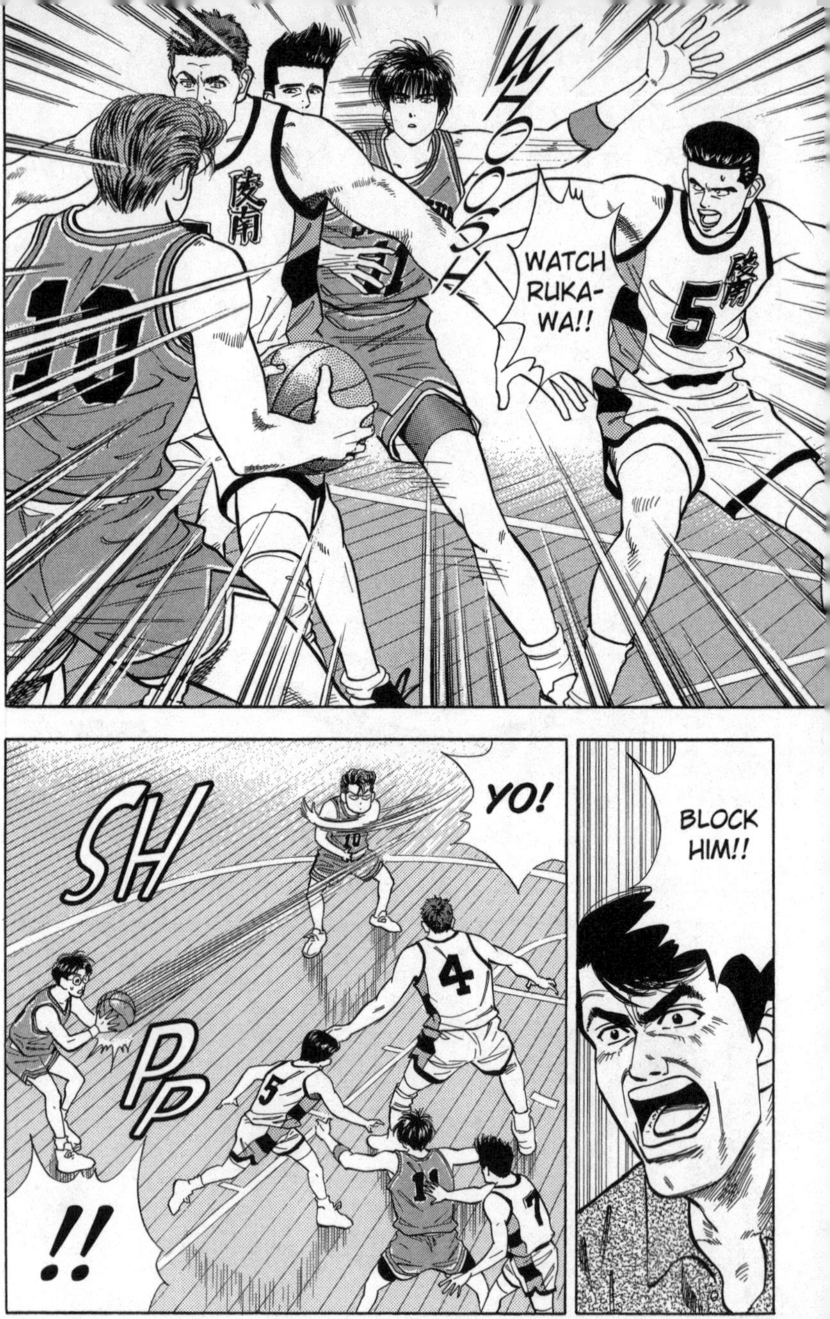
WHOOOSH
WATCH RUKAWA!!
BLOCK HIM!!
YO!
SHPP
!!

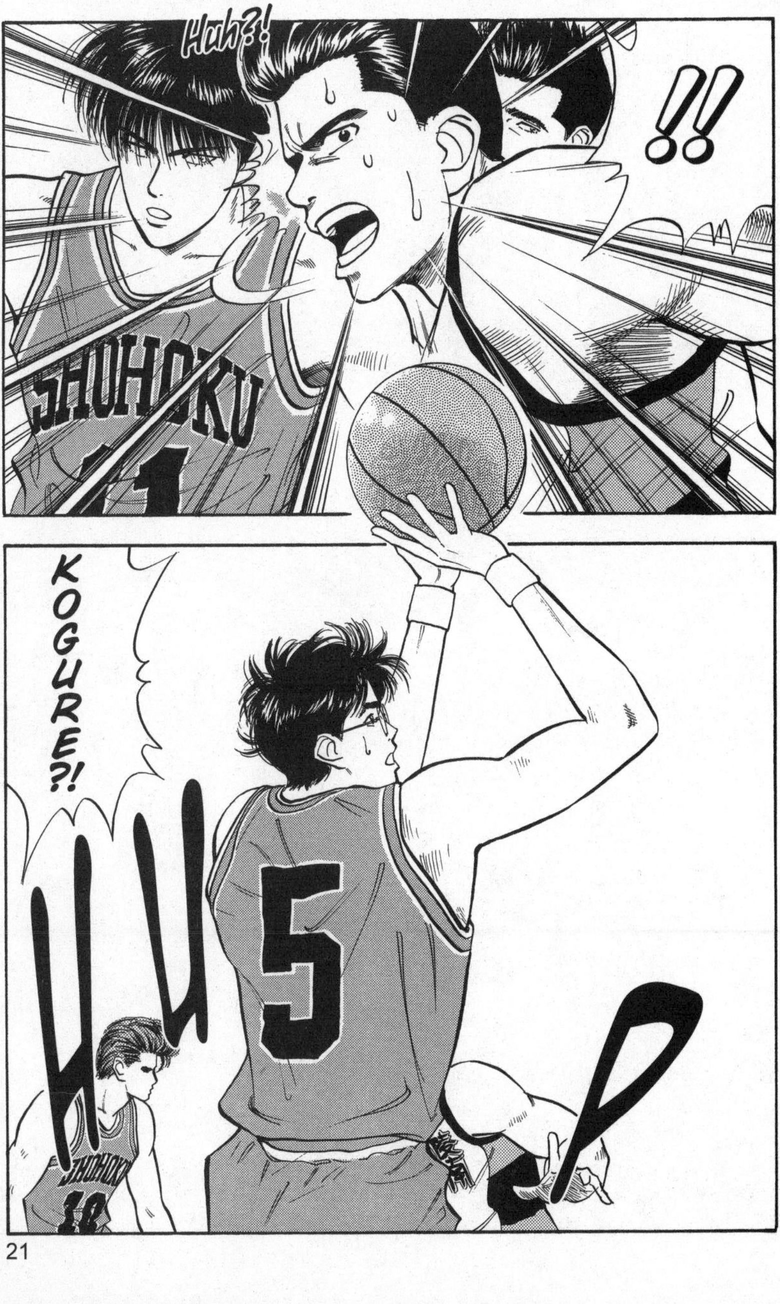
!!
Huh?!
SHOHOKU
KOGURE?!
HUP
SHOHOKU

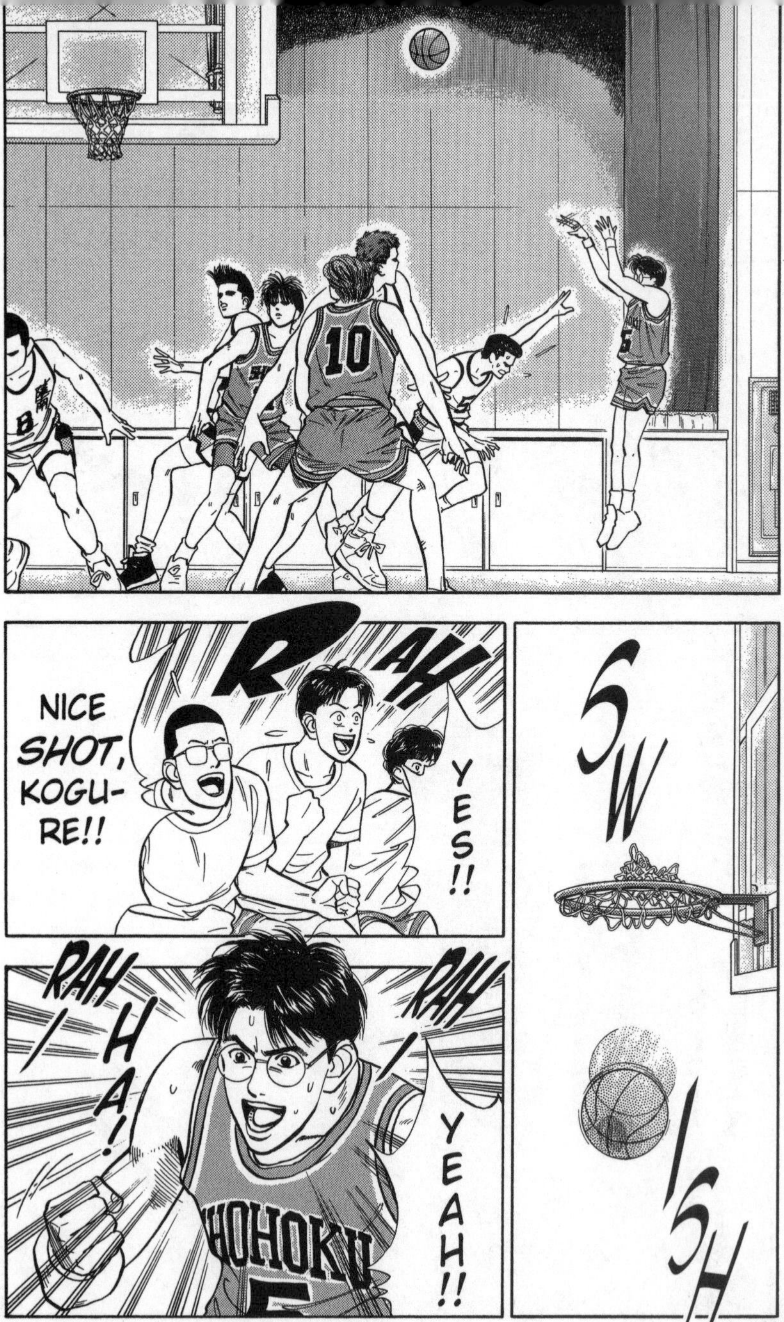
SWISH
RAH
YES!!
NICE SHOT, KOGURE!!
RAH!
YEAH!!
RAH!
HAHA!

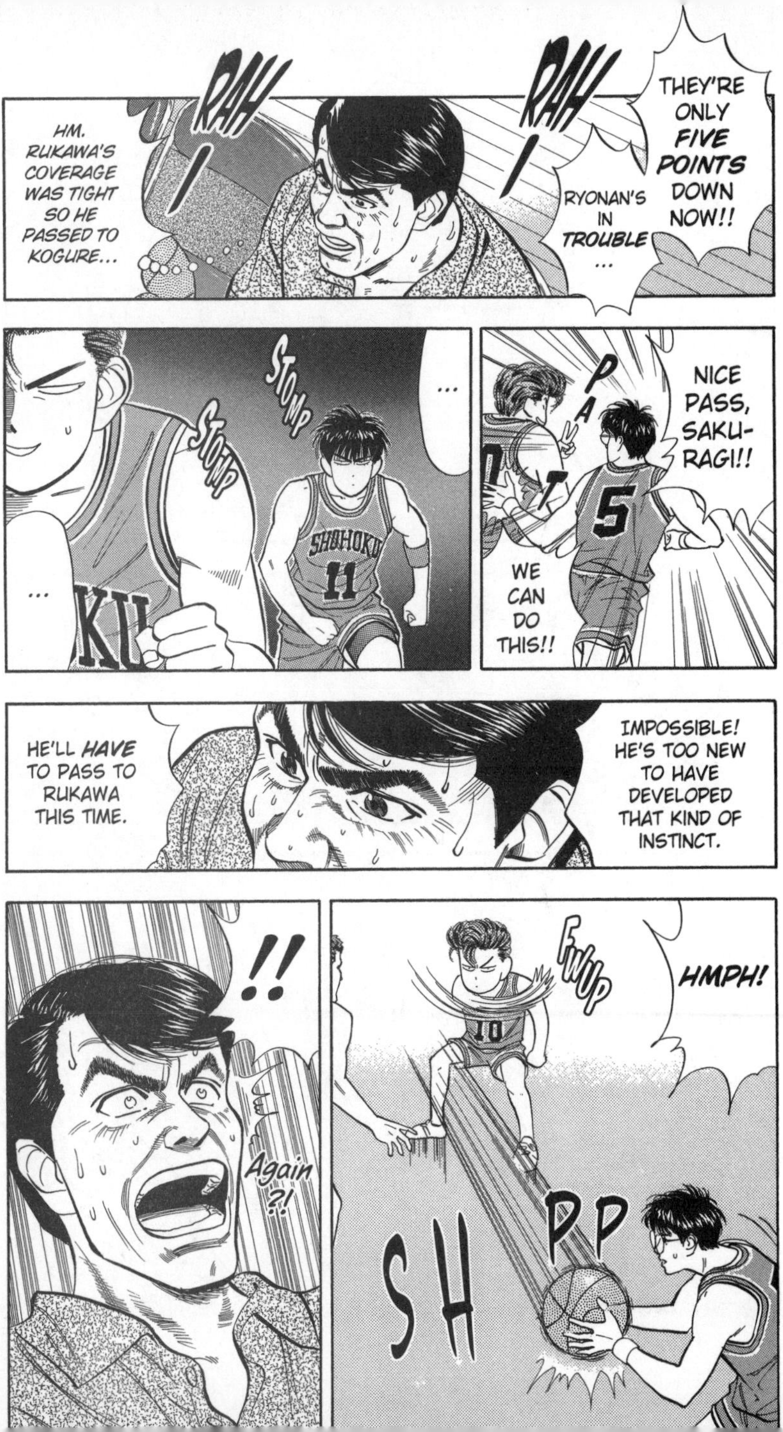
THEY'RE ONLY ***FIVE POINTS*** DOWN NOW!!
RYONAN'S IN ***TROUBLE***...
RAH
RAH
HM. RUKAWA'S COVERAGE WAS TIGHT SO HE PASSED TO KOGURE...
NICE PASS, SAKURAGI!!
PAT
WE CAN DO THIS!!
...
STOMP
STOMP
...
IMPOSSIBLE! HE'S TOO NEW TO HAVE DEVELOPED THAT KIND OF INSTINCT.
HE'LL ***HAVE*** TO PASS TO RUKAWA THIS TIME.
HMPH!
FWUP
SHPP
!!
Again?!

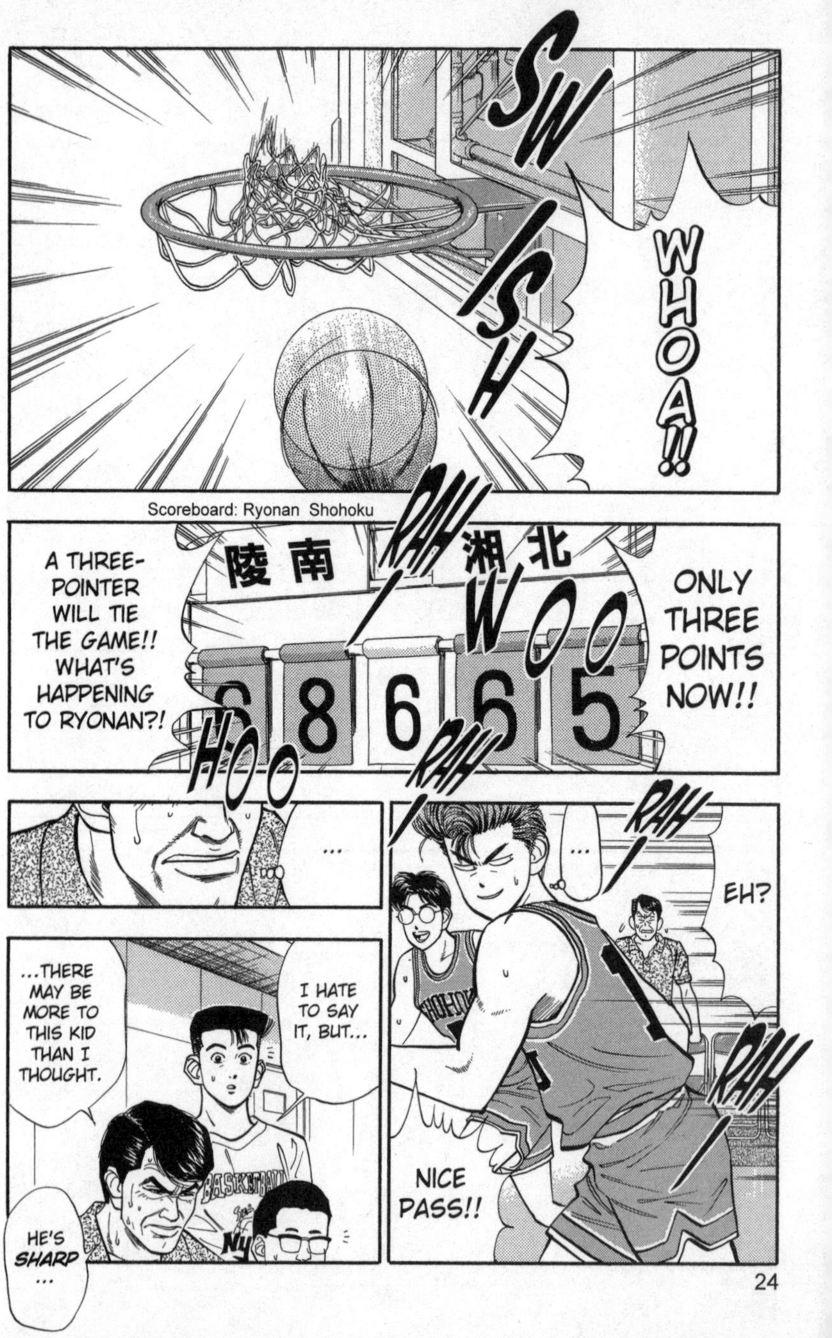
SWISH
WHOA!!
Scoreboard: Ryonan Shohoku
ONLY THREE POINTS NOW!!
陵南 湘北
68 66 65
A THREE-POINTER WILL TIE THE GAME!! WHAT'S HAPPENING TO RYONAN?!
RAH WOO HOO RAH
...
RAH
EH?
RAH
NICE PASS!!
...
I HATE TO SAY IT, BUT...
...THERE MAY BE MORE TO THIS KID THAN I THOUGHT.
HE'S *SHARP* ...

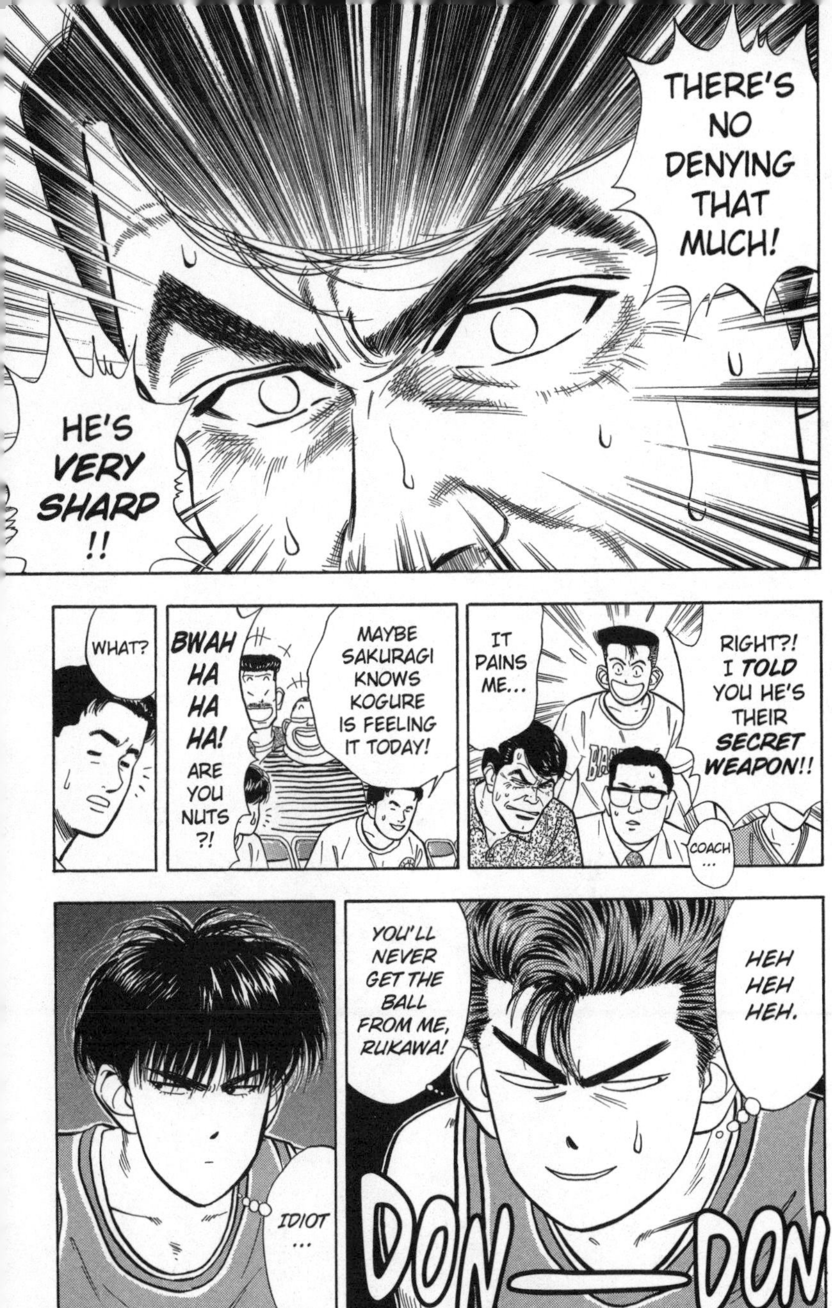
THERE'S NO DENYING THAT MUCH!
HE'S VERY SHARP!!
RIGHT?! I TOLD YOU HE'S THEIR SECRET WEAPON!!
IT PAINS ME...
COACH...
MAYBE SAKURAGI KNOWS KOGURE IS FEELING IT TODAY!
BWAH HA HA HA! ARE YOU NUTS?!
WHAT?
HEH HEH HEH.
YOU'LL NEVER GET THE BALL FROM ME, RUKAWA!
DON—DON
IDIOT...

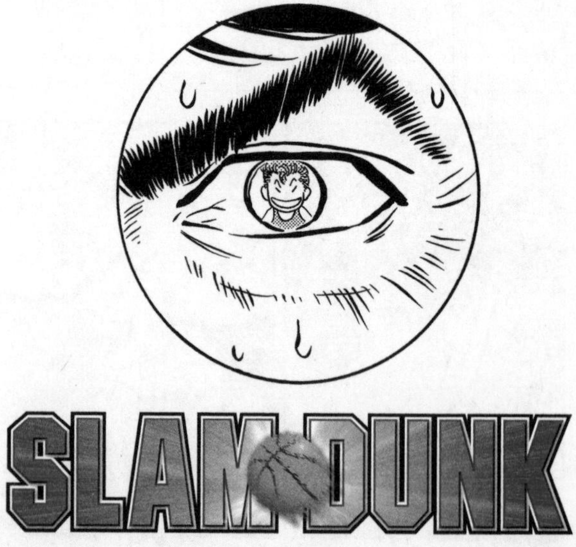

SLAM DUNK

#37
WHEN GORI'S AWAY...

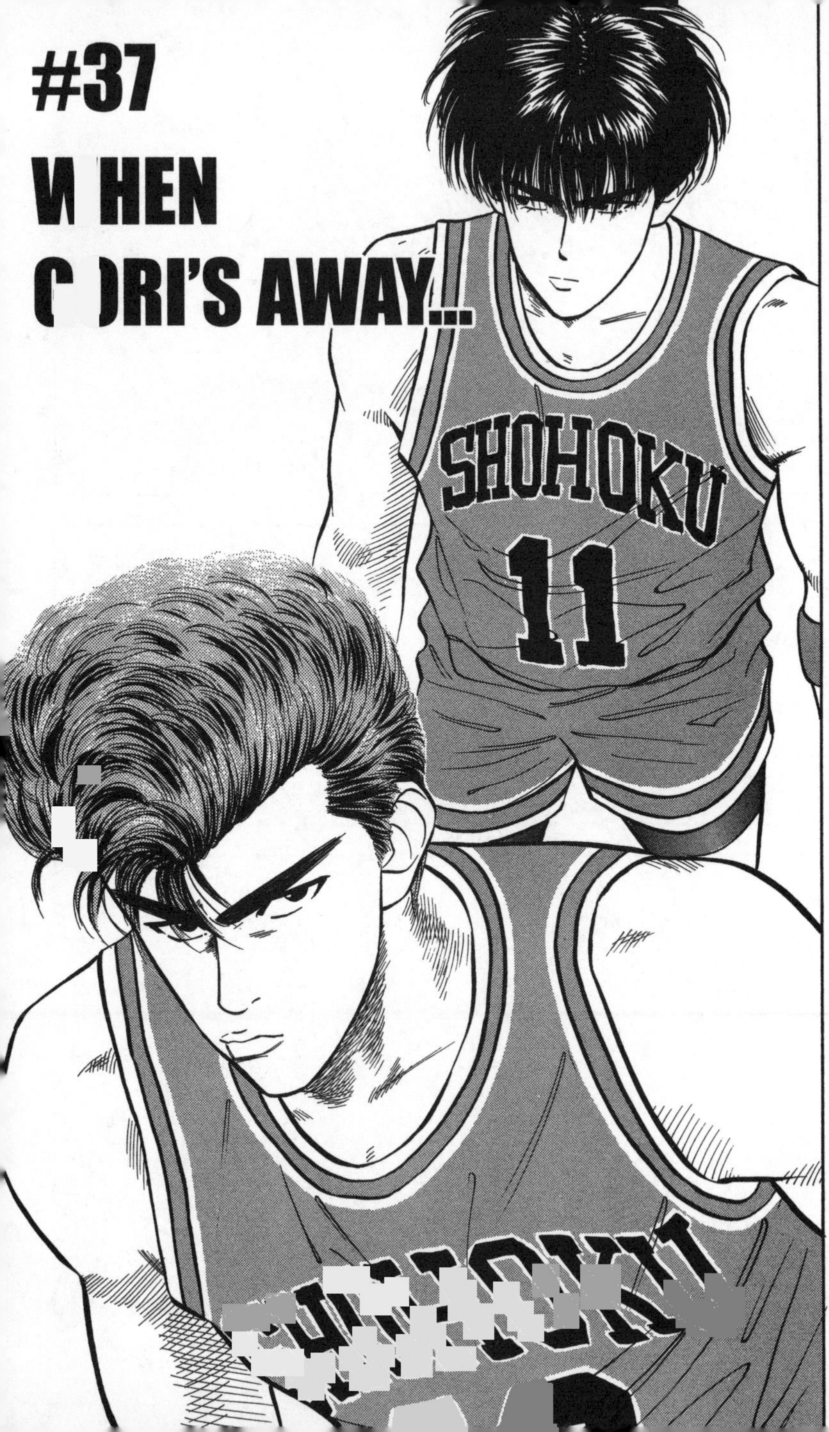
SHOHOKU
11

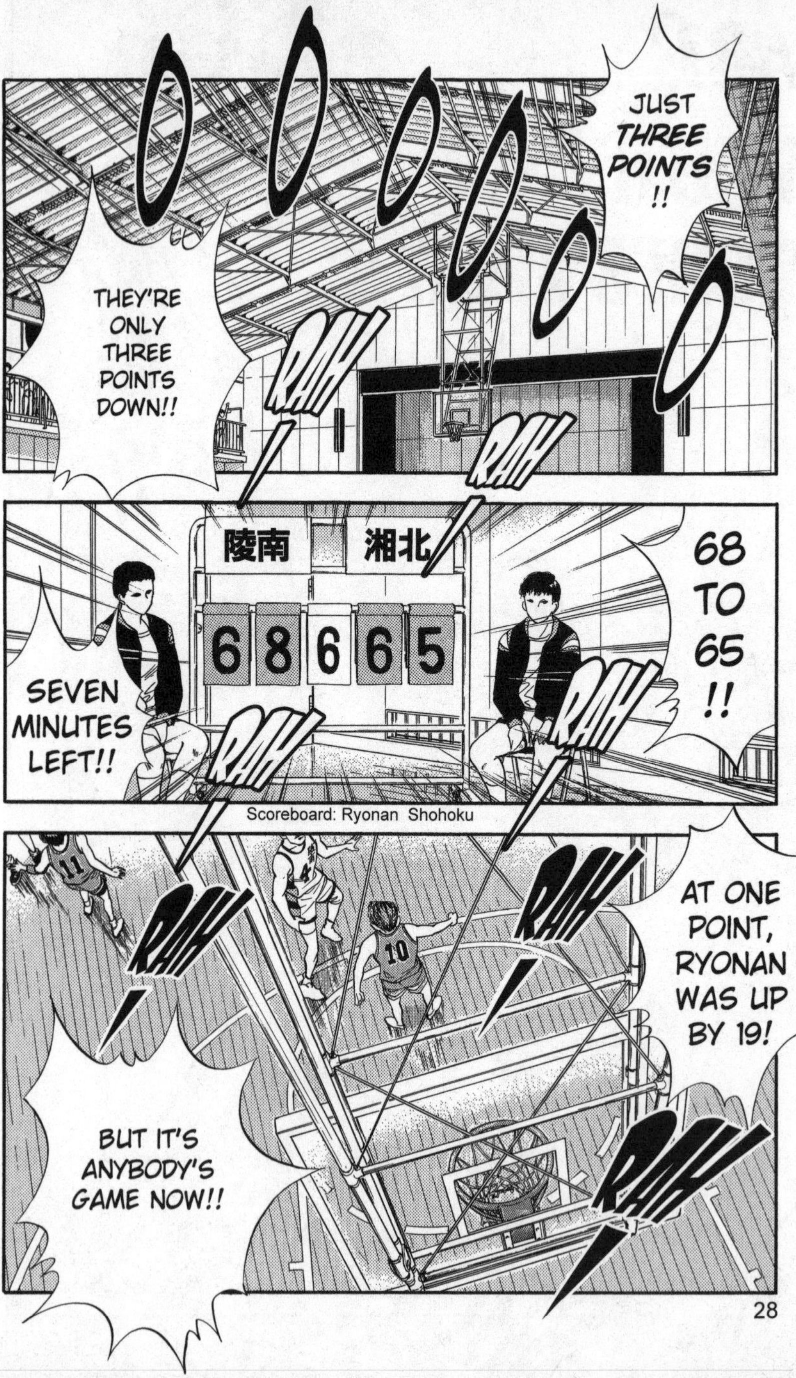
JUST THREE POINTS!!
OOOOOOOOO
THEY'RE ONLY THREE POINTS DOWN!!
RAH
RAH
陵南 湘北
68 TO 65!!
68 66 5
RAH
RAH
SEVEN MINUTES LEFT!!
Scoreboard: Ryonan Shohoku
AT ONE POINT, RYONAN WAS UP BY 19!
RAH
RAH
BUT IT'S ANYBODY'S GAME NOW!!
RAH

READ THIS WAY

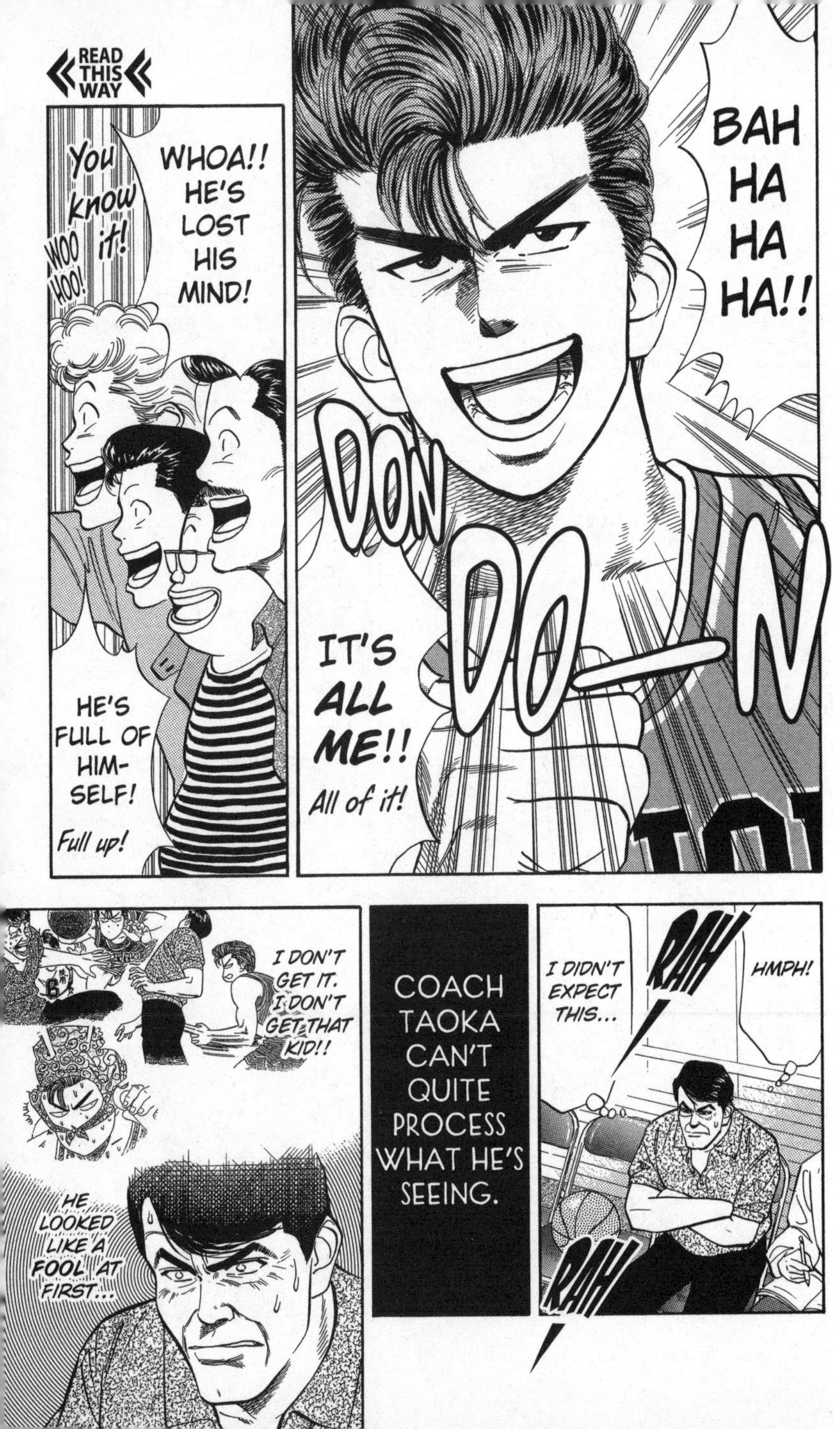

BAH HA HA HA!!
IT'S ALL ME!!
All of it!
DON
DO—N
WHOA!! HE'S LOST HIS MIND!
You know it!
WOO HOO!
HE'S FULL OF HIM-SELF!
Full up!
HMPH!
RAH
I DIDN'T EXPECT THIS...
RAH
COACH TAOKA CAN'T QUITE PROCESS WHAT HE'S SEEING.
I DON'T GET IT. I DON'T GET THAT KID!!
HE LOOKED LIKE A FOOL AT FIRST...

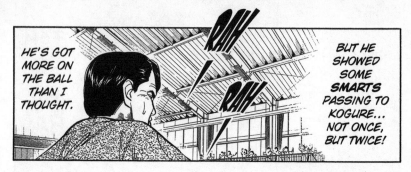

BUT HE SHOWED SOME SMARTS PASSING TO KOGURE... NOT ONCE, BUT TWICE!
RAH! RAH!
HE'S GOT MORE ON THE BALL THAN I THOUGHT.
HE'S THEIR SECRET WEAPON!!
Check him out!!
RIDING MY LAST NERVE...
IF HE REALLY IS AS GOOD AS RUKAWA, SHOHOKU COULD BE OUR BIGGEST RIVAL!!
What are you up to, Anzai?
I can never tell!!
HO HO HO!
YO, GRANDPA! YOU KNOW A SECRET WEAPON WHEN YOU SEE ONE, EH?
HA HA HA!
HO HO HO HO
DO YOU, NOW?
WHOA...!
A SECOND AGO HE WAS STIFF AS A BOARD!
Look who's talking!
YOU ALMOST BLEW IT, BUT I FORGIVE YOU!

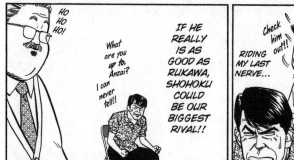

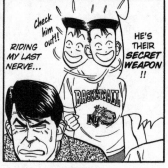

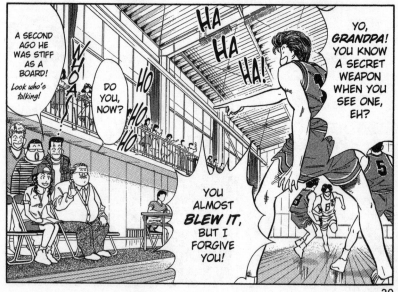

READ THIS WAY

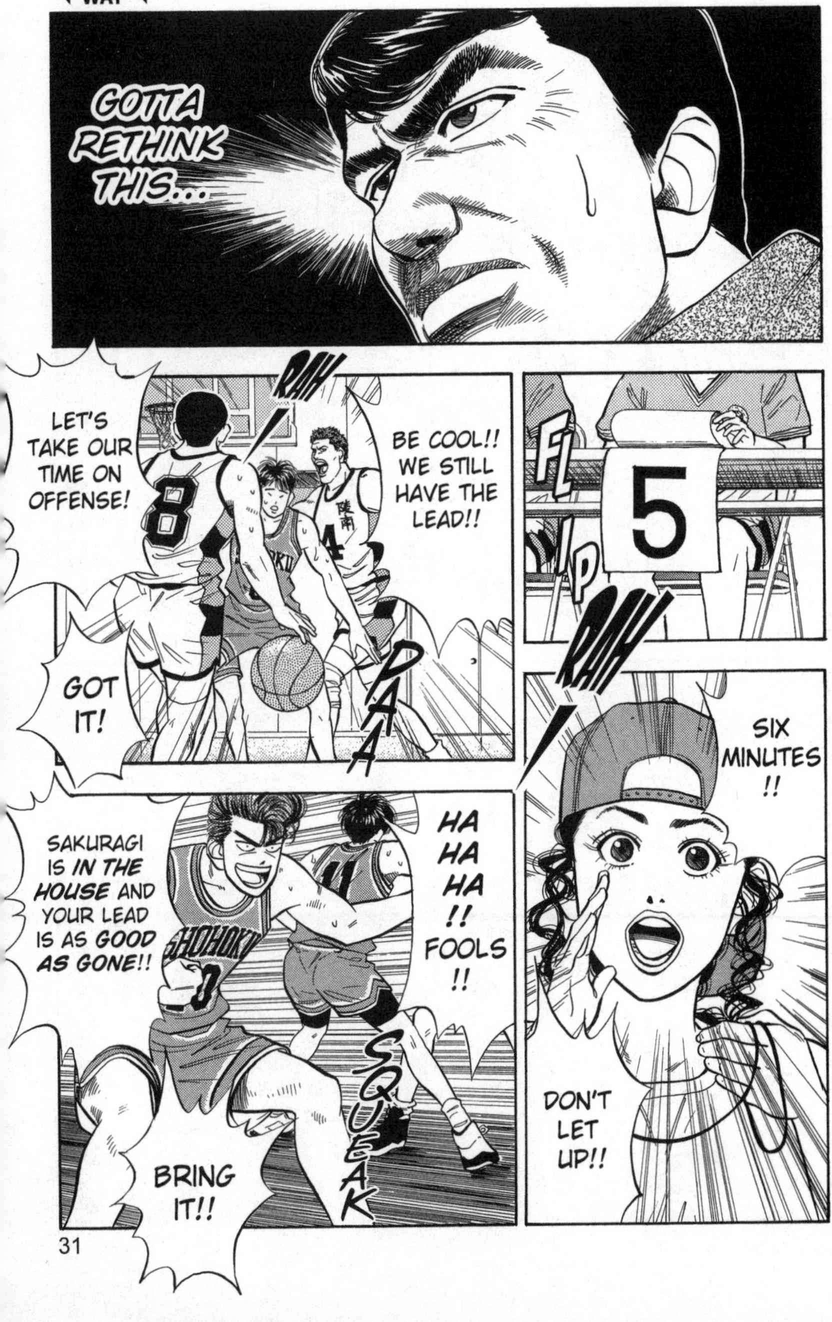

GOTTA RETHINK THIS...
FLIP
5
RAH
BE COOL!! WE STILL HAVE THE LEAD!!
LET'S TAKE OUR TIME ON OFFENSE!
GOT IT!
PAAA
RAH
SIX MINUTES!!
DON'T LET UP!!
HA HA HA!! FOOLS!!
SAKURAGI IS *IN THE HOUSE* AND YOUR LEAD IS AS *GOOD AS GONE*!!
SQUEAK
BRING IT!!

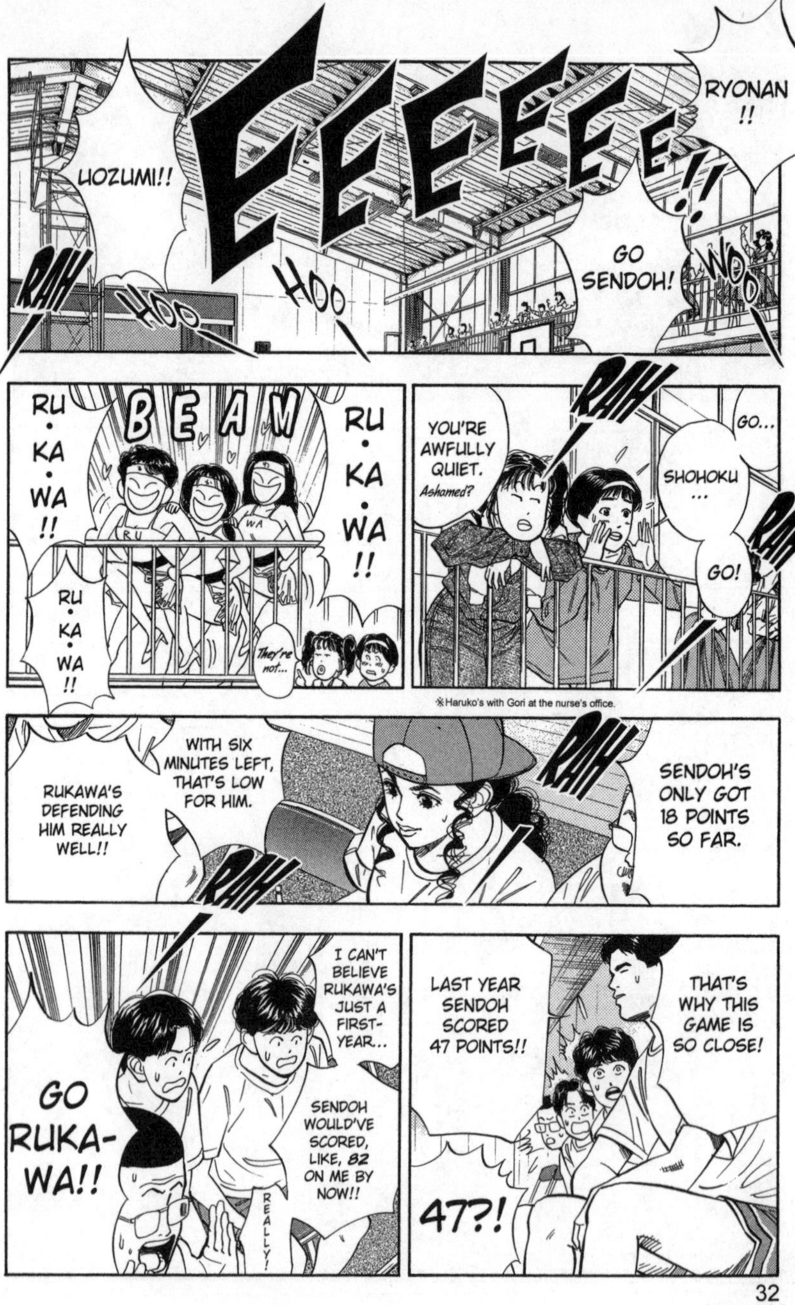
RYONAN!!
EEEEEE!!
GO SENDOH!
WOO
UOZUMI!!
HOO
HOO
RAH
RAH
GO...
SHOHOKU...
GO!
RAH
YOU'RE AWFULLY QUIET.
Ashamed?
※Haruko's with Gori at the nurse's office.
RU·KA·WA!!
BEAM
RU·KA·WA!!
RU·KA·WA!!
They're not...
RAH
SENDOH'S ONLY GOT 18 POINTS SO FAR.
WITH SIX MINUTES LEFT, THAT'S LOW FOR HIM.
RUKAWA'S DEFENDING HIM REALLY WELL!!
RAH
THAT'S WHY THIS GAME IS SO CLOSE!
LAST YEAR SENDOH SCORED 47 POINTS!!
47?!
I CAN'T BELIEVE RUKAWA'S JUST A FIRST-YEAR...
SENDOH WOULD'VE SCORED, LIKE, 82 ON ME BY NOW!!
REALLY!
GO RUKAWA!!

READ THIS WAY

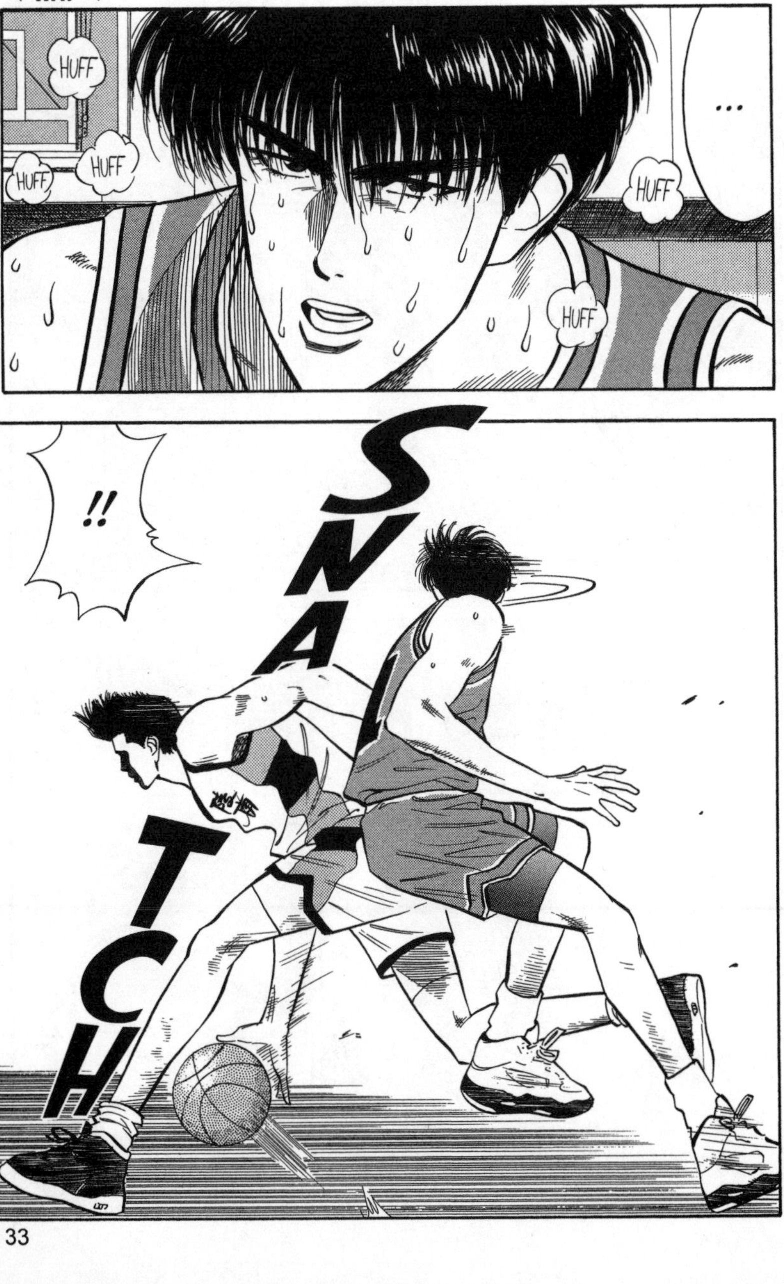
...
HUFF
HUFF
HUFF
HUFF
HUFF
SNATCH
!!

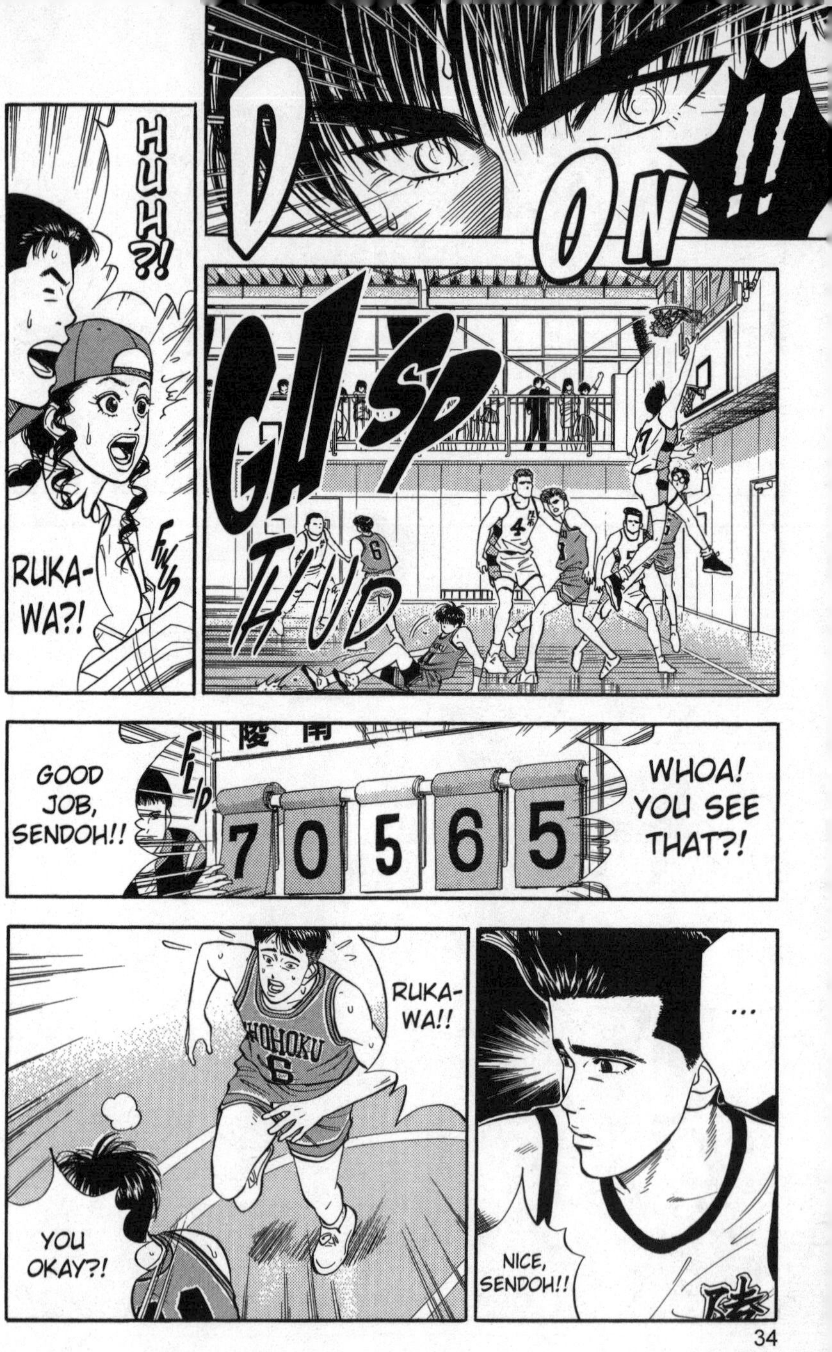
DOON!!
GASP
THUD
HUH?!
FWUP
RUKA-WA?!
WHOA! YOU SEE THAT?!
70565
FLIP
GOOD JOB, SENDOH!!
...
NICE, SENDOH!!
RUKA-WA!!
SHOHOKU
YOU OKAY?!

READ THIS WAY

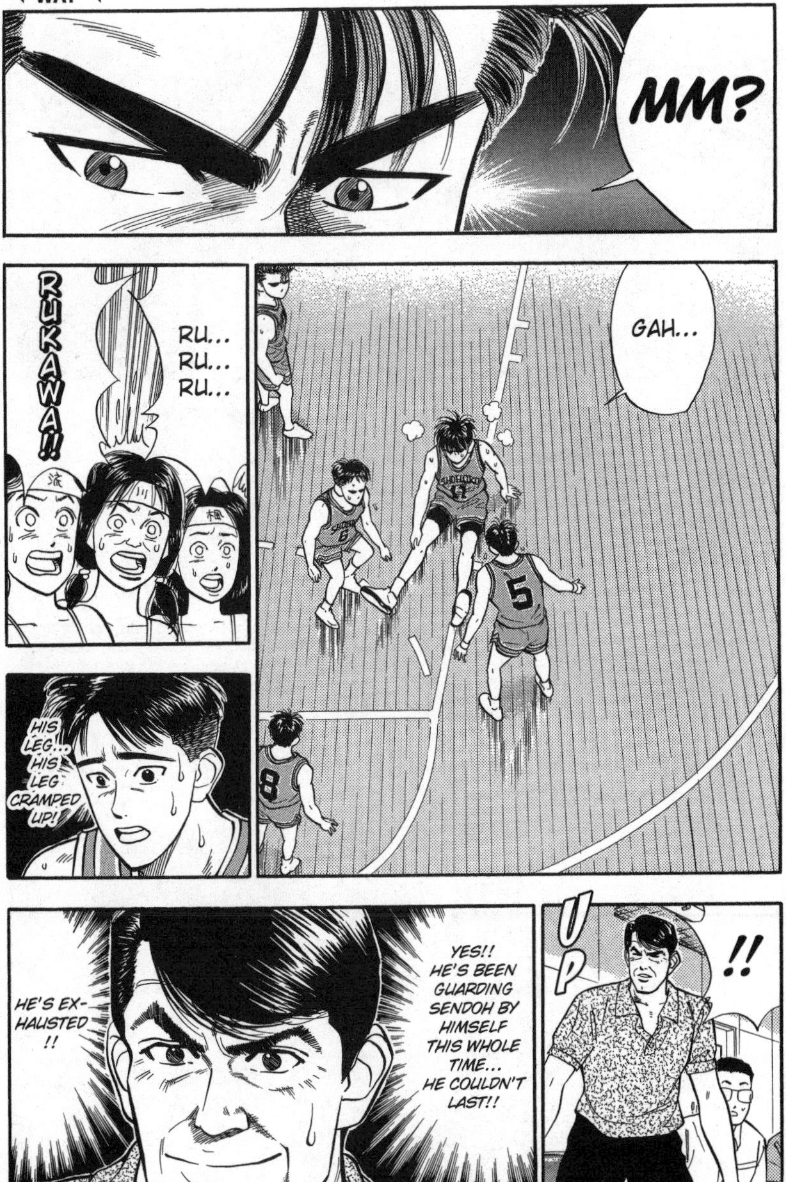
MM?
GAH...
RU... RU... RU...
RUKAWA!!
HIS LEG... HIS LEG CRAMPED UP!
UP
!!
YES!! HE'S BEEN GUARDING SENDOH BY HIMSELF THIS WHOLE TIME... HE COULDN'T LAST!!
HE'S EX-HAUSTED !!

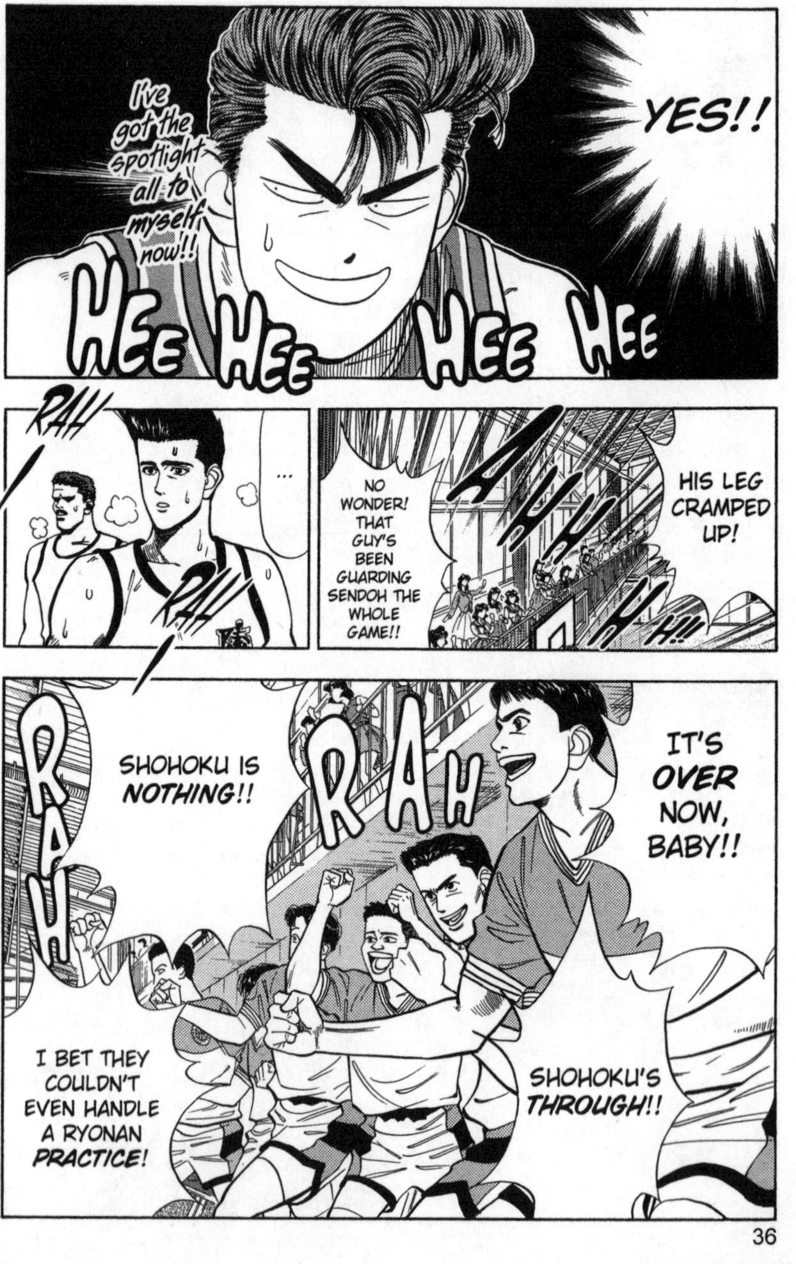
YES!!
I've got the spotlight all to myself now!!
HEE HEE HEE HEE
HIS LEG CRAMPED UP!
AHHHHH!!
NO WONDER! THAT GUY'S BEEN GUARDING SENDOH THE WHOLE GAME!!
...
RAH
RAH
IT'S OVER NOW, BABY!!
RAH
SHOHOKU IS NOTHING!!
RAH
SHOHOKU'S THROUGH!!
I BET THEY COULDN'T EVEN HANDLE A RYONAN PRACTICE!

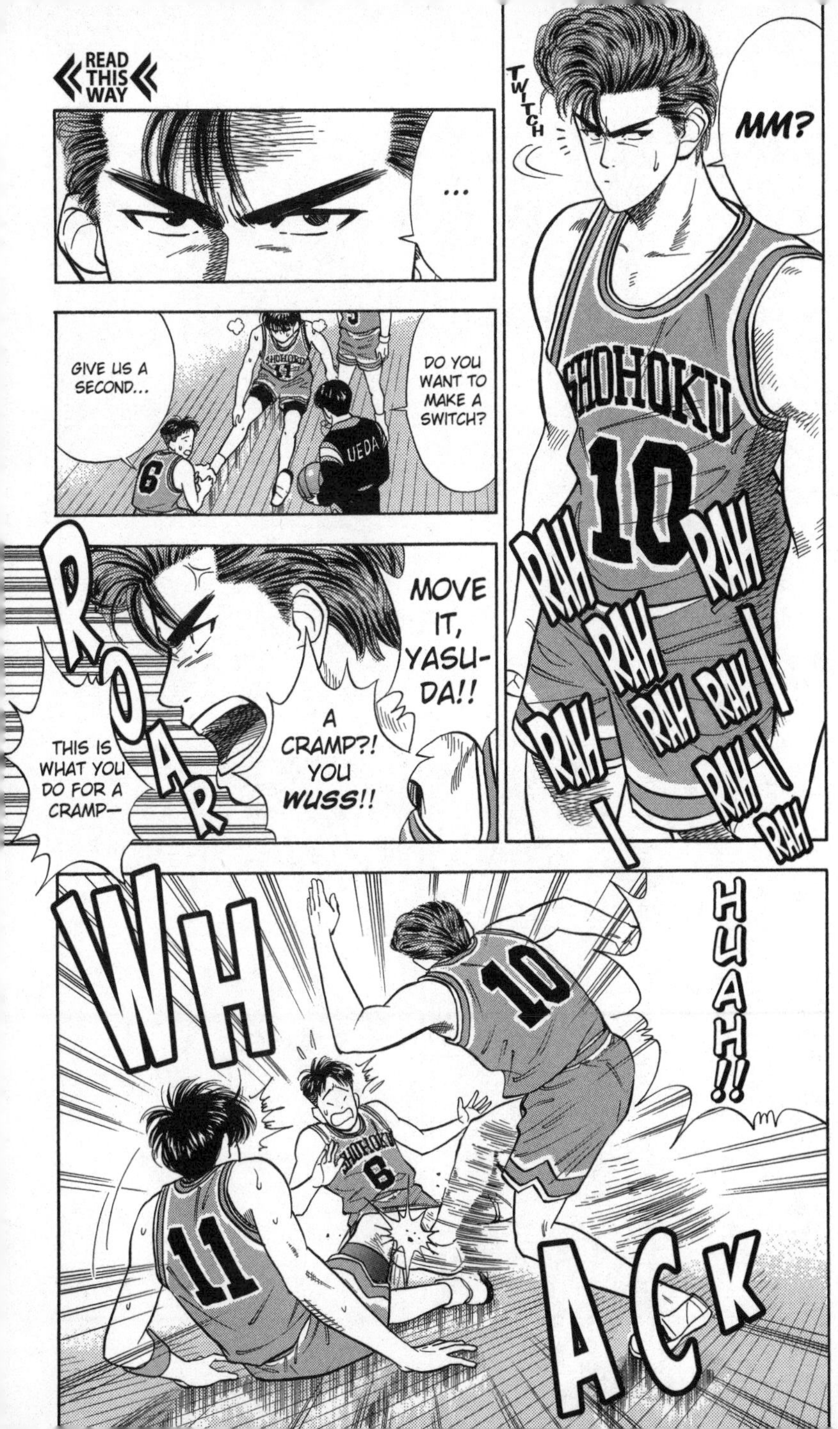
READ THIS WAY
TWITCH
MM?
RAH RAH RAH RAH RAH RAH RAH RAH
...
DO YOU WANT TO MAKE A SWITCH?
GIVE US A SECOND...
MOVE IT, YASUDA!!
A CRAMP?! YOU WUSS!!
ROAR
THIS IS WHAT YOU DO FOR A CRAMP—
HUAH!!
WHACK

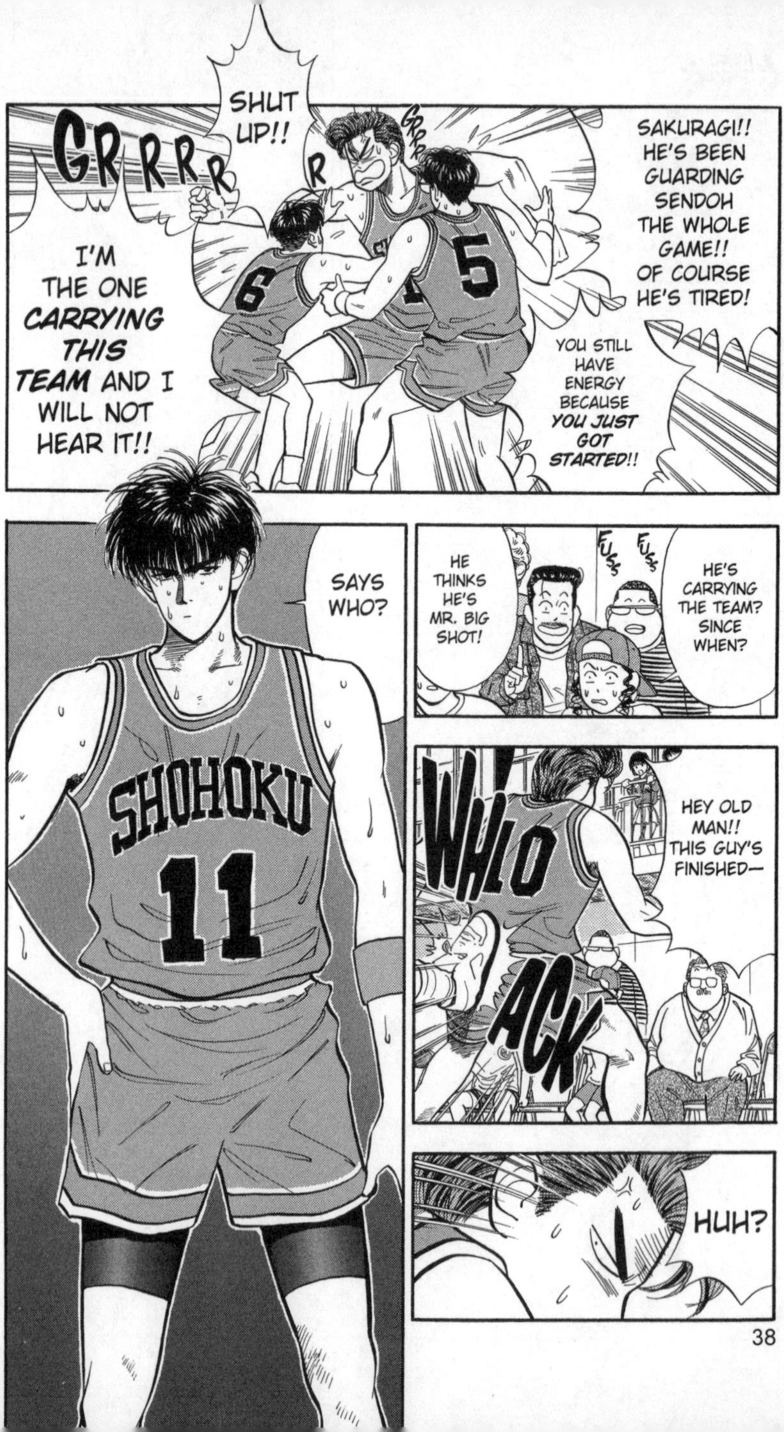
SAKURAGI!! HE'S BEEN GUARDING SENDOH THE WHOLE GAME!! OF COURSE HE'S TIRED!
YOU STILL HAVE ENERGY BECAUSE YOU JUST GOT STARTED!!
GRRR
SHUT UP!!
GRRRRR
I'M THE ONE CARRYING THIS TEAM AND I WILL NOT HEAR IT!!
FUSS FUSS
HE'S CARRYING THE TEAM? SINCE WHEN?
HE THINKS HE'S MR. BIG SHOT!
HEY OLD MAN!! THIS GUY'S FINISHED—
WHLO
ACK
HUH?
SAYS WHO?

READ THIS WAY

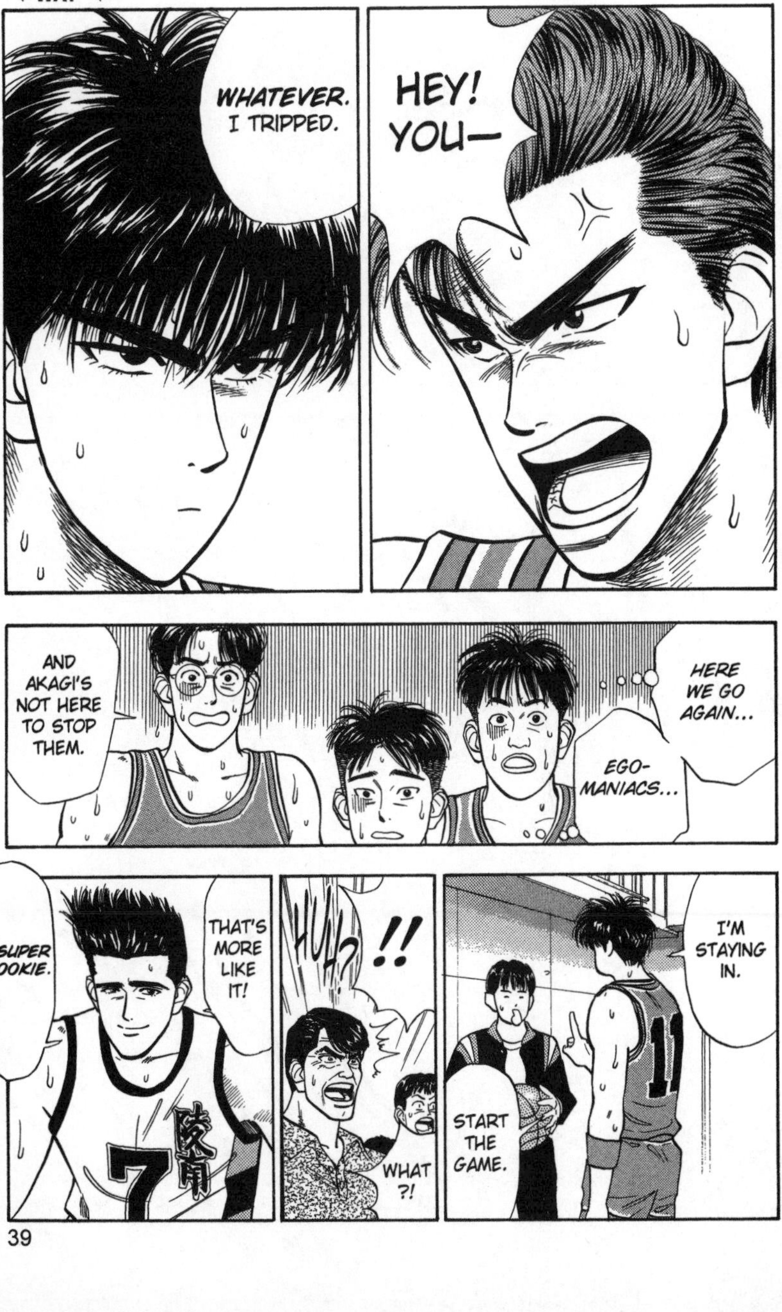
HEY! YOU—
WHATEVER. I TRIPPED.
HERE WE GO AGAIN...
EGO-MANIACS...
AND AKAGI'S NOT HERE TO STOP THEM.
I'M STAYING IN.
START THE GAME.
HUH?
!!
WHAT?!
THAT'S MORE LIKE IT!
...SUPER ROOKIE.

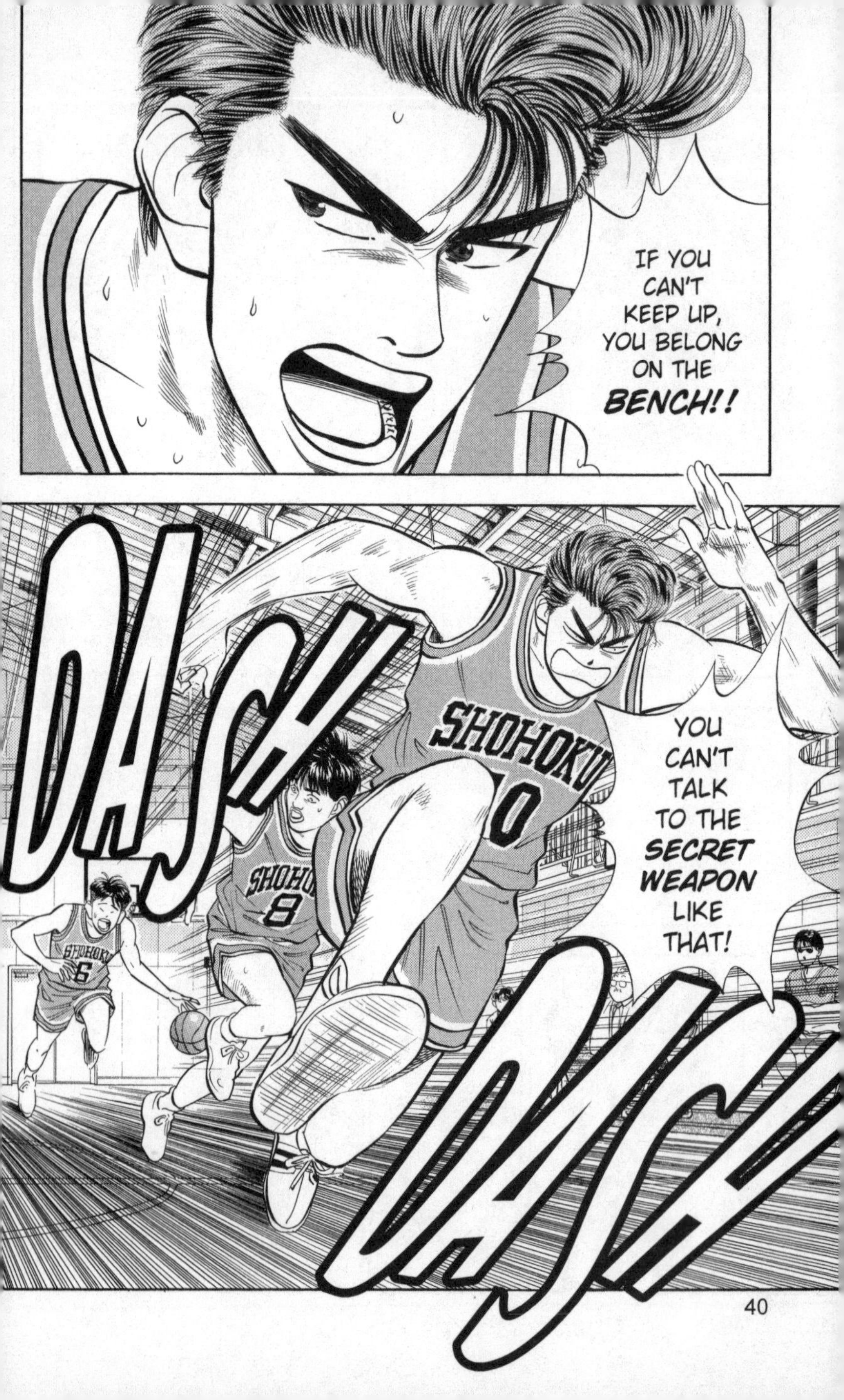
IF YOU CAN'T KEEP UP, YOU BELONG ON THE BENCH!!
YOU CAN'T TALK TO THE SECRET WEAPON LIKE THAT!
DASH
DASH
SHOHOKU
SHOHOKU
SHOHOKU

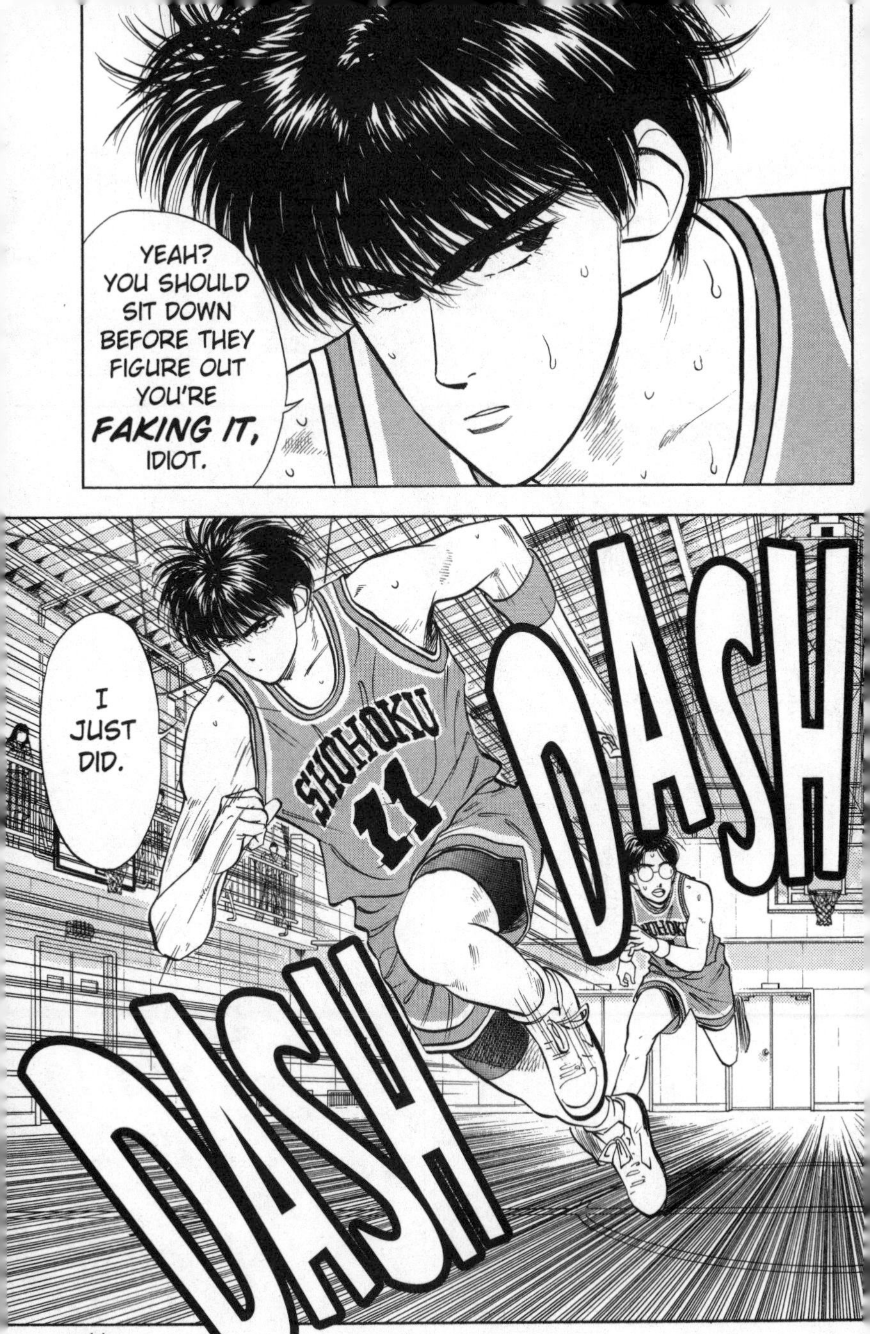
YEAH? YOU SHOULD SIT DOWN BEFORE THEY FIGURE OUT YOU'RE ***FAKING IT,*** IDIOT.
I JUST DID.
DASH
DASH
SHOHOKU 11

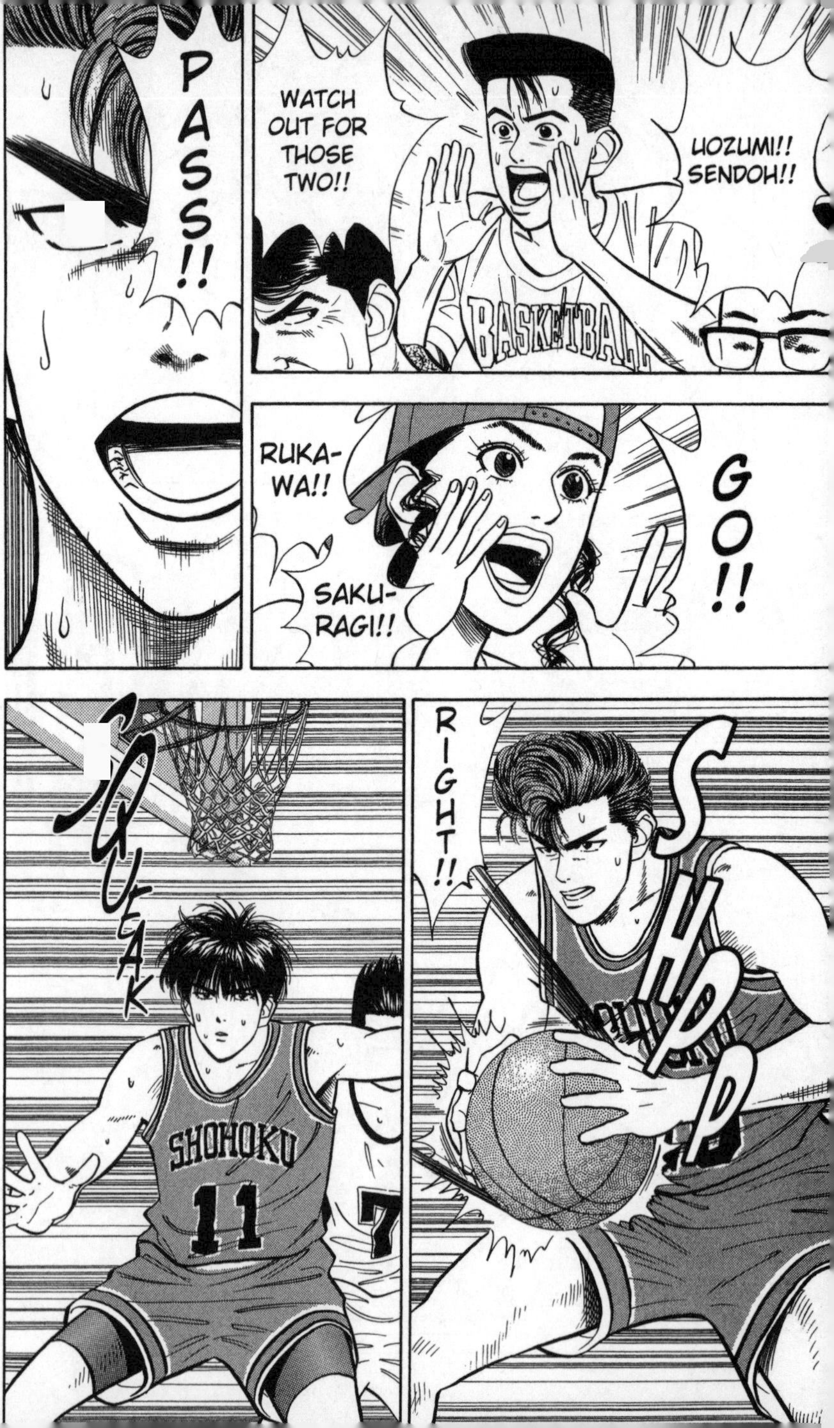
UOZUMI!! SENDOH!!
WATCH OUT FOR THOSE TWO!!
BASKETBALL
GO!!
RUKA-WA!!
SAKU-RAGI!!
PASS!!
RIGHT!!
SHPP
SQUEAK
SHOHOKU
11
7

READ THIS WAY

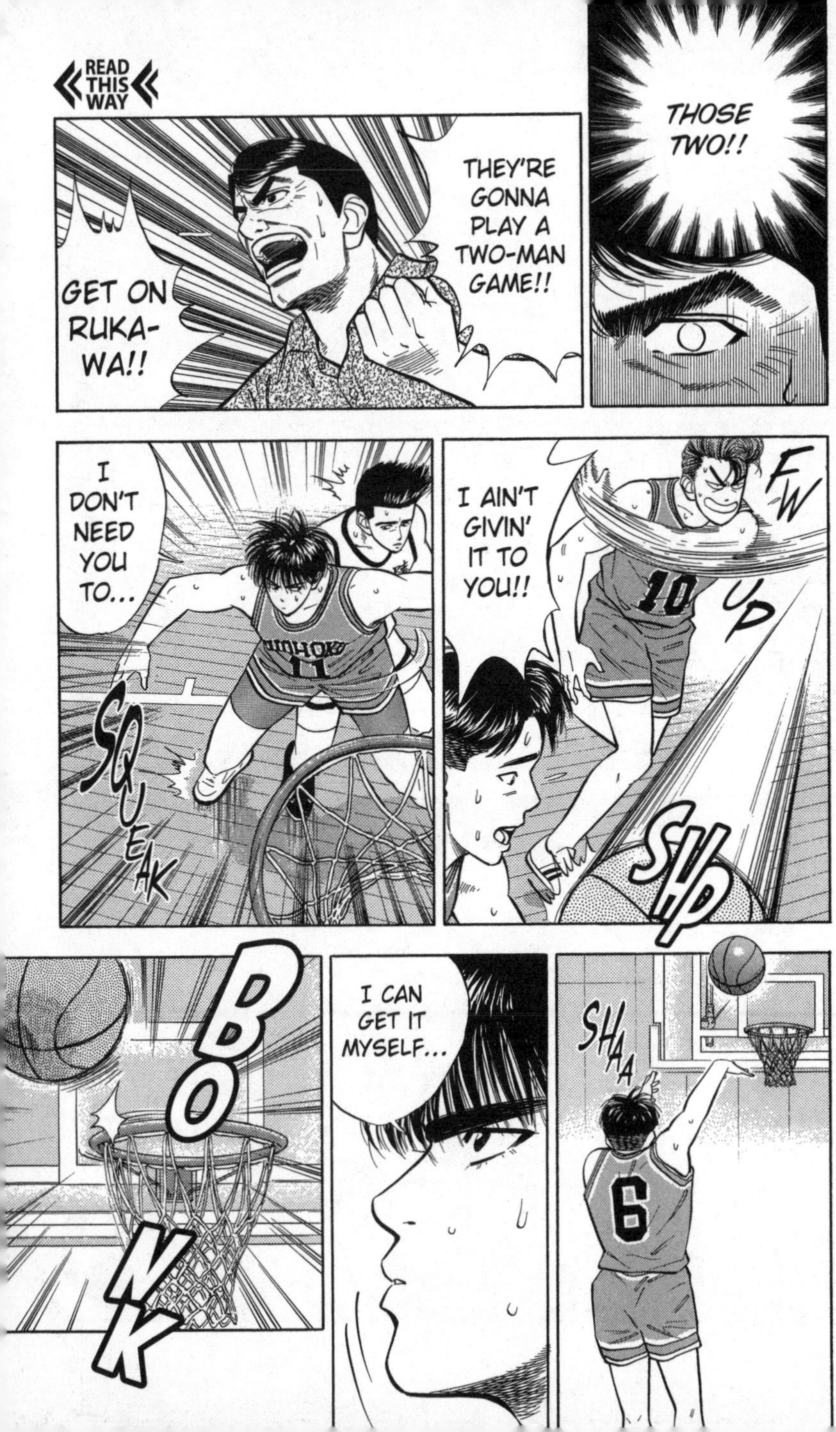
THOSE TWO!!
THEY'RE GONNA PLAY A TWO-MAN GAME!!
GET ON RUKAWA!!
I AIN'T GIVIN' IT TO YOU!!
FW
UP
SHP
I DON'T NEED YOU TO...
SQUEAK
SHAA
I CAN GET IT MYSELF...
BONK

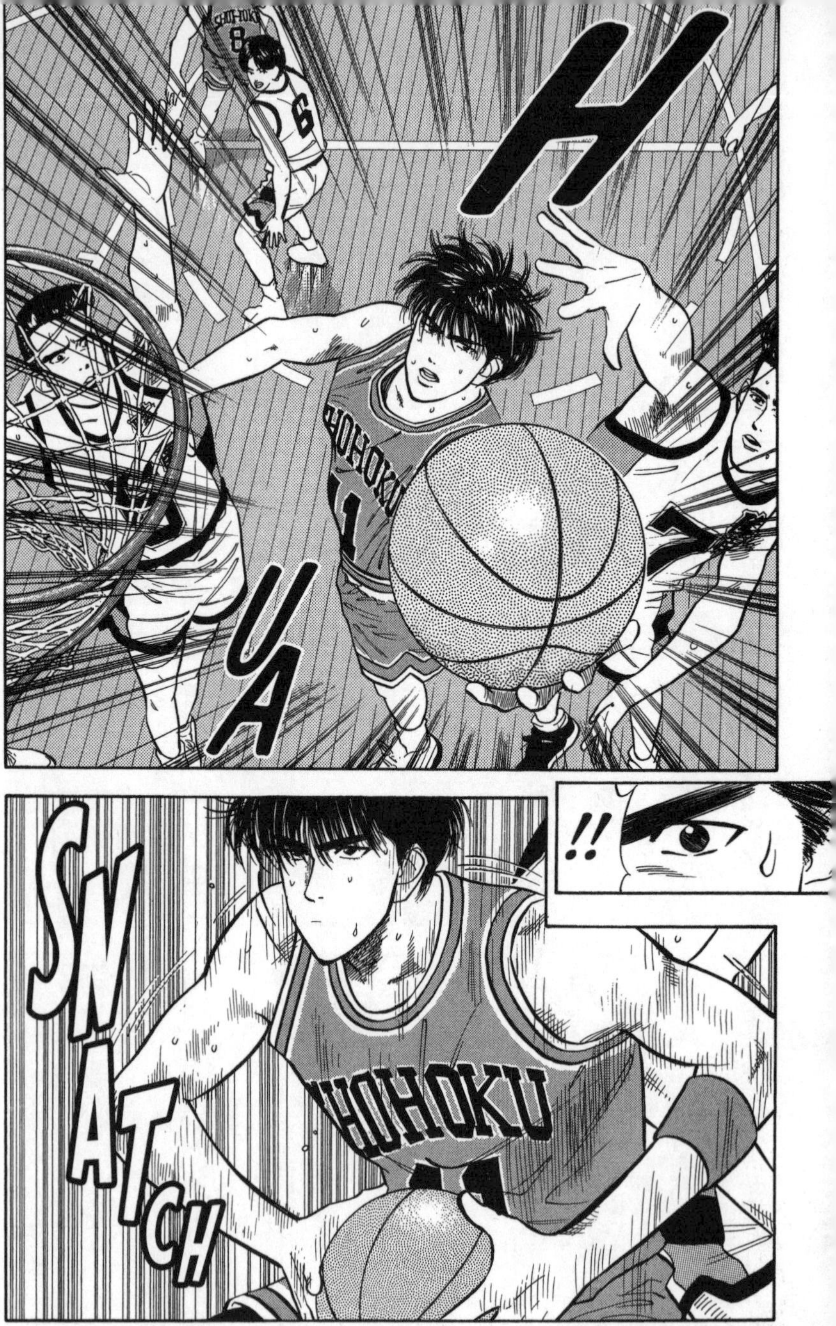
HUA
!!
SNATCH

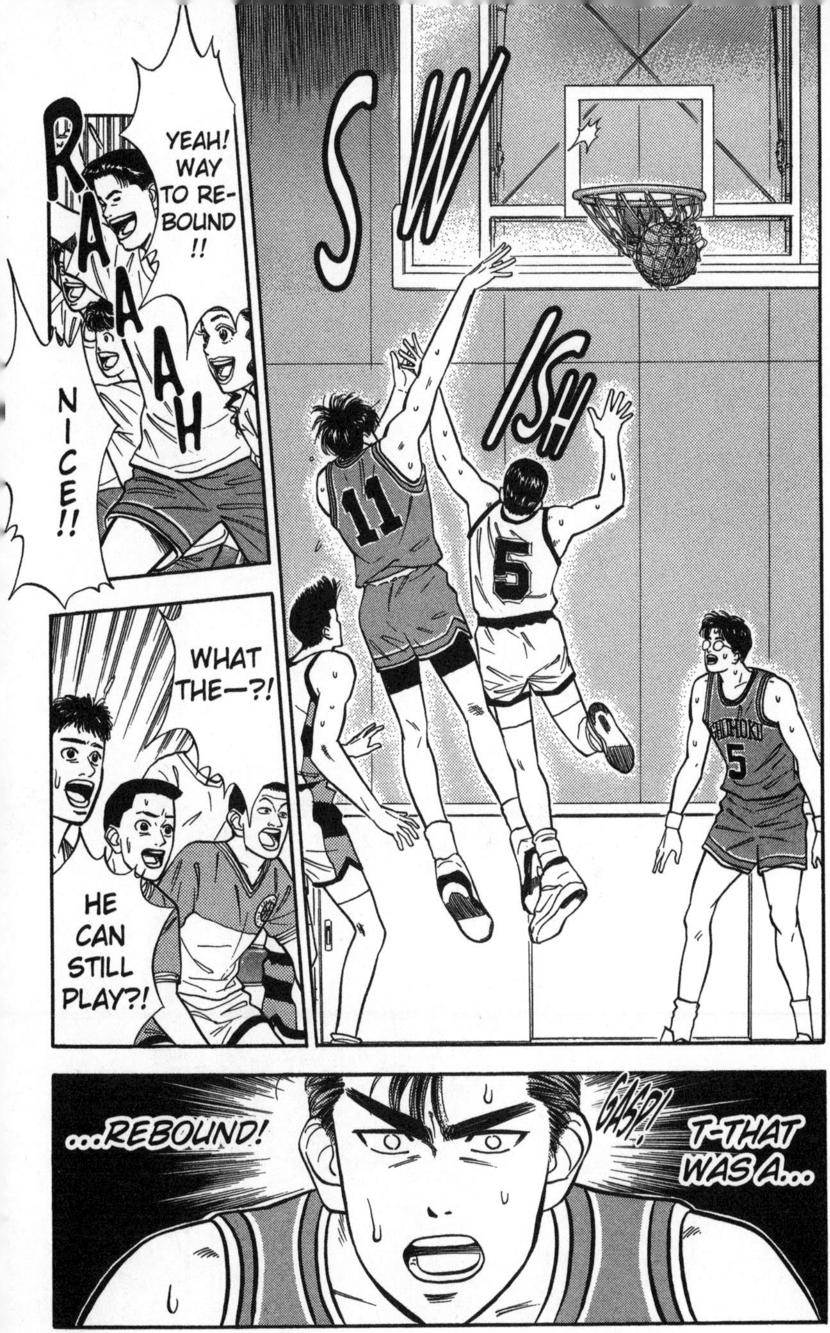
SWISH
YEAH! WAY TO RE-BOUND!!
RAAAAH
NICE!!
WHAT THE—?!
HE CAN STILL PLAY?!
T-THAT WAS A...
GASP!
...REBOUND!

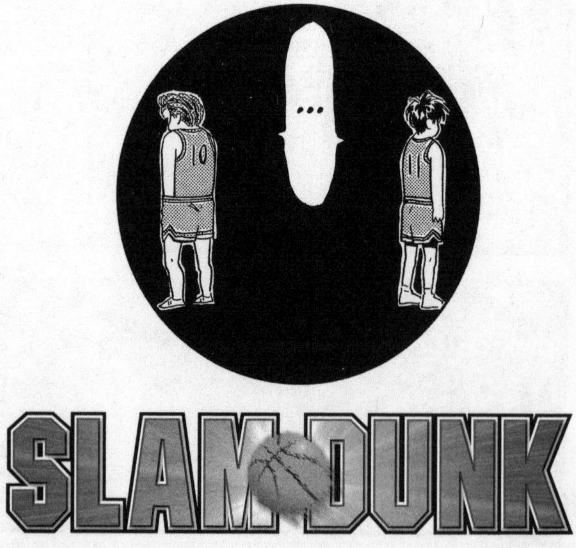
...

SLAM DUNK

#38 REBOUND

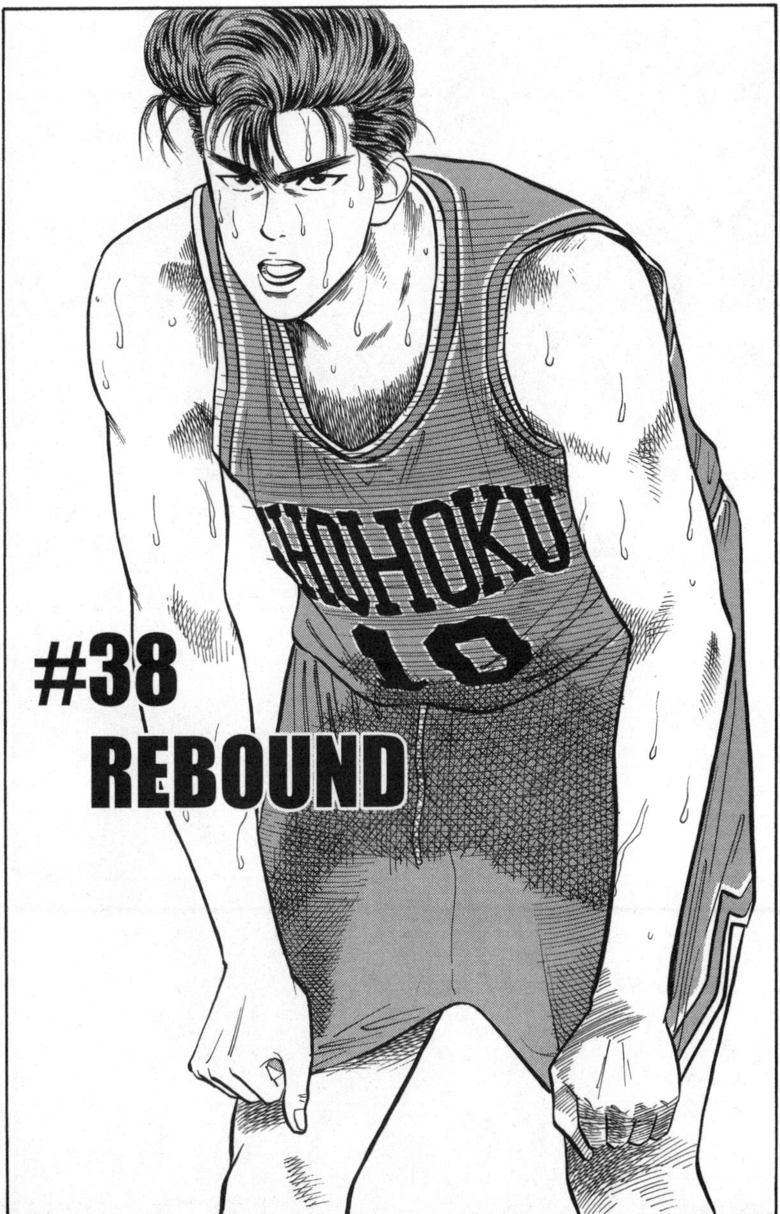

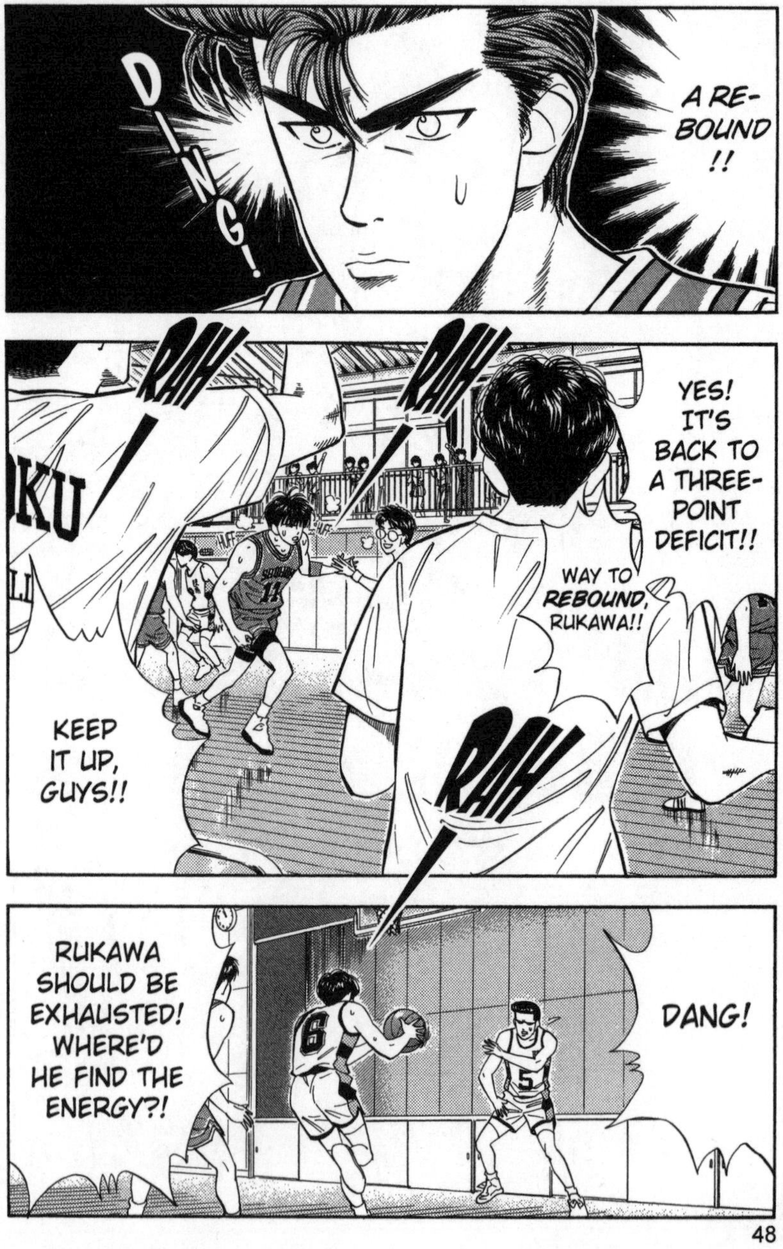
A RE-BOUND!!
DING!
RAH
RAH
YES! IT'S BACK TO A THREE-POINT DEFICIT!!
WAY TO REBOUND, RUKAWA!!
RAH
KEEP IT UP, GUYS!!
DANG!
RUKAWA SHOULD BE EXHAUSTED! WHERE'D HE FIND THE ENERGY?!

READ THIS WAY

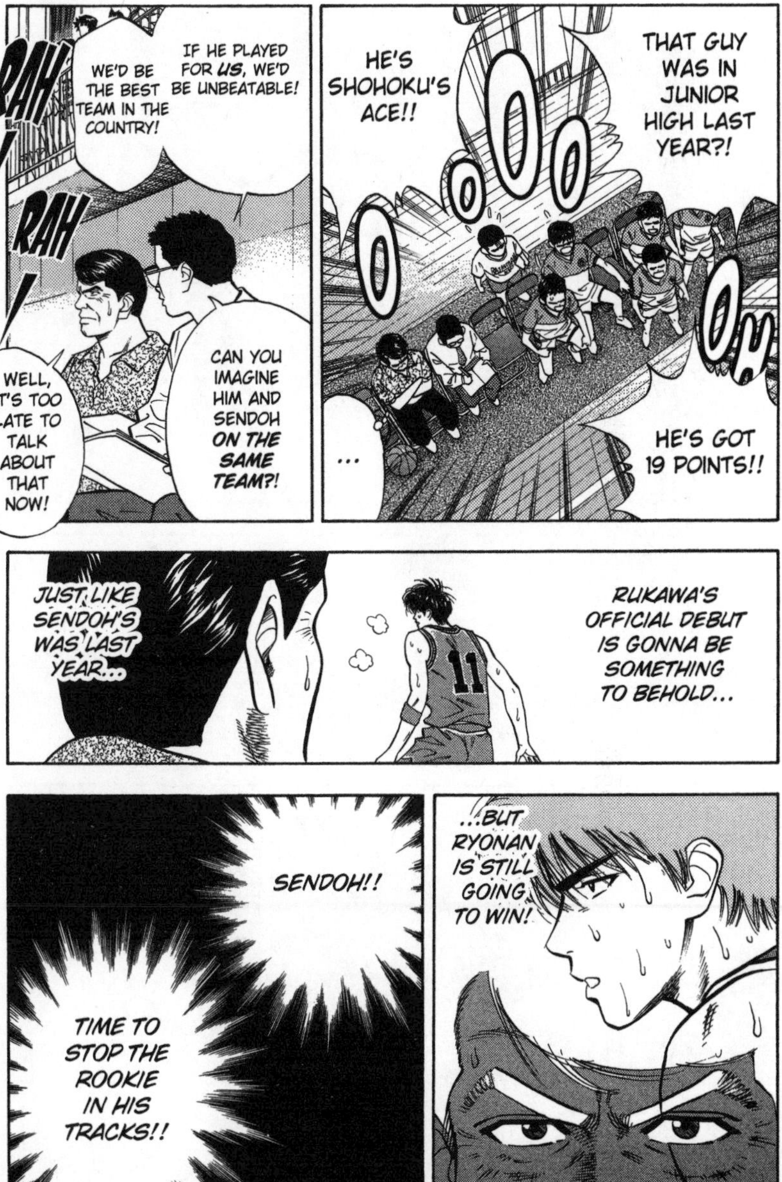
THAT GUY WAS IN JUNIOR HIGH LAST YEAR?!
HE'S SHOHOKU'S ACE!!
HE'S GOT 19 POINTS!!
...
IF HE PLAYED FOR US, WE'D BE UNBEATABLE!
WE'D BE THE BEST TEAM IN THE COUNTRY!
RAH
RAH
CAN YOU IMAGINE HIM AND SENDOH ON THE SAME TEAM?!
WELL, IT'S TOO LATE TO TALK ABOUT THAT NOW!
RUKAWA'S OFFICIAL DEBUT IS GONNA BE SOMETHING TO BEHOLD...
JUST LIKE SENDOH'S WAS LAST YEAR...
...BUT RYONAN IS STILL GOING TO WIN!
SENDOH!!
TIME TO STOP THE ROOKIE IN HIS TRACKS!!

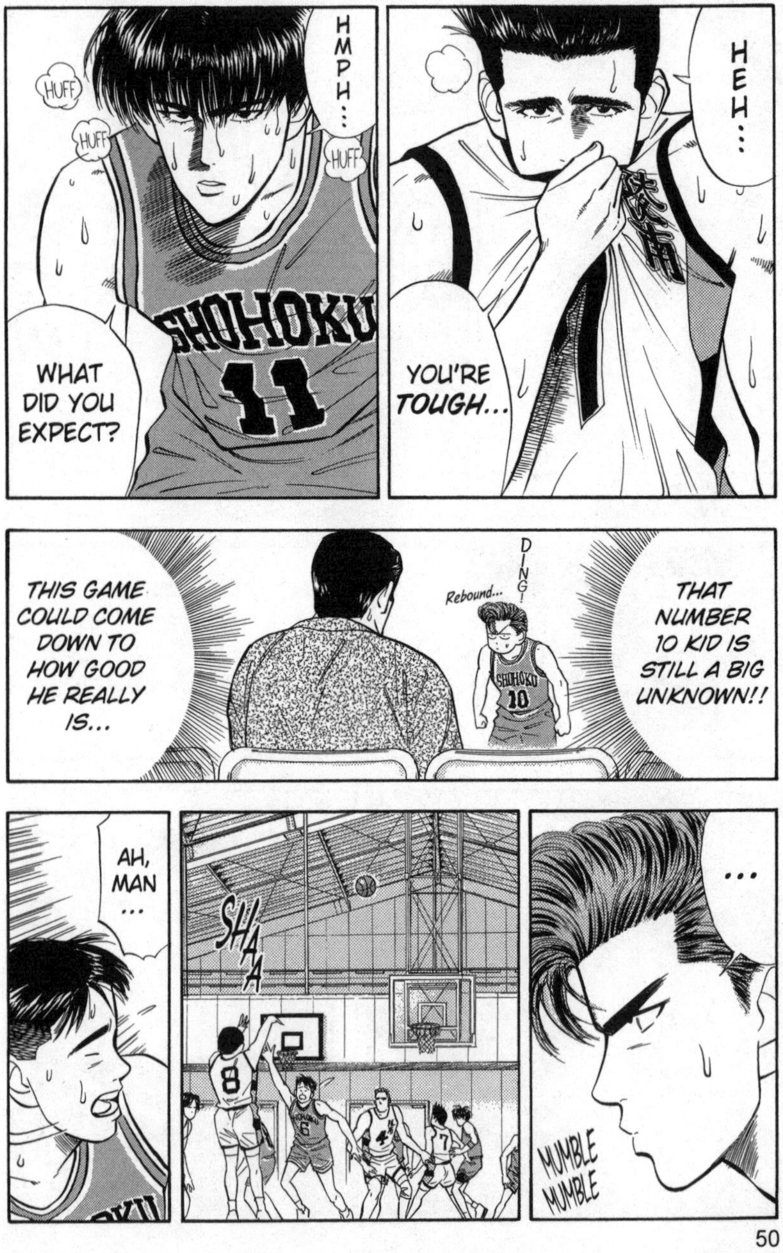
HEH...
YOU'RE TOUGH...
HMPH...
HUFF
HUFF
HUFF
WHAT DID YOU EXPECT?
THAT NUMBER 10 KID IS STILL A BIG UNKNOWN!!
DING!
Rebound...
THIS GAME COULD COME DOWN TO HOW GOOD HE REALLY IS...
...
MUMBLE MUMBLE
SHAA
AH, MAN...

READ THIS WAY

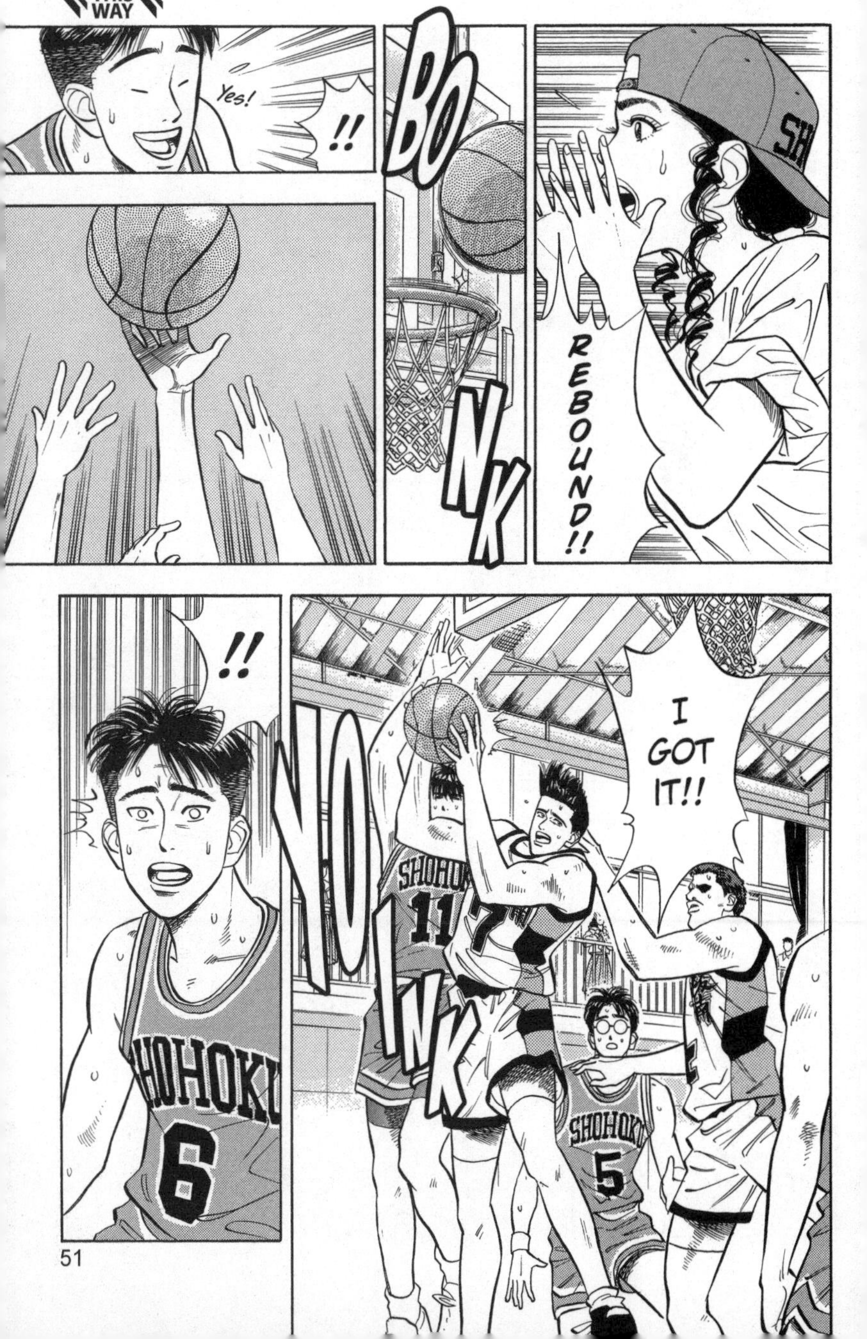
REBOUND!!
BONK
Yes!
!!
I GOT IT!!
YOINK
!!

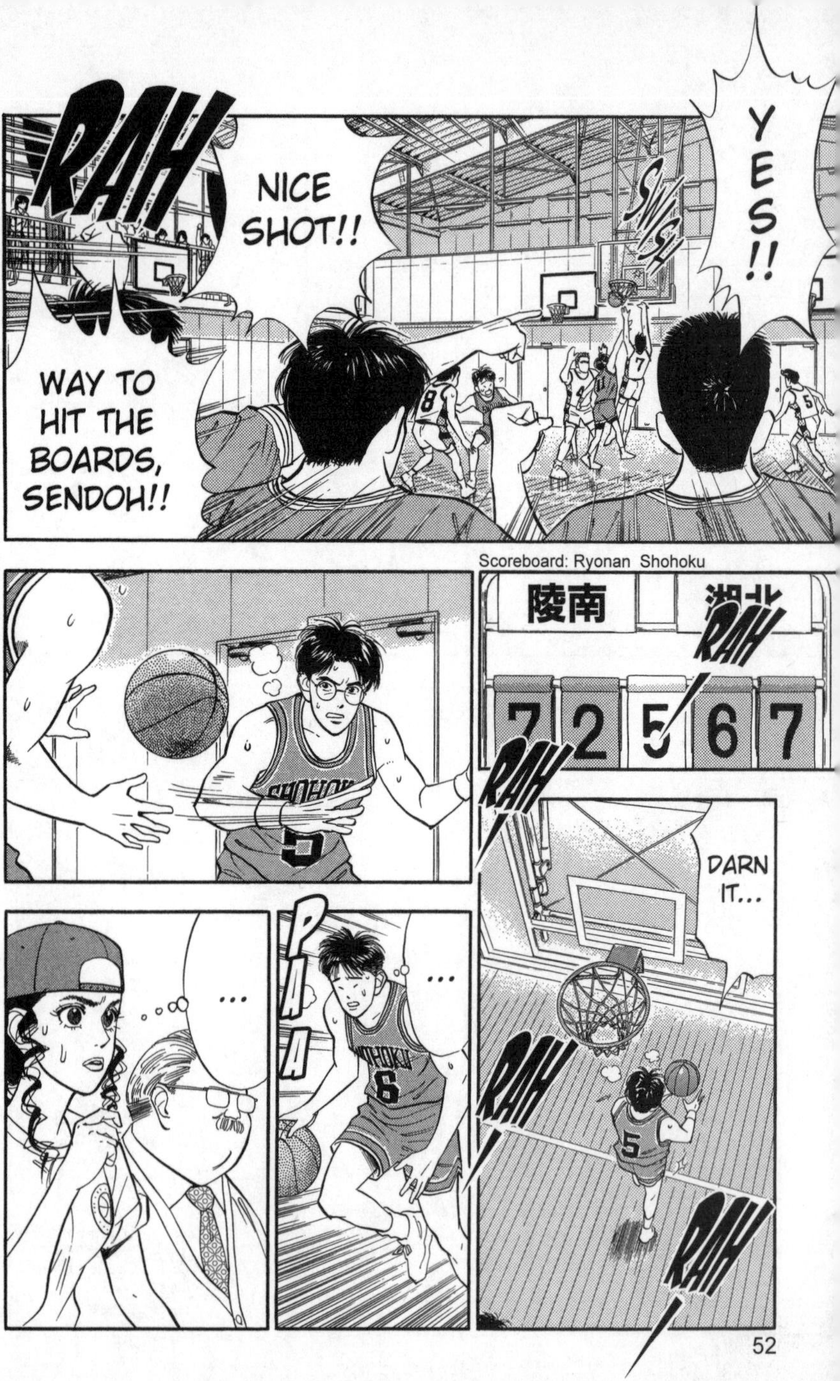
YES!!
SWISH
NICE SHOT!!
RAH
WAY TO HIT THE BOARDS, SENDOH!!
Scoreboard: Ryonan Shohoku
陵南
湘北
RAH
7 2 5 6 7
RAH
DARN IT...
RAH
RAH
...
PAH
...

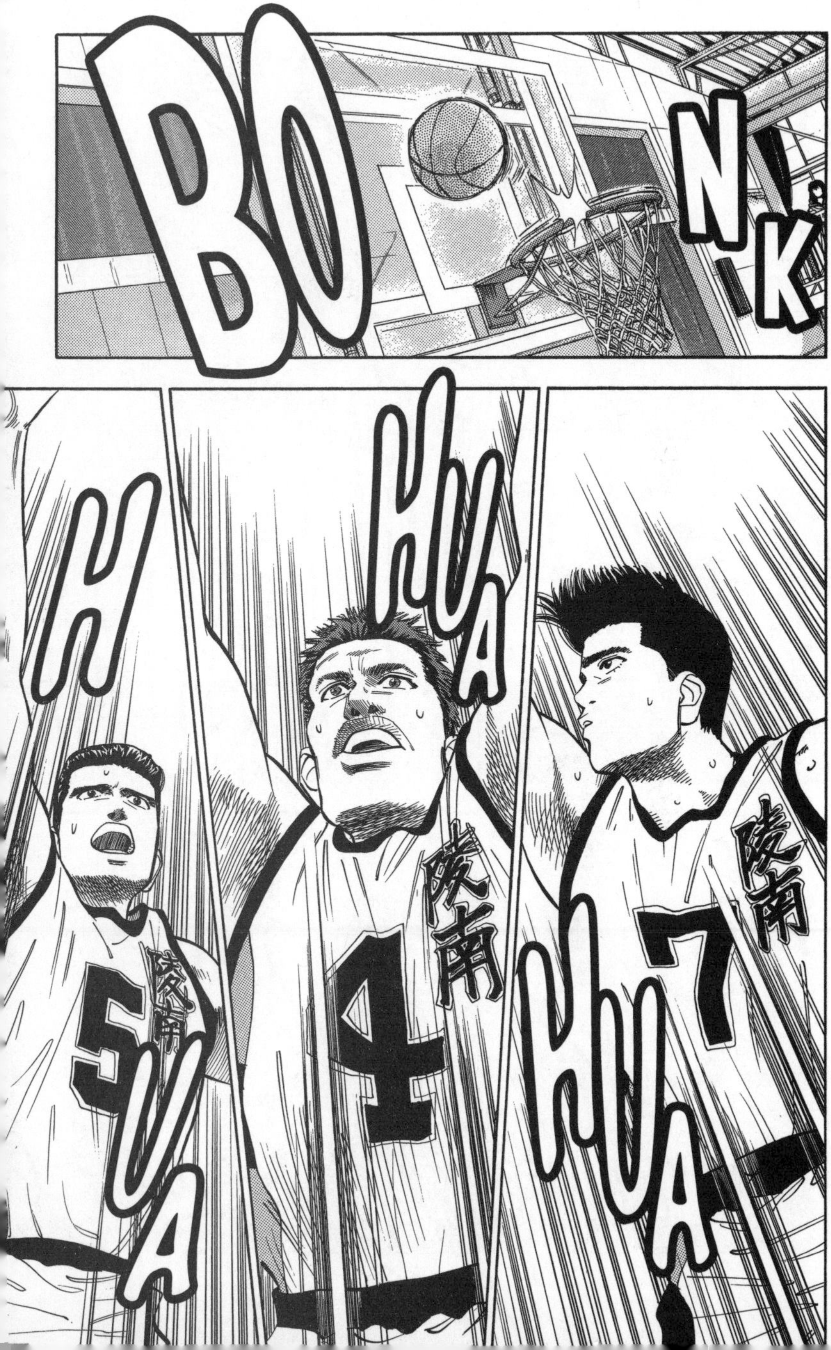
BONK
HUA
HUA
HUA

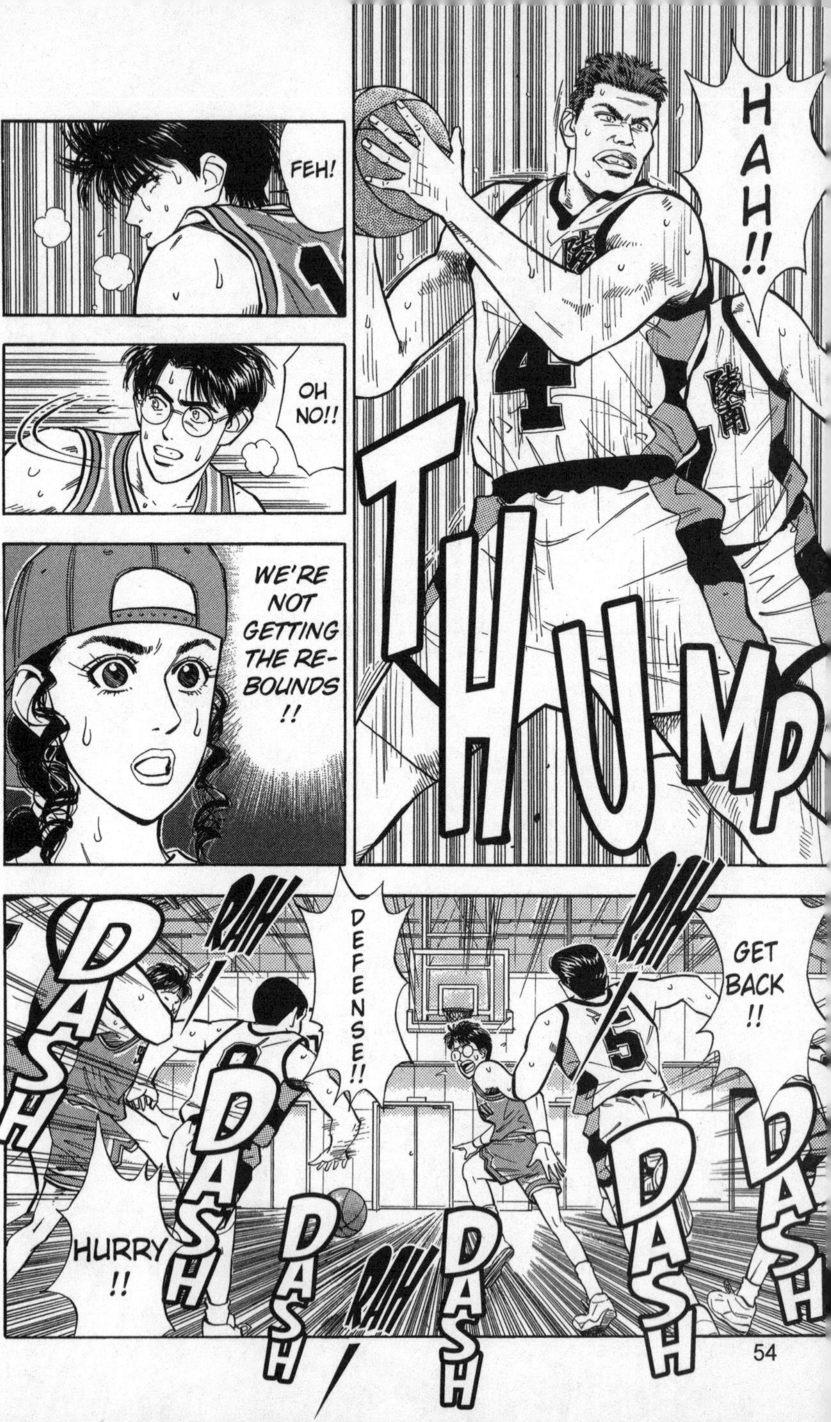
HAH!!
THUMP
FEH!
OH NO!!
WE'RE NOT GETTING THE RE-BOUNDS !!
GET BACK !!
DASH
DASH
RAH
DASH
RAH
DEFENSE!!
DASH
RAH
DASH
DASH
HURRY !!

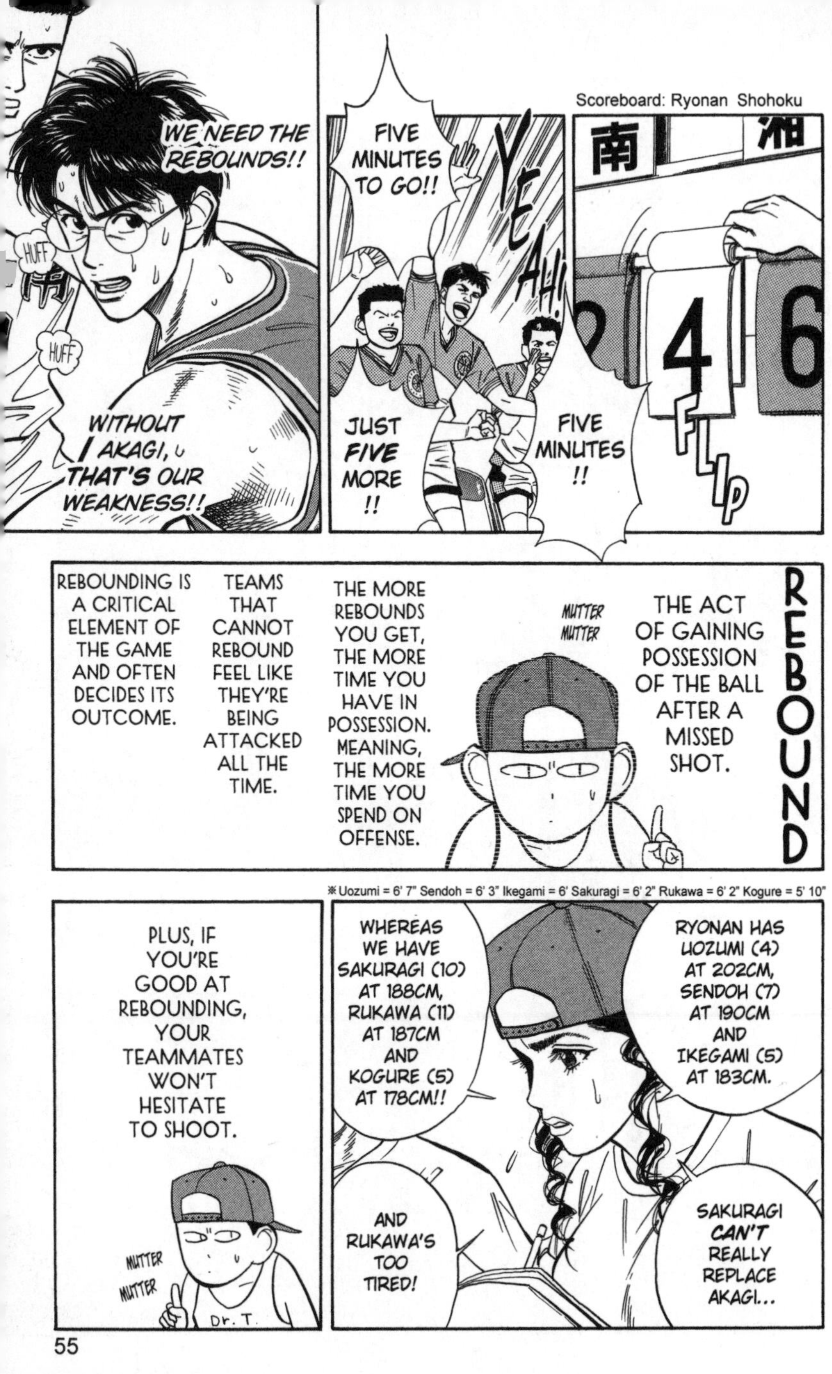
Scoreboard: Ryonan Shohoku
南
湘
4
6
FLIP
FIVE MINUTES TO GO!!
YEAH!
FIVE MINUTES!!
JUST FIVE MORE!!
WE NEED THE REBOUNDS!!
HUFF
HUFF
WITHOUT AKAGI, THAT'S OUR WEAKNESS!!
REBOUND
THE ACT OF GAINING POSSESSION OF THE BALL AFTER A MISSED SHOT.
MUTTER MUTTER
THE MORE REBOUNDS YOU GET, THE MORE TIME YOU HAVE IN POSSESSION. MEANING, THE MORE TIME YOU SPEND ON OFFENSE.
TEAMS THAT CANNOT REBOUND FEEL LIKE THEY'RE BEING ATTACKED ALL THE TIME.
REBOUNDING IS A CRITICAL ELEMENT OF THE GAME AND OFTEN DECIDES ITS OUTCOME.
※Uozumi = 6' 7" Sendoh = 6' 3" Ikegami = 6' Sakuragi = 6' 2" Rukawa = 6' 2" Kogure = 5' 10"
RYONAN HAS UOZUMI (4) AT 202CM, SENDOH (7) AT 190CM AND IKEGAMI (5) AT 183CM.
WHEREAS WE HAVE SAKURAGI (10) AT 188CM, RUKAWA (11) AT 187CM AND KOGURE (5) AT 178CM!!
SAKURAGI CAN'T REALLY REPLACE AKAGI...
AND RUKAWA'S TOO TIRED!
PLUS, IF YOU'RE GOOD AT REBOUNDING, YOUR TEAMMATES WON'T HESITATE TO SHOOT.
MUTTER
MUTTER
Dr. T.

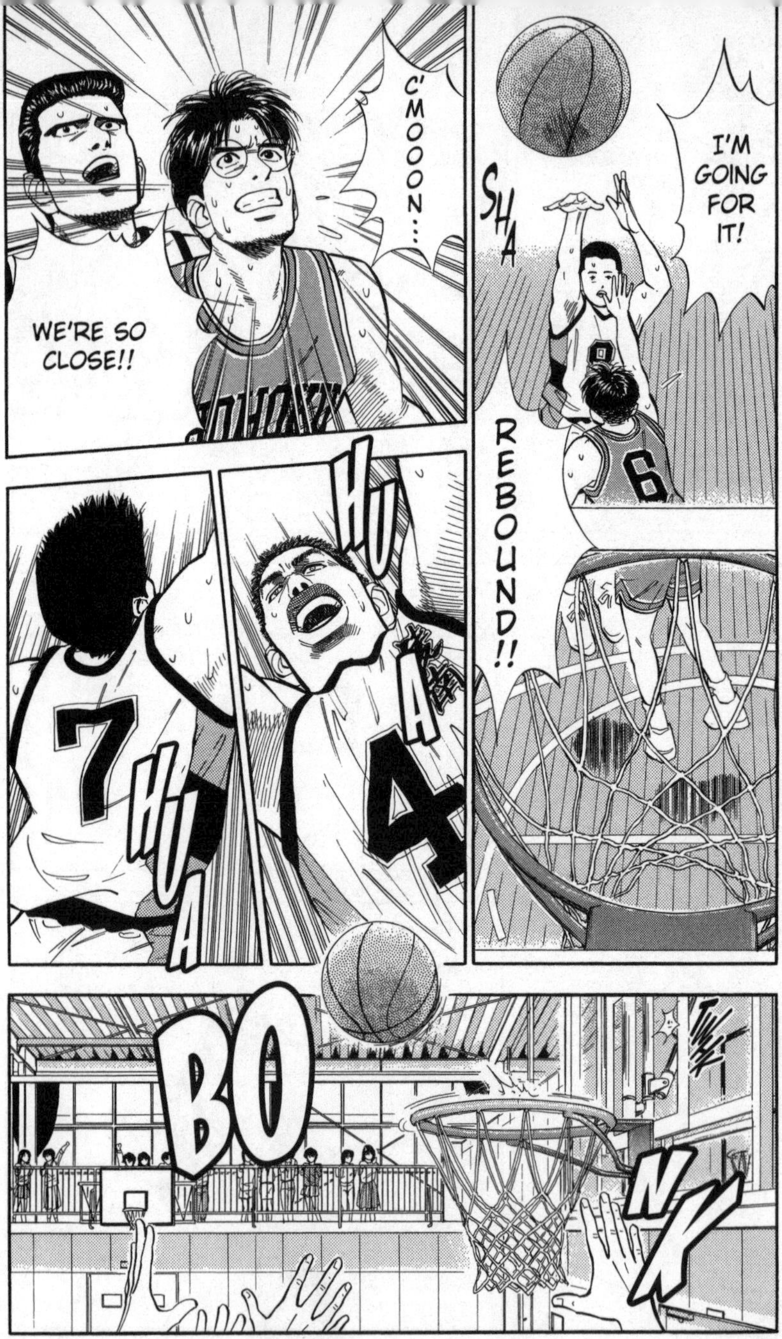
I'M GOING FOR IT!
SHA
REBOUND!!
C'MOOOON...
WE'RE SO CLOSE!!
HUA
HUA
BONK

READ THIS WAY

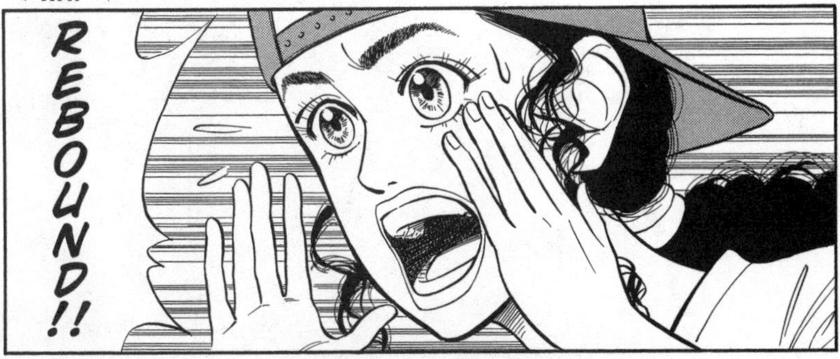
REBOUND!!

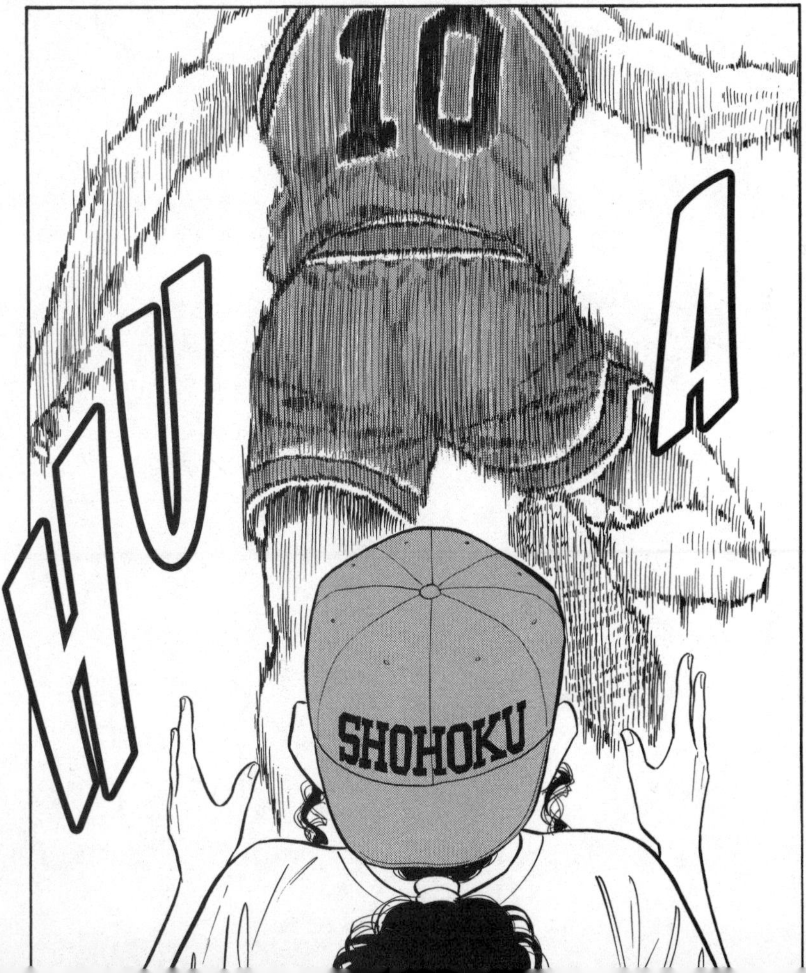
10
HUA
SHOHOKU

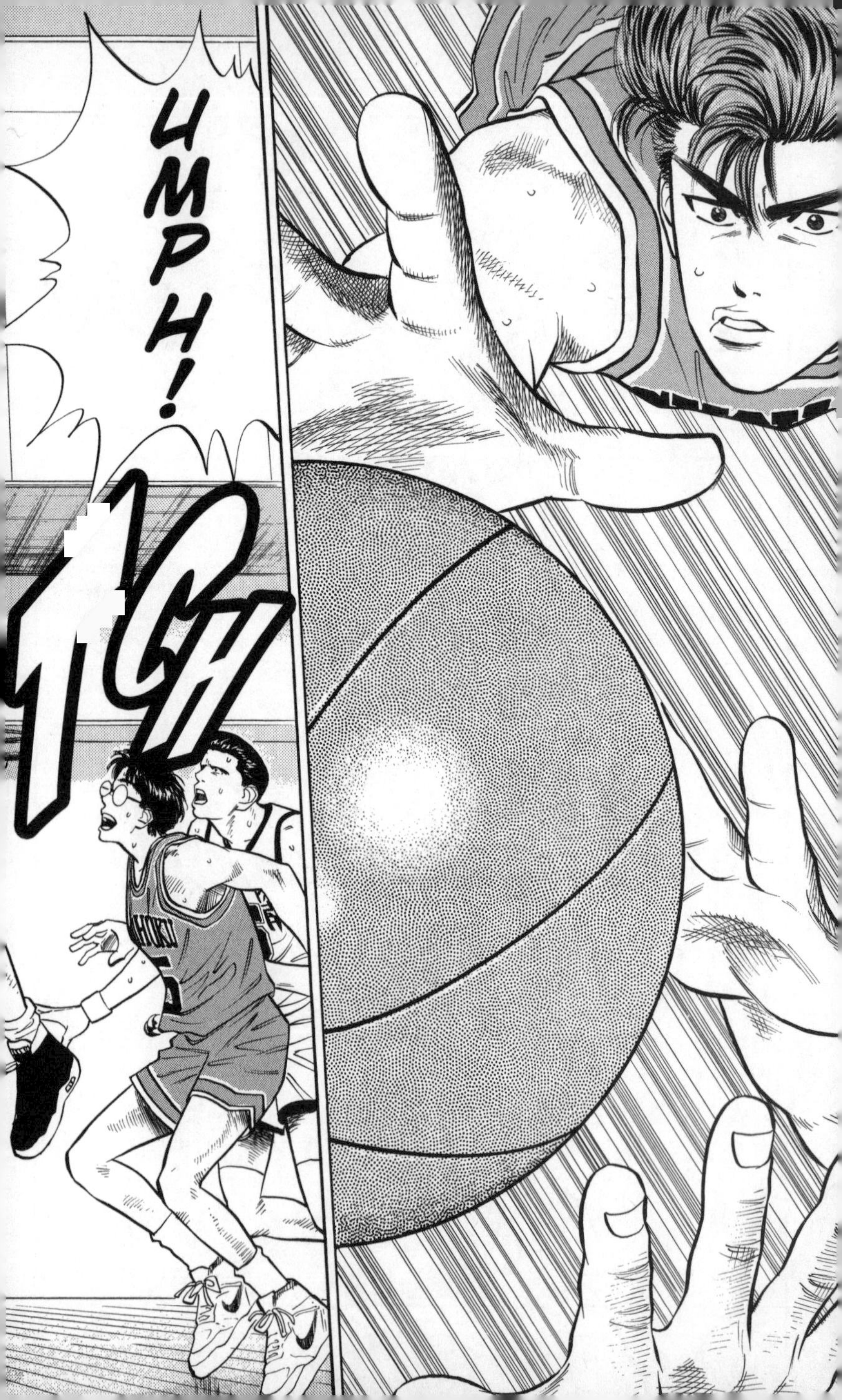
UMPH!

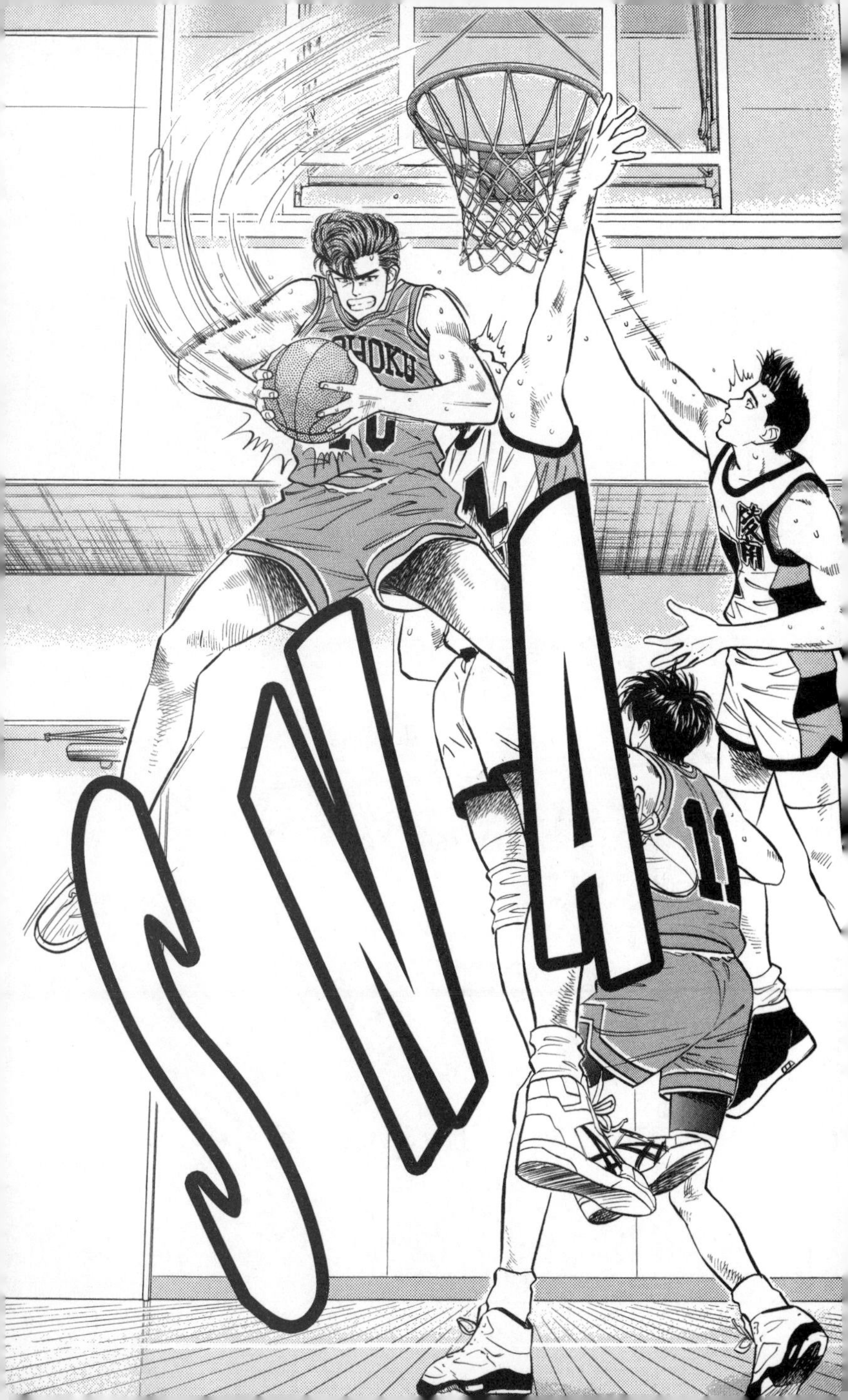
SNA

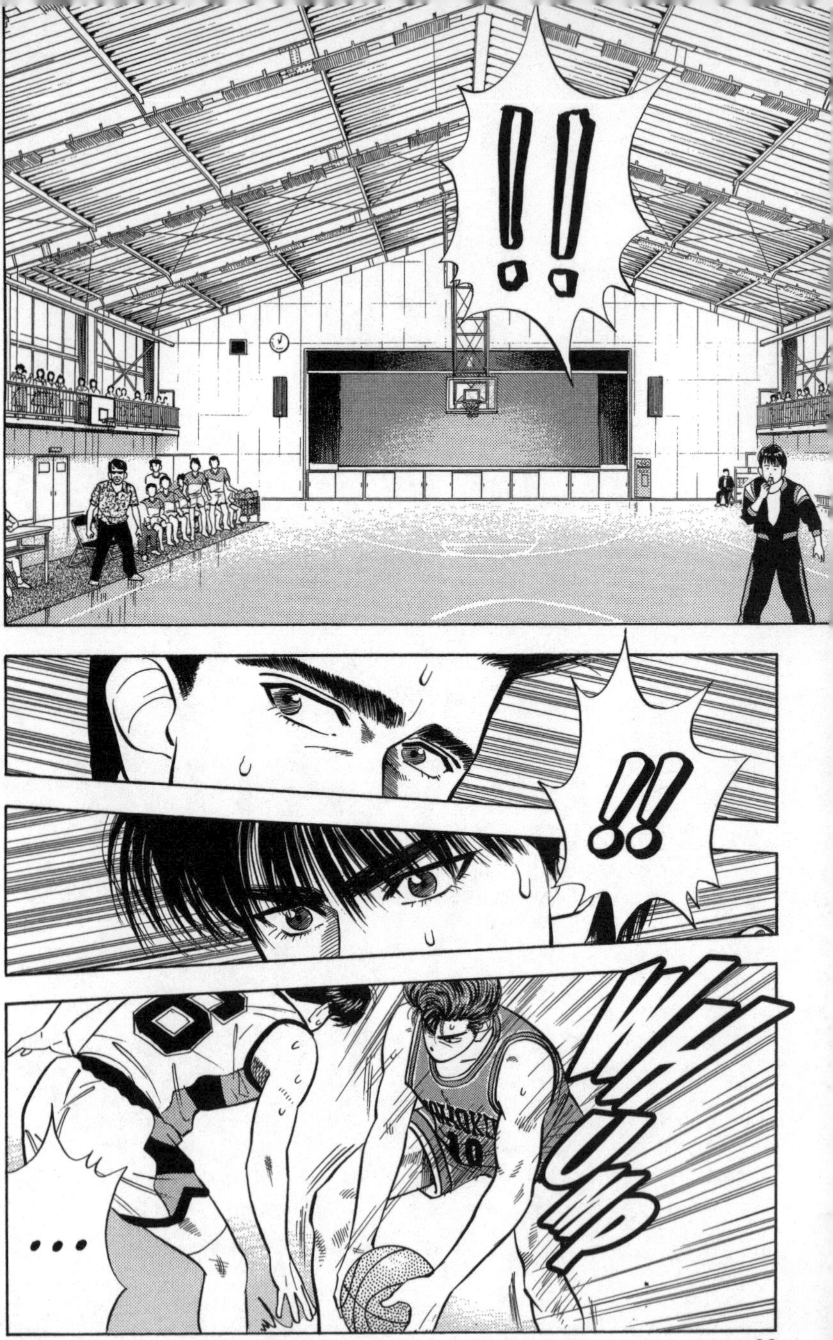
!!
!!
WHUMP
...

READ THIS WAY

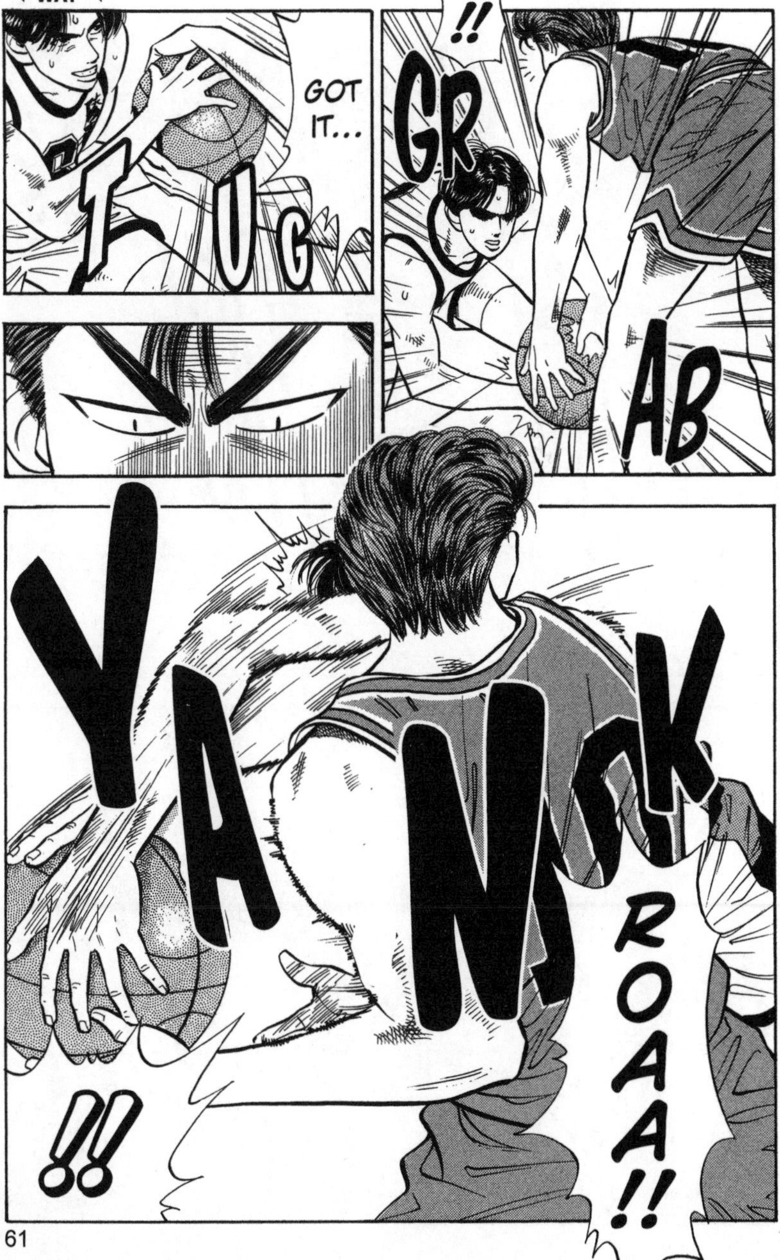
!!
GR
AB
GOT IT...
TUG
YANK
ROAA!!
!!

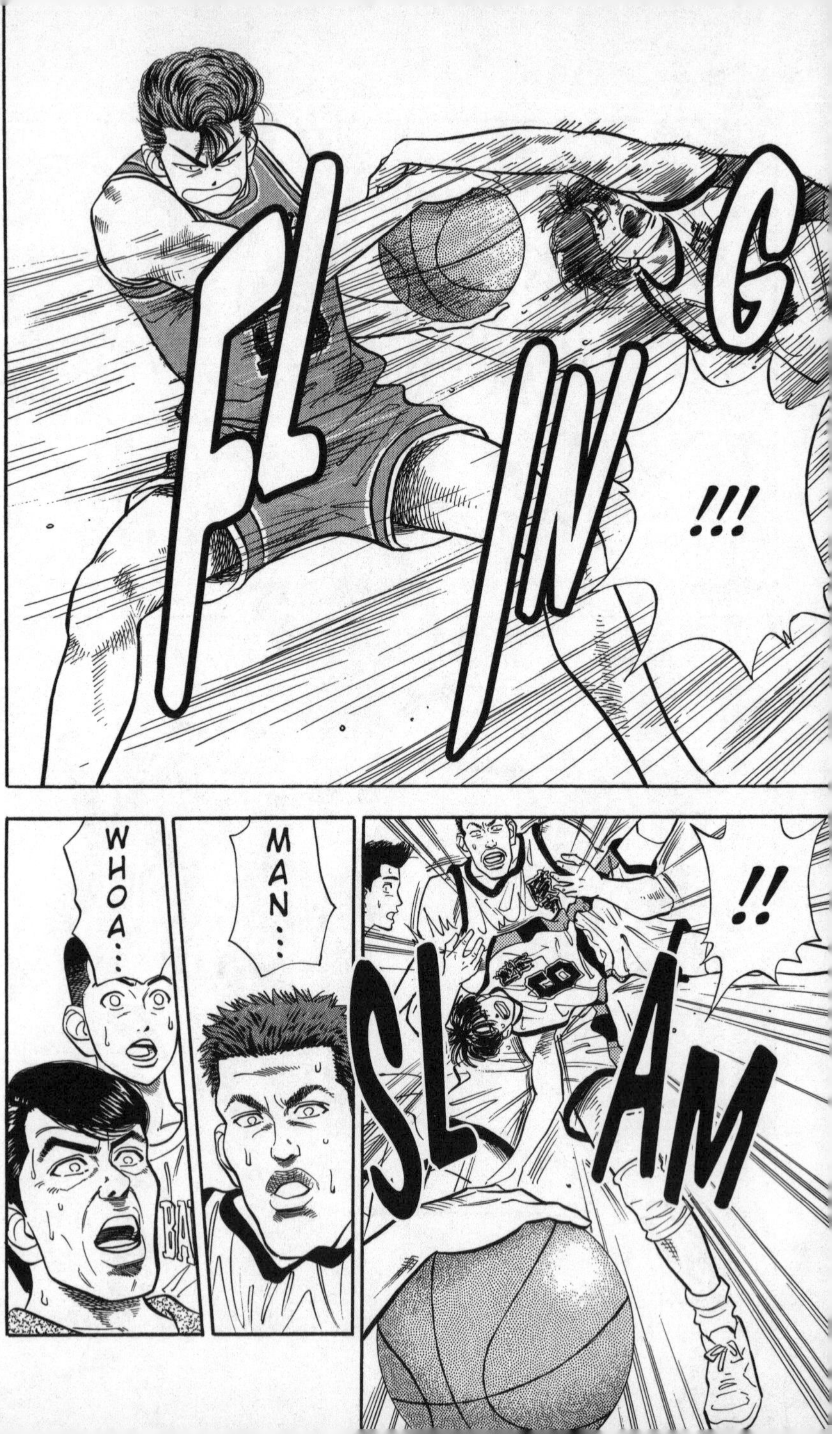
FLING
!!!
SLAM
!!
MAN...
WHOA...

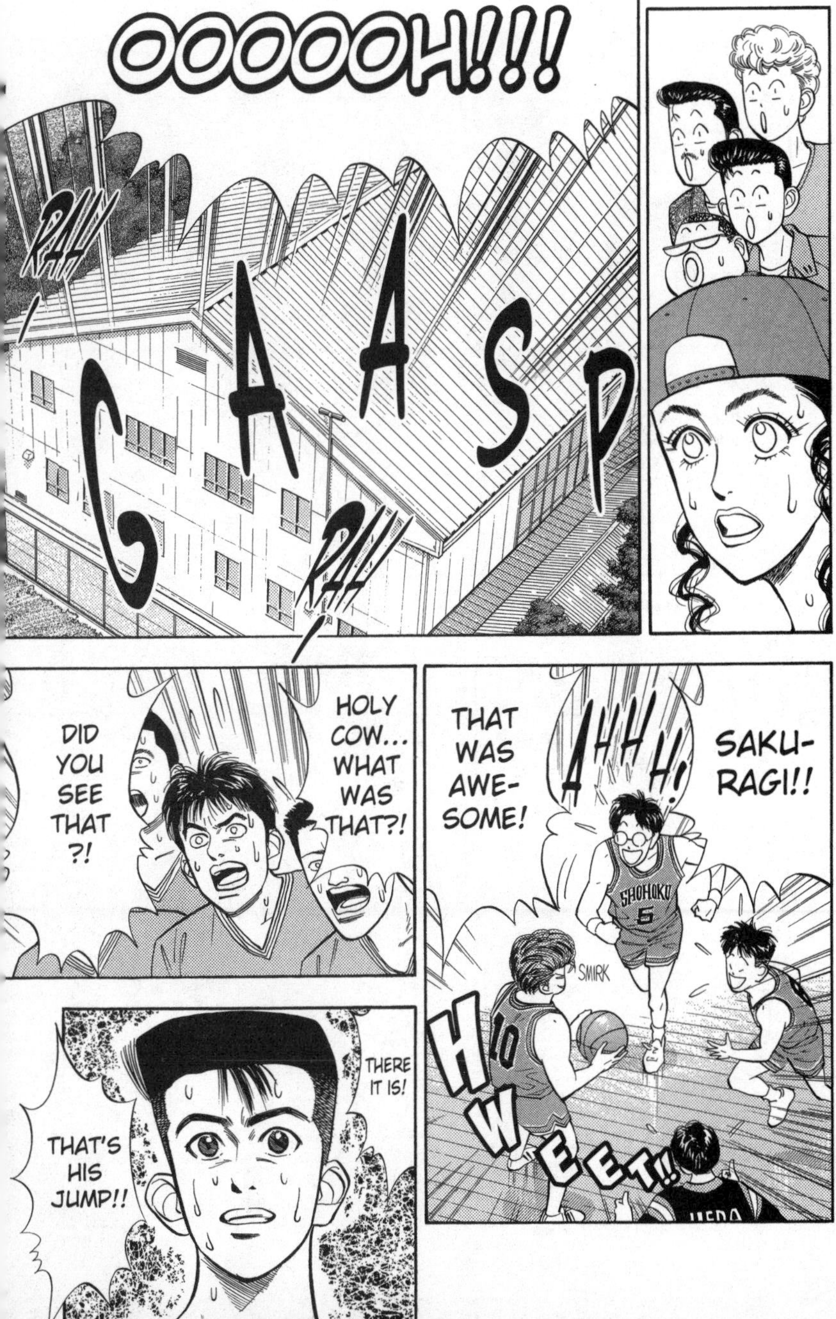
OOOOOH!!!
RAH
GAASP
RAH
SAKU-
RAGI!!
AHHH!
THAT
WAS
AWE-
SOME!
SMIRK
HWEET!!
HOLY
COW...
WHAT
WAS
THAT?!
DID
YOU
SEE
THAT
?!
THERE
IT IS!
THAT'S
HIS
JUMP!!

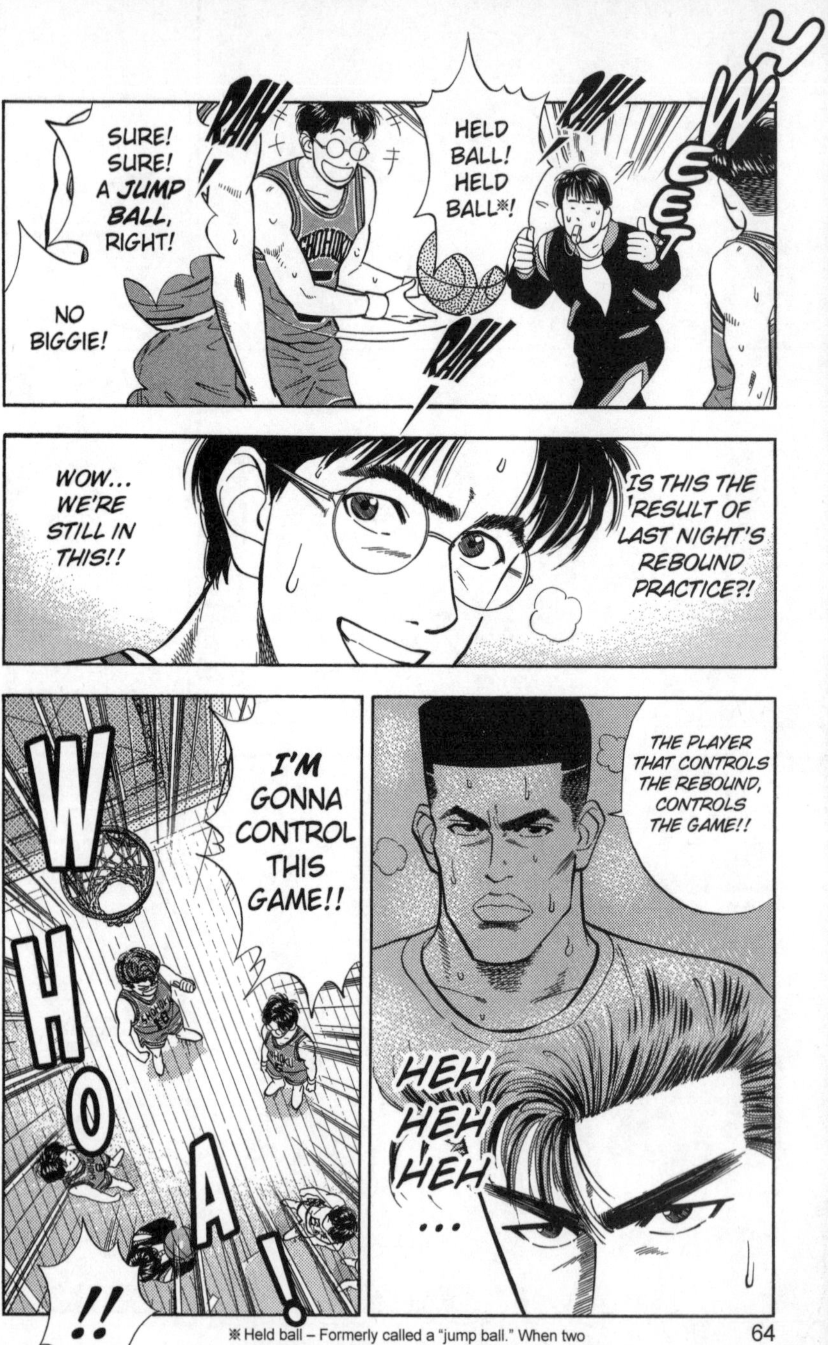
WHEET
RAH
HELD BALL! HELD BALL※!
RAH
SURE! SURE! A JUMP BALL, RIGHT!
NO BIGGIE!
RAH
IS THIS THE RESULT OF LAST NIGHT'S REBOUND PRACTICE?!
WOW... WE'RE STILL IN THIS!!
THE PLAYER THAT CONTROLS THE REBOUND, CONTROLS THE GAME!!
HEH HEH HEH...
I'M GONNA CONTROL THIS GAME!!
WHOA!
!!

※ Held ball – Formerly called a "jump ball." When two players on opposite teams are in joint control of the ball.

READ THIS WAY

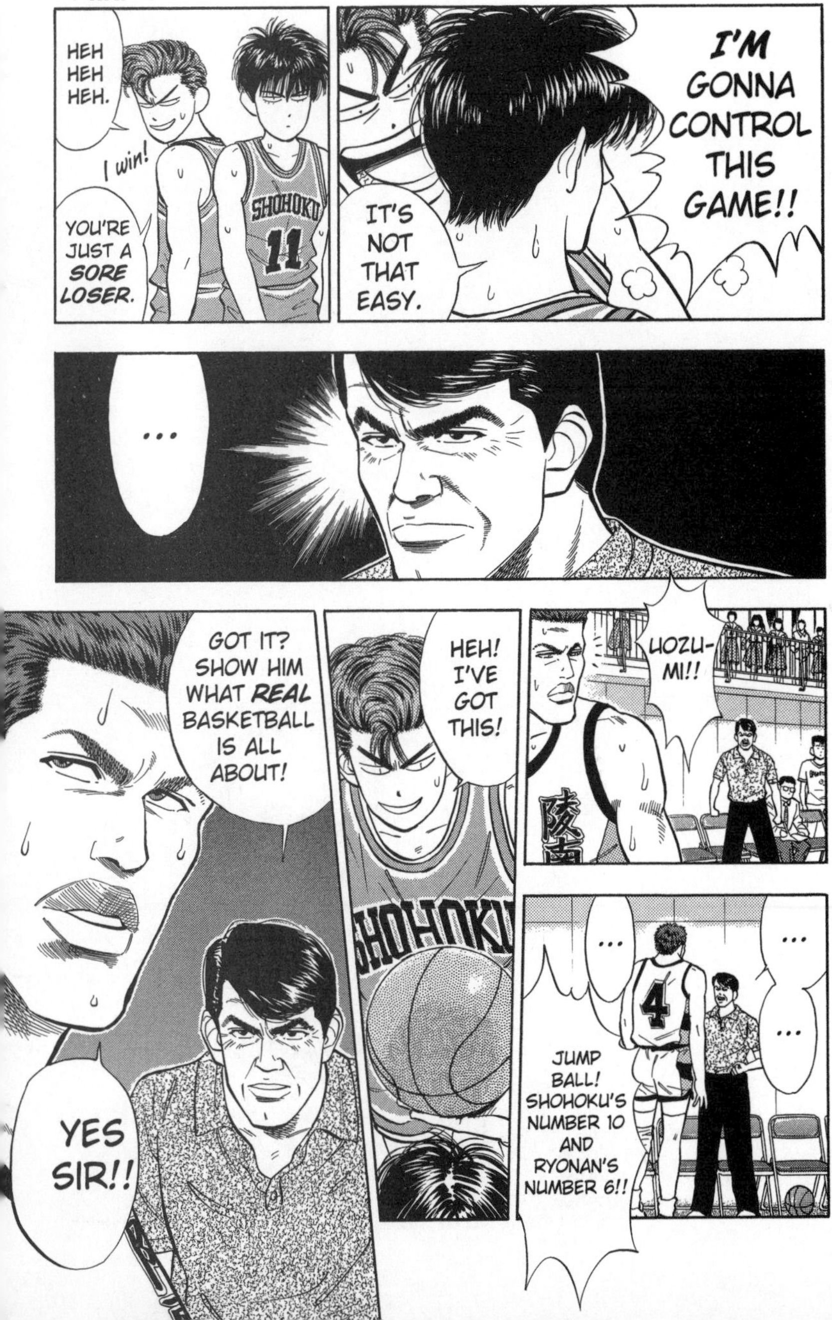
I'M GONNA CONTROL THIS GAME!!
IT'S NOT THAT EASY.
HEH HEH HEH.
I win!
YOU'RE JUST A SORE LOSER.
...
UOZU-MI!!
...
...
...
JUMP BALL! SHOHOKU'S NUMBER 10 AND RYONAN'S NUMBER 6!!
HEH! I'VE GOT THIS!
GOT IT? SHOW HIM WHAT REAL BASKETBALL IS ALL ABOUT!
YES SIR!!

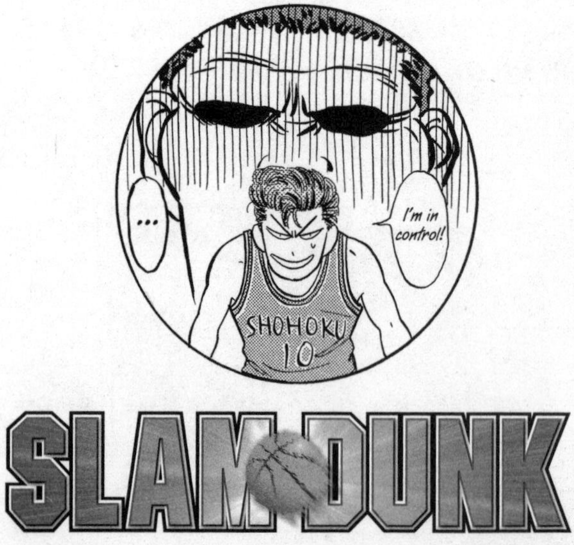
I'm in control!
...
SHOHOKU
10

SLAM DUNK

#39 TROUBLE IN THE REBOUND KING'S COURT

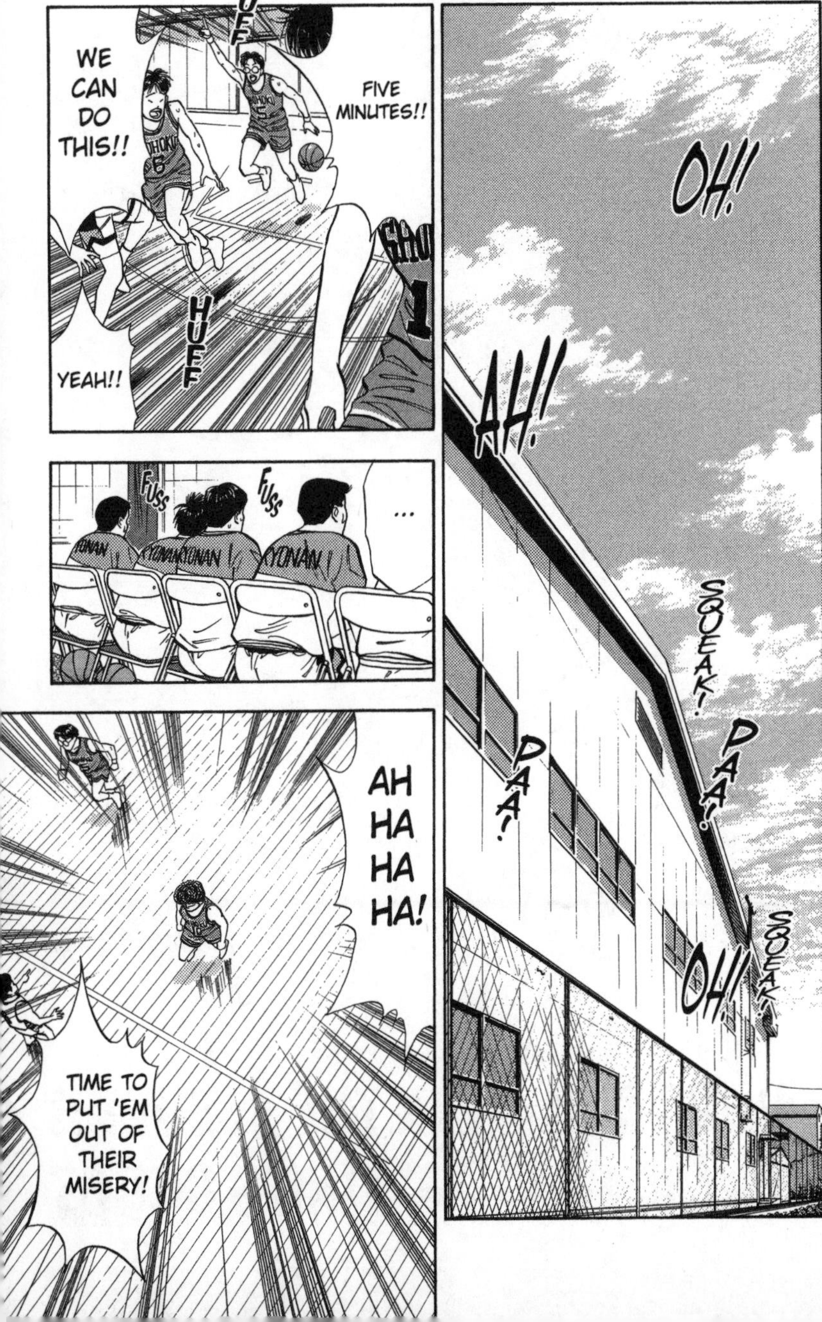
OH!
AH!
SQUEAK!
PAA!
DAA!
SQUEAK!
OH!
FIVE MINUTES!!
HUFF
WE CAN DO THIS!!
HUFF
YEAH!!
...
FUSS
FUSS
AH HA HA HA HA!
TIME TO PUT 'EM OUT OF THEIR MISERY!

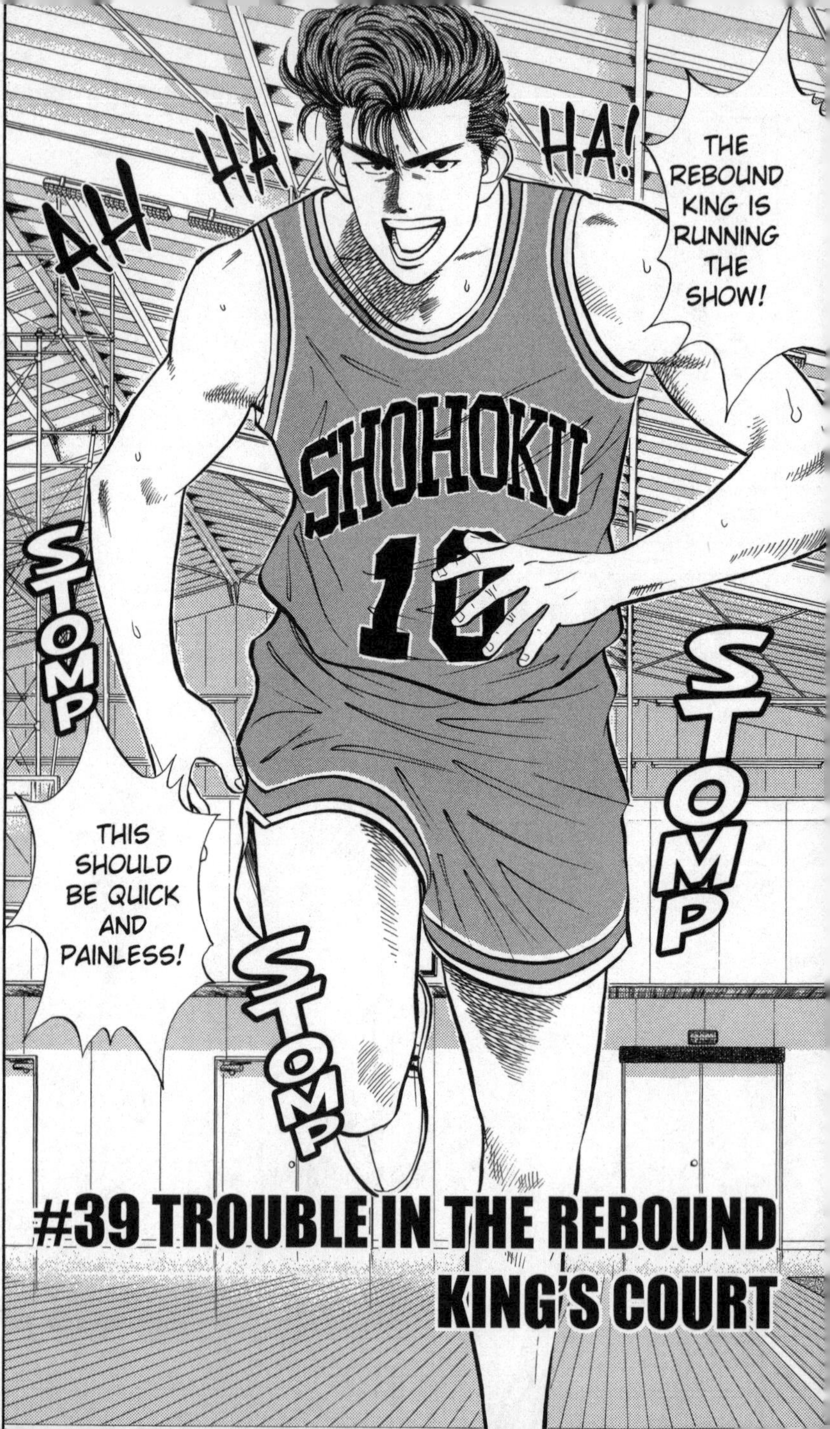
THE REBOUND KING IS RUNNING THE SHOW!
AH HA HA HA!
STOMP
STOMP
STOMP
THIS SHOULD BE QUICK AND PAINLESS!

#39 TROUBLE IN THE REBOUND KING'S COURT

READ THIS WAY

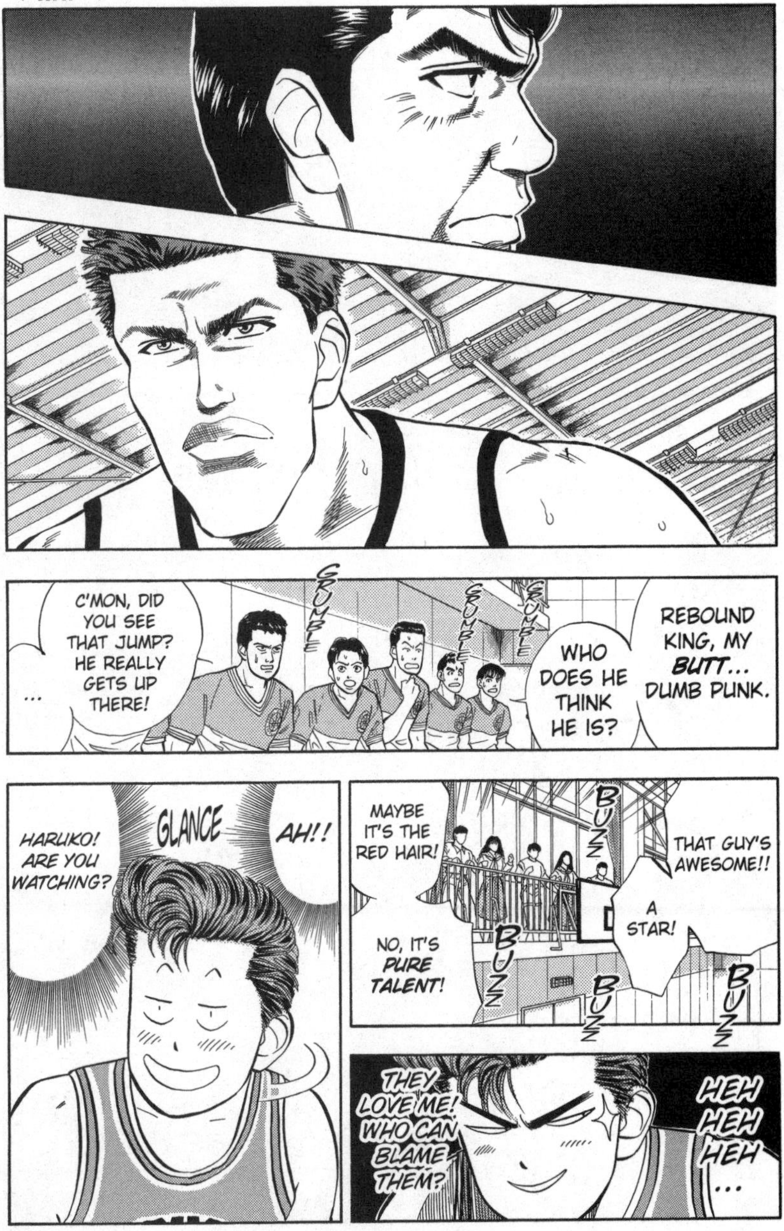
REBOUND KING, MY **BUTT**... DUMB PUNK.
WHO DOES HE THINK HE IS?
GRUMBLE
GRUMBLE
GRUMBLE
C'MON, DID YOU SEE THAT JUMP? HE REALLY GETS UP THERE!
...
THAT GUY'S AWESOME!!
A STAR!
MAYBE IT'S THE RED HAIR!
NO, IT'S **PURE TALENT**!
BUZZ
BUZZ
BUZZ
BUZZ
HEH HEH HEH ...
THEY LOVE ME! WHO CAN BLAME THEM?
AH!!
GLANCE
HARUKO! ARE YOU WATCHING?

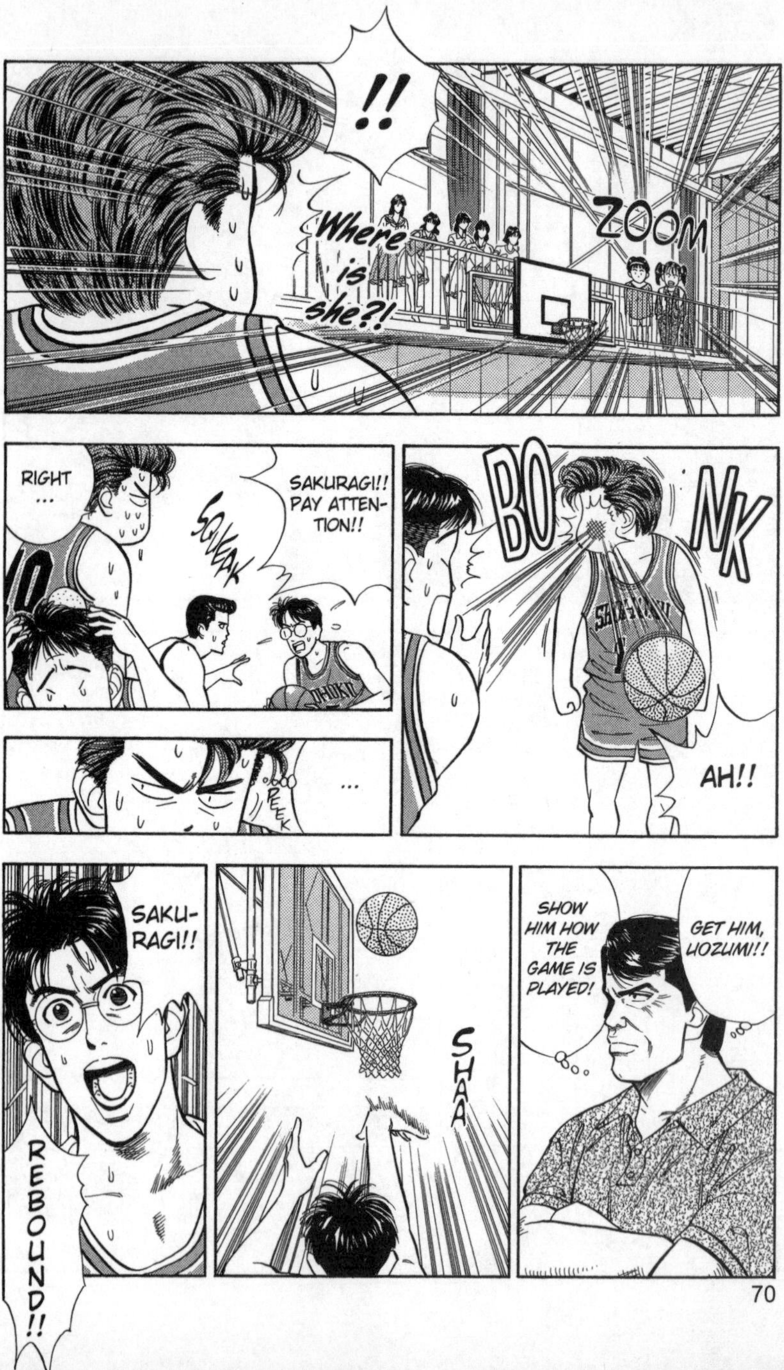
!!
ZOOM
Where is she?!
BONK
AH!!
SAKURAGI!! PAY ATTENTION!!
SQUEAK
RIGHT ...
...
PEEK
GET HIM, UOZUMI!!
SHOW HIM HOW THE GAME IS PLAYED!
SHAA
SAKU-RAGI!!
REBOUND!!

READ THIS WAY

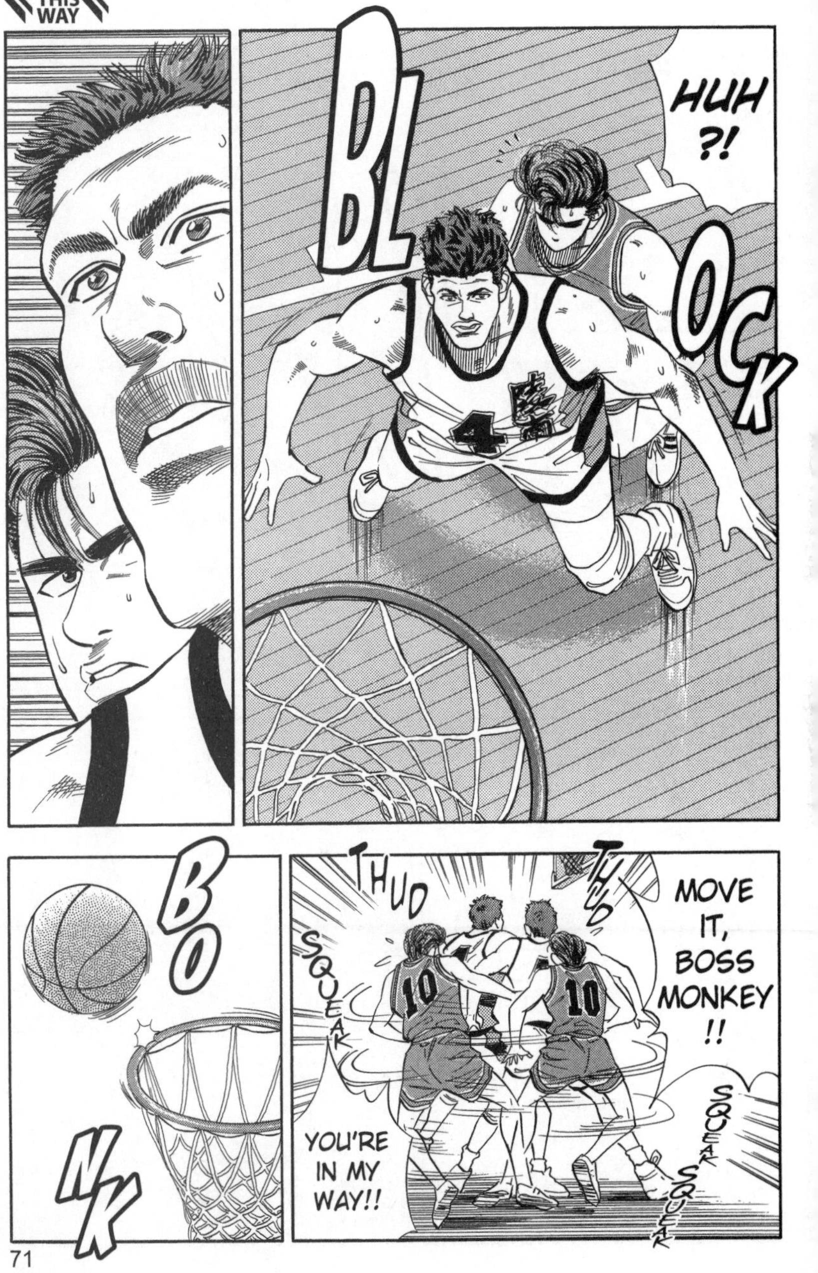
BLOCK
HUH?!
THUD
THUD
MOVE IT, BOSS MONKEY!!
SQUEAK
YOU'RE IN MY WAY!!
SQUEAK
SQUEAK
BONK

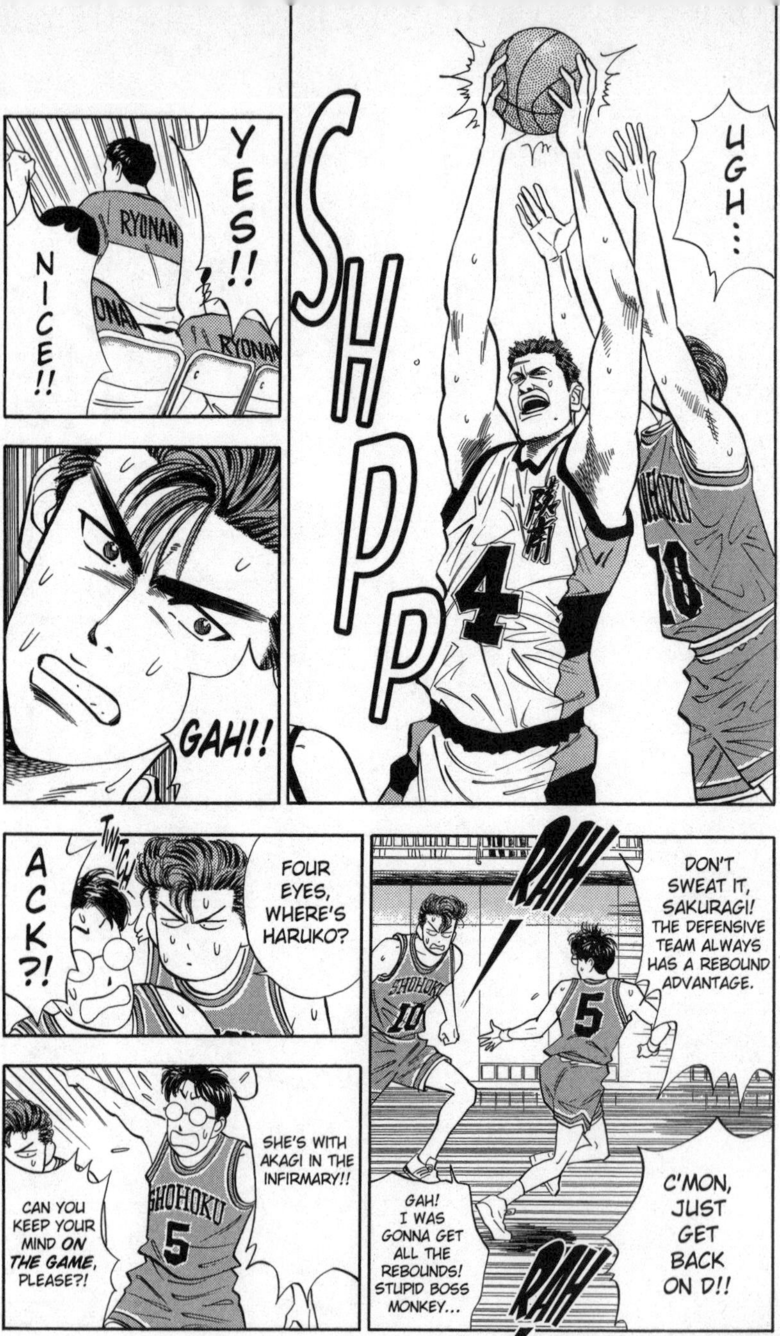
UGH...
SHPP
YES!!
NICE!!
GAH!!
DON'T SWEAT IT, SAKURAGI! THE DEFENSIVE TEAM ALWAYS HAS A REBOUND ADVANTAGE.
RAH
C'MON, JUST GET BACK ON D!!
GAH! I WAS GONNA GET ALL THE REBOUNDS! STUPID BOSS MONKEY...
RAH
FOUR EYES, WHERE'S HARUKO?
TWITCH
ACK?!
SHE'S WITH AKAGI IN THE INFIRMARY!!
CAN YOU KEEP YOUR MIND ***ON THE GAME***, PLEASE?!

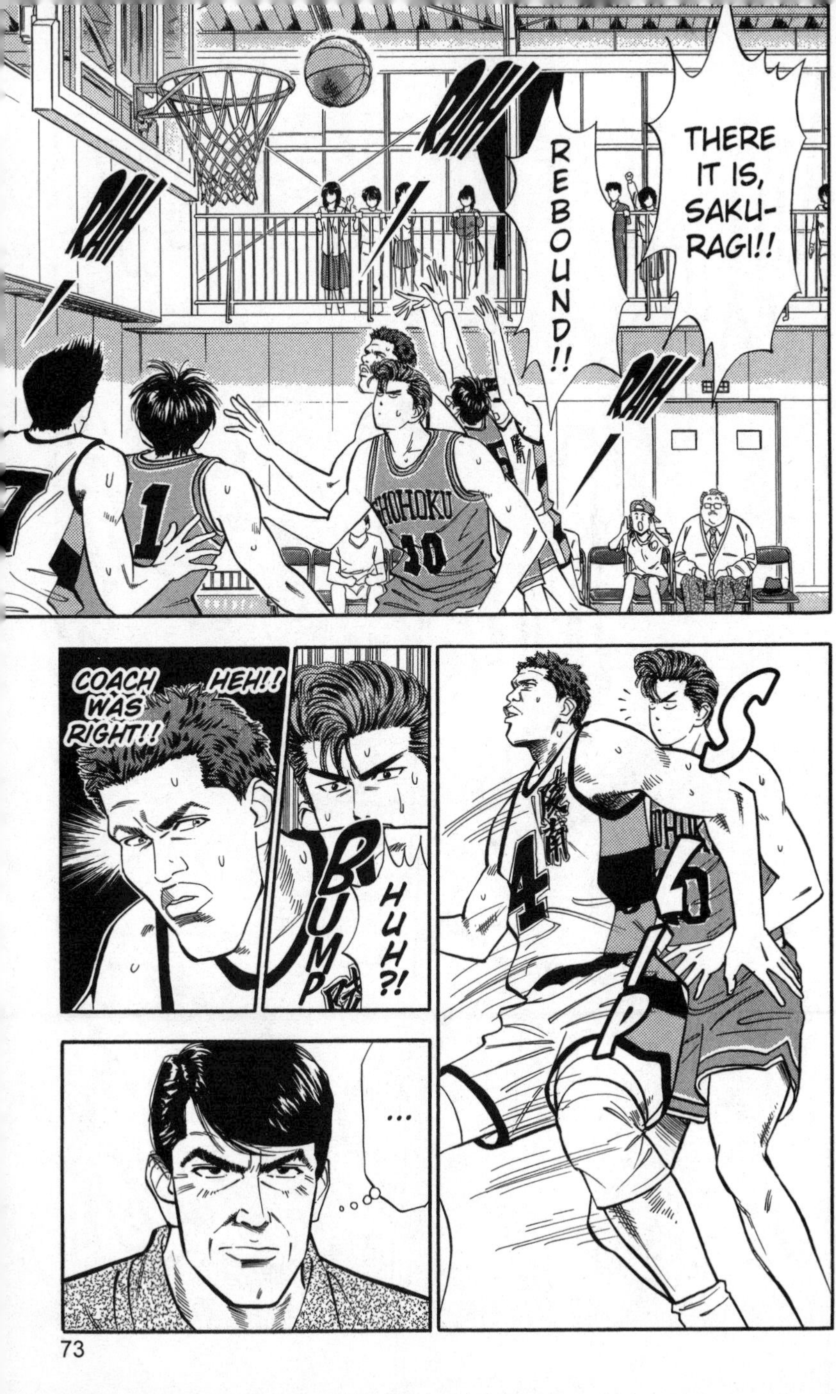
THERE IT IS, SAKURAGI!!
REBOUND!!
RAH
RAH
RAH
SLIP
HUH?!
BUMP
HEH!!
COACH WAS RIGHT!!
...

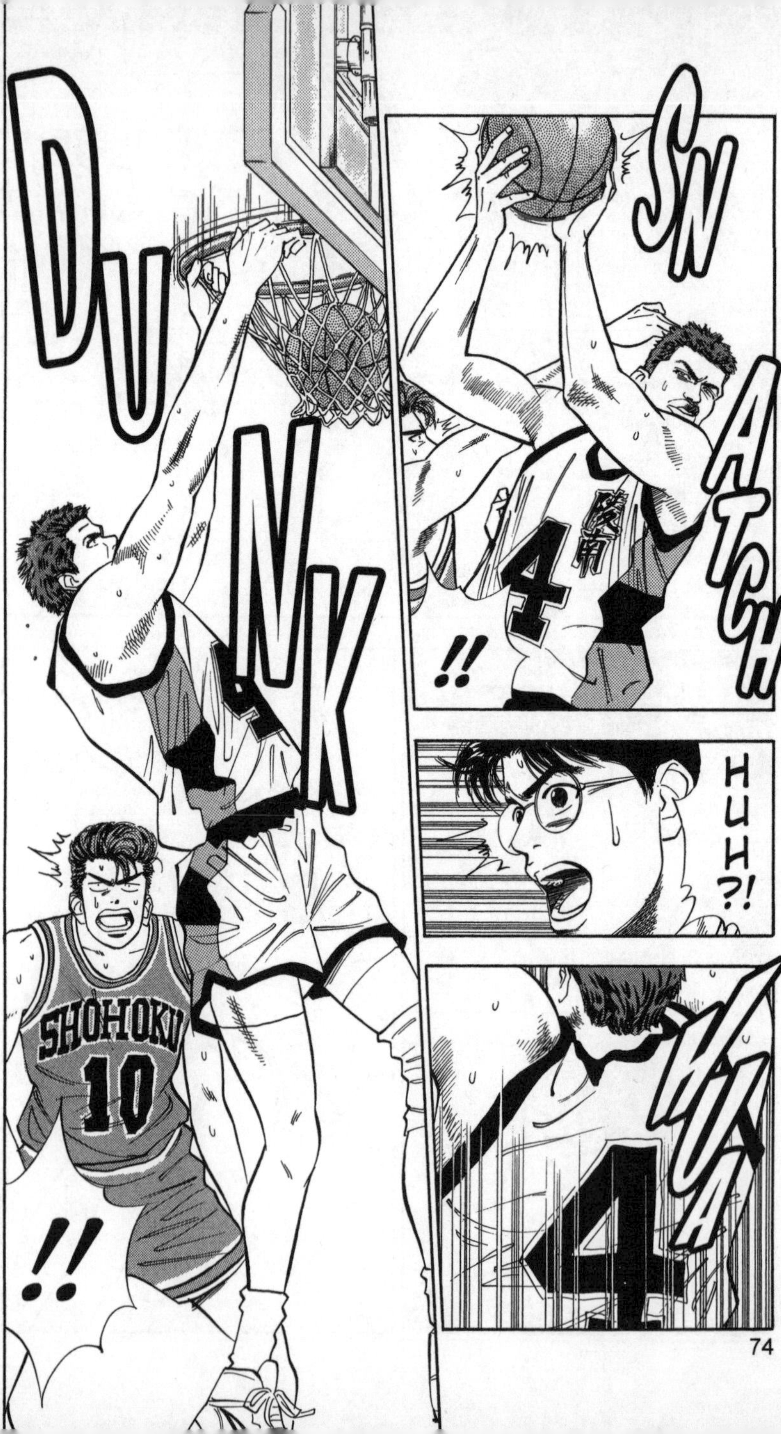
SNATCH
!!
HUH?!
DUNK
SHOHOKU 10
!!

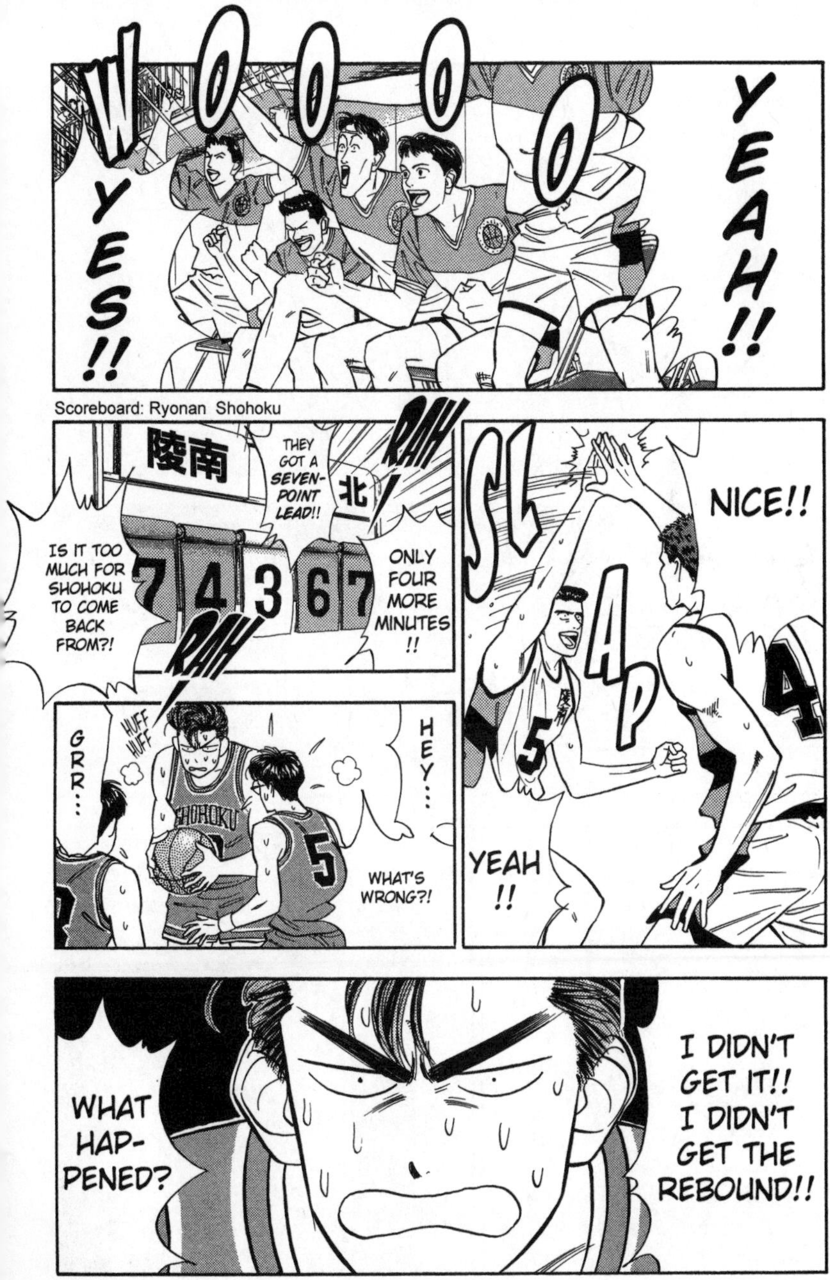
WOOOOO
YEAH!!
YES!!
Scoreboard: Ryonan Shohoku
SLAP
NICE!!
YEAH!!
RAH
THEY GOT A SEVEN-POINT LEAD!!
ONLY FOUR MORE MINUTES!!
陵南
北
7 4 3 6 7
IS IT TOO MUCH FOR SHOHOKU TO COME BACK FROM?!
RAH
HEY...
WHAT'S WRONG?!
HUFF HUFF
GRR...
SHOHOKU
I DIDN'T GET IT!! I DIDN'T GET THE REBOUND!!
WHAT HAPPENED?

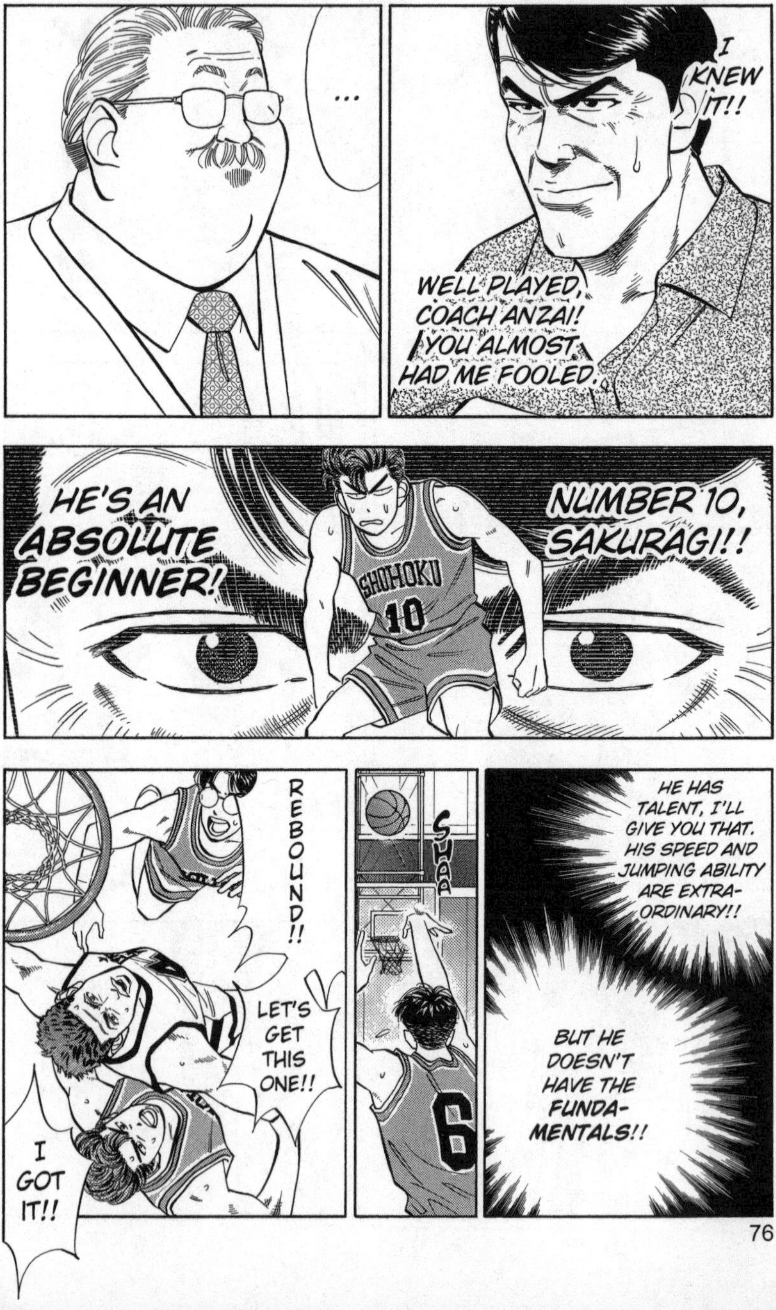
I KNEW IT!!
WELL PLAYED, COACH ANZAI! YOU ALMOST HAD ME FOOLED.
...
NUMBER 10, SAKURAGI!!
HE'S AN ABSOLUTE BEGINNER!
HE HAS TALENT, I'LL GIVE YOU THAT. HIS SPEED AND JUMPING ABILITY ARE EXTRA-ORDINARY!!
BUT HE DOESN'T HAVE THE FUNDA-MENTALS!!
SHAA
REBOUND!!
LET'S GET THIS ONE!!
I GOT IT!!

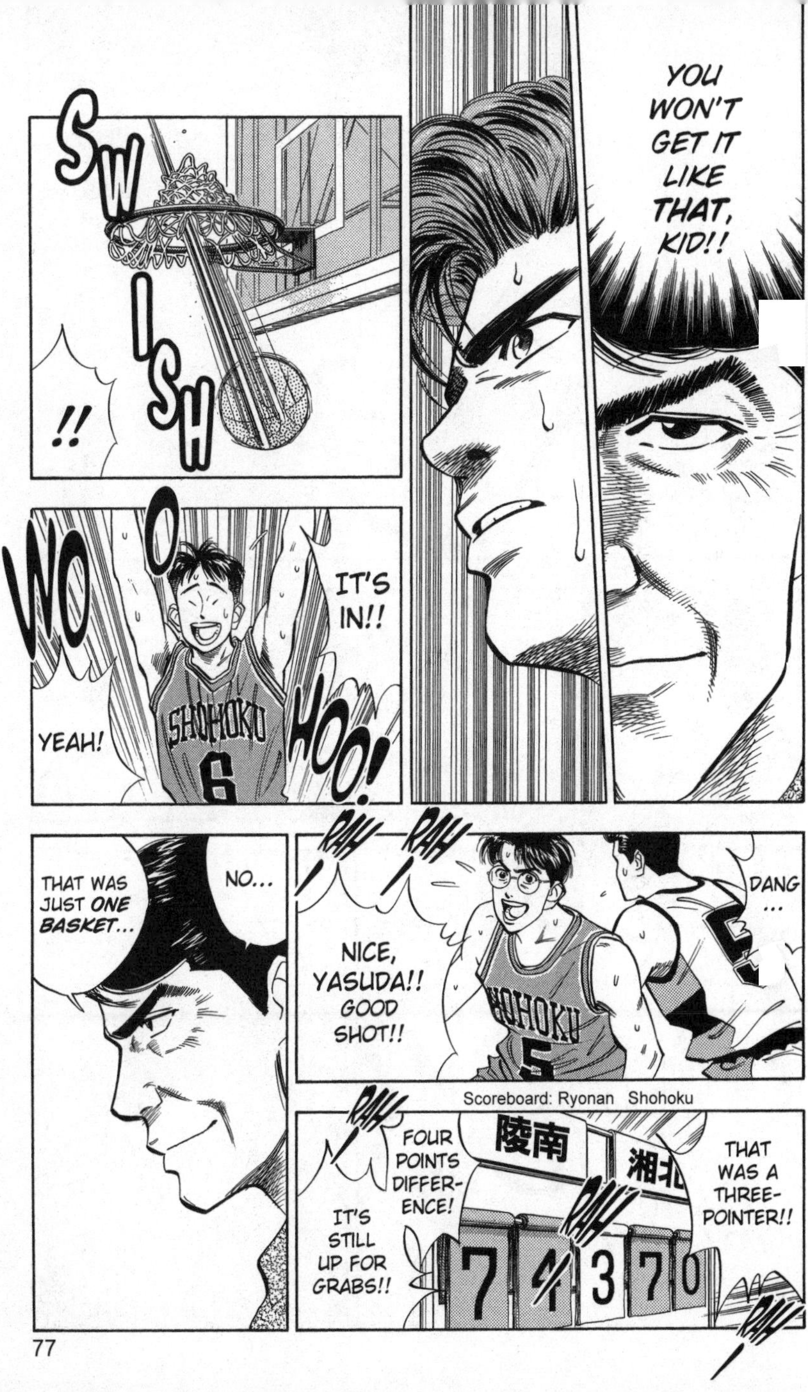
YOU WON'T GET IT LIKE THAT, KID!!
SWISH
!!
WOOO
HOO!
IT'S IN!!
YEAH!
DANG...
RAH!
RAH!
NICE, YASUDA!! GOOD SHOT!!
Scoreboard: Ryonan Shohoku
THAT WAS A THREE-POINTER!!
陵南
湘北
RAH
FOUR POINTS DIFFERENCE!
RAH
IT'S STILL UP FOR GRABS!!
RAH
NO...
THAT WAS JUST ONE BASKET...

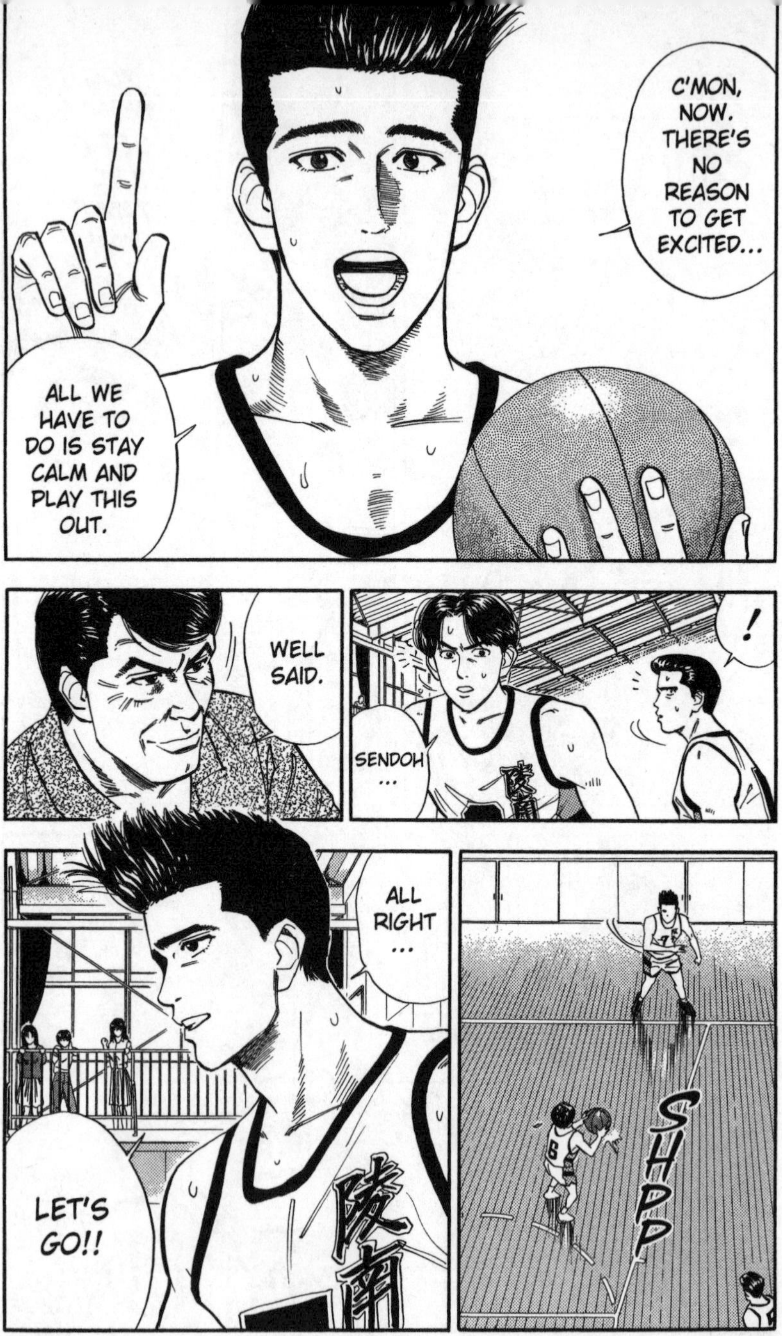
C'MON, NOW. THERE'S NO REASON TO GET EXCITED...
ALL WE HAVE TO DO IS STAY CALM AND PLAY THIS OUT.
!
SENDOH ...
WELL SAID.
SHPP
ALL RIGHT ...
LET'S GO!!

READ THIS WAY

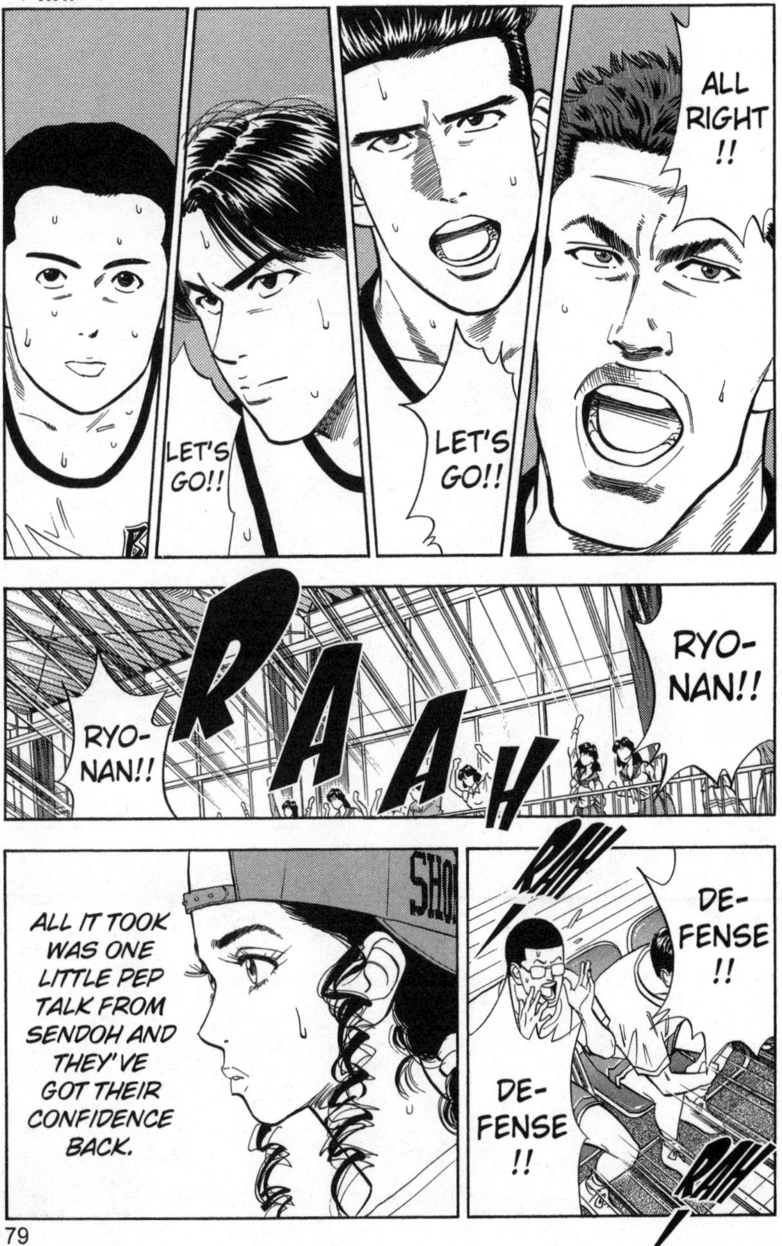

ALL RIGHT!!
LET'S GO!!
LET'S GO!!
RYO-NAN!!
RAAAH
RYO-NAN!!
RAH
DE-FENSE!!
DE-FENSE!!
RAH
ALL IT TOOK WAS ONE LITTLE PEP TALK FROM SENDOH AND THEY'VE GOT THEIR CONFIDENCE BACK.

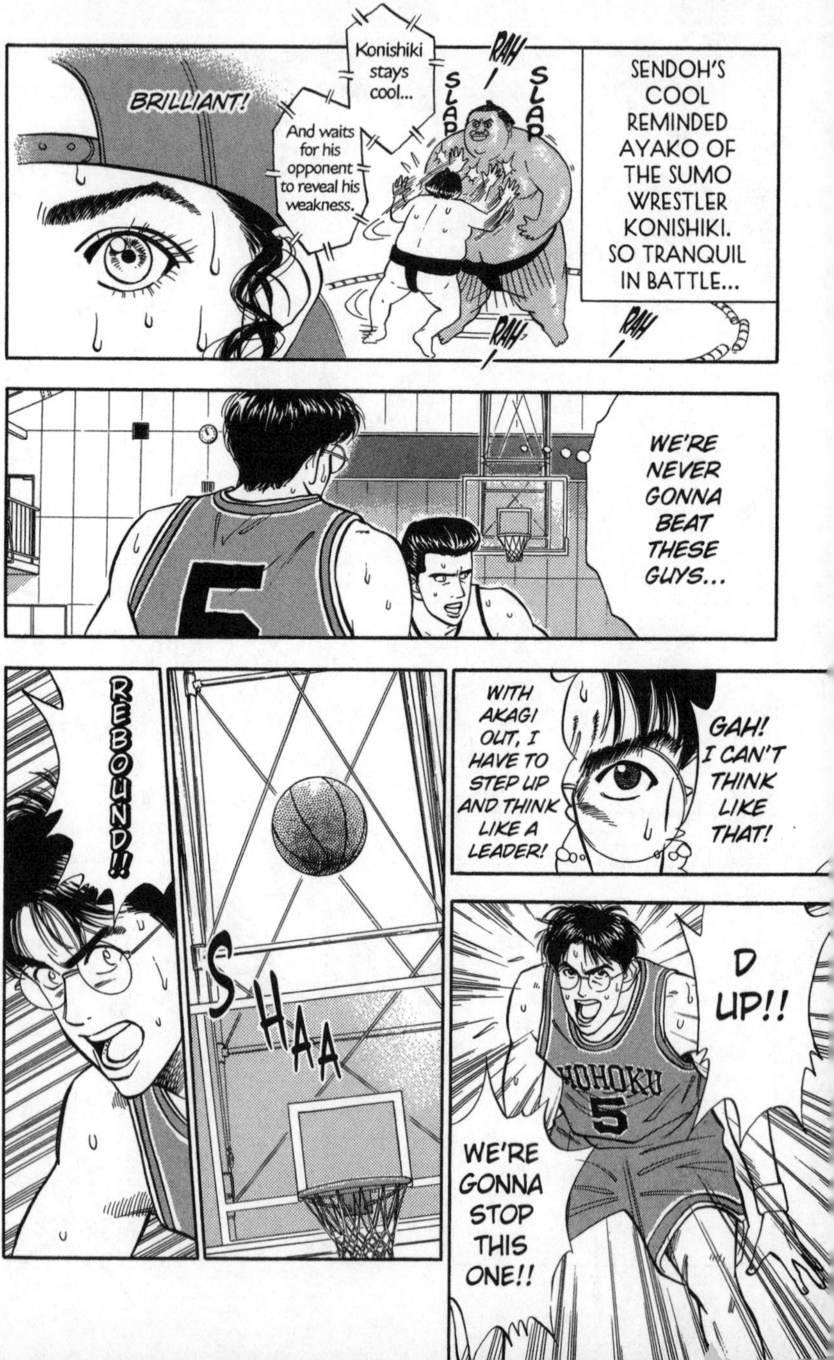
SENDOH'S COOL REMINDED AYAKO OF THE SUMO WRESTLER KONISHIKI. SO TRANQUIL IN BATTLE...
SLAP
RAH!
SLAP
Konishiki stays cool...
And waits for his opponent to reveal his weakness.
BRILLIANT!
RAH!
RAH!
WE'RE NEVER GONNA BEAT THESE GUYS...
GAH! I CAN'T THINK LIKE THAT!
WITH AKAGI OUT, I HAVE TO STEP UP AND THINK LIKE A LEADER!
D UP!!
WE'RE GONNA STOP THIS ONE!!
SHAA
REBOUND!!

READ THIS WAY

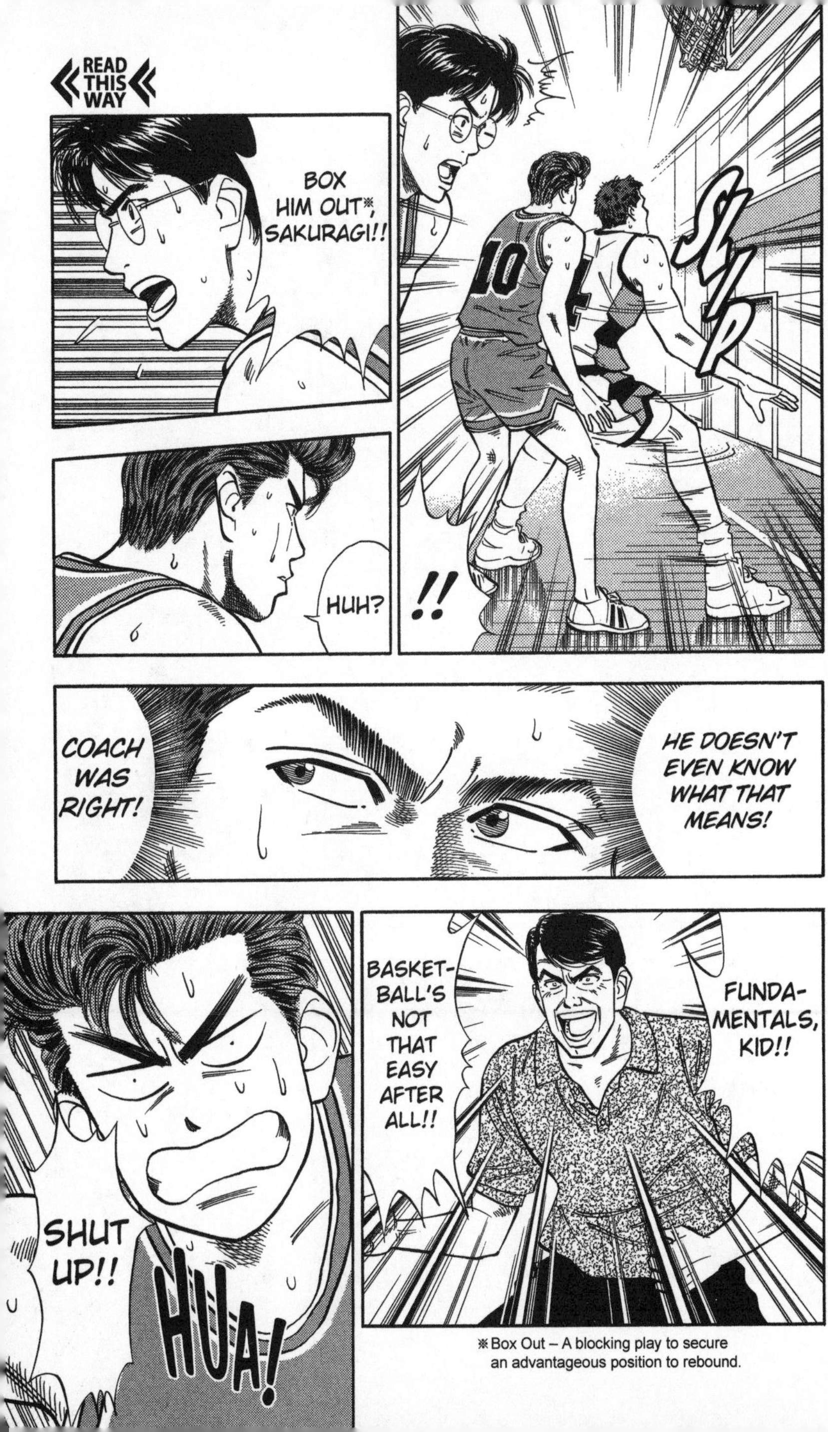
SLIP
!!
BOX HIM OUT※, SAKURAGI!!
HUH?
HE DOESN'T EVEN KNOW WHAT THAT MEANS!
COACH WAS RIGHT!
FUNDA-MENTALS, KID!!
BASKET-BALL'S NOT THAT EASY AFTER ALL!!
SHUT UP!!
HUA!

※Box Out – A blocking play to secure an advantageous position to rebound.

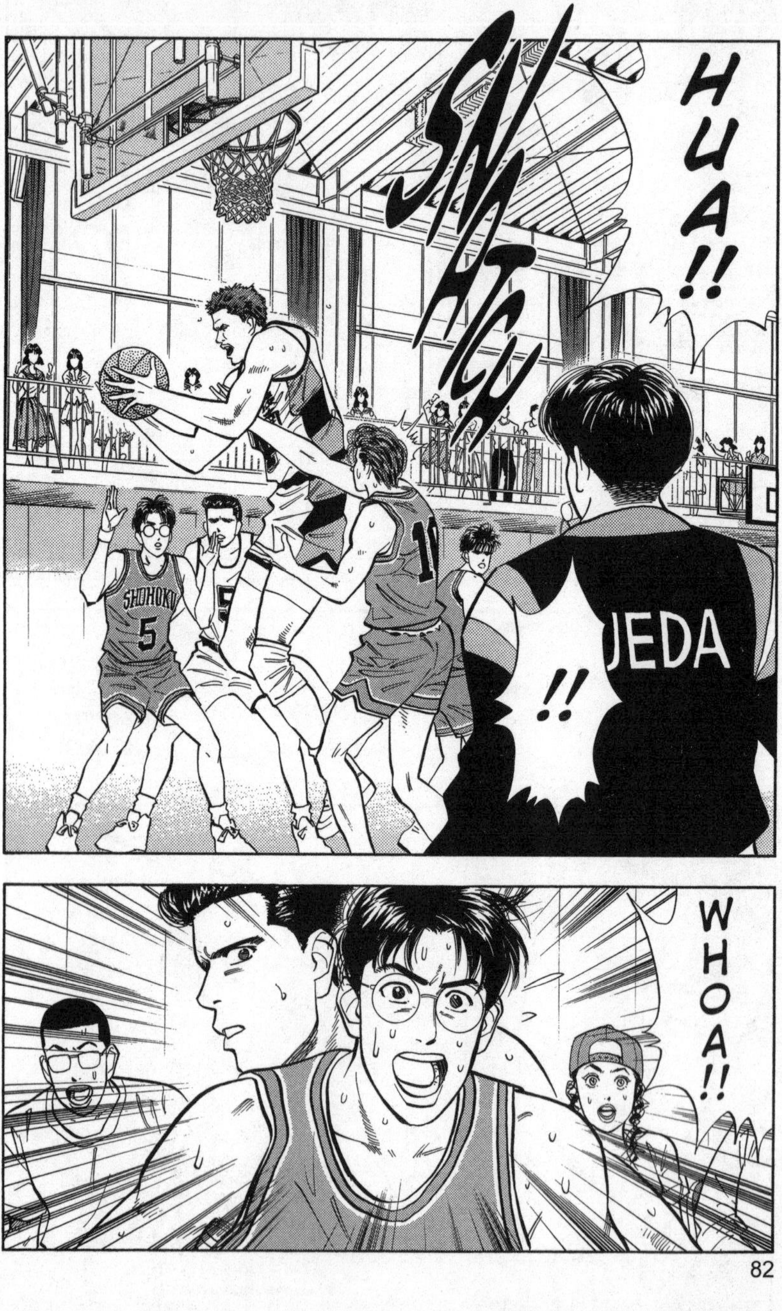
HUAA!!
SMATCH
!!
WHOA!!

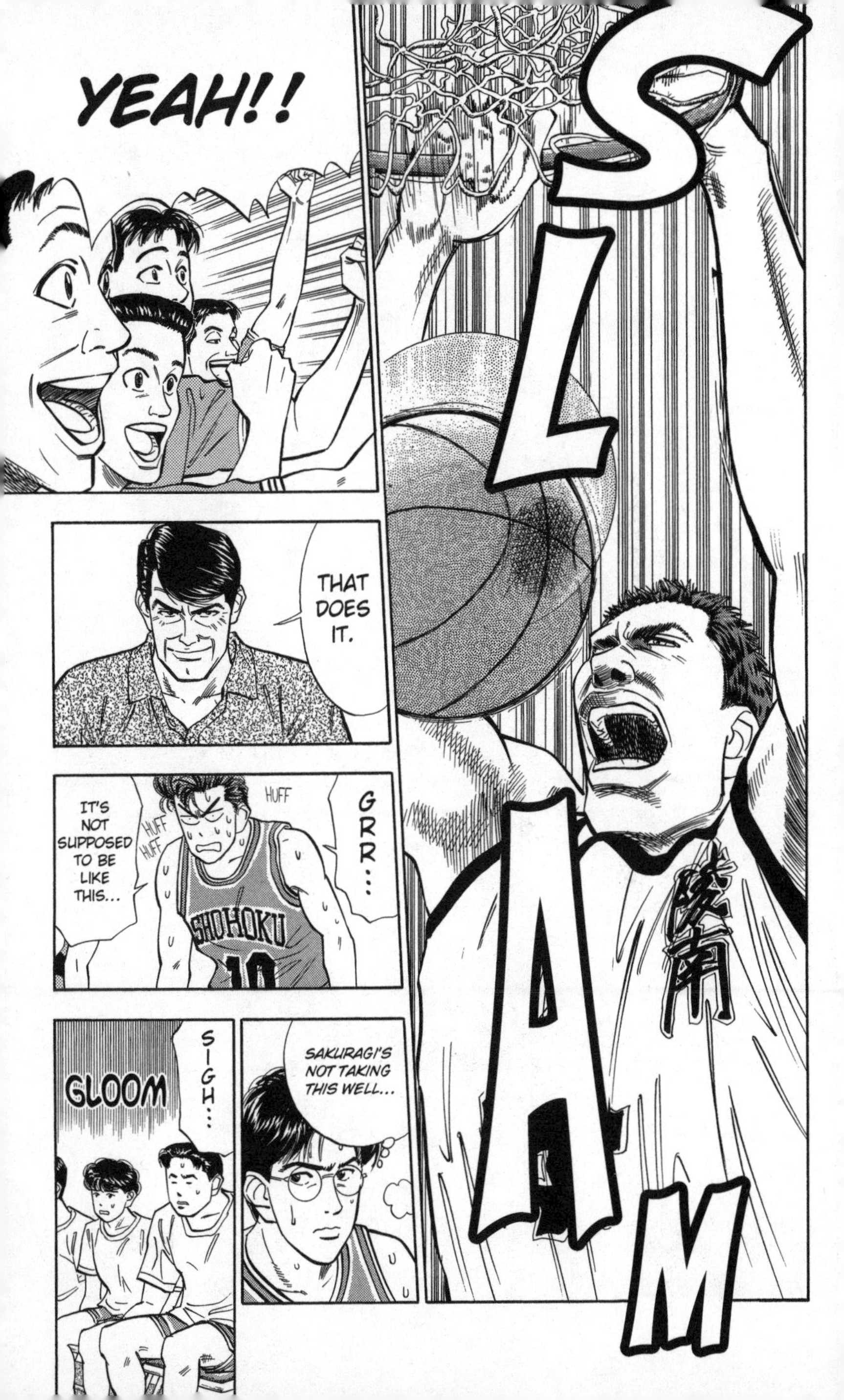
SLAM
陵南
YEAH!!
THAT DOES IT.
GRR...
HUFF
HUFF HUFF
IT'S NOT SUPPOSED TO BE LIKE THIS...
SAKURAGI'S NOT TAKING THIS WELL...
SIGH...
GLOOM
SHOHOKU 10

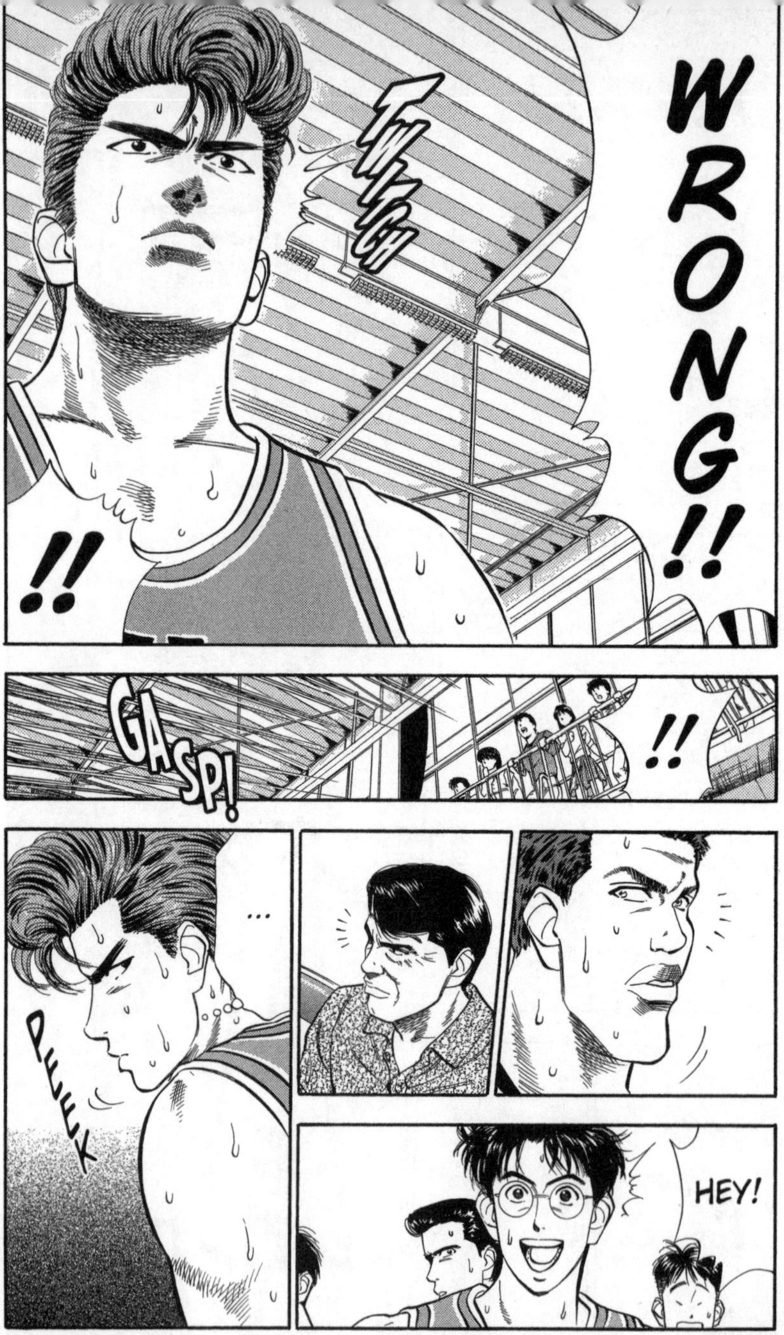
WRONG!!
TWITCH
!!
!!
GASP!
...
QUEEK
HEY!

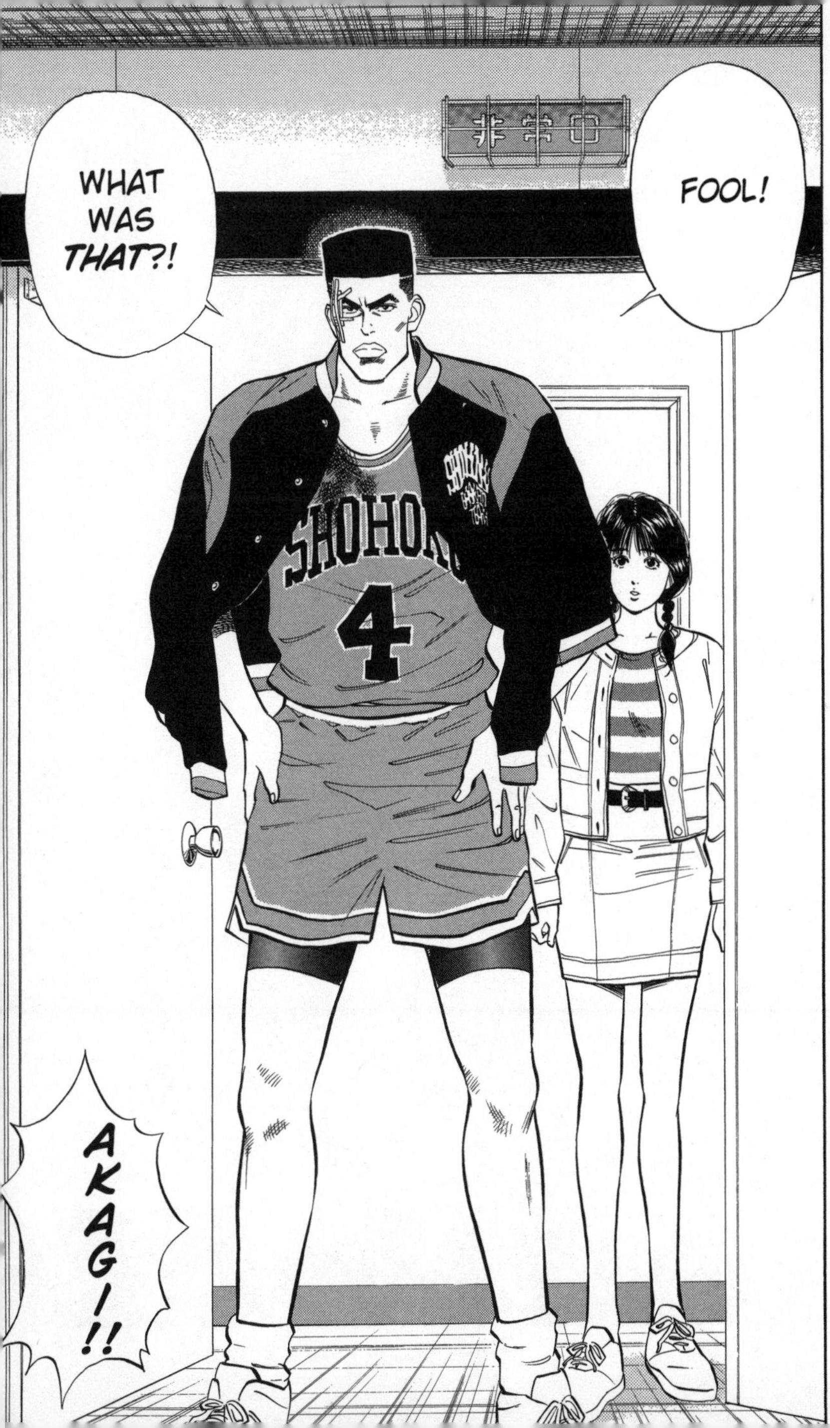
FOOL!
WHAT WAS THAT?!
AKAGI!!

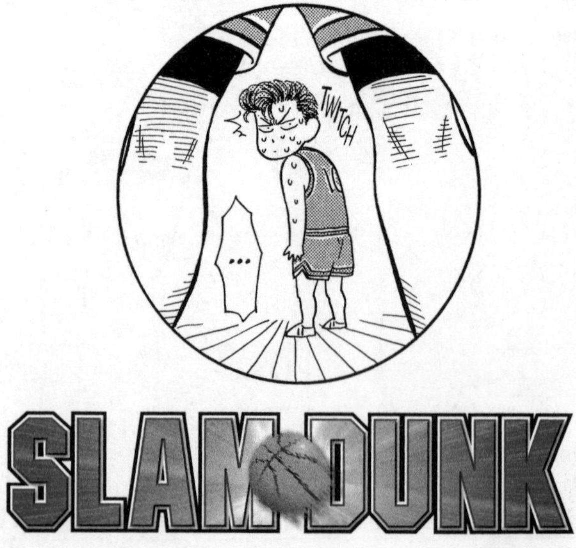
TWITCH
...

SLAM DUNK

#40 WRONG!

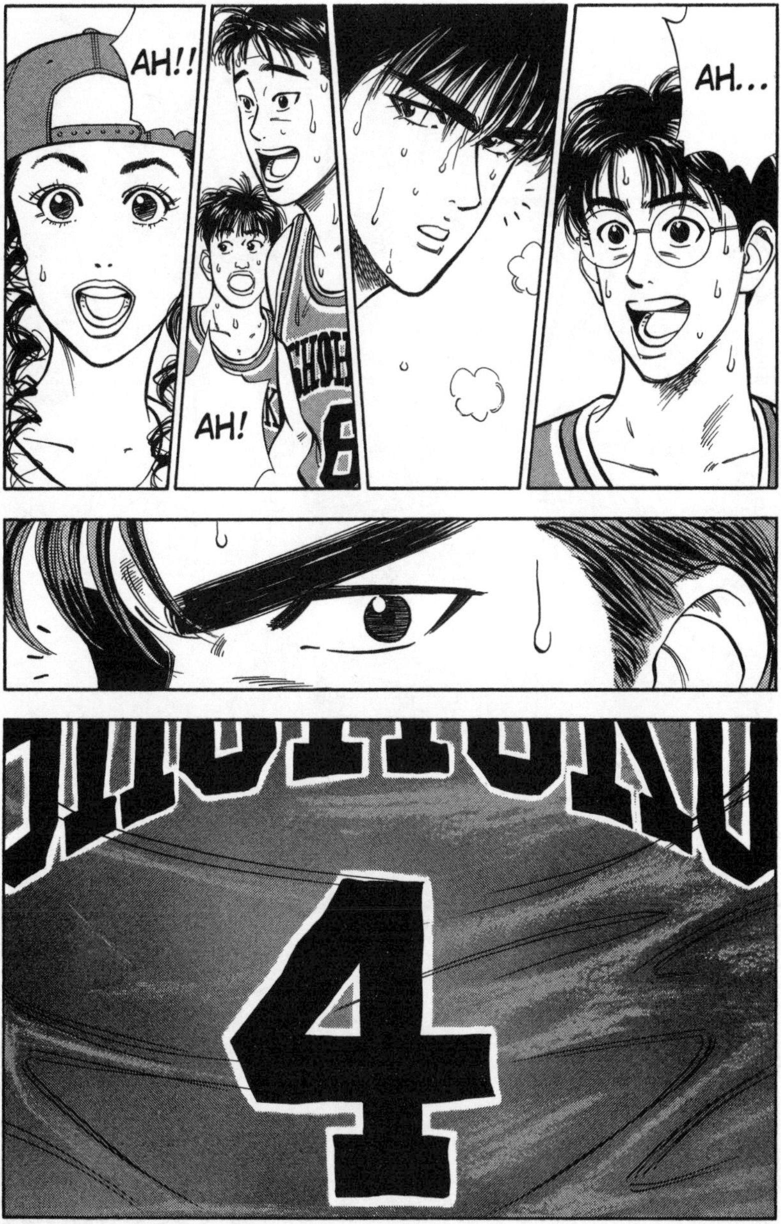
AH...
AH!
AH!!

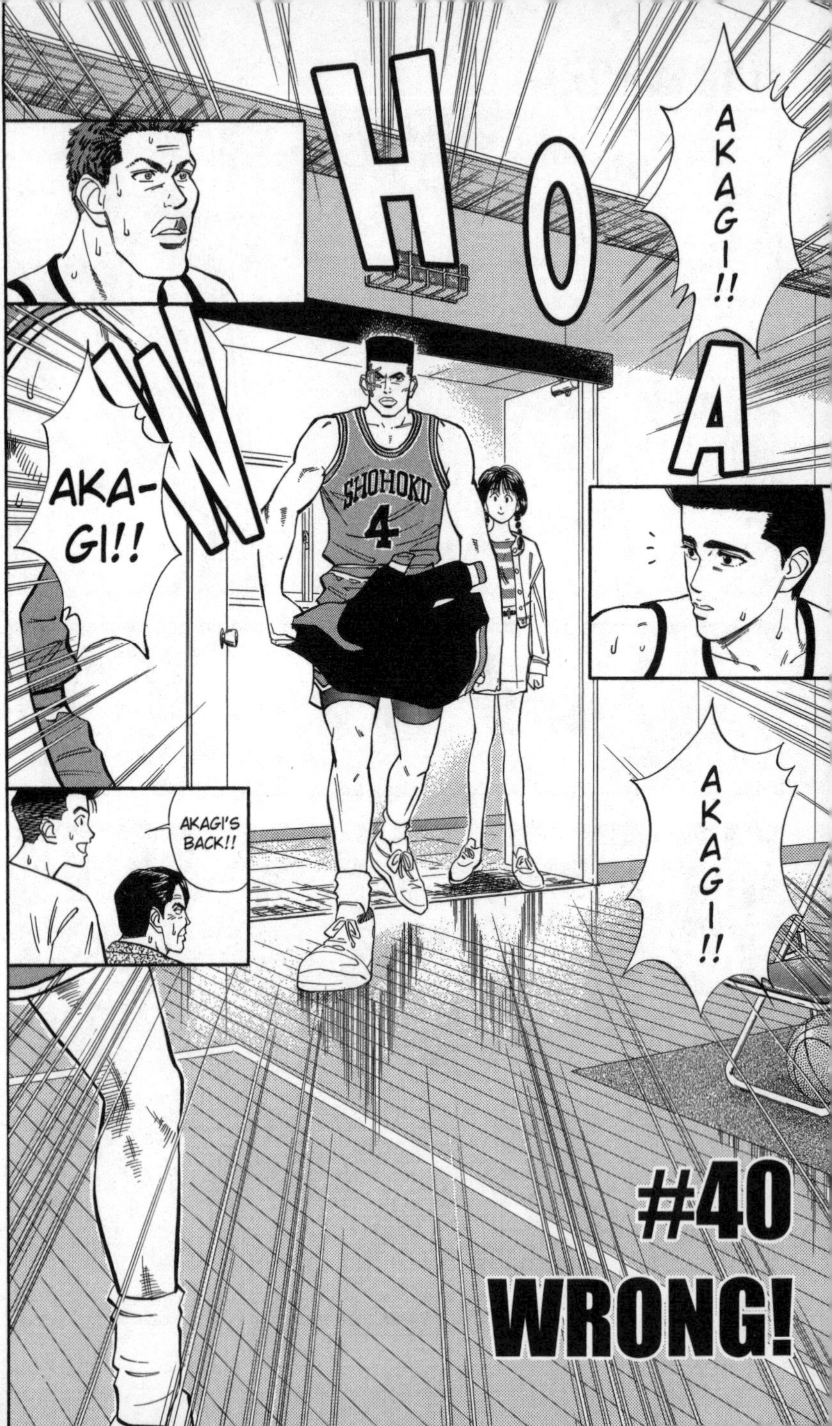
AKAGI!!
WHOA
AKA-GI!!
AKAGI!!
AKAGI'S BACK!!
#40 WRONG!

READ THIS WAY

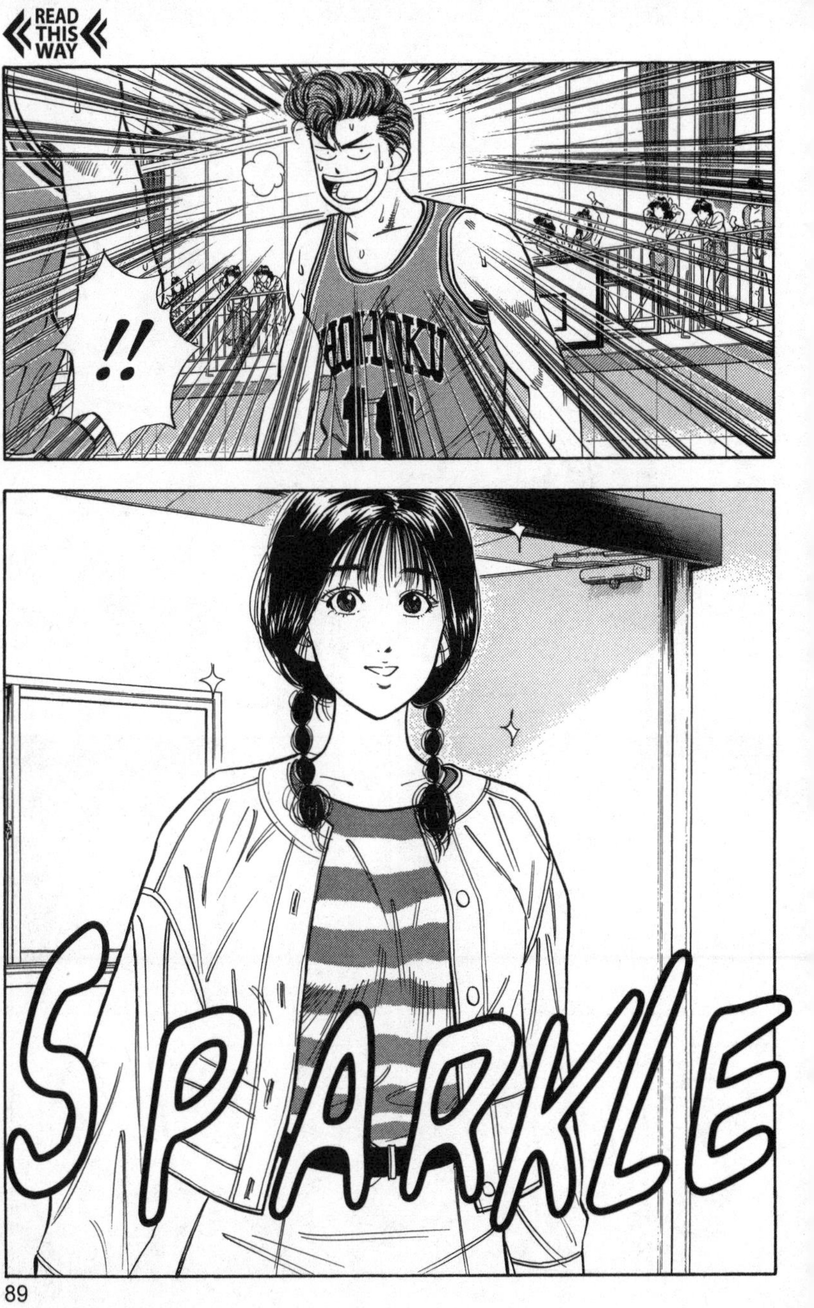
!!
SHOHOKU
SPARKLE

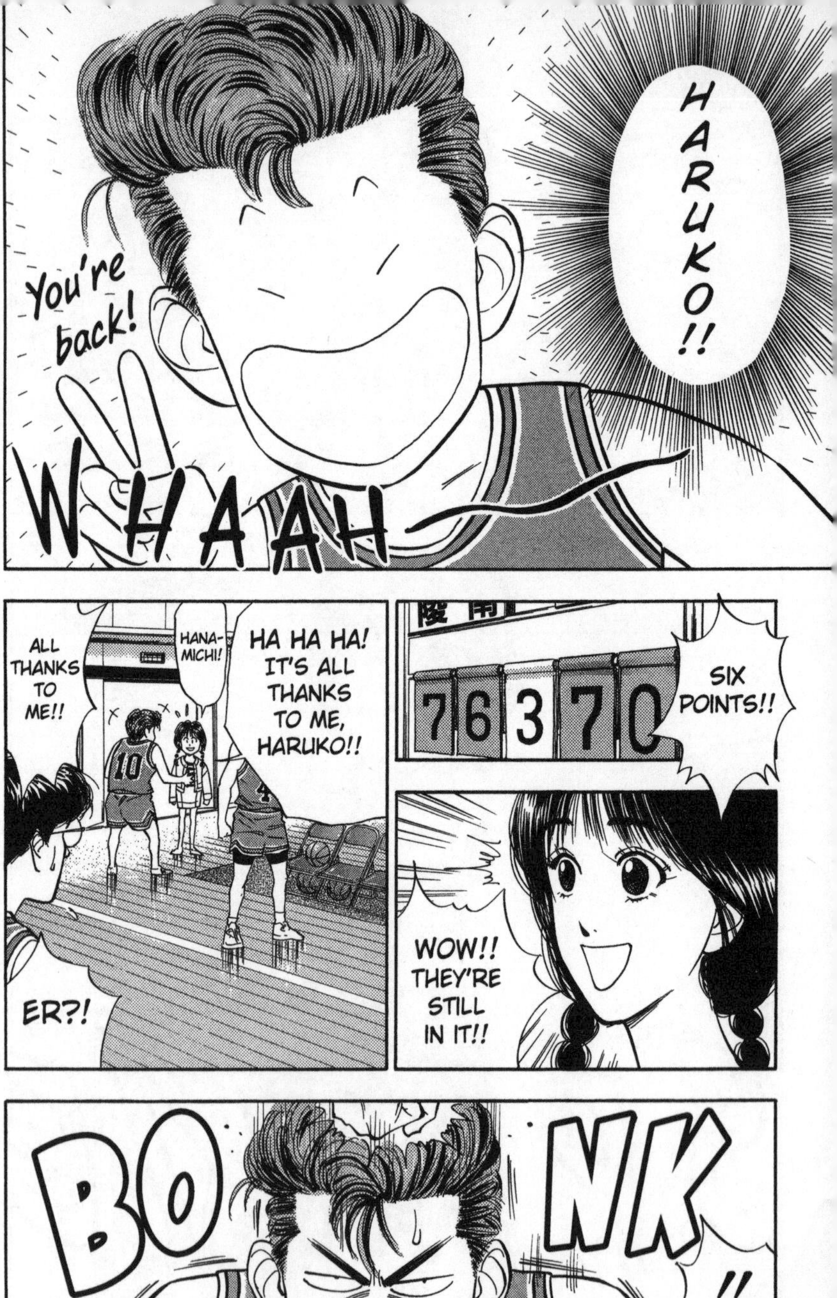
HARUKO!!
You're back!
WHAAH
SIX POINTS!!
WOW!! THEY'RE STILL IN IT!!
HA HA HA! IT'S ALL THANKS TO ME, HARUKO!!
HANA-MICHI!
ALL THANKS TO ME!!
ER?!
BONK!!

READ THIS WAY

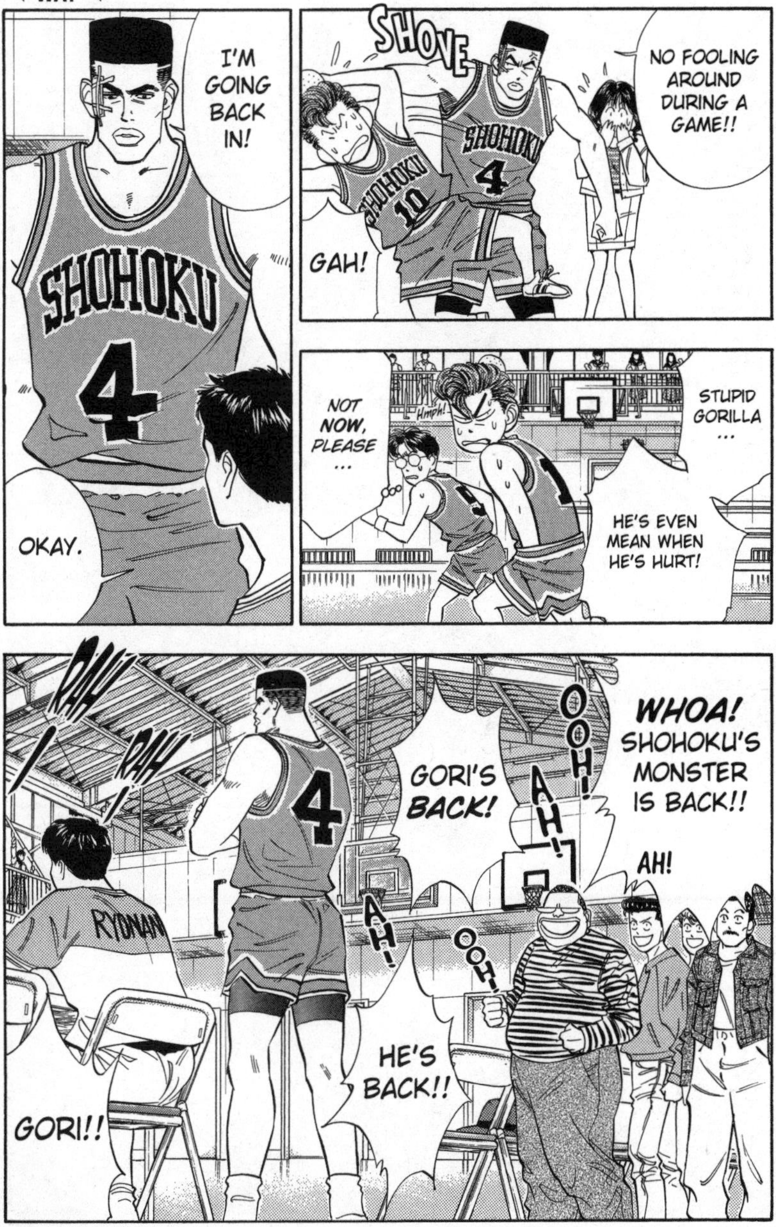

NO FOOLING AROUND DURING A GAME!!
SHOVE
GAH!
STUPID GORILLA ...
Hmph!
NOT NOW, PLEASE ...
HE'S EVEN MEAN WHEN HE'S HURT!
I'M GOING BACK IN!
OKAY.
WHOA! SHOHOKU'S MONSTER IS BACK!!
AH!
OOH! AH!
GORI'S BACK!
RAH! RAH!
AH!
OOH!
HE'S BACK!!
RYONAN
GORI!!

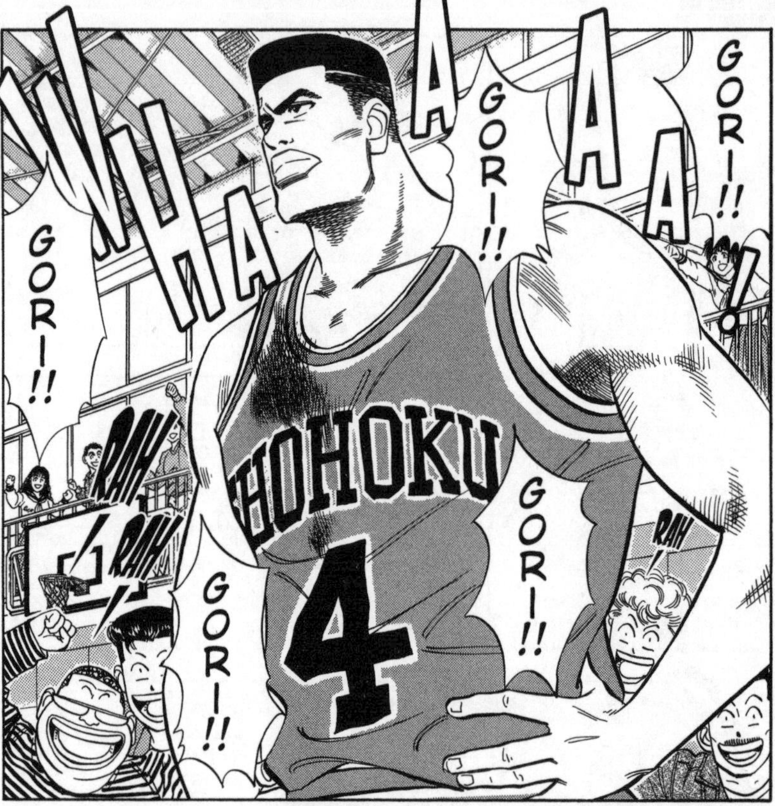
GORI!!
WHAAAA!
GORI!!
GORI!!
GORI!!
RAH
SHOHOKU
4
GORI!!
RAH, RAH, RAH
GORI!!

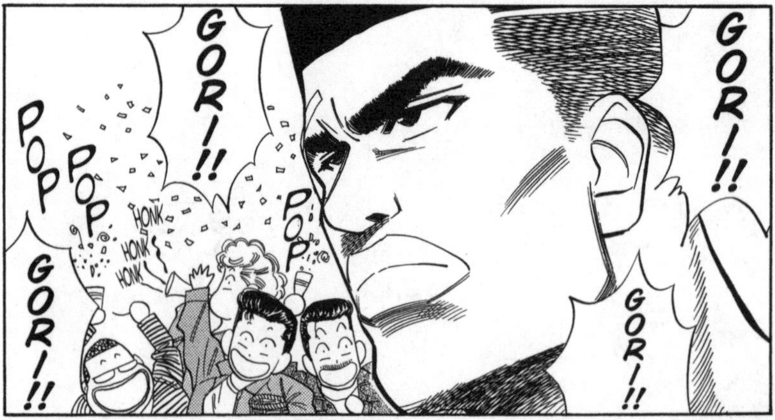
GORI!!
GORI!!
GORI!!
POP
HONK HONK HONK
POP
POP
GORI!!

READ THIS WAY

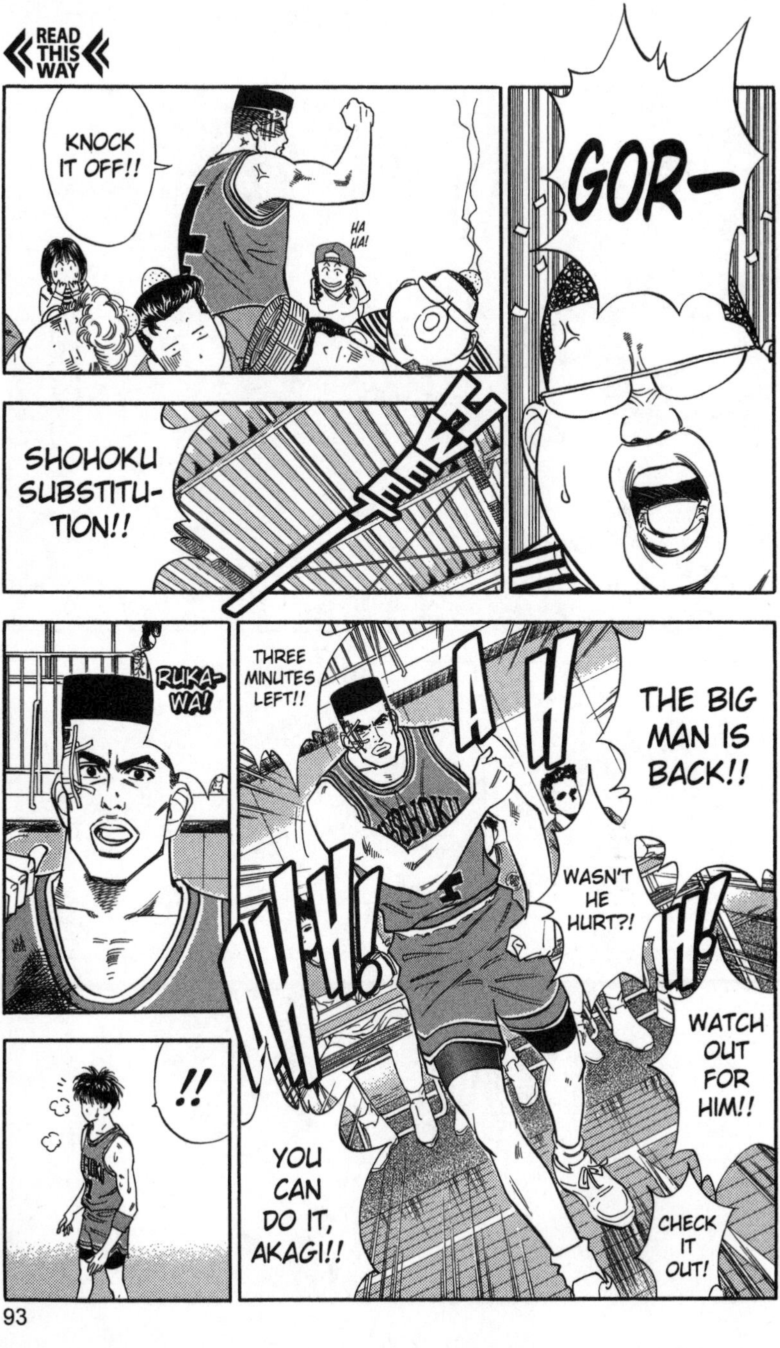
GOR-
KNOCK IT OFF!!
HA HA!
SHOHOKU SUBSTITUTION!!
THE BIG MAN IS BACK!!
THREE MINUTES LEFT!!
WASN'T HE HURT?!
WATCH OUT FOR HIM!!
YOU CAN DO IT, AKAGI!!
CHECK IT OUT!
RUKAWA!
!!

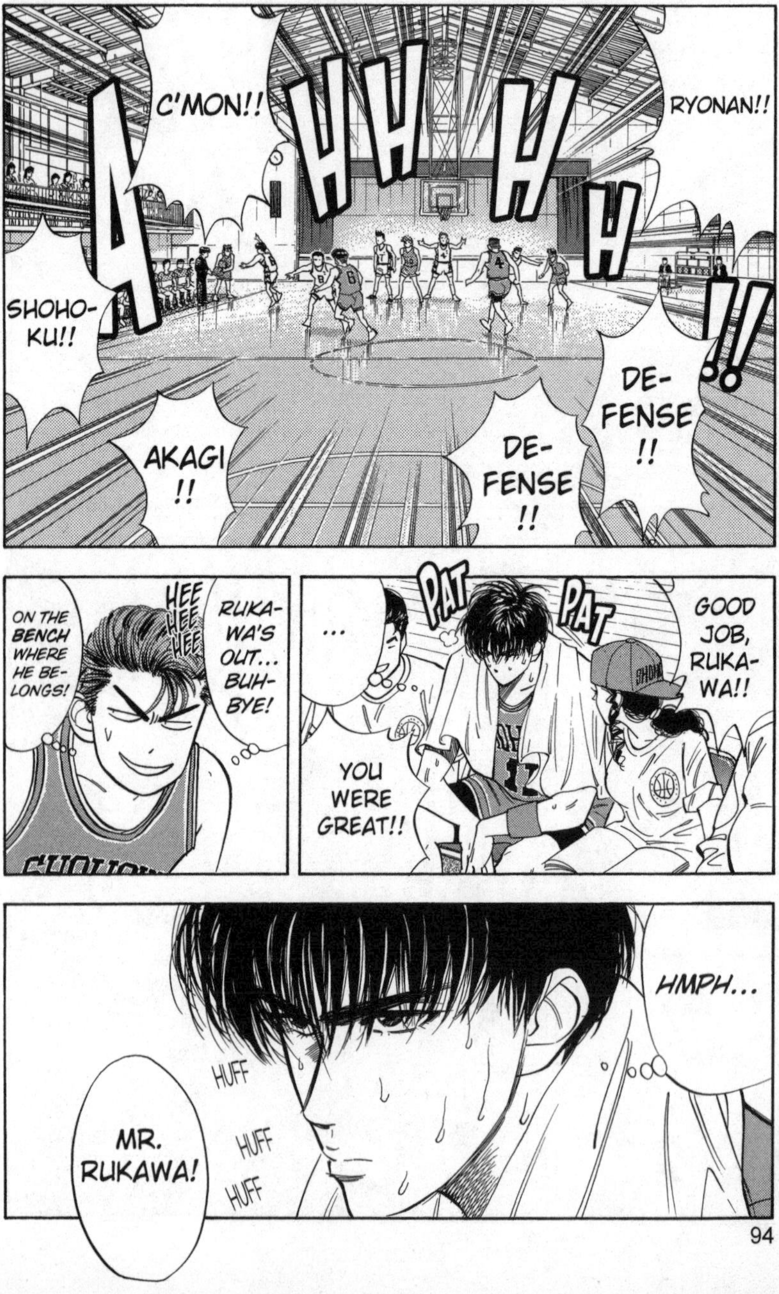

RYONAN!!
C'MON!!
AHHHHH!!
SHOHOKU!!
DE-FENSE!!
DE-FENSE!!
AKAGI!!
GOOD JOB, RUKAWA!!
PAT PAT
...
YOU WERE GREAT!!
RUKAWA'S OUT... BUH-BYE!
HEE HEE HEE
ON THE BENCH WHERE HE BELONGS!
HMPH...
HUFF HUFF HUFF
MR. RUKAWA!

READ THIS WAY

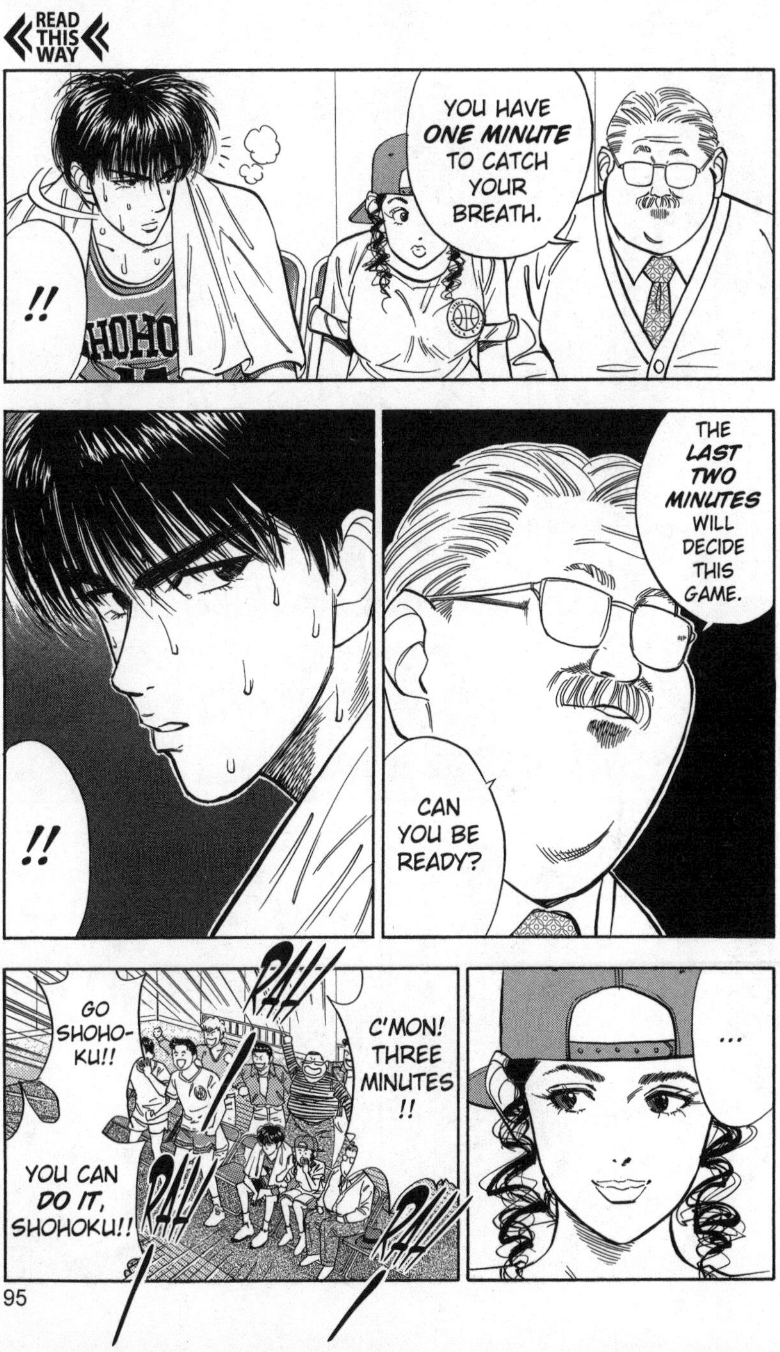
YOU HAVE ONE MINUTE TO CATCH YOUR BREATH.
!!
THE LAST TWO MINUTES WILL DECIDE THIS GAME.
CAN YOU BE READY?
!!
...
C'MON! THREE MINUTES!!
RAH!
GO SHOHO-KU!!
RAH!
RAH!
YOU CAN DO IT, SHOHOKU!!

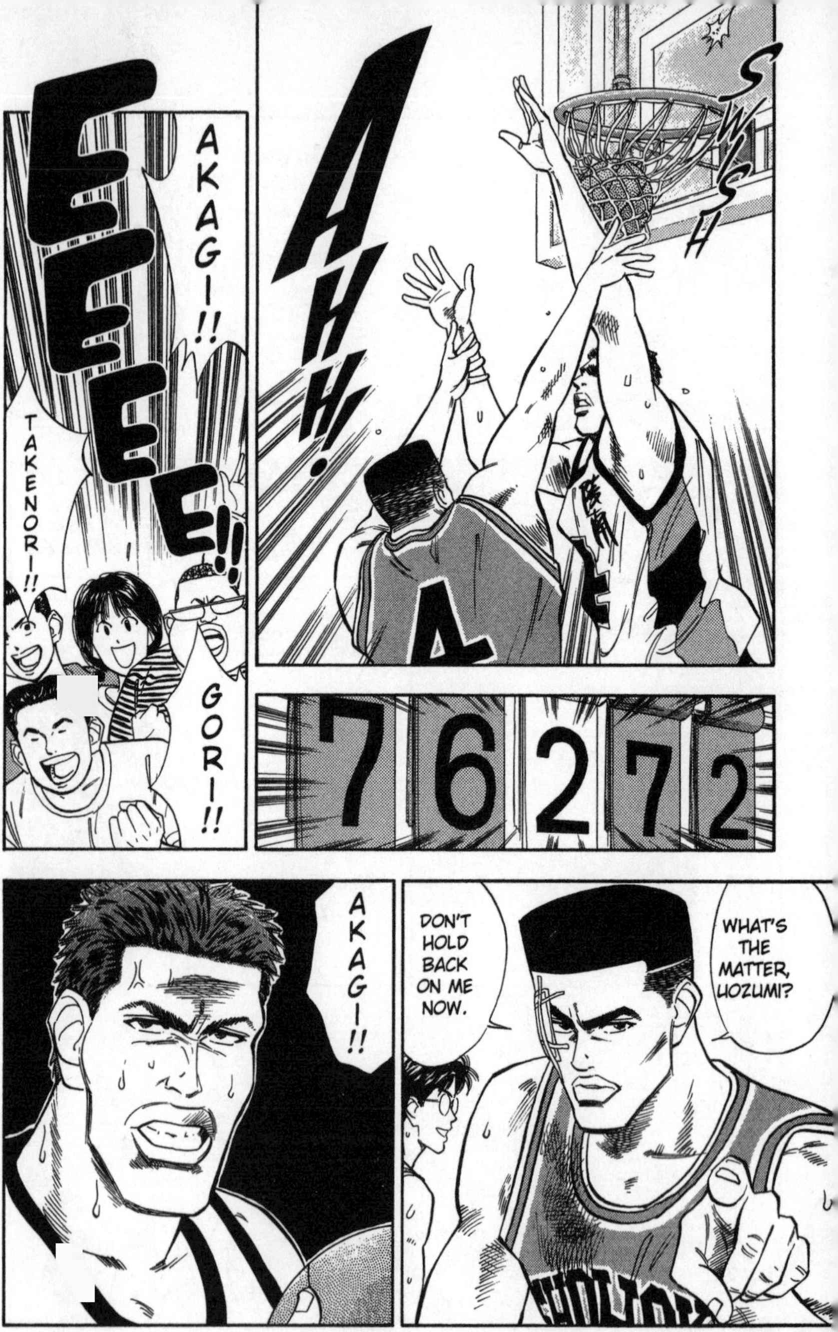
SWISH
AHHH!
76
62
72
EEEE!!
AKAGI!!
TAKENORI!!
GORI!!
WHAT'S THE MATTER, UOZUMI?
DON'T HOLD BACK ON ME NOW.
AKAGI!!

READ THIS WAY

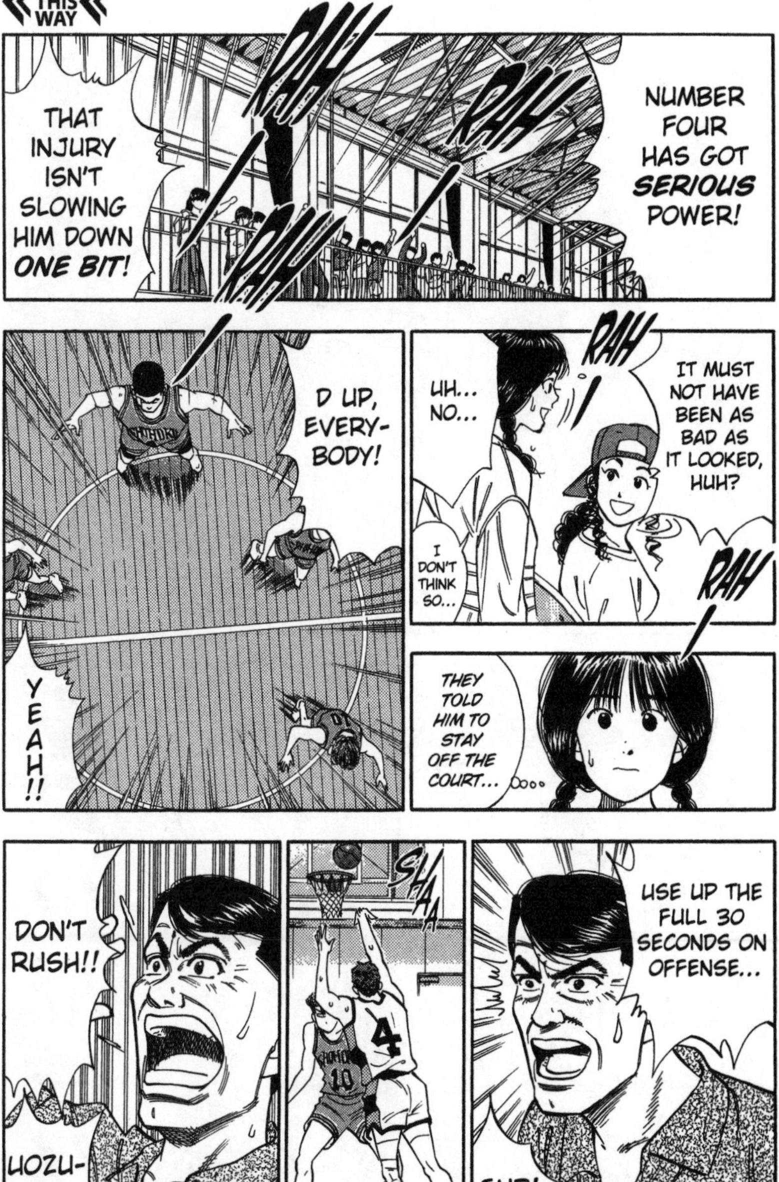
RAH
RAH
NUMBER FOUR HAS GOT SERIOUS POWER!
RAH
THAT INJURY ISN'T SLOWING HIM DOWN ONE BIT!
RAH
IT MUST NOT HAVE BEEN AS BAD AS IT LOOKED, HUH?
UH... NO...
RAH
I DON'T THINK SO...
THEY TOLD HIM TO STAY OFF THE COURT...
D UP, EVERY-BODY!
YEAH!!
USE UP THE FULL 30 SECONDS ON OFFENSE...
EH?!
SHAA
DON'T RUSH!!
UOZU-MI!!

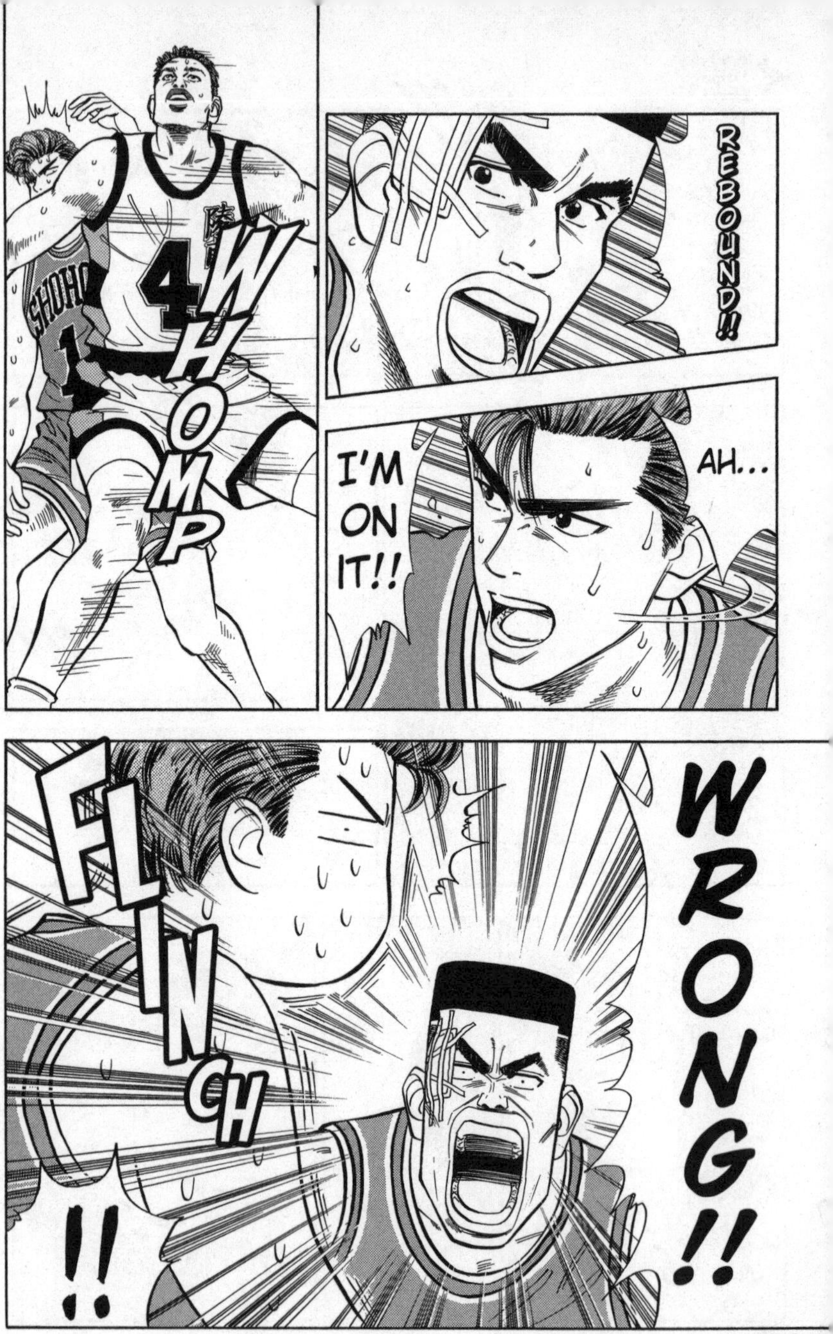

REBOUND!!
AH...
I'M ON IT!!
WHOMP
WRONG!!
FLINCH!!

ULP...

WRONG
!!

P
A
A

IDIOT!!

YOU WON'T GET THE REBOUND IF YOUR POSITIONING SUCKS!

HOW MANY TIMES DO I HAVE TO EXPLAIN THIS?!

BONK

OW!

99

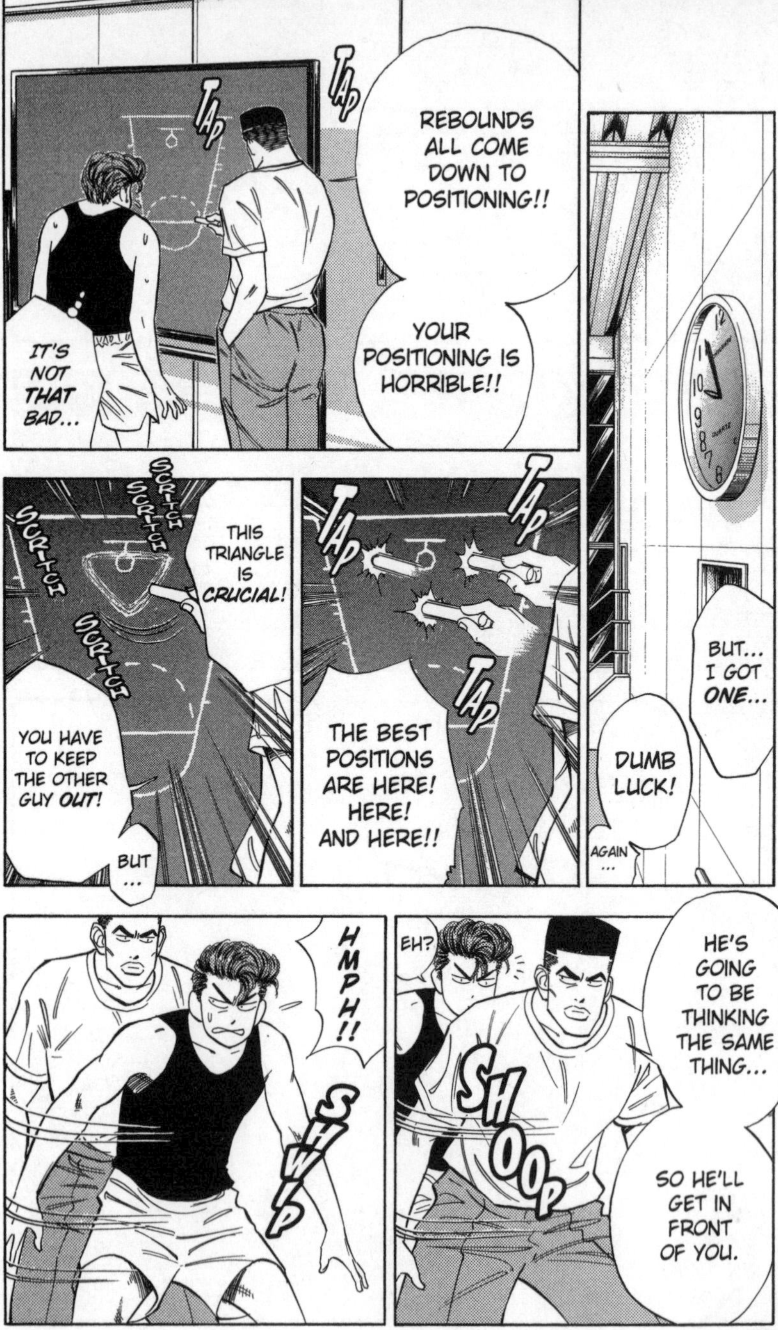
TAP
TAP
REBOUNDS ALL COME DOWN TO POSITIONING!!
YOUR POSITIONING IS HORRIBLE!!
IT'S NOT THAT BAD...
SCRITCH
SCRITCH
SCRITCH
SCRITCH
THIS TRIANGLE IS CRUCIAL!
YOU HAVE TO KEEP THE OTHER GUY OUT!
BUT ...
TAP
TAP
TAP
THE BEST POSITIONS ARE HERE! HERE! AND HERE!!
BUT... I GOT ONE...
DUMB LUCK!
AGAIN ...
HMPH!!
SHWIP
EH?
HE'S GOING TO BE THINKING THE SAME THING...
SHOOOP
SO HE'LL GET IN FRONT OF YOU.

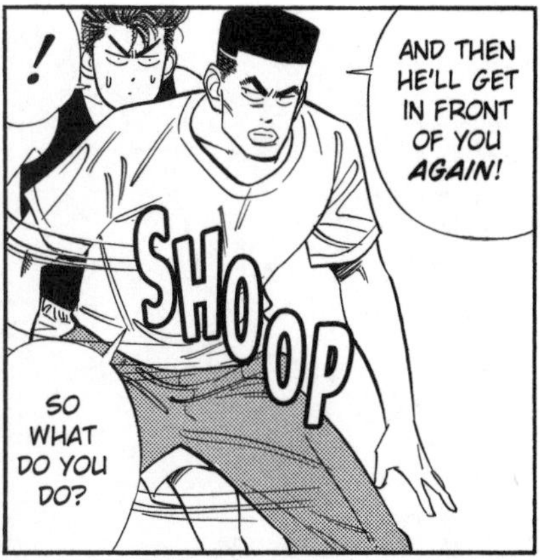
AND THEN HE'LL GET IN FRONT OF YOU *AGAIN!*
!
SHOOP
SO WHAT DO YOU DO?
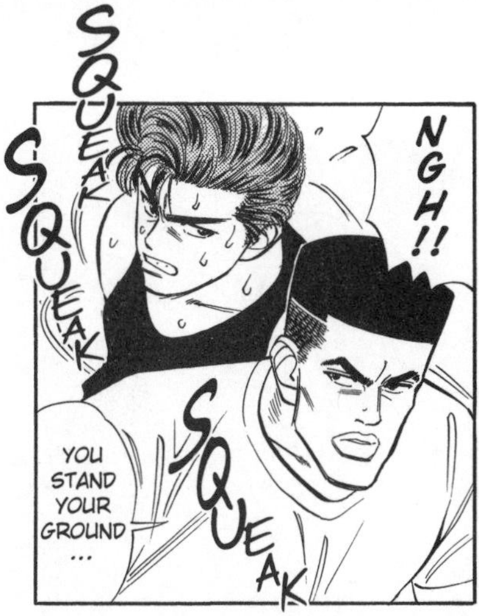
NGH!!
SQUEAK SQUEAK
YOU STAND YOUR GROUND ...
SQUEAK
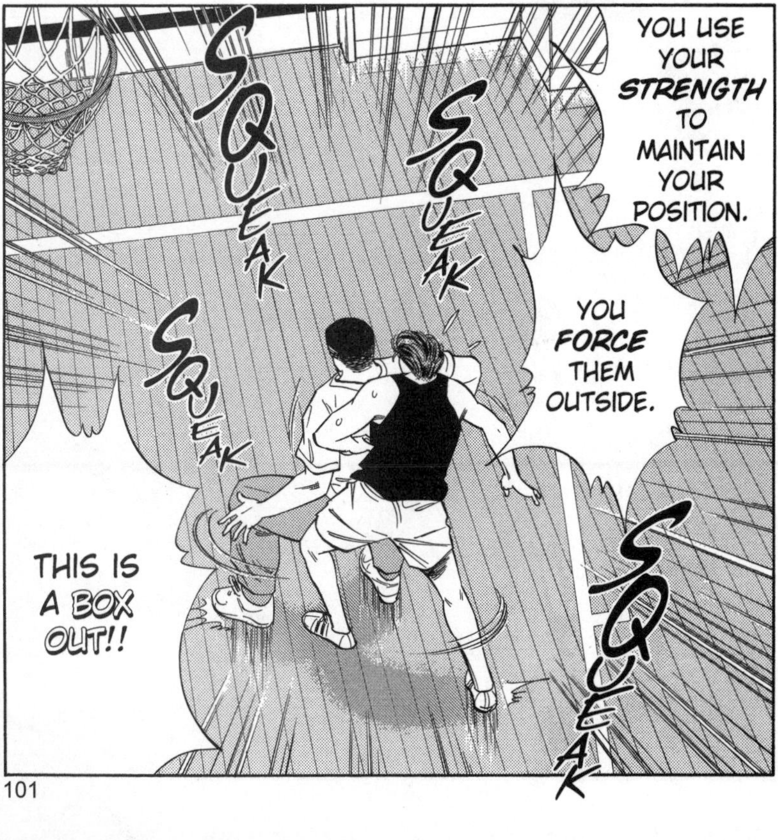
YOU USE YOUR *STRENGTH* TO MAINTAIN YOUR POSITION.
SQUEAK
SQUEAK
YOU *FORCE* THEM OUTSIDE.
SQUEAK
THIS IS A BOX OUT!!
SQUEAK

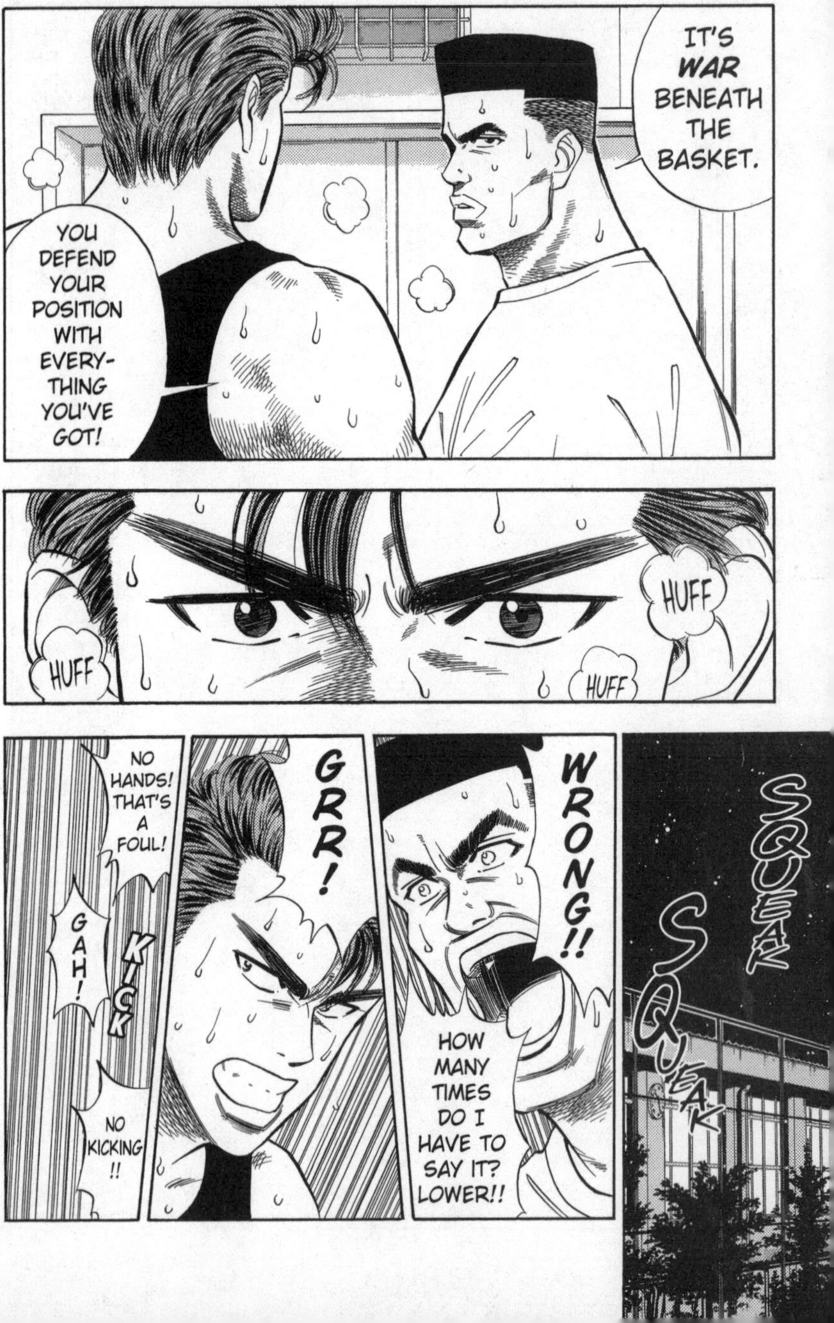
IT'S **WAR** BENEATH THE BASKET.
YOU DEFEND YOUR POSITION WITH EVERY-THING YOU'VE GOT!
HUFF
HUFF
HUFF
SQUEAK
SQUEAK
WRONG!!
HOW MANY TIMES DO I HAVE TO SAY IT? LOWER!!
GRR!
NO HANDS! THAT'S A FOUL!
GAH!
KICK
NO KICKING!!

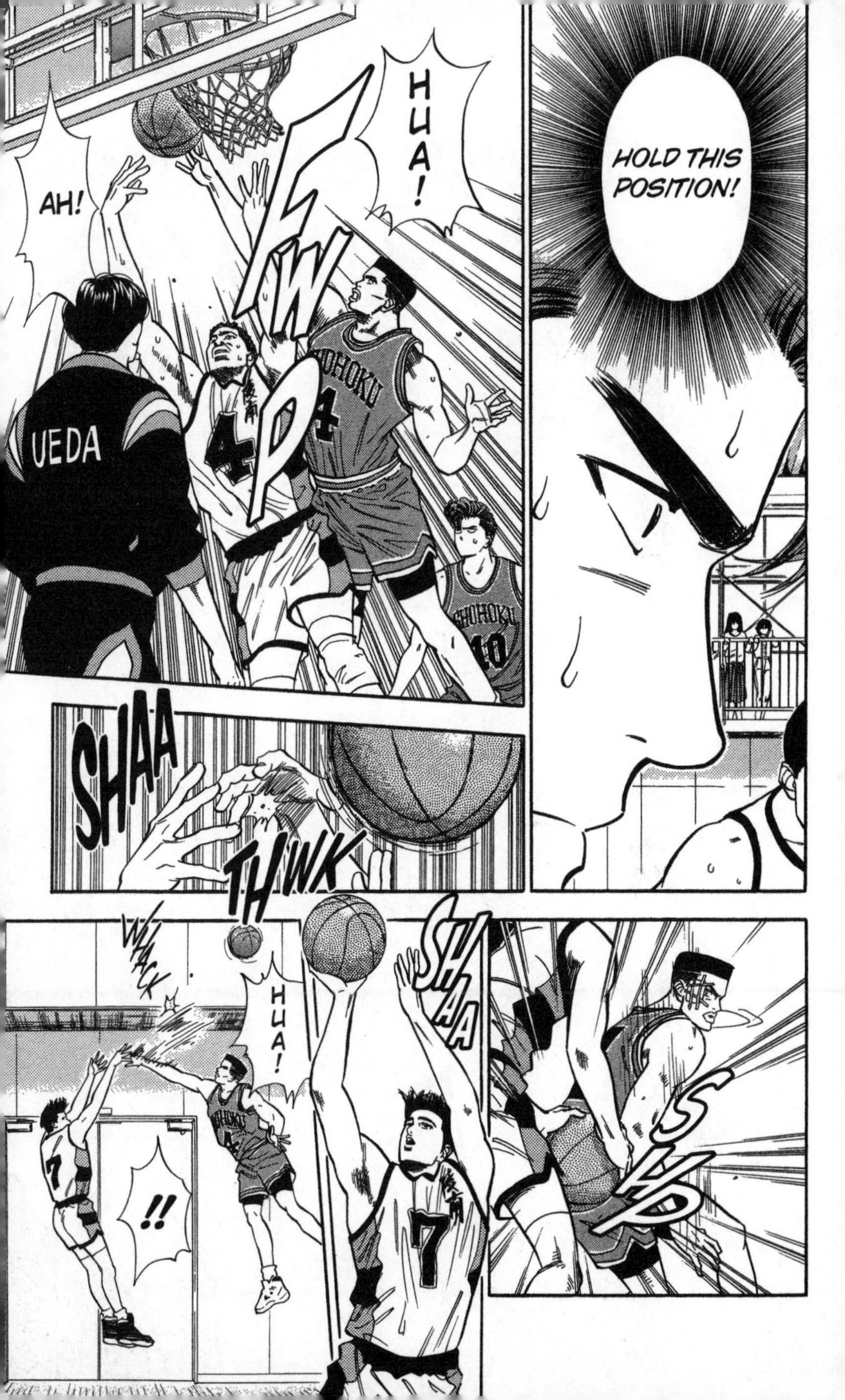
HOLD THIS POSITION!
HUA!
AH!
UEDA
SHAA
THWK
SHAA
WHACK
HUA!
!!

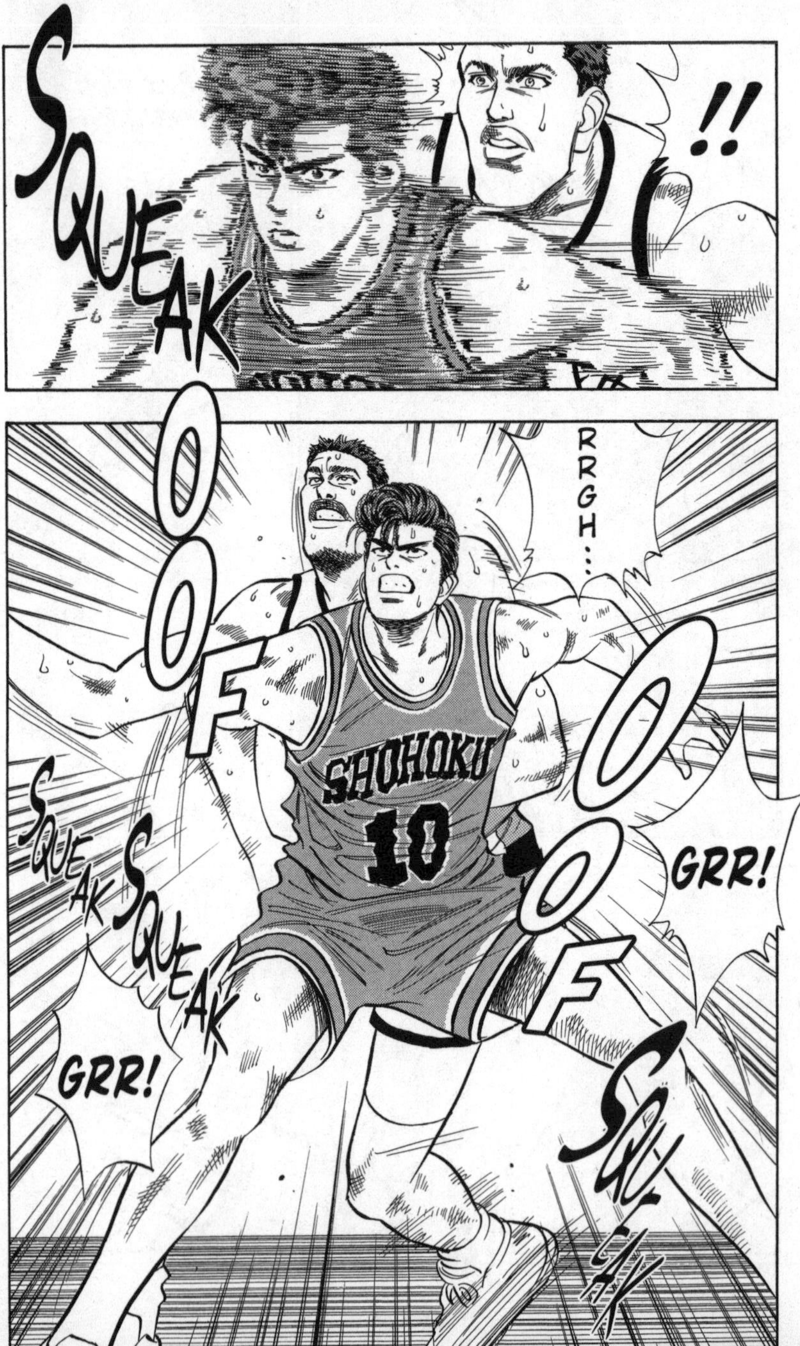
!!
SQUEAK
RRGH...
GRR!
OOOF
SQUEAK
OOOF
SQUEAK
SQUEAK
GRR!

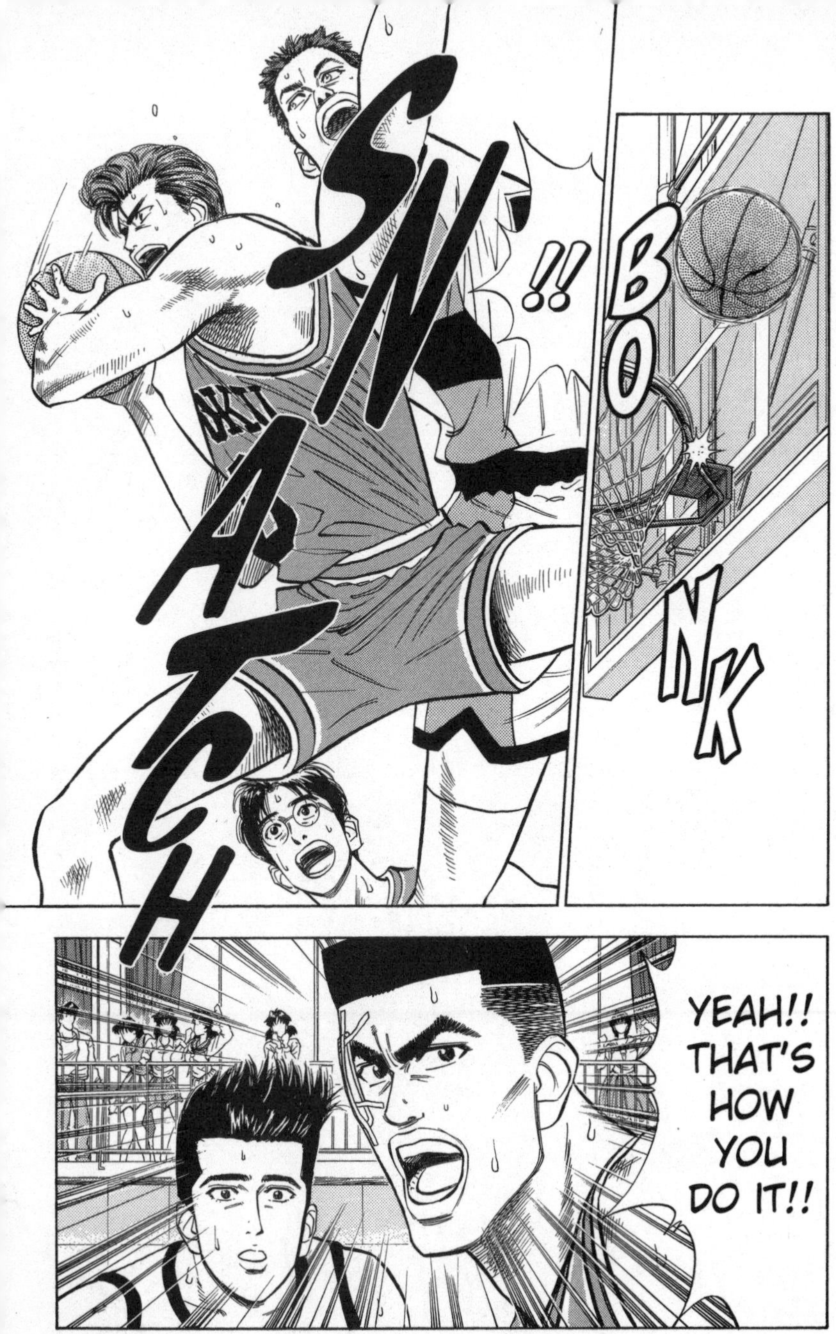
BONK
!!
SNATCH
YEAH!! THAT'S HOW YOU DO IT!!

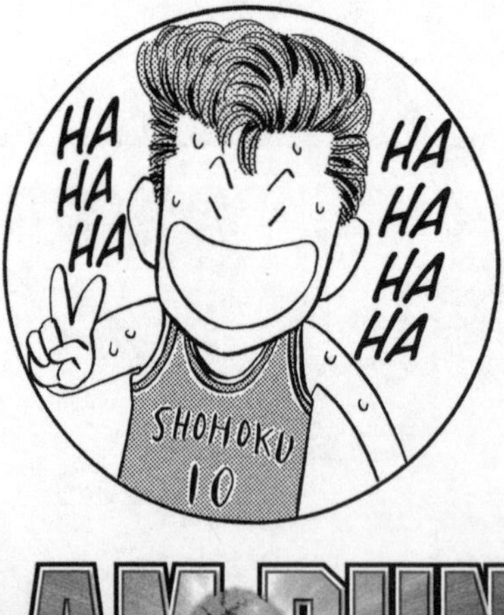
HA HA HA HA HA
HA HA HA
SHOHOKU 10

SLAM DUNK

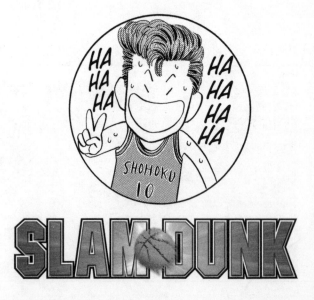

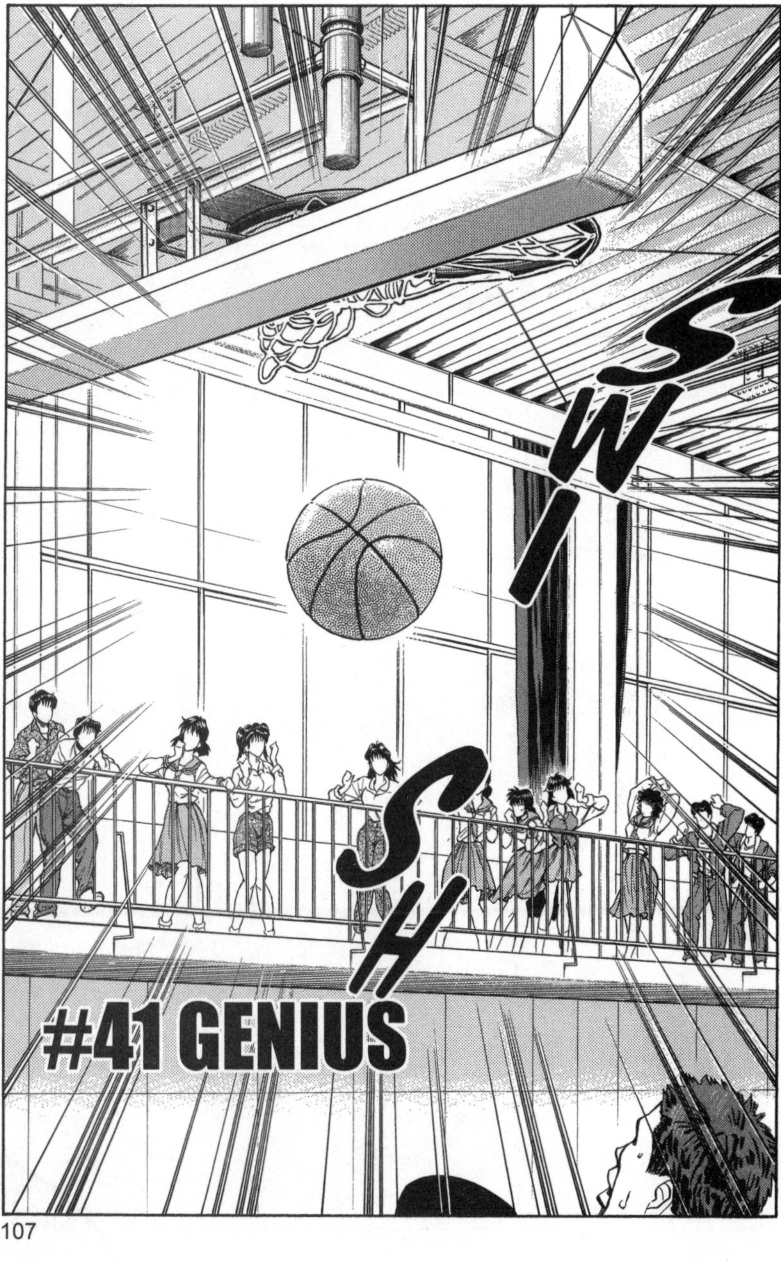
SWISH
#41 GENIUS

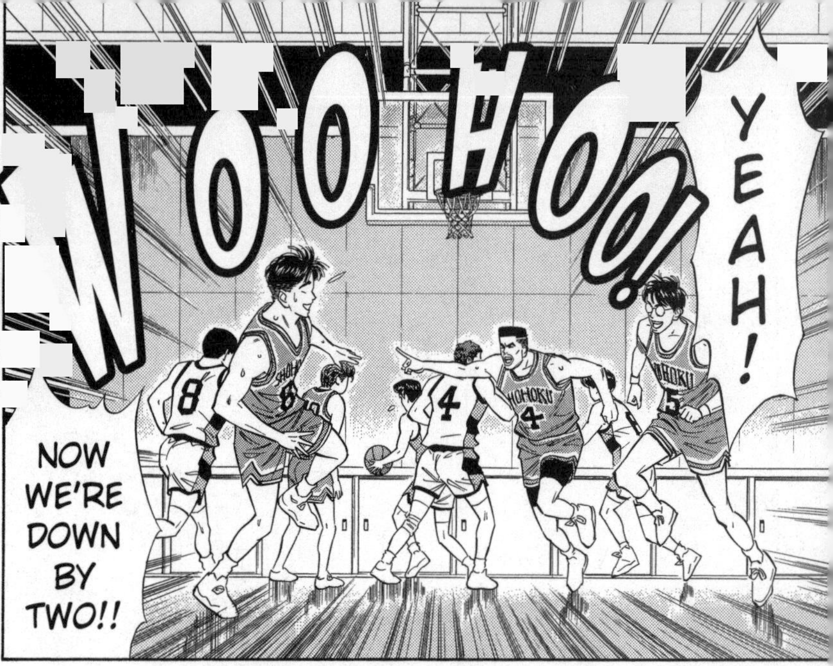
YEAH!
WOOOHOO!
NOW WE'RE DOWN BY TWO!!

Scoreboard: Ryonan Shohoku

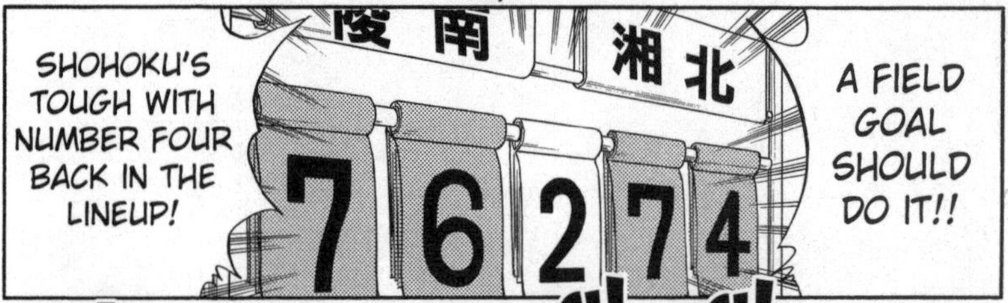
A FIELD GOAL SHOULD DO IT!!
陵南
湘北
76274
SHOHOKU'S TOUGH WITH NUMBER FOUR BACK IN THE LINEUP!

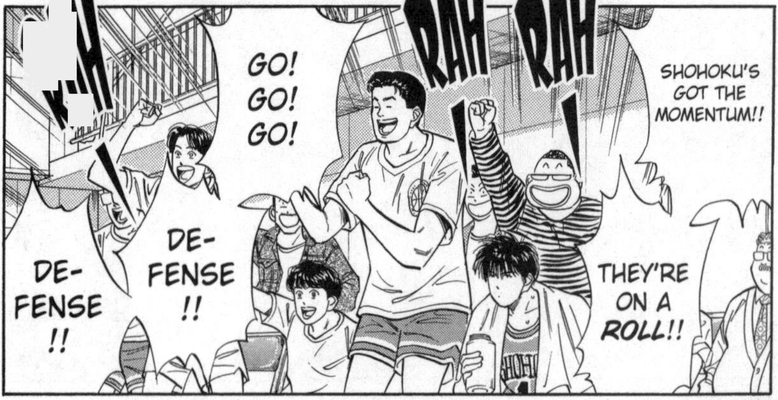
SHOHOKU'S GOT THE MOMENTUM!!
THEY'RE ON A *ROLL*!!
RAH!
RAH!
GO! GO! GO!
DE-FENSE!!
DE-FENSE!!

READ THIS WAY

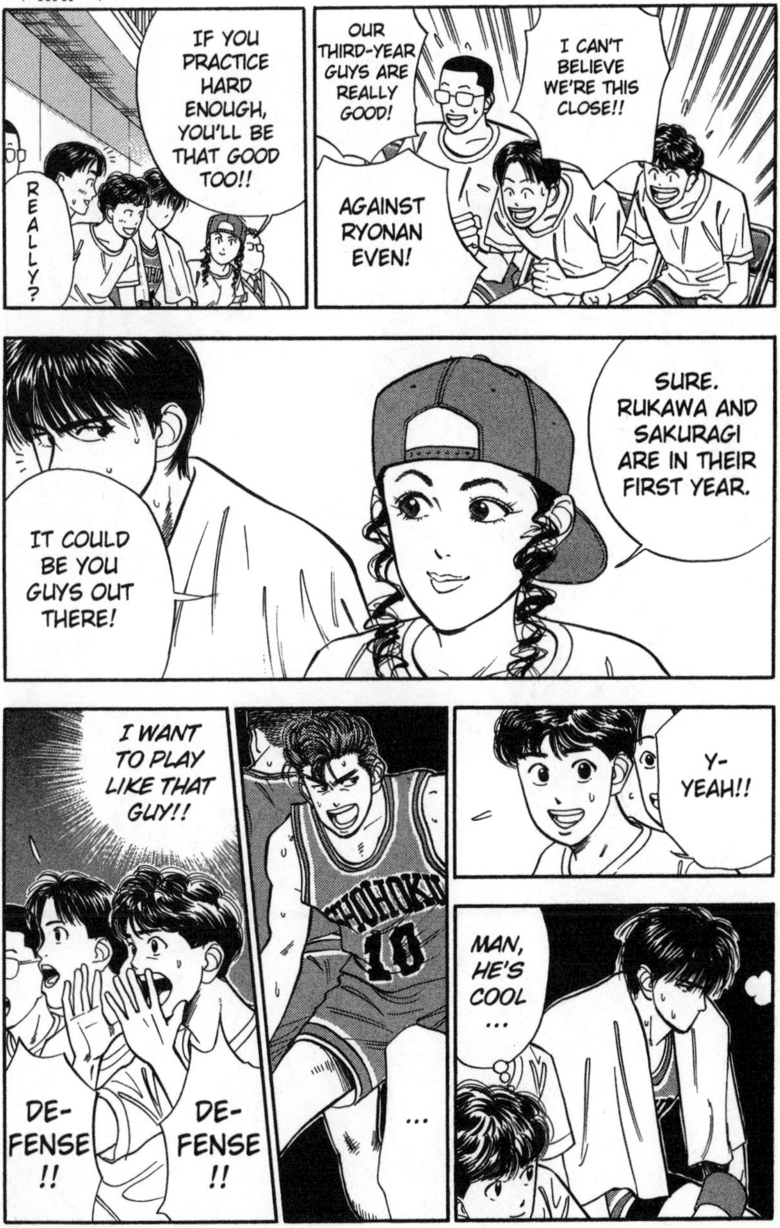

I CAN'T BELIEVE WE'RE THIS CLOSE!!
OUR THIRD-YEAR GUYS ARE REALLY GOOD!
AGAINST RYONAN EVEN!
IF YOU PRACTICE HARD ENOUGH, YOU'LL BE THAT GOOD TOO!!
REALLY?
SURE. RUKAWA AND SAKURAGI ARE IN THEIR FIRST YEAR.
IT COULD BE YOU GUYS OUT THERE!
Y-YEAH!!
MAN, HE'S COOL ...
...
I WANT TO PLAY LIKE THAT GUY!!
DE-FENSE!!
DE-FENSE!!

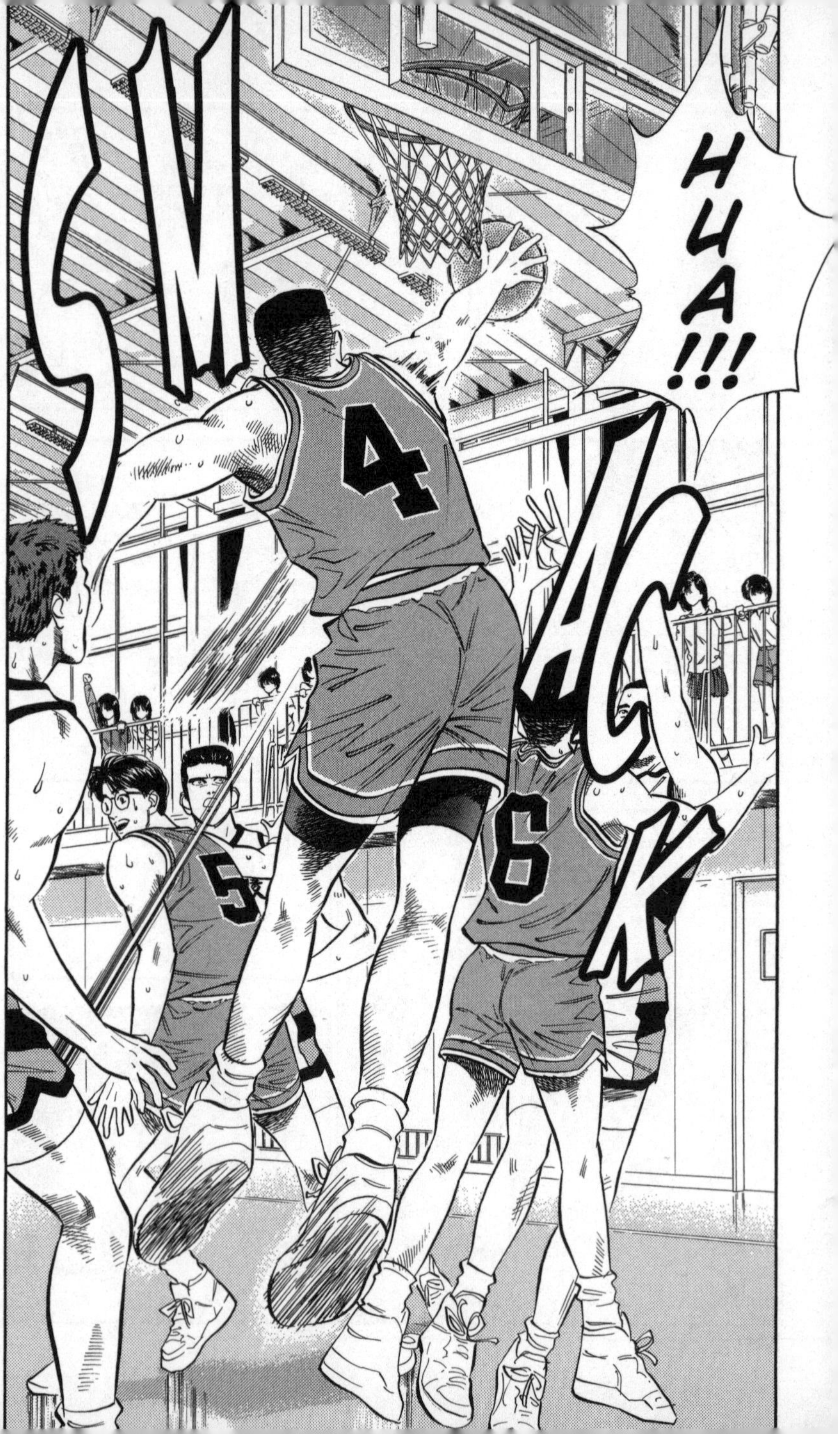
HUA!!!
SMACK

READ THIS WAY

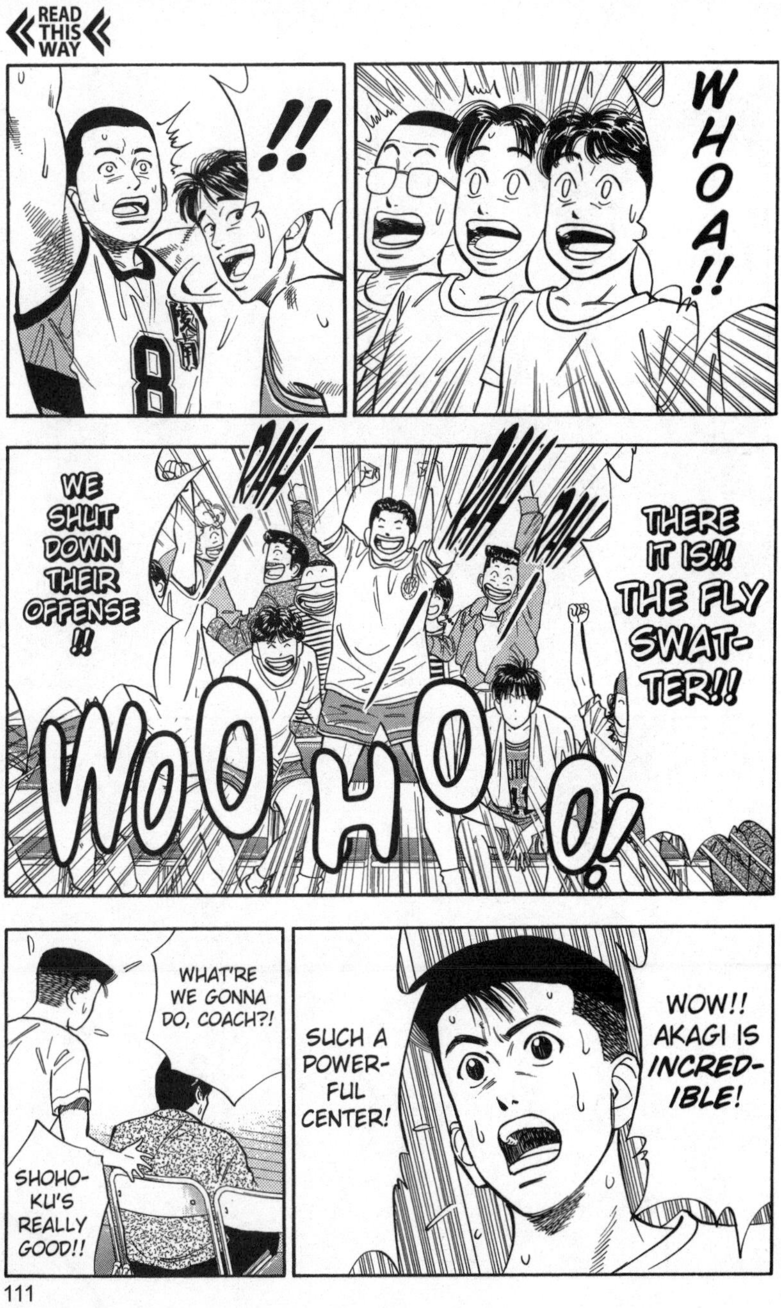

WHOA!!
!!
RAH
RAH
RAH
THERE IT IS!! THE FLY SWATTER!!
WE SHUT DOWN THEIR OFFENSE!!
WOOHOO!
WOW!! AKAGI IS INCREDIBLE!
SUCH A POWERFUL CENTER!
WHAT'RE WE GONNA DO, COACH?!
SHOHOKU'S REALLY GOOD!!

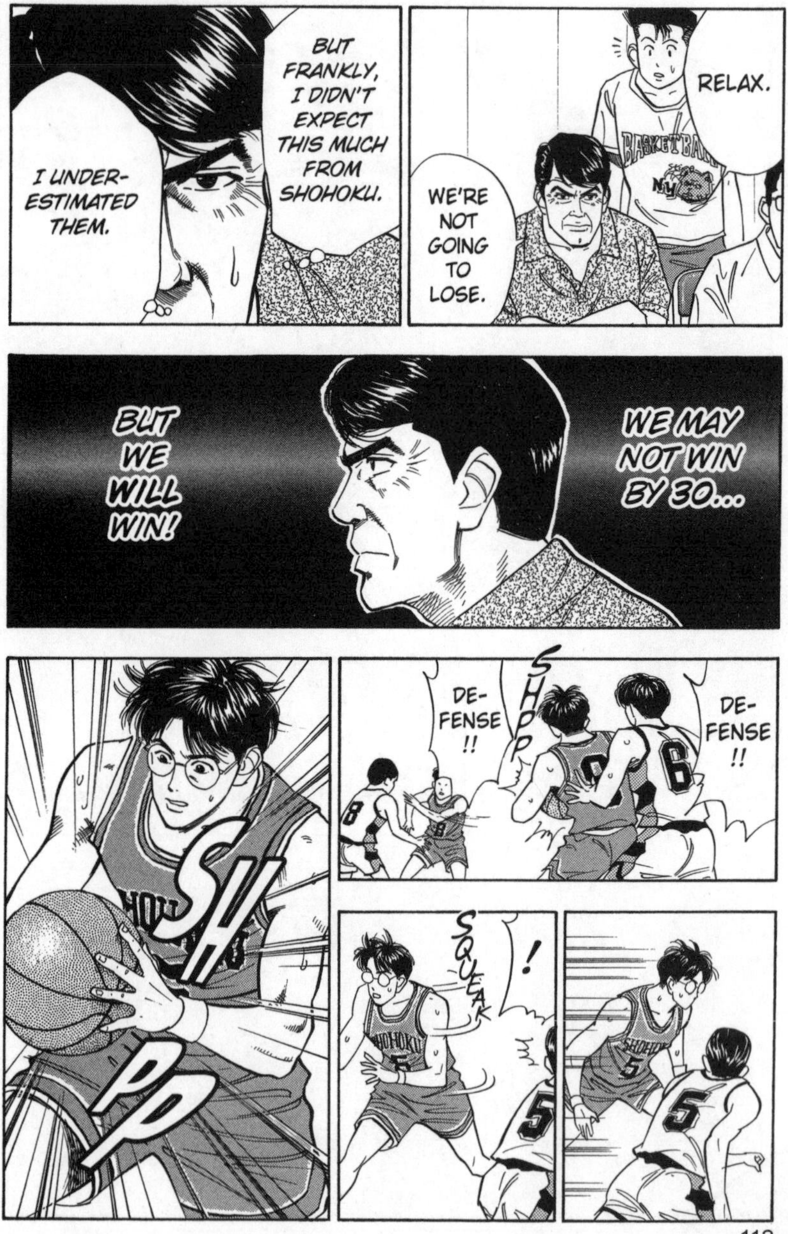
RELAX.
WE'RE NOT GOING TO LOSE.
BUT FRANKLY, I DIDN'T EXPECT THIS MUCH FROM SHOHOKU.
I UNDER-ESTIMATED THEM.
WE MAY NOT WIN BY 30...
BUT WE WILL WIN!
DE-FENSE !!
SHPP
DE-FENSE !!
!
SQUEAK
SHPP

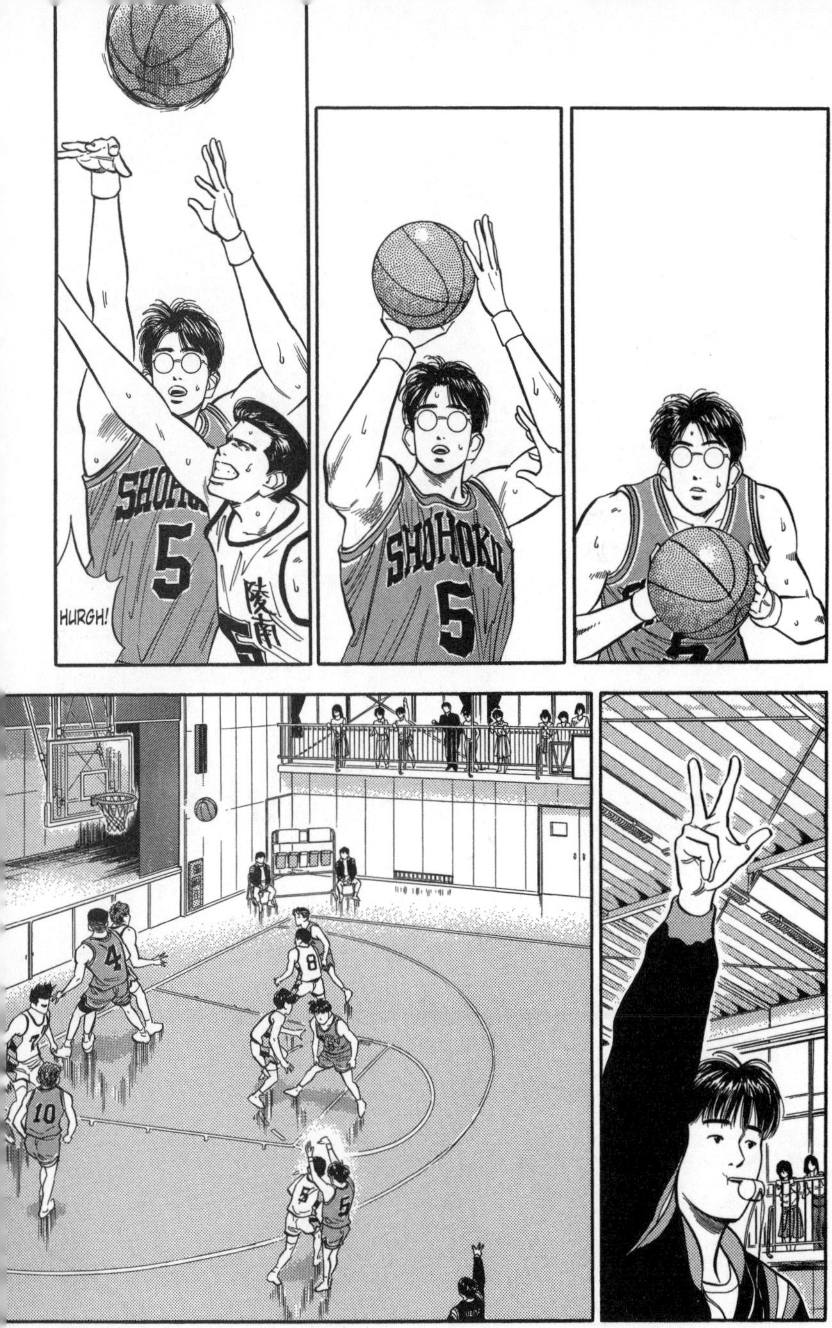
HURGH!

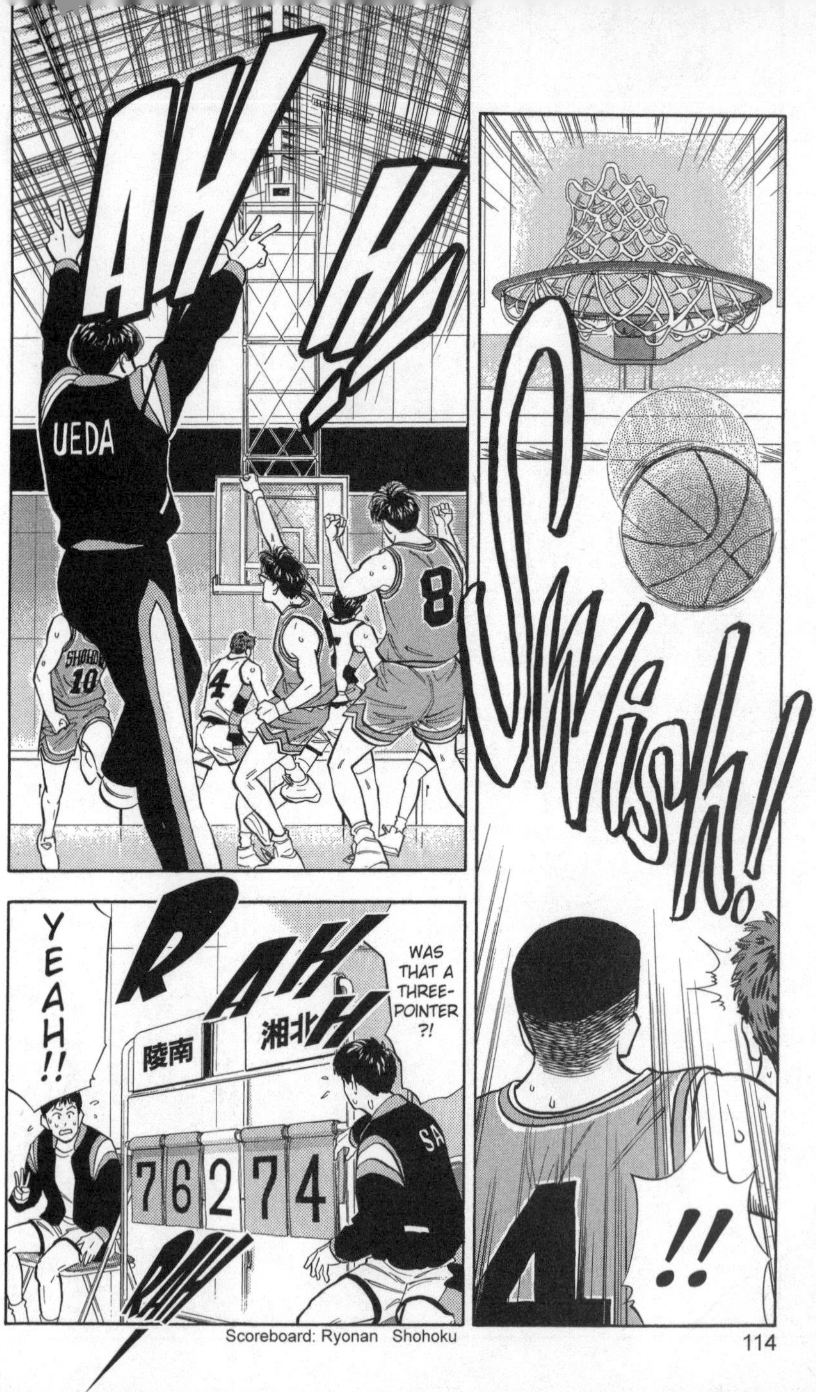
Swish!
!!
AHH!!
UEDA
RAHH
RAHH
WAS THAT A THREE-POINTER?!
YEAH!!
陵南
湘北
76274

Scoreboard: Ryonan Shohoku

READ THIS WAY

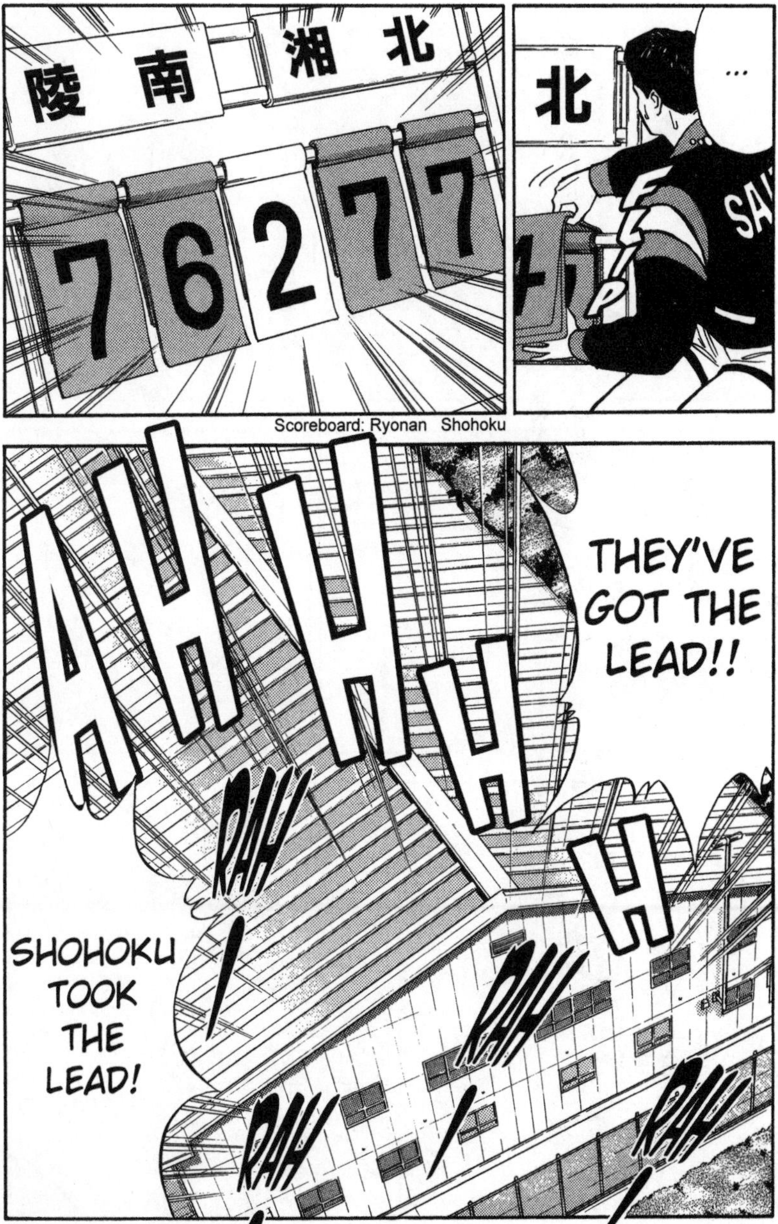
...
FLIP
北
湘北
陵南
76
2
77
THEY'VE GOT THE LEAD!!
AHHHHH
RAH!
SHOHOKU TOOK THE LEAD!
RAH!
RAH!
RAH!
Scoreboard: Ryonan Shohoku

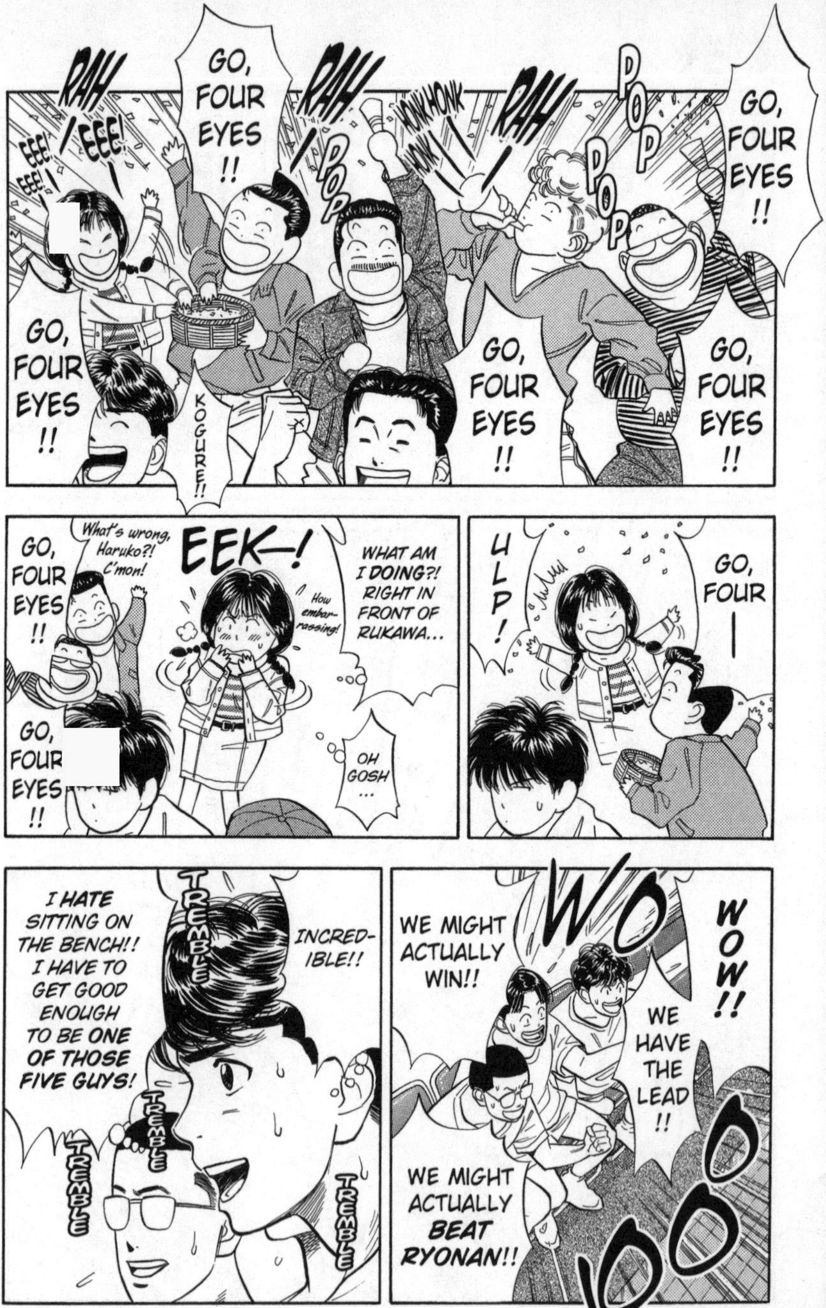
GO, FOUR EYES!!
POP POP POP POP
RAH!
HONK HONK HONK
RAH!
POP
GO, FOUR EYES!!
RAH! EEE!
EEE! EEE!
GO, FOUR EYES!!
GO, FOUR EYES!!
KOGURE!!
GO, FOUR EYES!!
GO, FOUR—
ULP!
WHAT AM I DOING?! RIGHT IN FRONT OF RUKAWA...
OH GOSH...
EEK—!
How embarrassing!
What's wrong, Haruko?! C'mon!
GO, FOUR EYES!!
GO, FOUR EYES!!
WOW!!
WOOO!
WE HAVE THE LEAD!!
WE MIGHT ACTUALLY WIN!!
WE MIGHT ACTUALLY BEAT RYONAN!!
INCREDIBLE!!
TREMBLE
I HATE SITTING ON THE BENCH!! I HAVE TO GET GOOD ENOUGH TO BE ONE OF THOSE FIVE GUYS!
TREMBLE
TREMBLE
TREMBLE

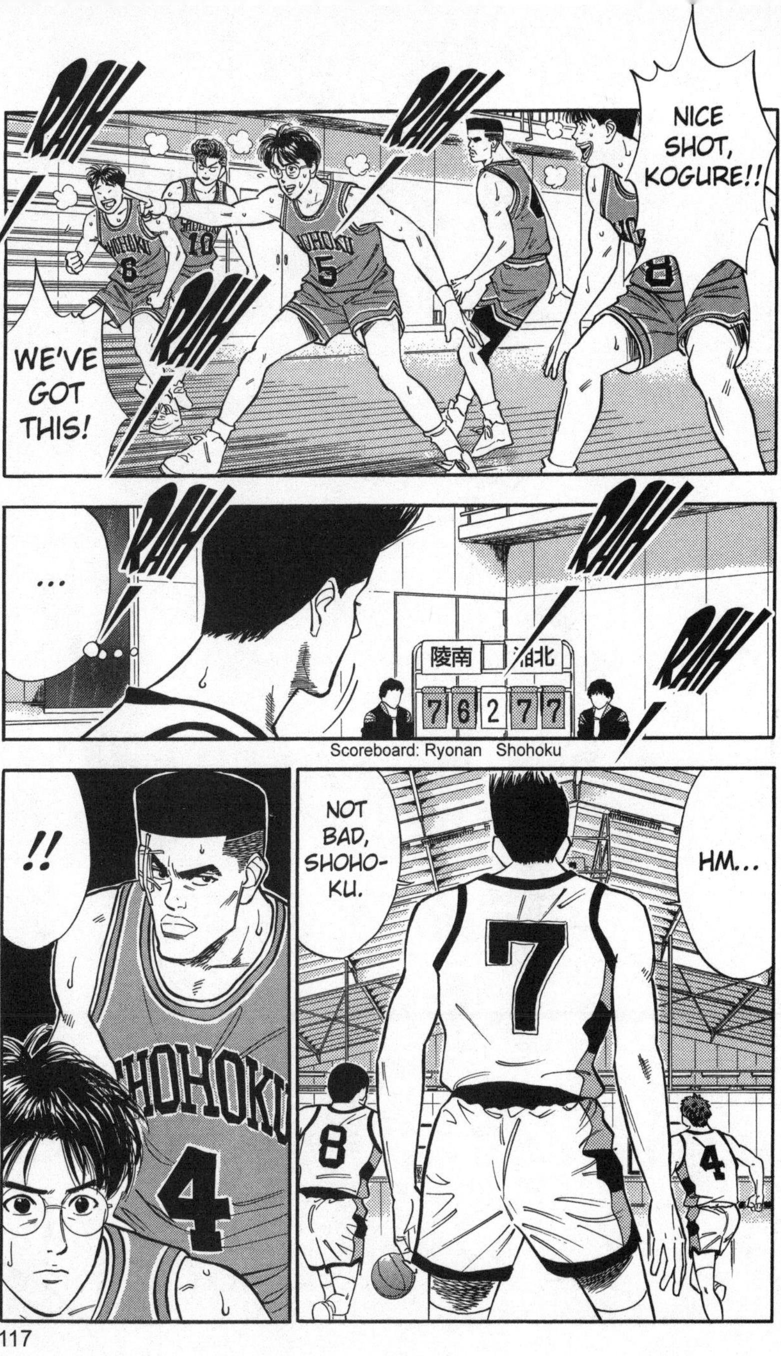
NICE SHOT, KOGURE!!
RAH
RAH
RAH
WE'VE GOT THIS!
RAH
RAH
陵南
湘北
7 6 2 7 7
RAH
...
Scoreboard: Ryonan Shohoku
HM...
NOT BAD, SHOHOKU.
!!

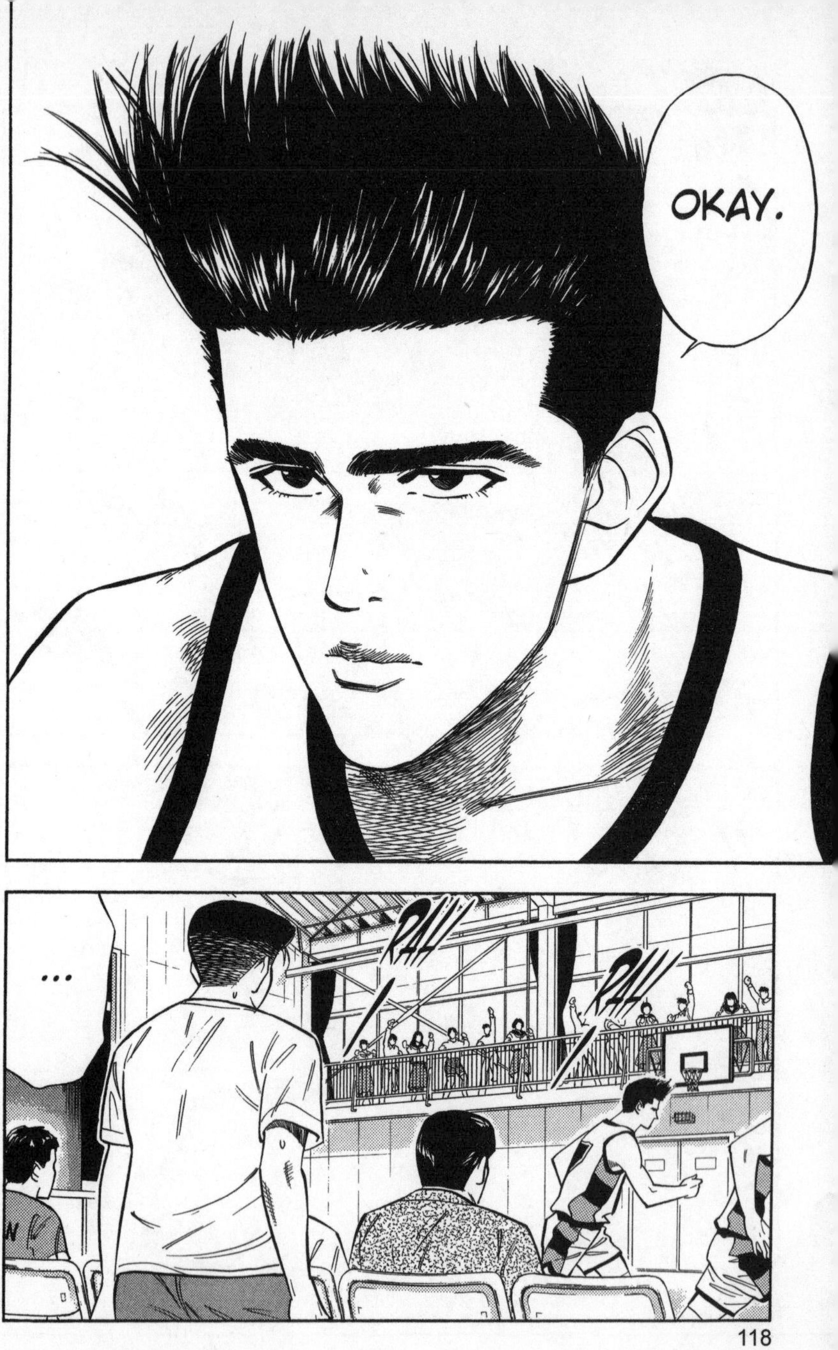
OKAY.
RAH
RAH
...

READ THIS WAY

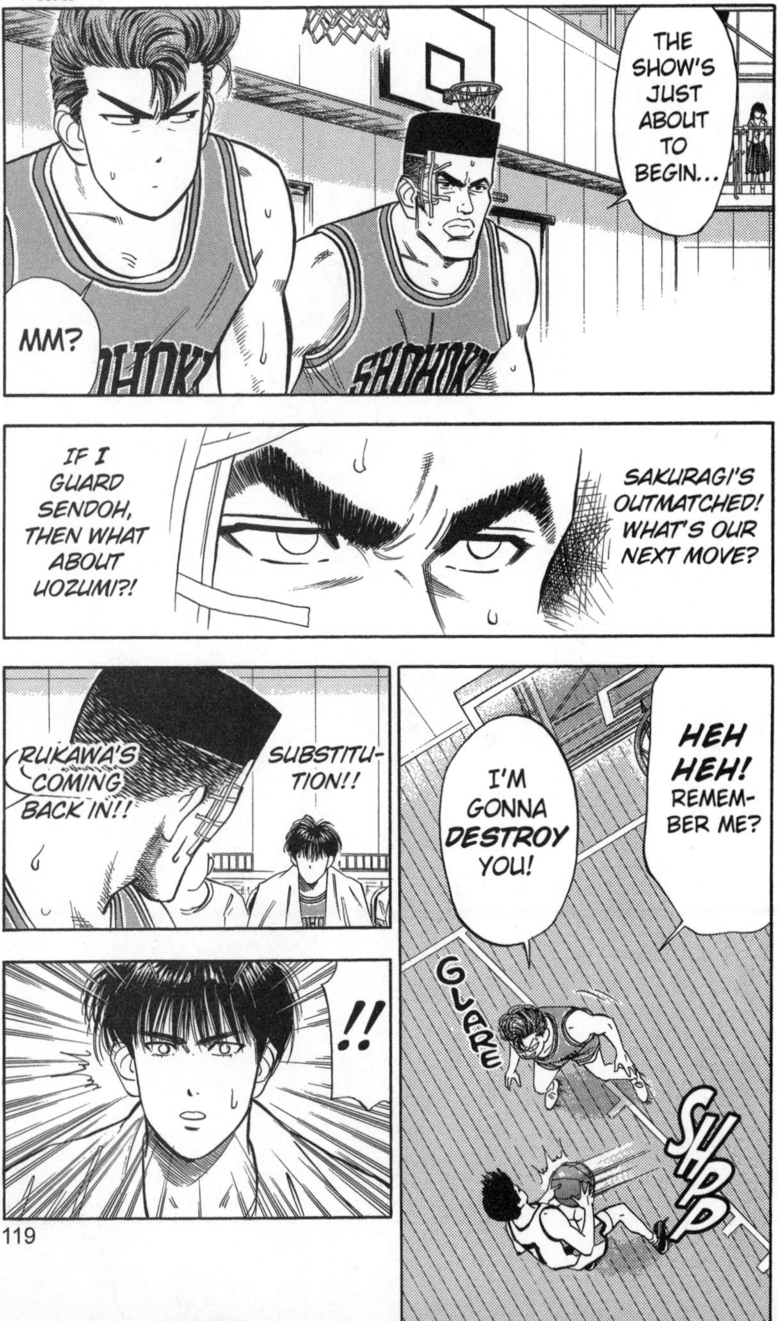
THE SHOW'S JUST ABOUT TO BEGIN...
MM?
SAKURAGI'S OUTMATCHED! WHAT'S OUR NEXT MOVE?
IF I GUARD SENDOH, THEN WHAT ABOUT UOZUMI?!
HEH HEH! REMEMBER ME?
I'M GONNA DESTROY YOU!
GLARE
SHPP
SUBSTITUTION!!
RUKAWA'S COMING BACK IN!!
!!

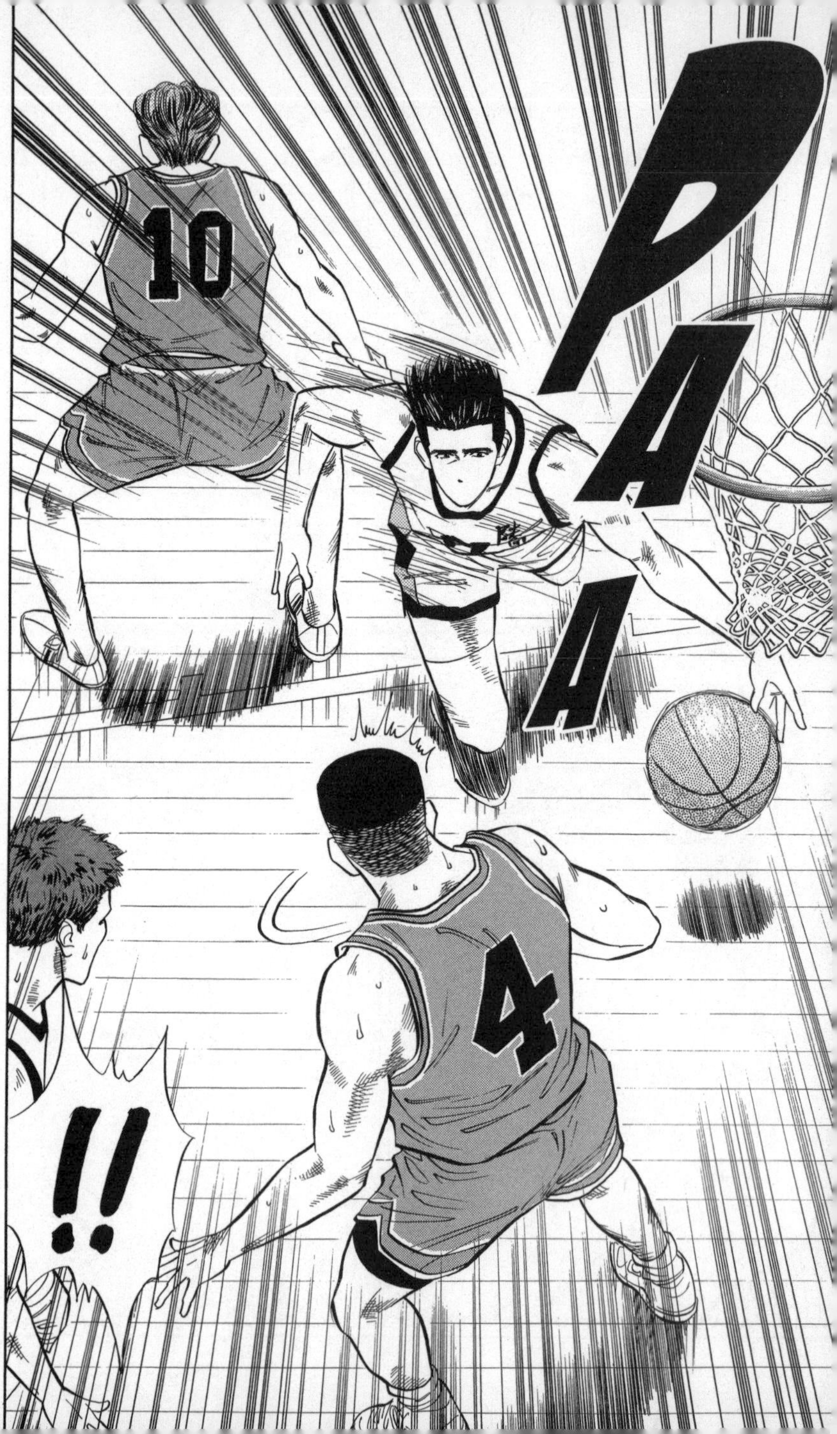
PAA
!!

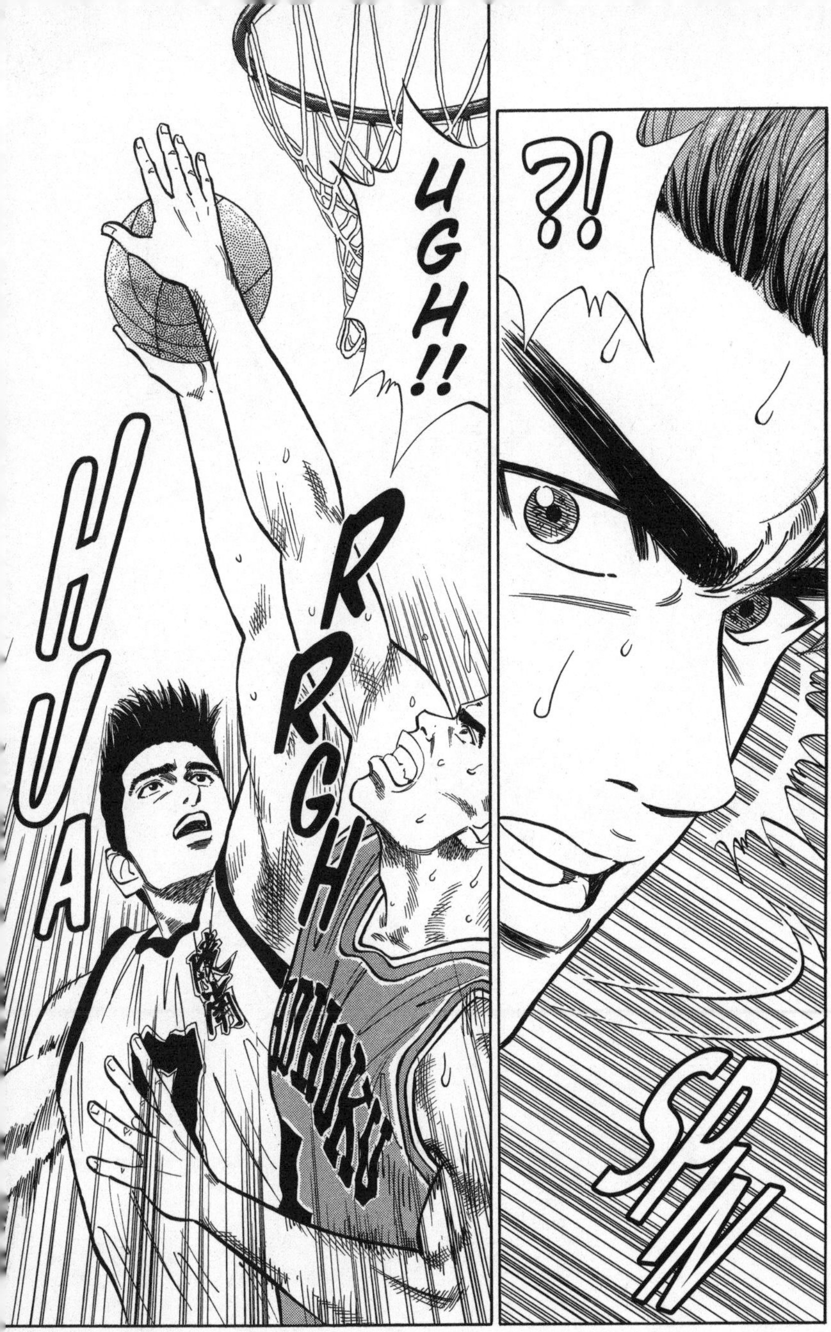
?!
SPIN
UGH!!
RRRGH
HUUA

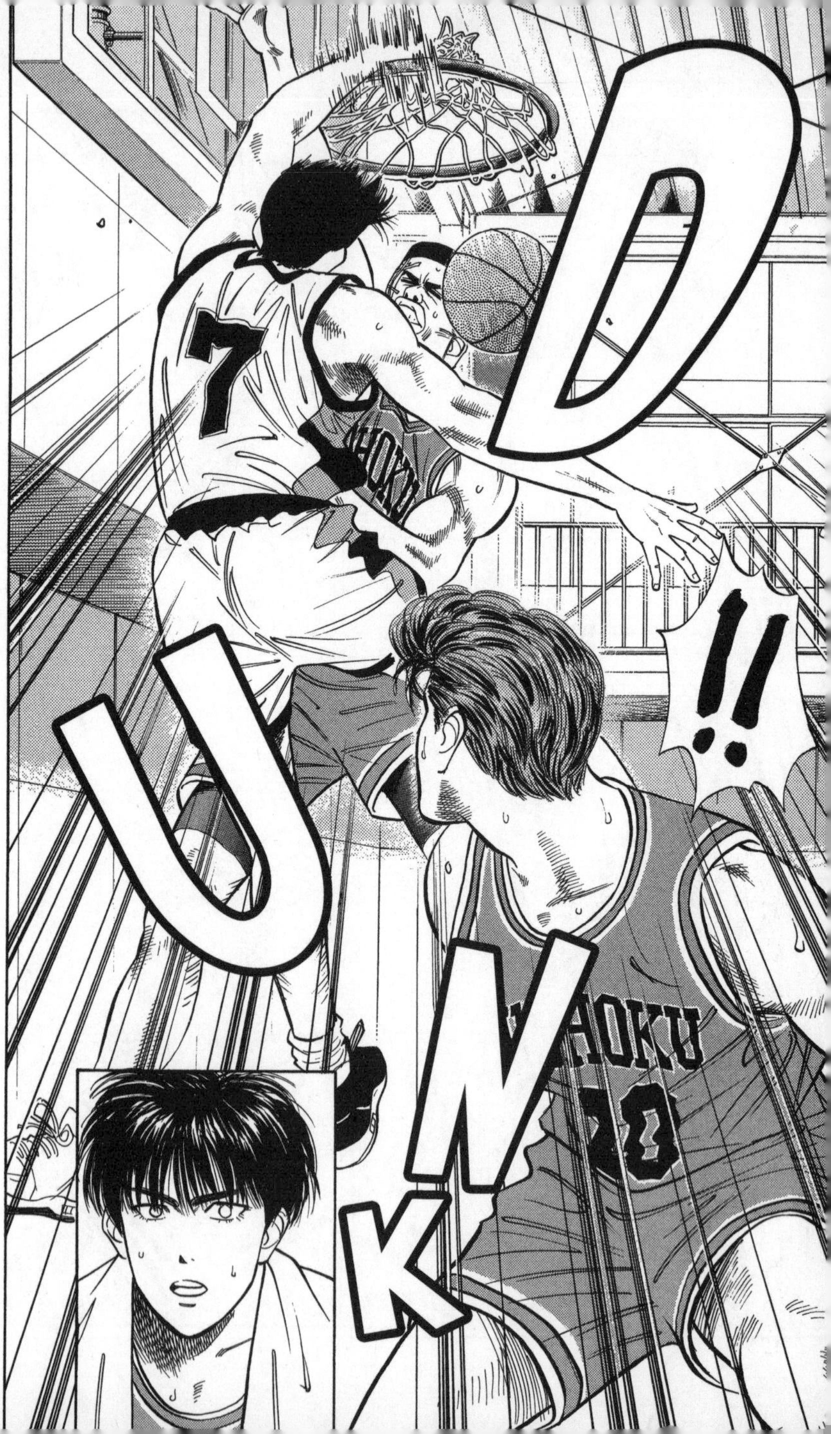
DUNK
!!

READ THIS WAY

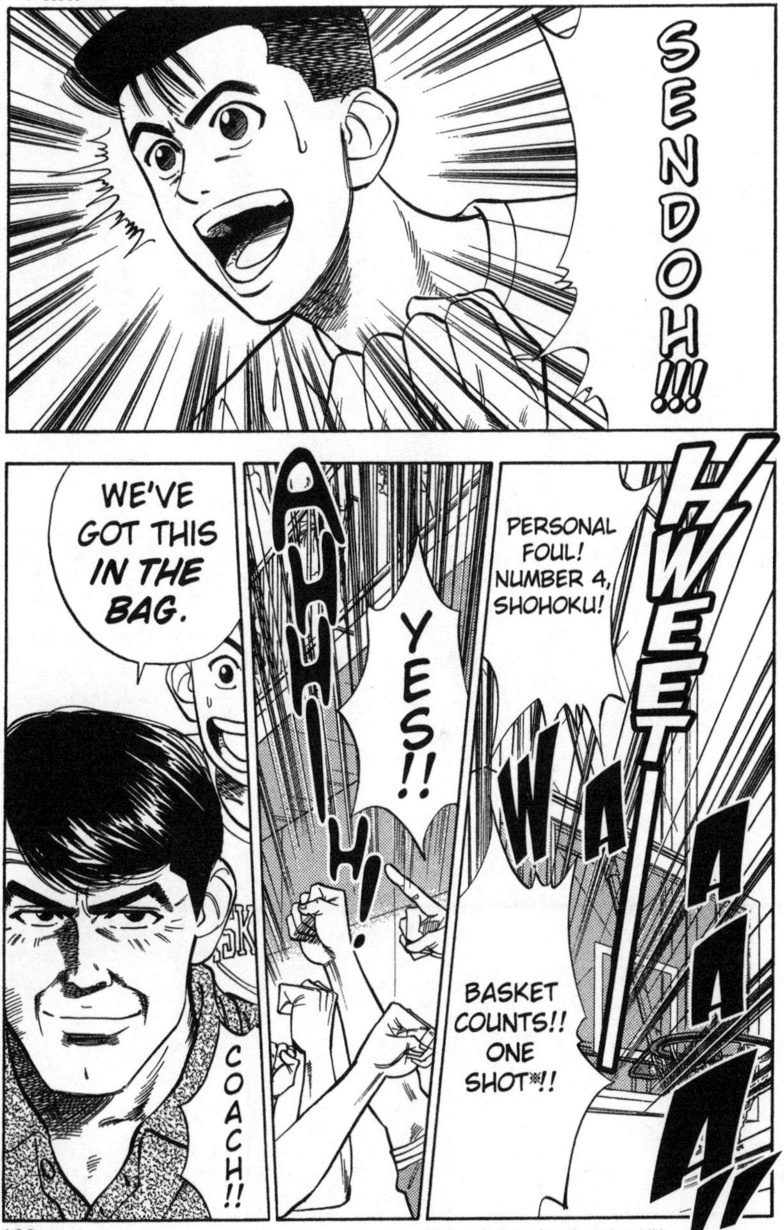
SENDOH!!!
HWEET!
PERSONAL FOUL! NUMBER 4, SHOHOKU!
WAAAAA!!
BASKET COUNTS!! ONE SHOT※!!
AHHIH!
YES!!
WE'VE GOT THIS *IN THE BAG*.
COACH!!

※ Awarded one free throw in addition to the field goal.

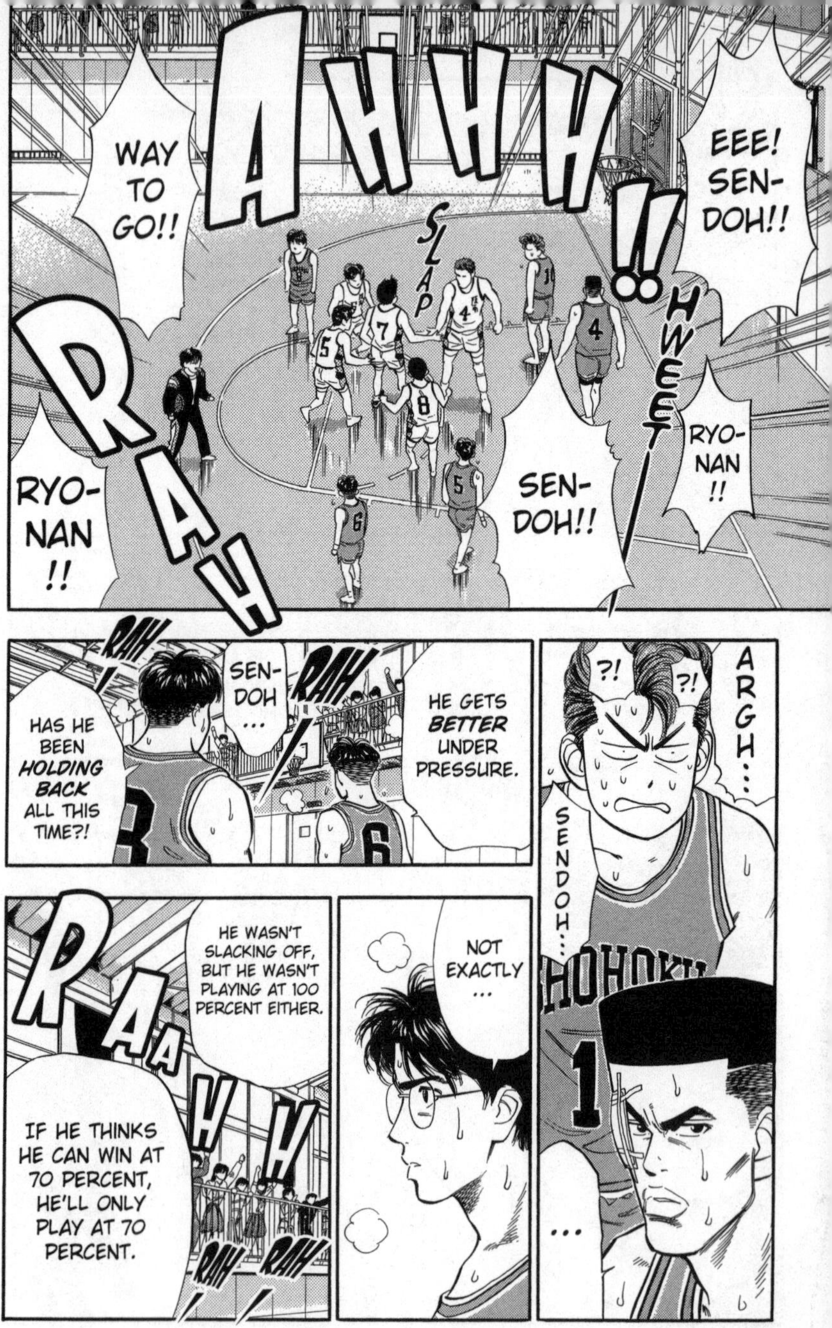
EEE! SEN-DOH!!
AHHHH!!
WAY TO GO!!
SLAP
HWEET
RYO-NAN!!
SEN-DOH!!
RAAH
RYO-NAN!!
ARGH...
?!
?!
SENDOH...
HE GETS BETTER UNDER PRESSURE.
RAH
SEN-DOH...
RAH
HAS HE BEEN HOLDING BACK ALL THIS TIME?!
...
NOT EXACTLY...
HE WASN'T SLACKING OFF, BUT HE WASN'T PLAYING AT 100 PERCENT EITHER.
RAAAHH
IF HE THINKS HE CAN WIN AT 70 PERCENT, HE'LL ONLY PLAY AT 70 PERCENT.
RAH
RAH

READ THIS WAY

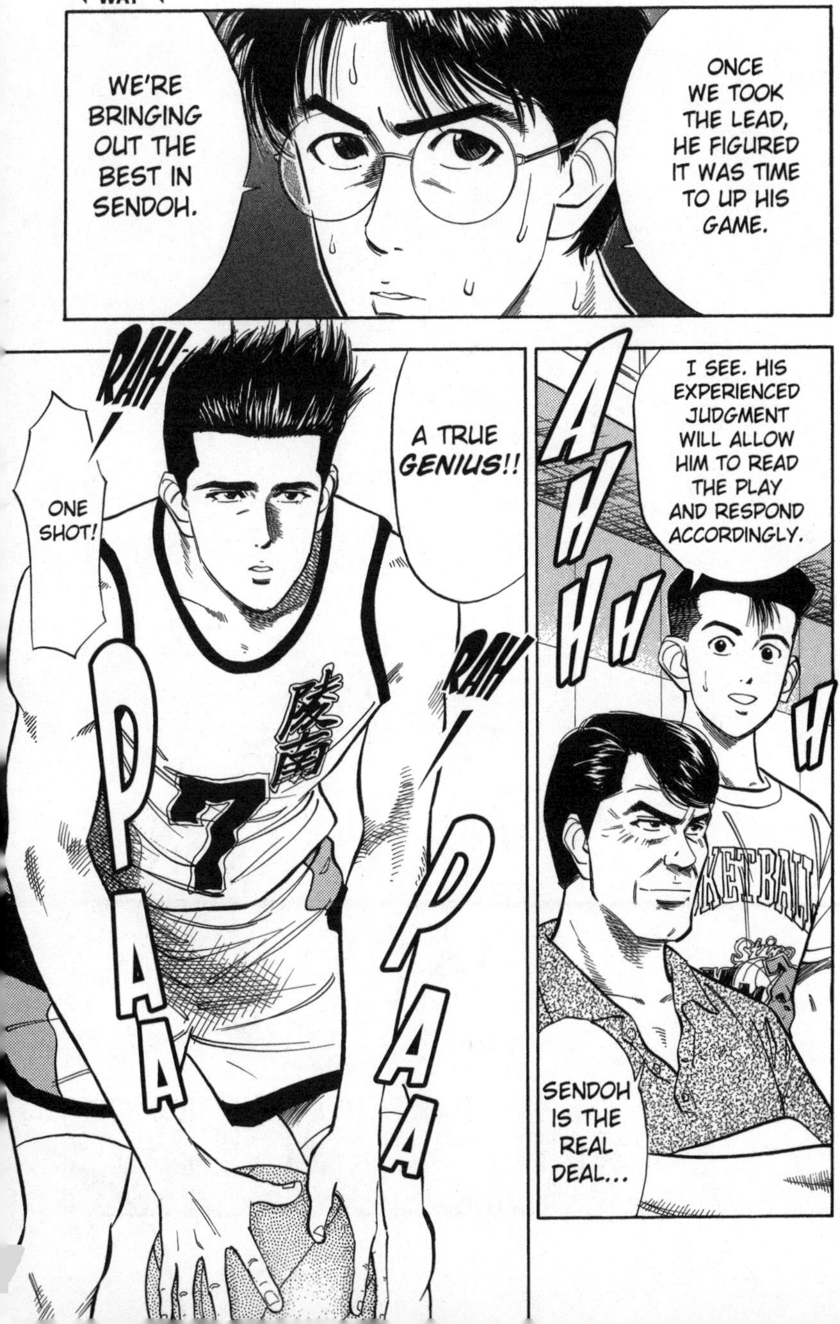
ONCE WE TOOK THE LEAD, HE FIGURED IT WAS TIME TO UP HIS GAME.
WE'RE BRINGING OUT THE BEST IN SENDOH.
AAHHHHH
I SEE. HIS EXPERIENCED JUDGMENT WILL ALLOW HIM TO READ THE PLAY AND RESPOND ACCORDINGLY.
SENDOH IS THE REAL DEAL...
A TRUE GENIUS!!
RAH
PAAA
RAH
ONE SHOT!
PAAA

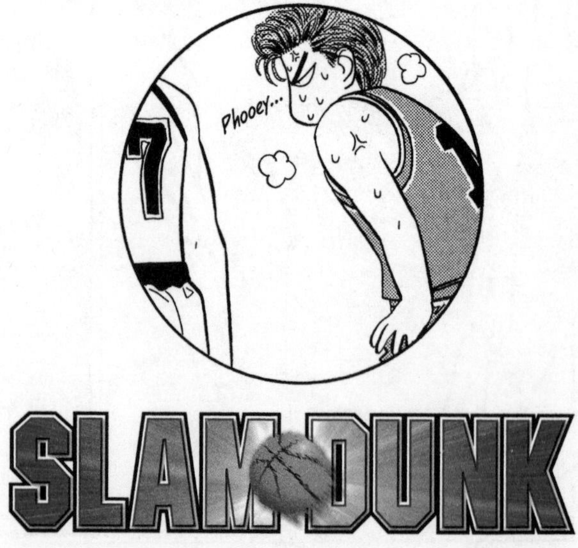
Phooey...

SLAM DUNK

#42 WINNERS WILL NOT BE DENIED

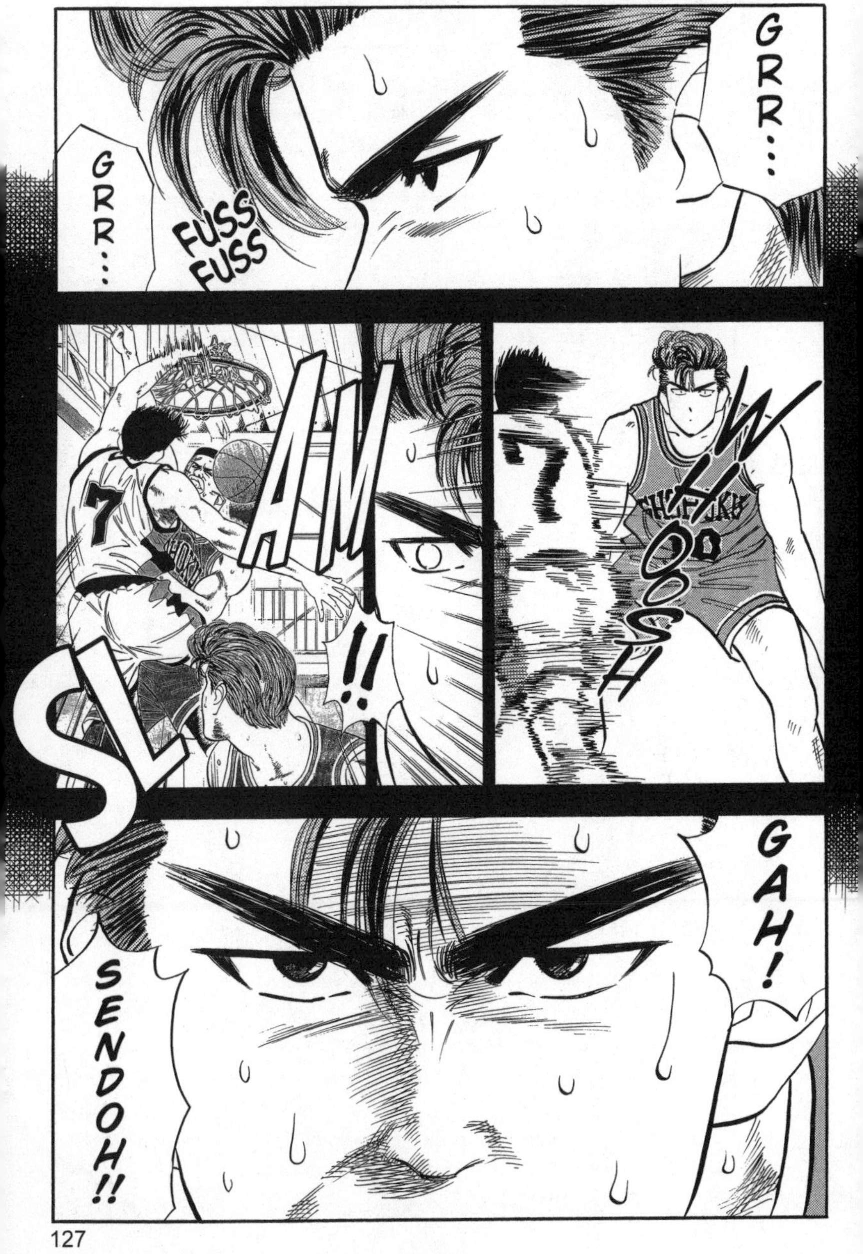
GRR...
GRR...
FUSS FUSS
WHOOOSH
SLAM!!
GAH!
SENDOH!!

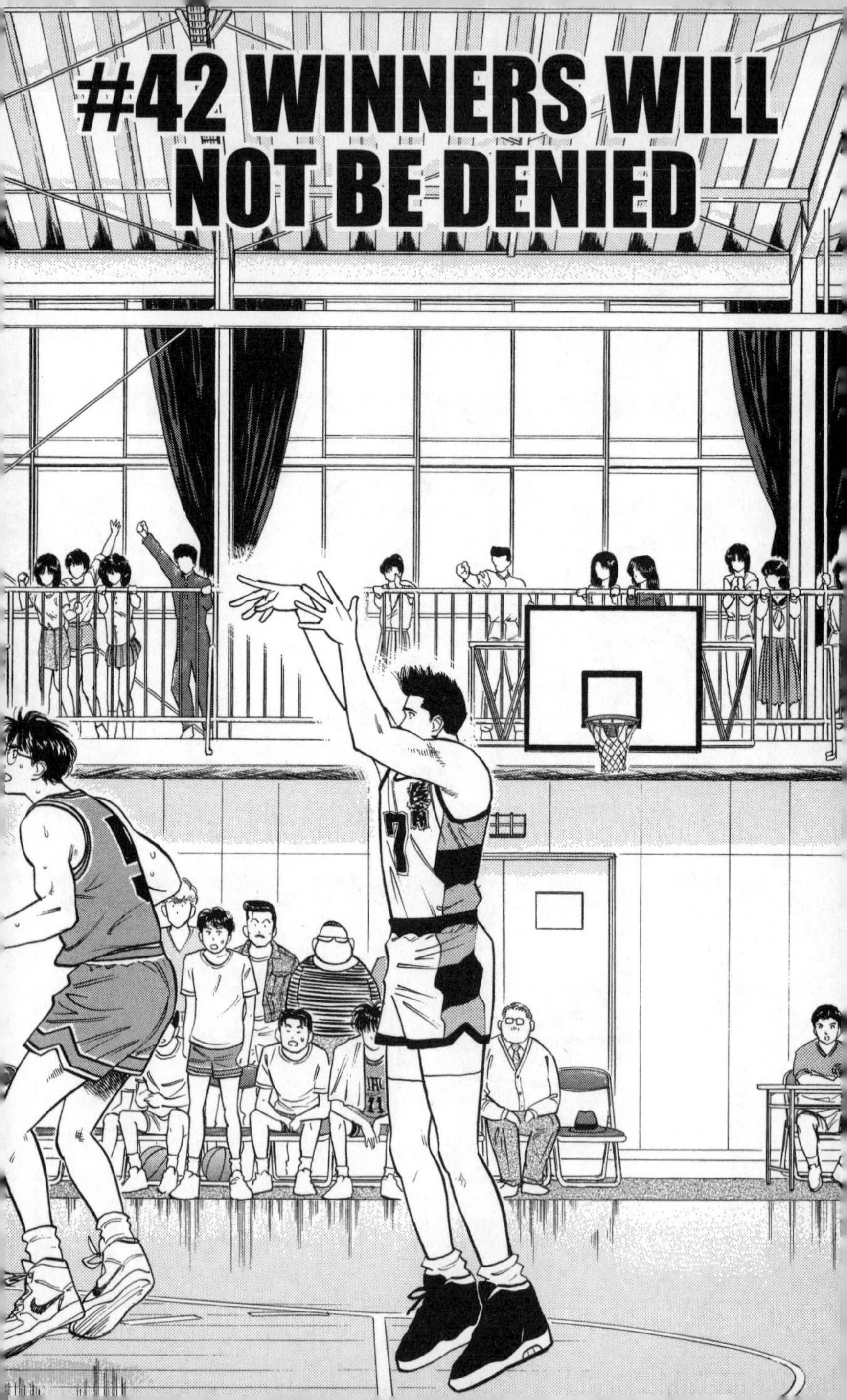
#42 WINNERS WILL NOT BE DENIED

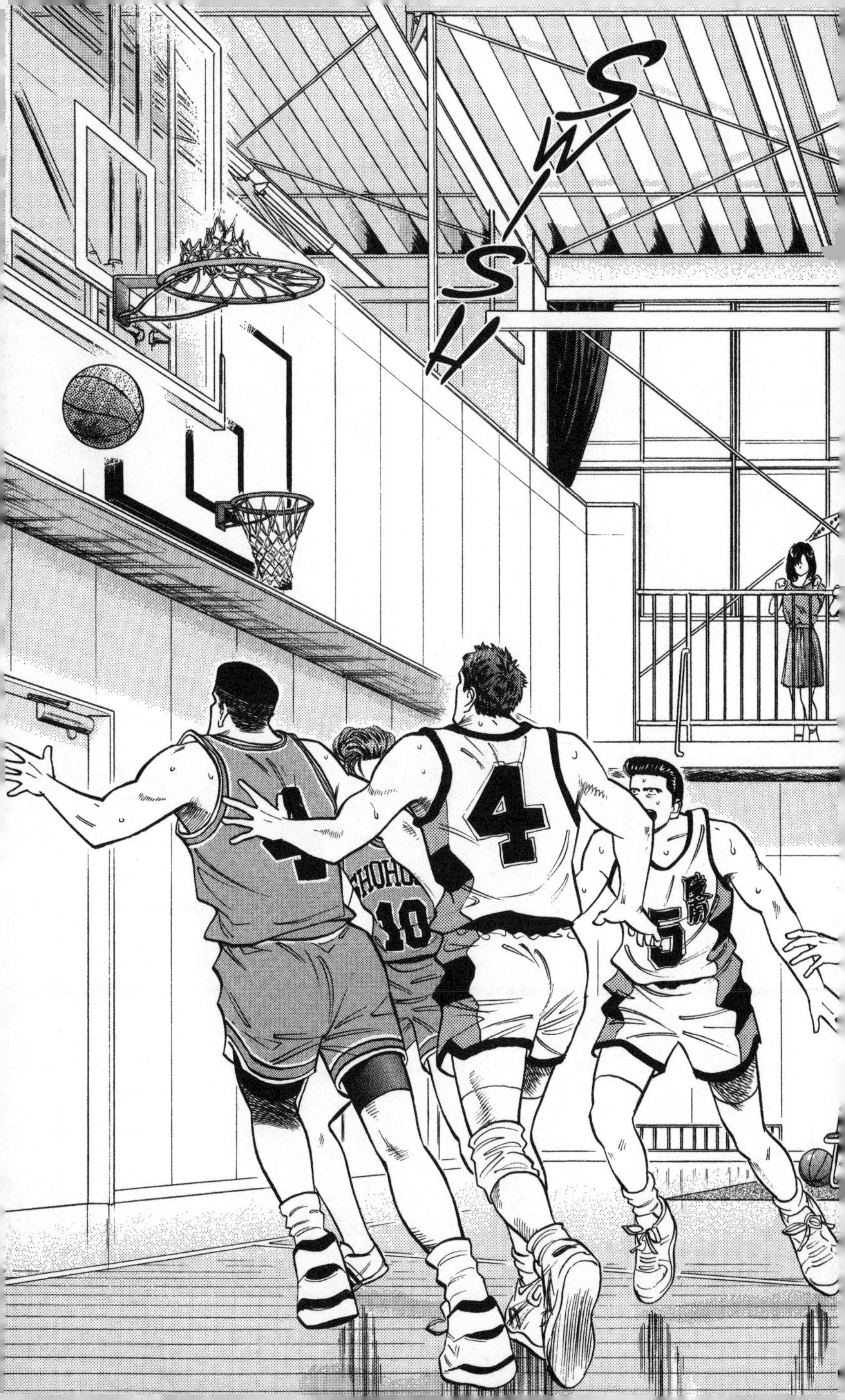
SWISH

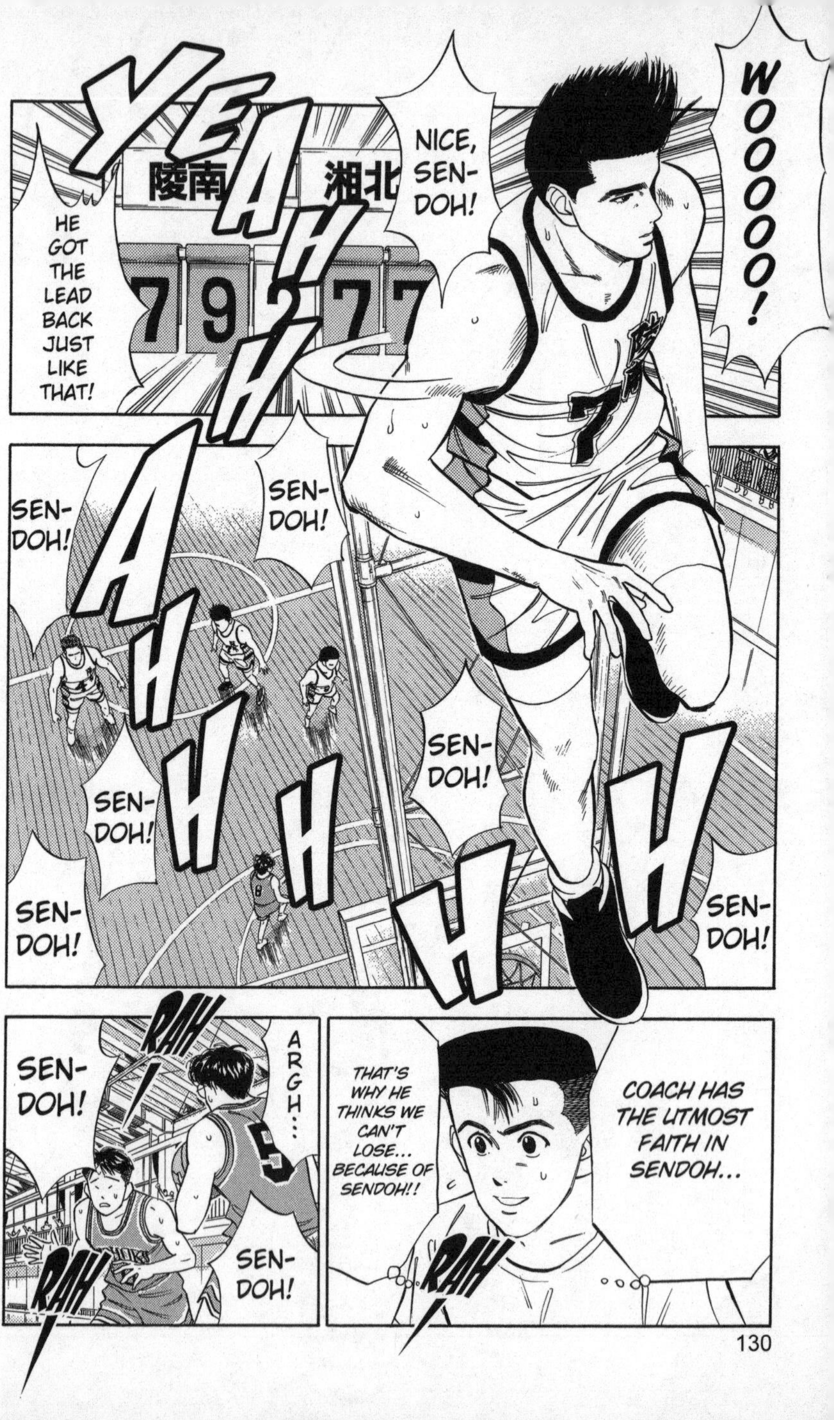
WOOOOOO!
NICE, SEN-DOH!
YEAHHH AHHHHH
HE GOT THE LEAD BACK JUST LIKE THAT!
SEN-DOH!
SEN-DOH!
SEN-DOH!
SEN-DOH!
SEN-DOH!
SEN-DOH!
COACH HAS THE UTMOST FAITH IN SENDOH...
THAT'S WHY HE THINKS WE CAN'T LOSE... BECAUSE OF SENDOH!!
RAH
ARGH...
RAH!
SEN-DOH!
SEN-DOH!
RAH

READ THIS WAY

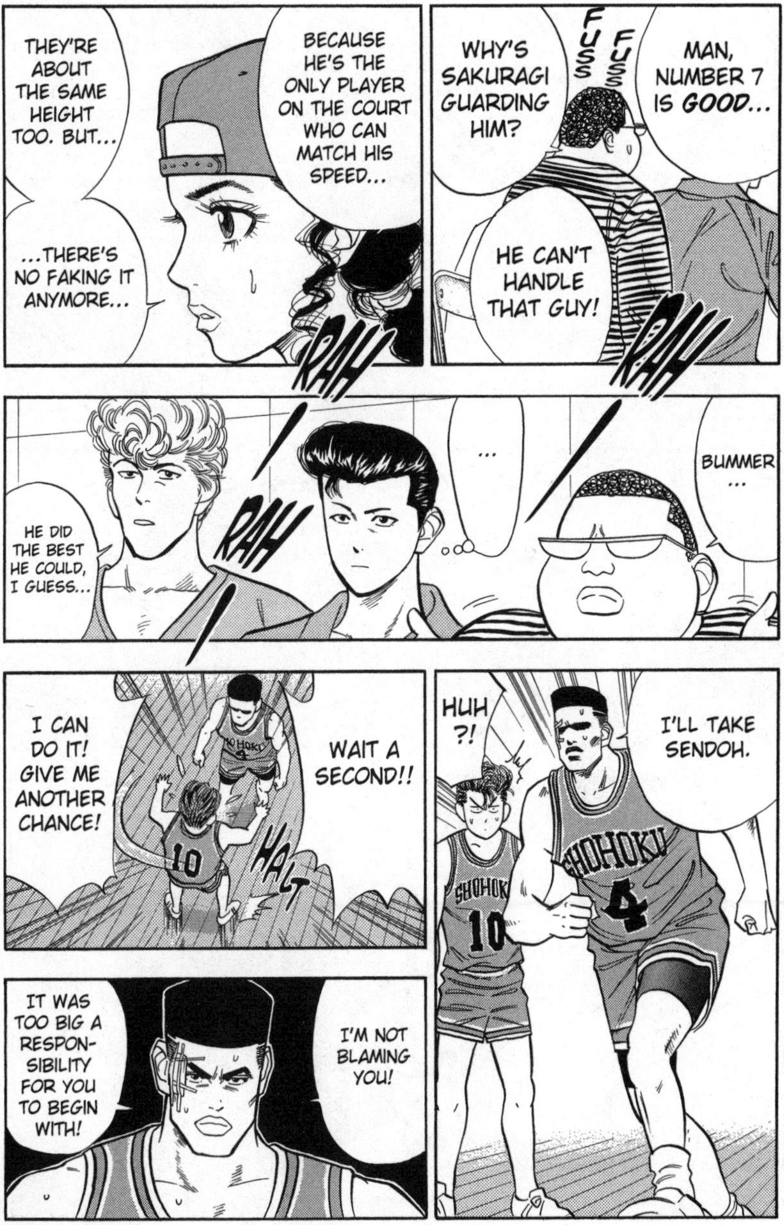

MAN, NUMBER 7 IS GOOD...
FUSS FUSS
WHY'S SAKURAGI GUARDING HIM?
HE CAN'T HANDLE THAT GUY!
RAH!
BECAUSE HE'S THE ONLY PLAYER ON THE COURT WHO CAN MATCH HIS SPEED...
THEY'RE ABOUT THE SAME HEIGHT TOO. BUT...
...THERE'S NO FAKING IT ANYMORE...
RAH!
BUMMER...
...
RAH!
HE DID THE BEST HE COULD, I GUESS...
I'LL TAKE SENDOH.
HUH?!
WAIT A SECOND!!
I CAN DO IT! GIVE ME ANOTHER CHANCE!
HALT
I'M NOT BLAMING YOU!
IT WAS TOO BIG A RESPON-SIBILITY FOR YOU TO BEGIN WITH!

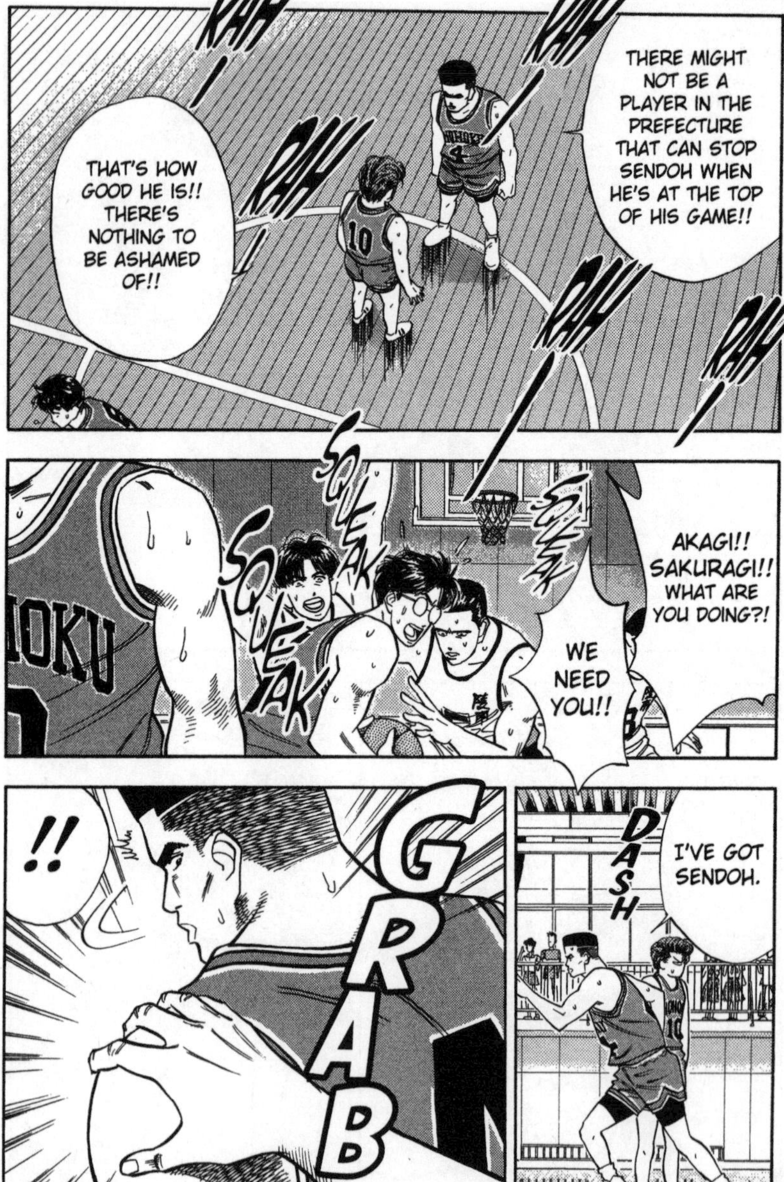
RAH
RAH
RAH
THERE MIGHT NOT BE A PLAYER IN THE PREFECTURE THAT CAN STOP SENDOH WHEN HE'S AT THE TOP OF HIS GAME!!
THAT'S HOW GOOD HE IS!! THERE'S NOTHING TO BE ASHAMED OF!!
RAH
RAH
AKAGI!! SAKURAGI!! WHAT ARE YOU DOING?!
WE NEED YOU!!
SQUEAK
SQUEAK
SQUEAK
DASH
I'VE GOT SENDOH.
!!
GRAB

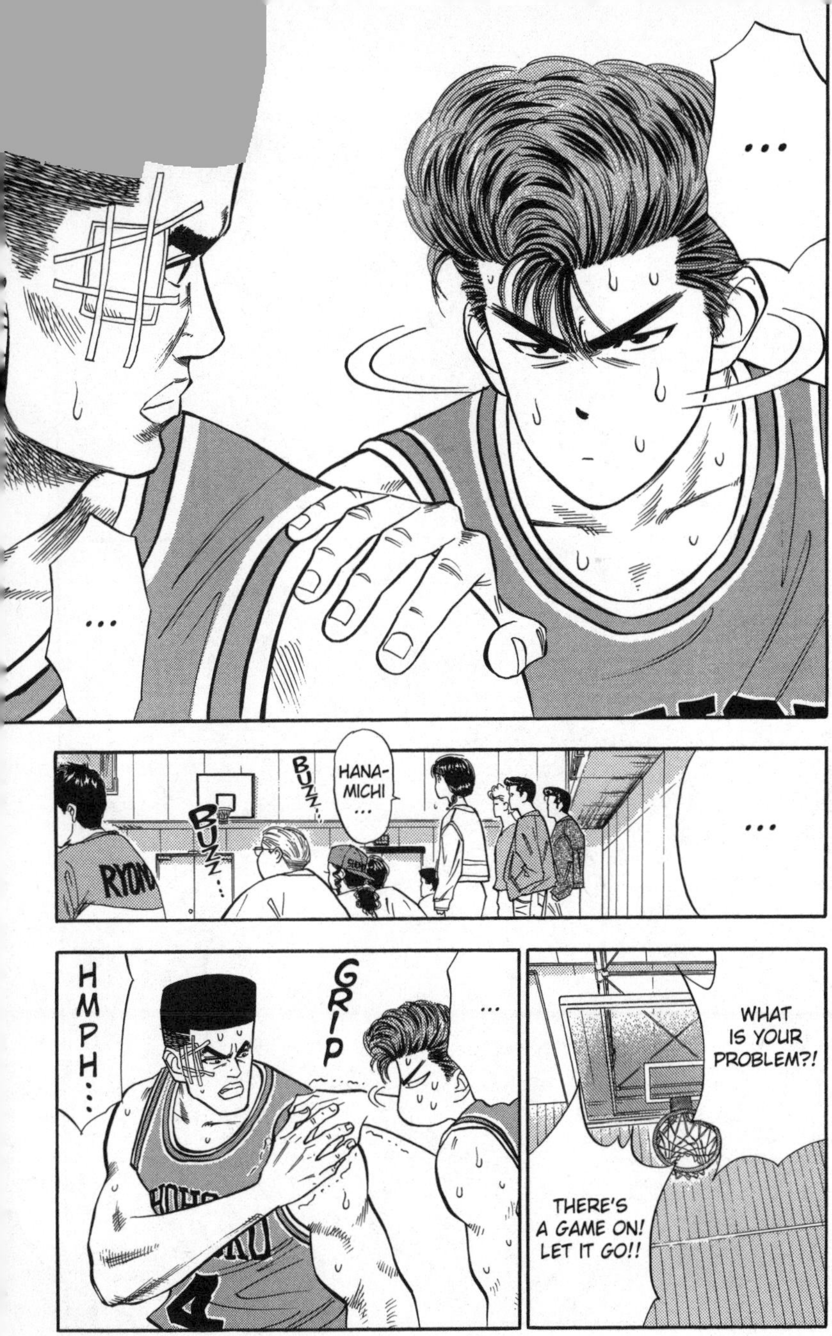
...
...
...
HANA-MICHI ...
BUZZ
BUZZ...
WHAT IS YOUR PROBLEM?!
THERE'S A GAME ON! LET IT GO!!
...
GRIP
HMPH...

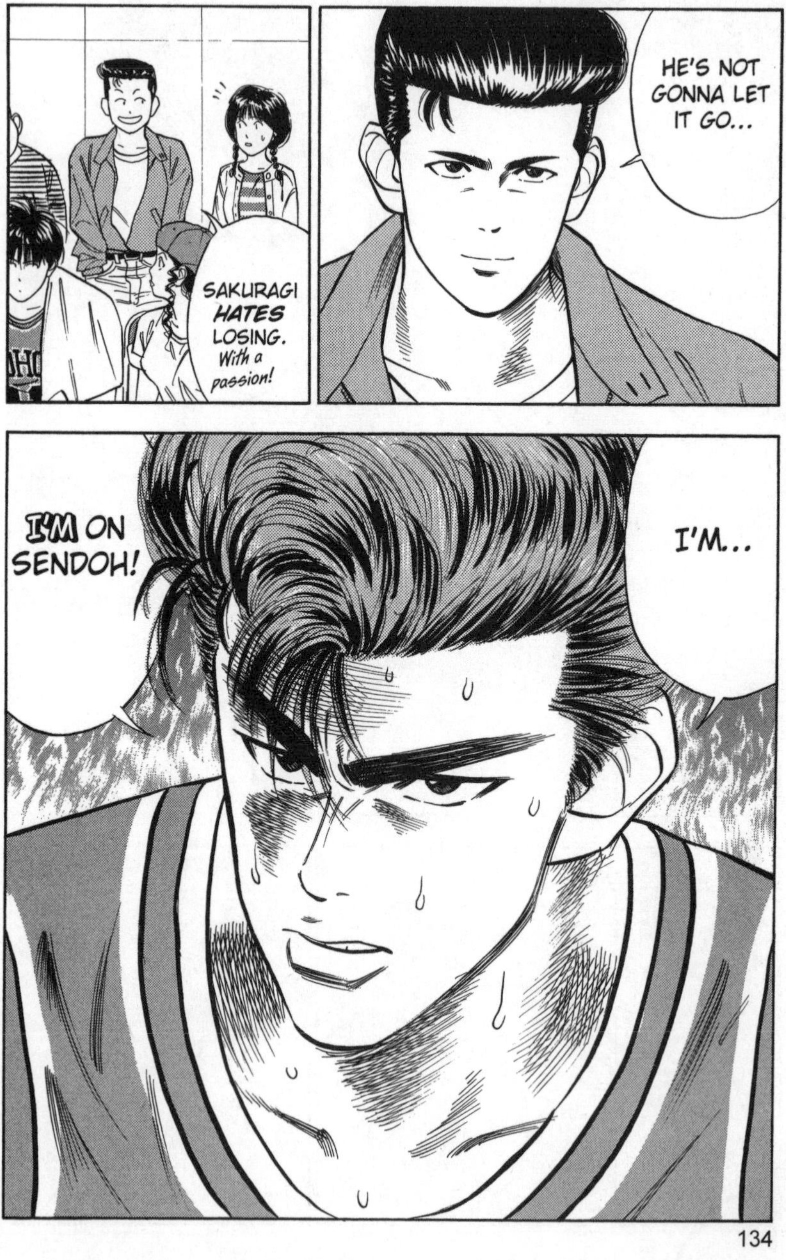
HE'S NOT GONNA LET IT GO...
SAKURAGI **HATES** LOSING. *With a passion!*
I'M...
I'M ON SENDOH!

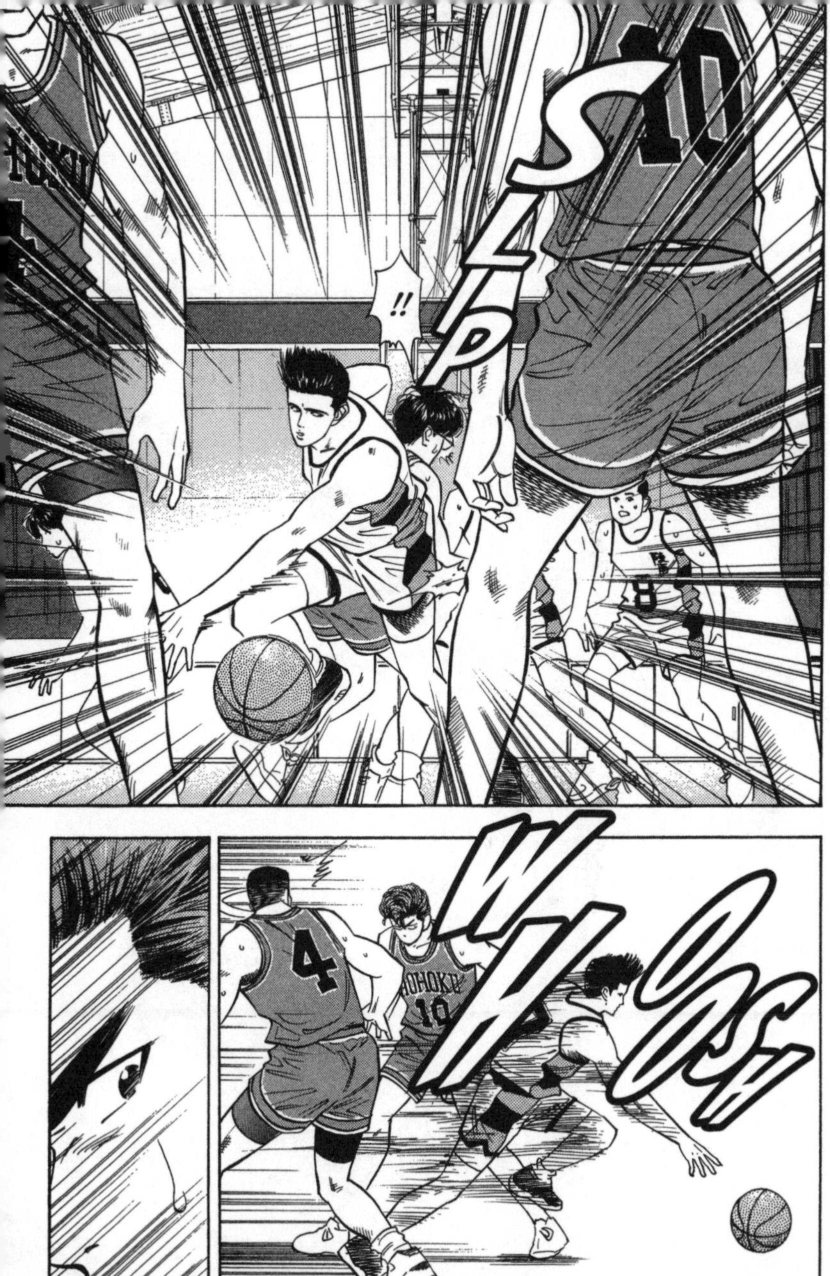
SLIP
!!
WHOOSH

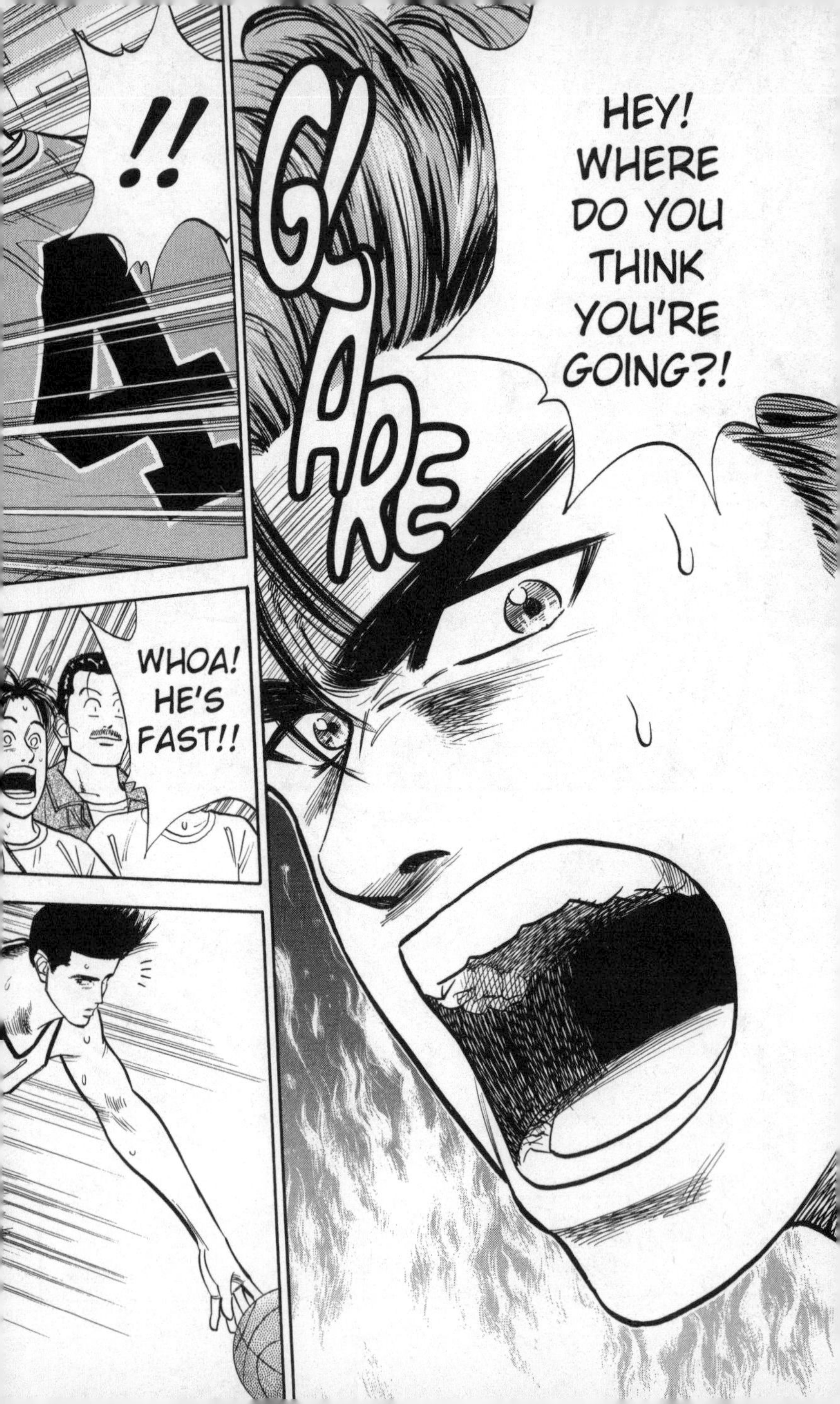
HEY! WHERE DO YOU THINK YOU'RE GOING?!
GLARE
!!
WHOA! HE'S FAST!!

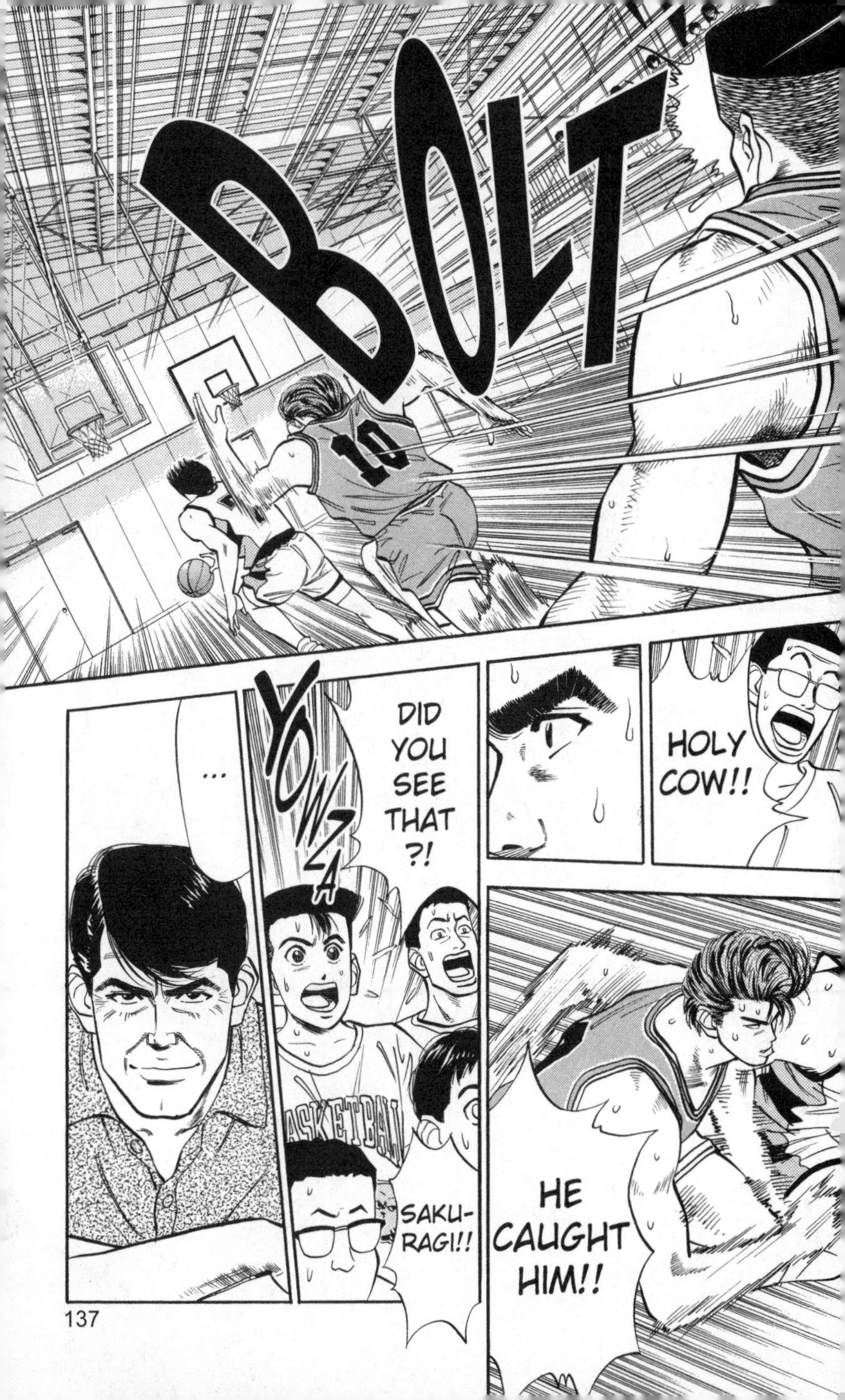
BOLT
HOLY COW!!
HE CAUGHT HIM!!
DID YOU SEE THAT?!
YOWZA
SAKU-RAGI!!
...

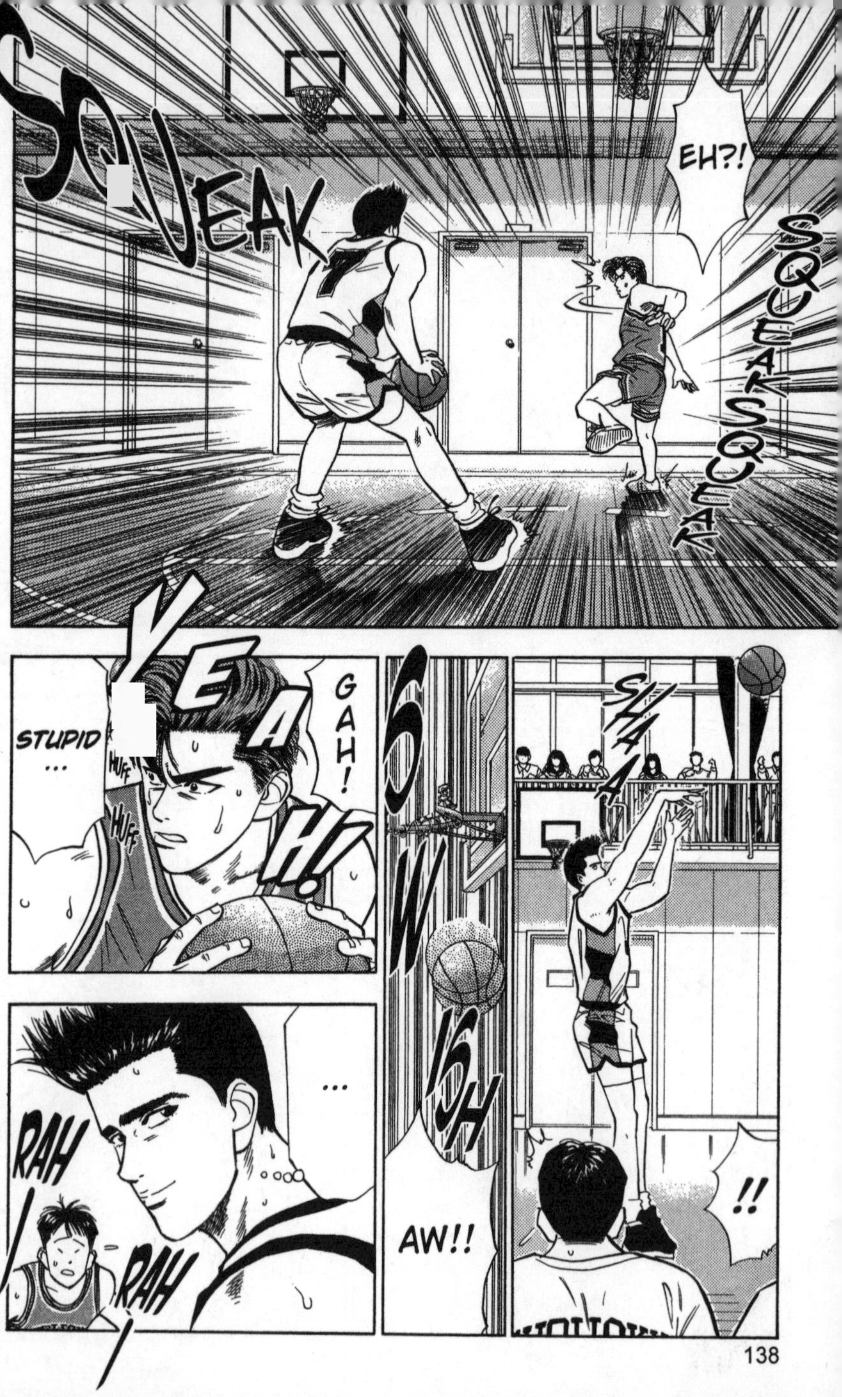
EH?!
SQUEAKSQUEAK
SQUEAK
SHAAA
!!
SWISH
AW!!
YEAH!
GAH!
STUPID ...
HUFF HUFF
...
RAH RAH

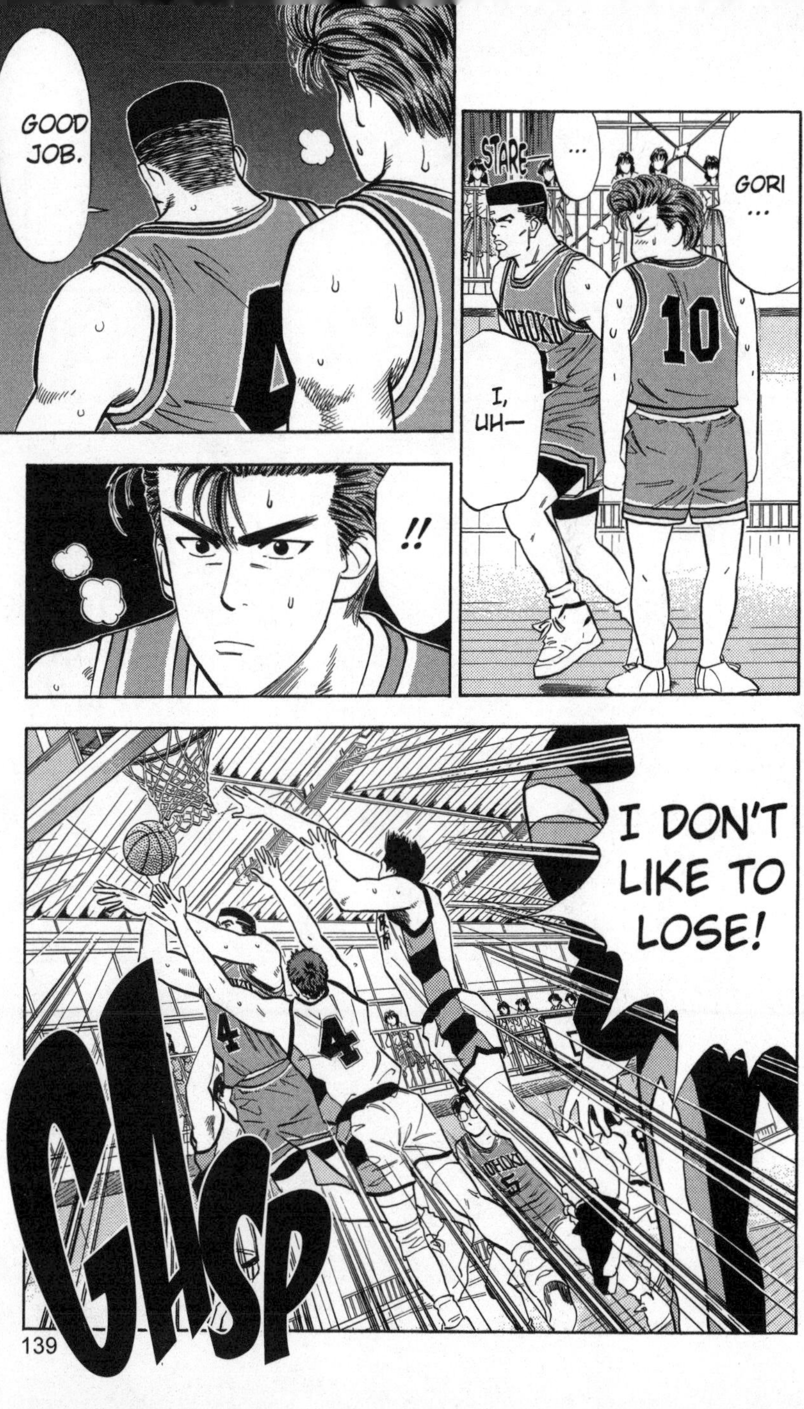
STARE
...
GORI ...
I, UH—
GOOD JOB.
!!
I DON'T LIKE TO LOSE!
GASP

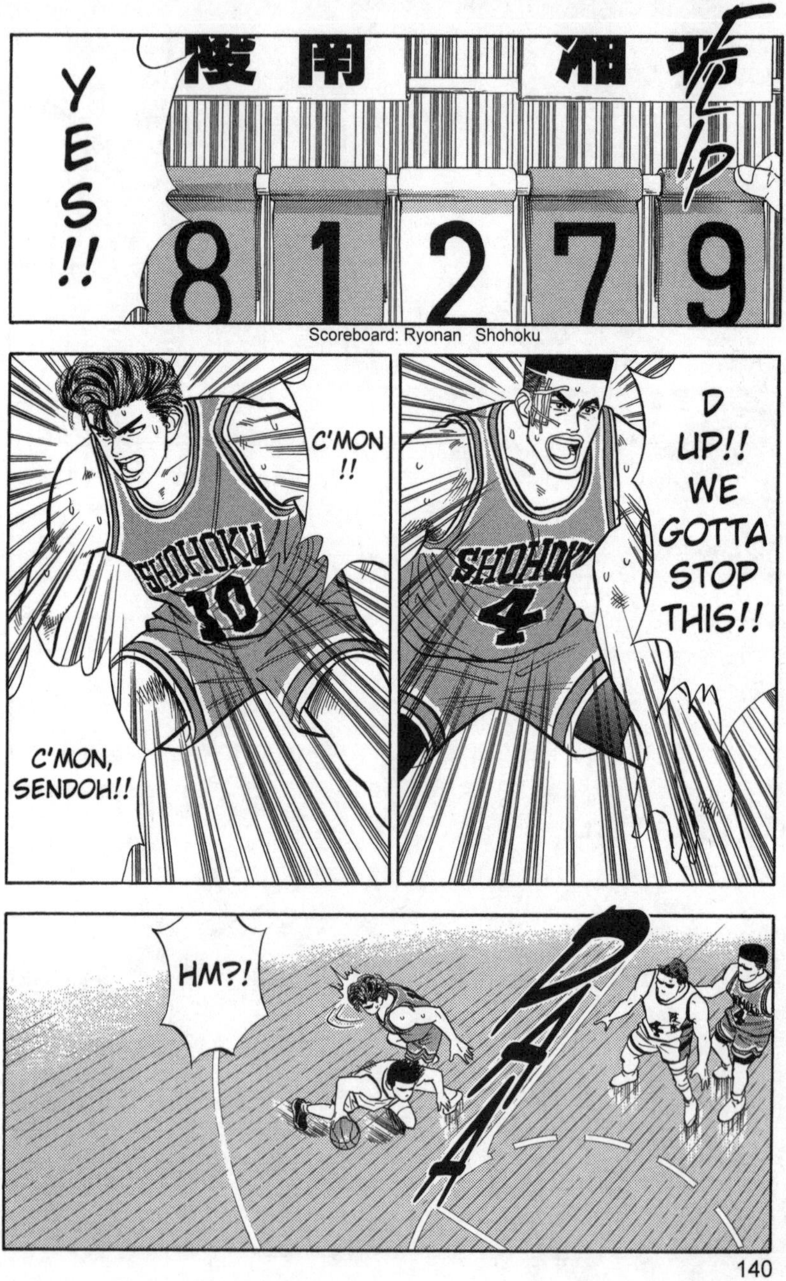
FLIP
YES!!
陵南
湘北
81
27
9
Scoreboard: Ryonan Shohoku
D UP!! WE GOTTA STOP THIS!!
C'MON!!
C'MON, SENDOH!!
HM?!

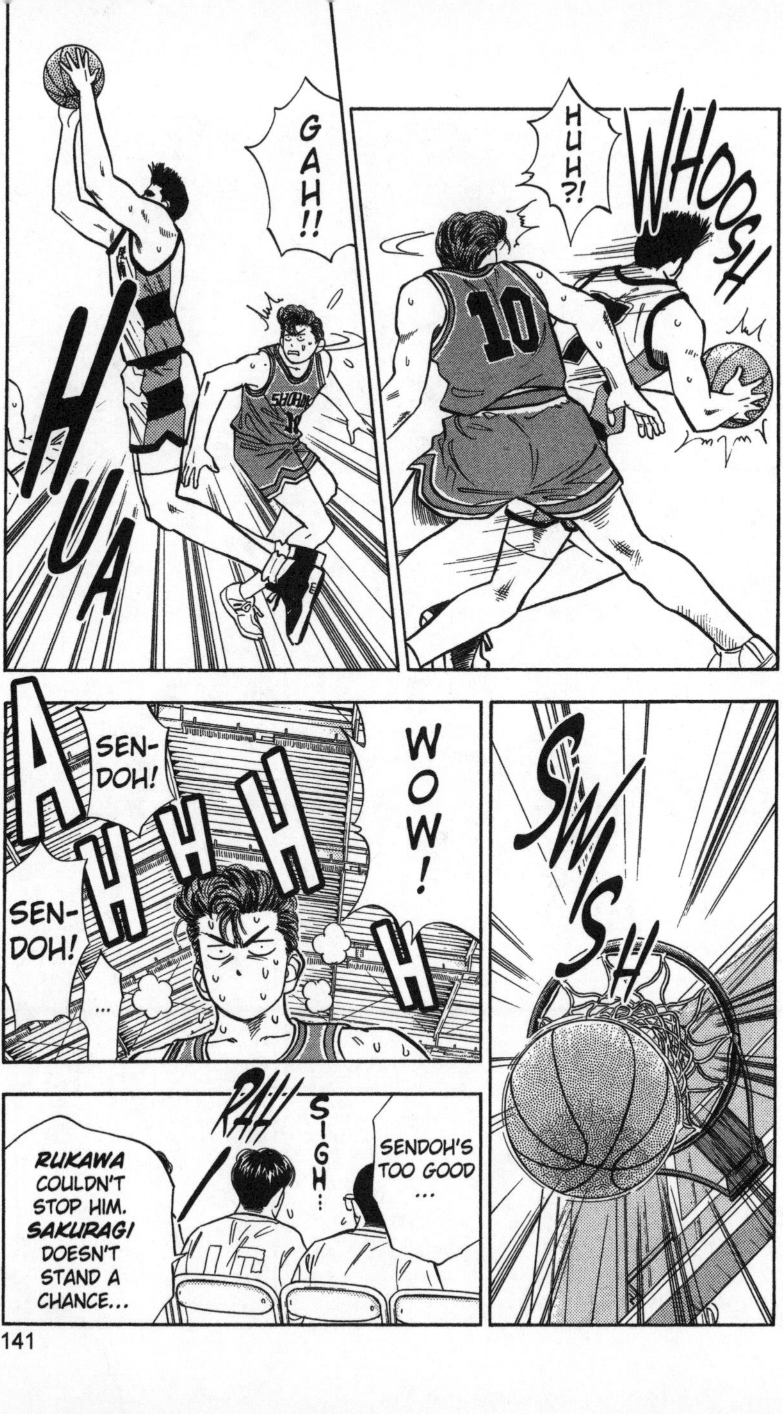
HUH?!
WHOOSH
GAH!!
HUUA
SWISH
WOW!
SEN-DOH!
AHHHHH
SEN-DOH!
...
SENDOH'S TOO GOOD...
SIGH...
RAH
RUKAWA COULDN'T STOP HIM. SAKURAGI DOESN'T STAND A CHANCE...

HE'S DEFENDING SENDOH...

...LIKE HE'S BEEN PLAYING FOR YEARS!!

RAH

RAH

B-BUT SAKURAGI'S DEFENSE ISN'T *THAT* BAD!!

!!

HUNH!!

SWAT

8

!!

YUP. AND HE'S GETTING *BETTER* AS THE GAME GOES ON!!

LOOK...

WHOA!!

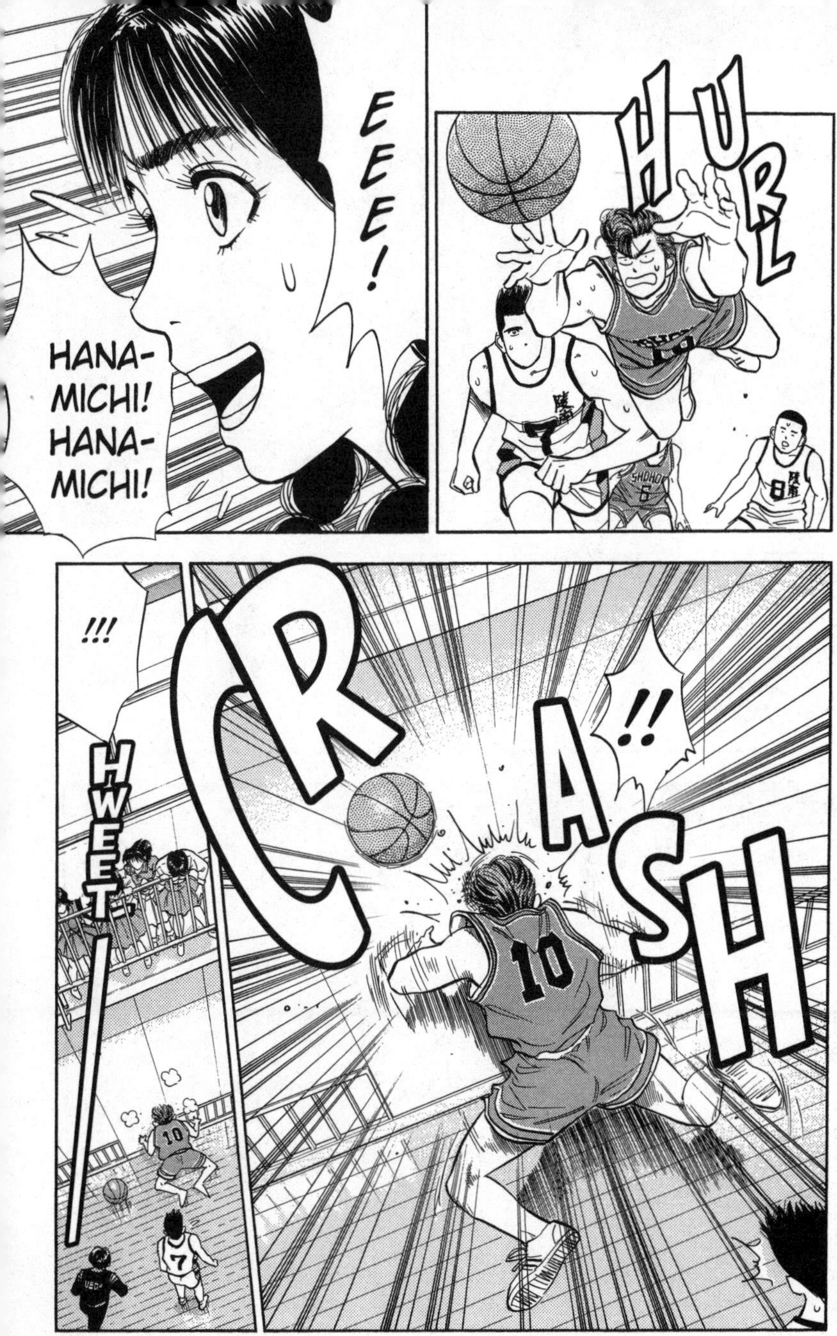
HURL
EEEE!
HANA-
MICHI!
HANA-
MICHI!
!!
CRASH
!!!
HWEET

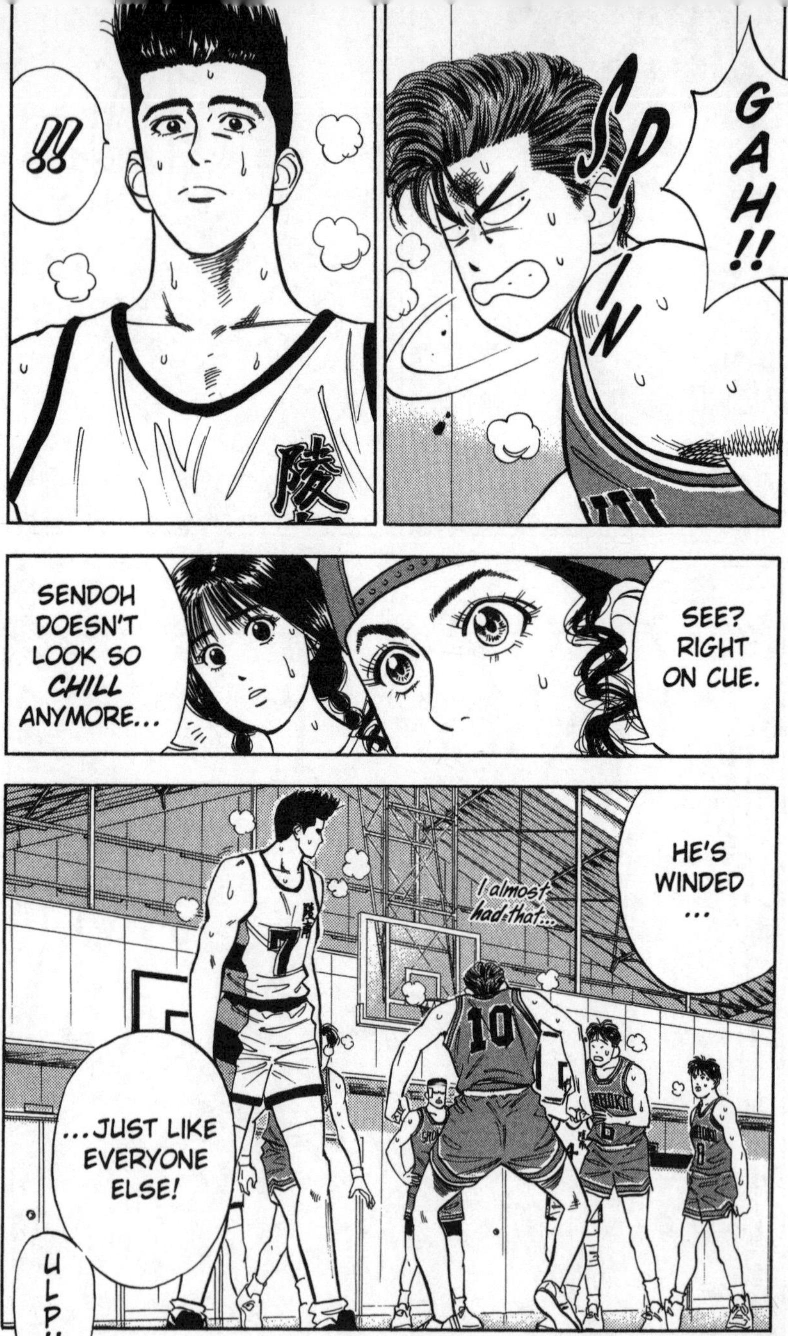

SPIN
GAH!!
!!
SEE? RIGHT ON CUE.
SENDOH DOESN'T LOOK SO CHILL ANYMORE...
HE'S WINDED ...
I almost had that...
...JUST LIKE EVERYONE ELSE!
ULP!!

READ THIS WAY

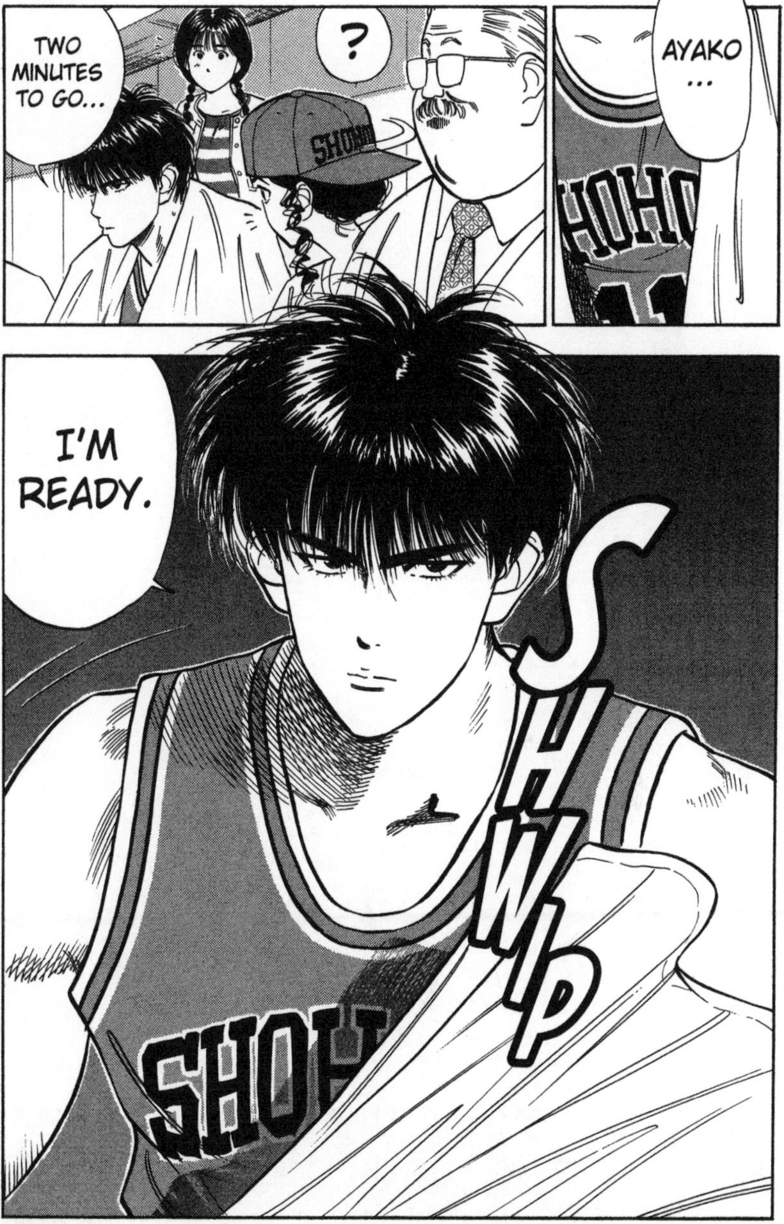

AYAKO ...
?
TWO MINUTES TO GO...
I'M READY.
SHWIP

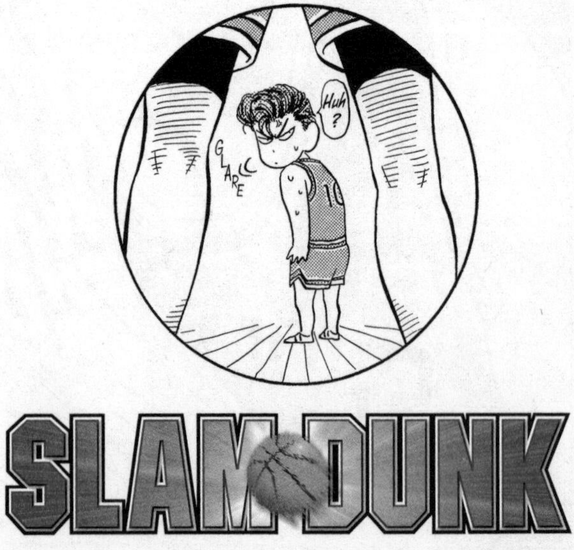
Huh ?
GLARE

SLAM DUNK

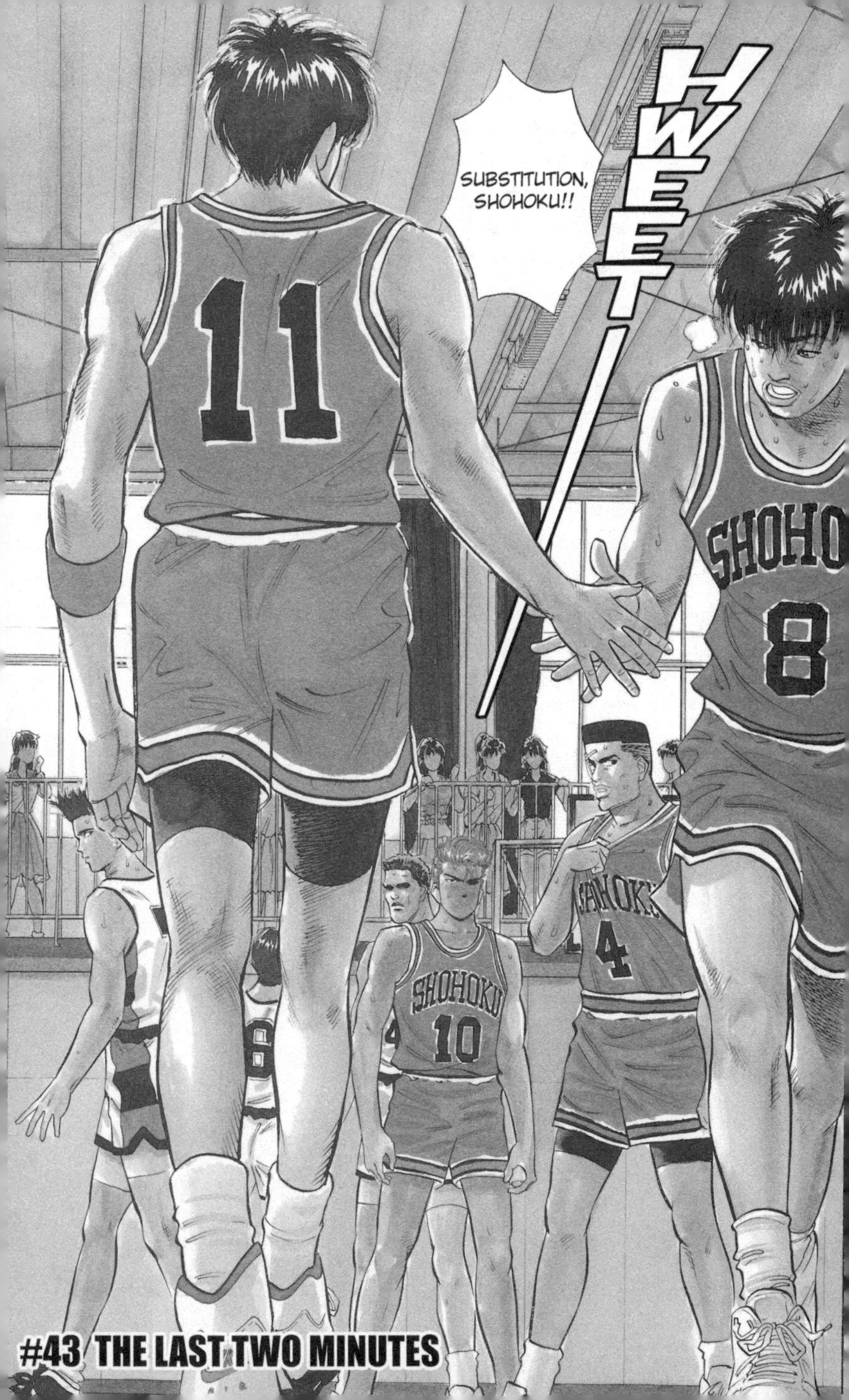
HWEET
SUBSTITUTION, SHOHOKU!!
SHOHOKU
8
SHOHOKU
4
SHOHOKU
10
11

#43 THE LAST TWO MINUTES

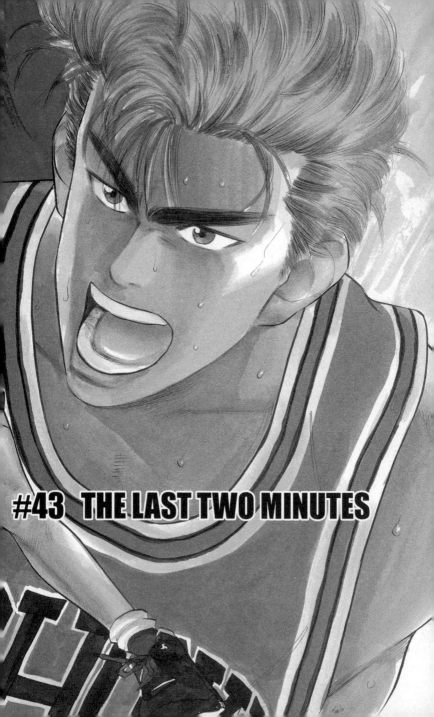

#43 THE LAST TWO MINUTES

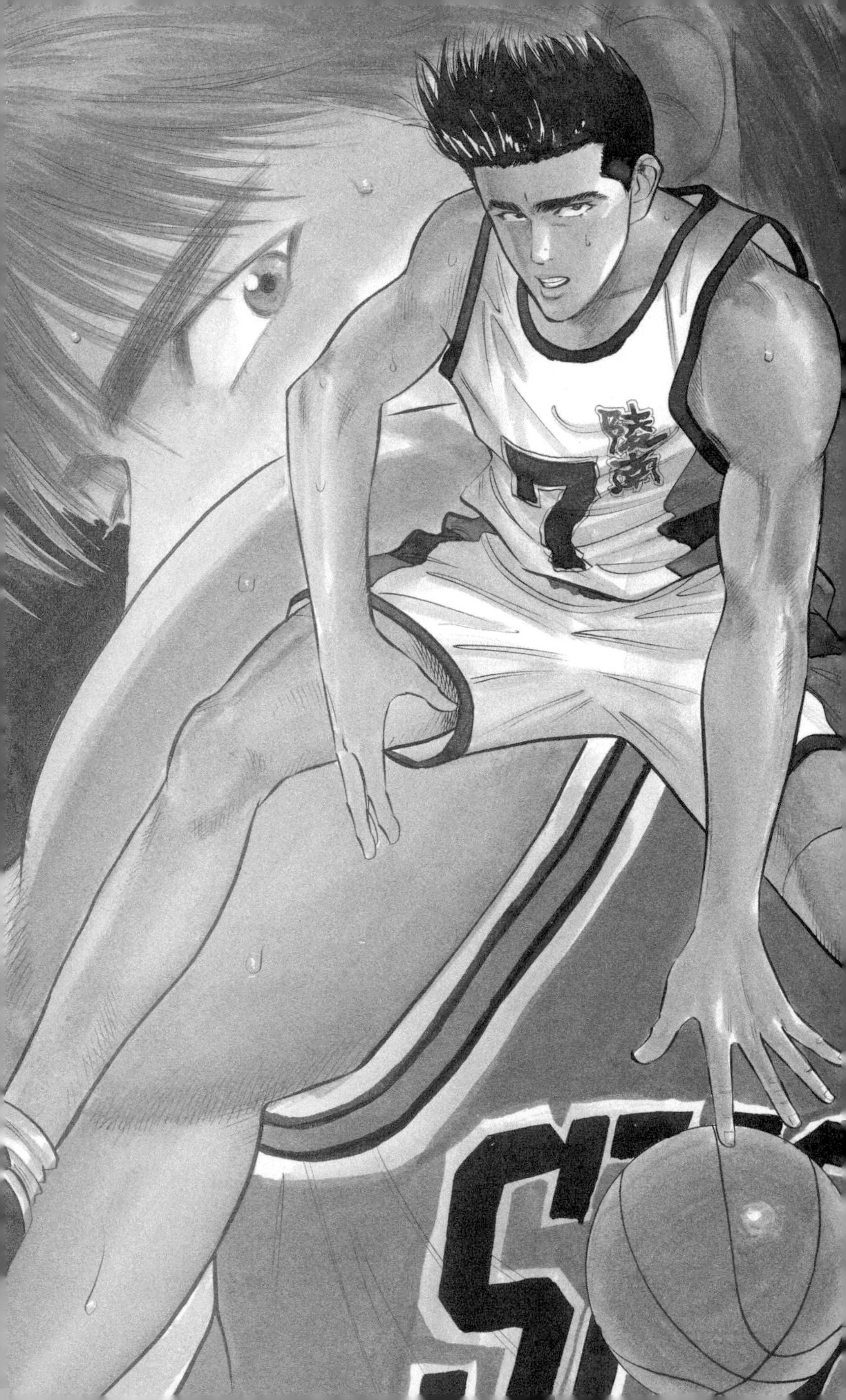
陵南
7

Scoreboard: Ryonan Shohoku

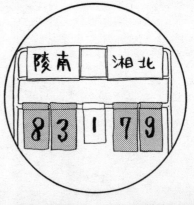

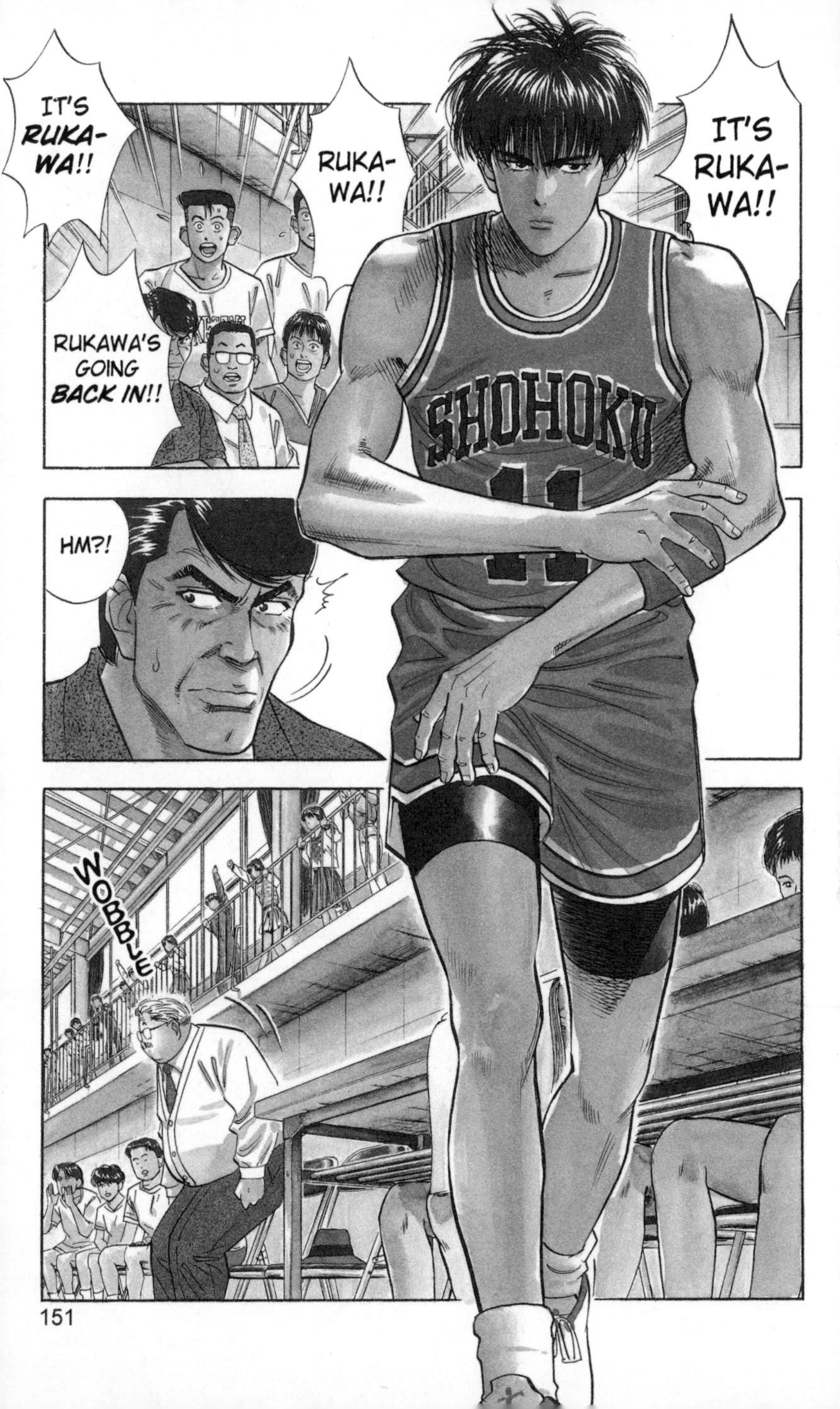
IT'S RUKAWA!!
RUKAWA!!
IT'S RUKAWA!!
RUKAWA'S GOING BACK IN!!
HM?!
WOBBLE

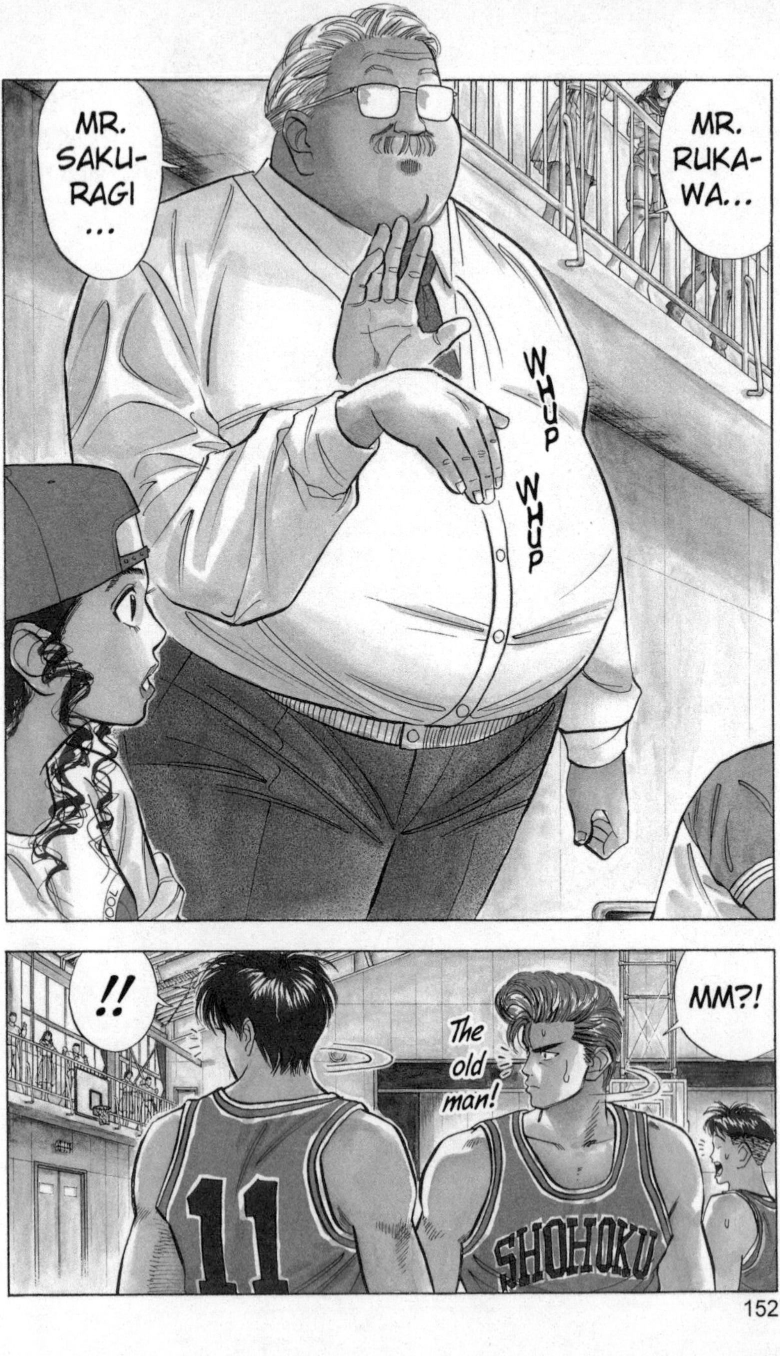
MR. RUKAWA...
MR. SAKURAGI...
WHUP WHUP
MM?!
The old man!
!!

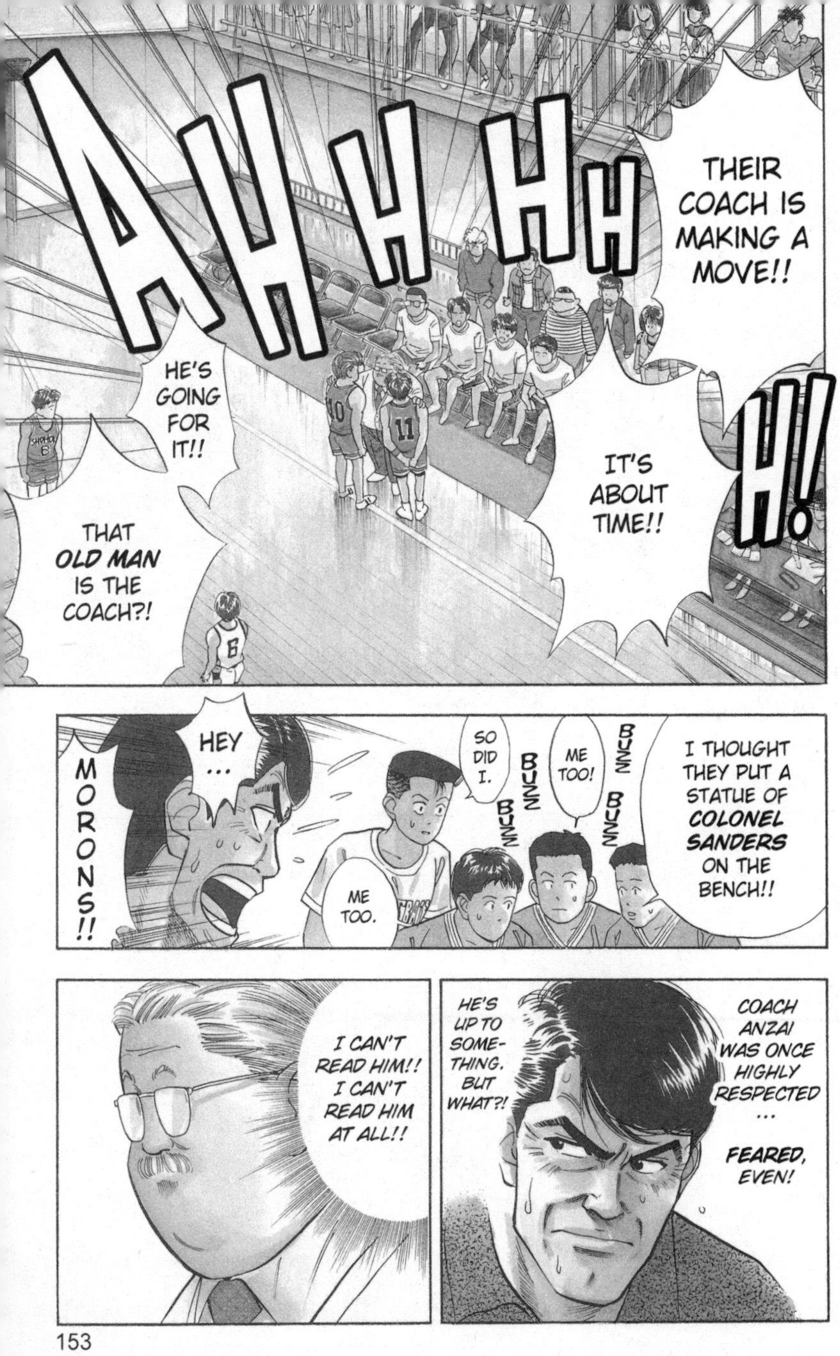
THEIR COACH IS MAKING A MOVE!!
AHHHHHH!!
IT'S ABOUT TIME!!
HE'S GOING FOR IT!!
THAT OLD MAN IS THE COACH?!
I THOUGHT THEY PUT A STATUE OF COLONEL SANDERS ON THE BENCH!!
BUZZ BUZZ
ME TOO!
BUZZ BUZZ
SO DID I.
ME TOO.
HEY ...
MORONS!!
COACH ANZAI WAS ONCE HIGHLY RESPECTED ... FEARED, EVEN!
HE'S UP TO SOMETHING. BUT WHAT?!
I CAN'T READ HIM!! I CAN'T READ HIM AT ALL!!

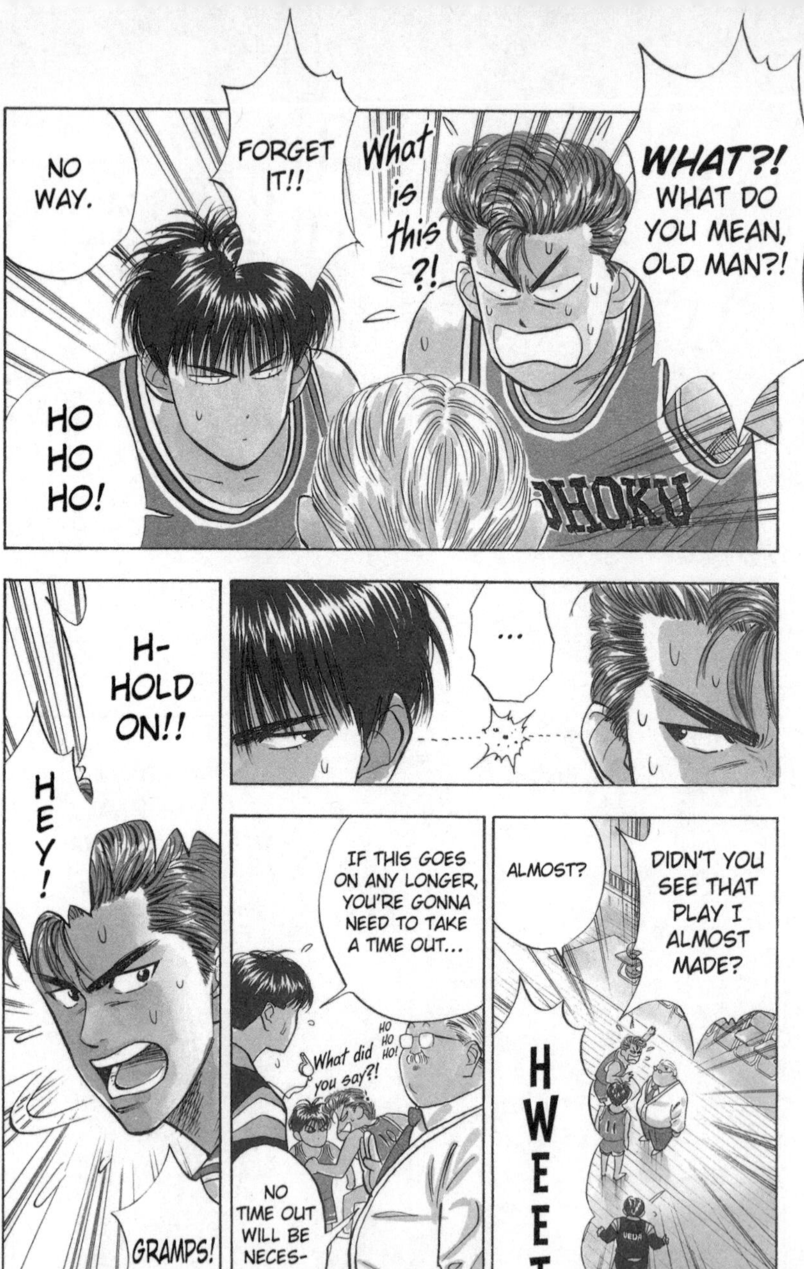

WHAT?! WHAT DO YOU MEAN, OLD MAN?!
What is this?!
FORGET IT!!
NO WAY.
HO HO HO!
JHOKU
...
DIDN'T YOU SEE THAT PLAY I ALMOST MADE?
ALMOST?
HWEET
IF THIS GOES ON ANY LONGER, YOU'RE GONNA NEED TO TAKE A TIME OUT...
HO HO HO!
What did you say?!
NO TIME OUT WILL BE NECES-SARY.
H-HOLD ON!!
HEY!
GRAMPS!

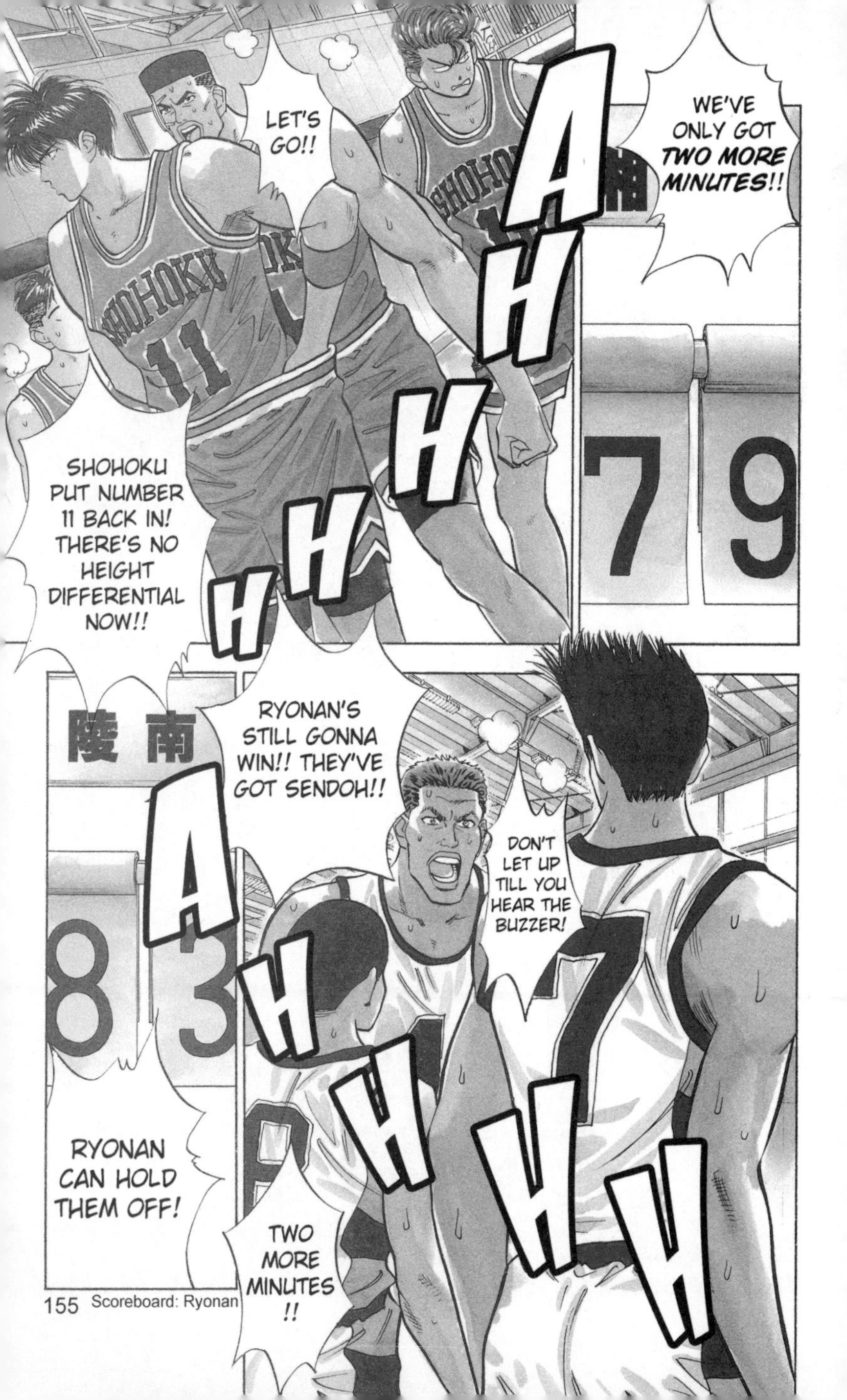
WE'VE ONLY GOT TWO MORE MINUTES!!
LET'S GO!!
AHHHHH
79
SHOHOKU PUT NUMBER 11 BACK IN! THERE'S NO HEIGHT DIFFERENTIAL NOW!!
DON'T LET UP TILL YOU HEAR THE BUZZER!
RYONAN'S STILL GONNA WIN!! THEY'VE GOT SENDOH!!
陵南
83
AHHHHH
TWO MORE MINUTES!!
RYONAN CAN HOLD THEM OFF!

Scoreboard: Ryonan

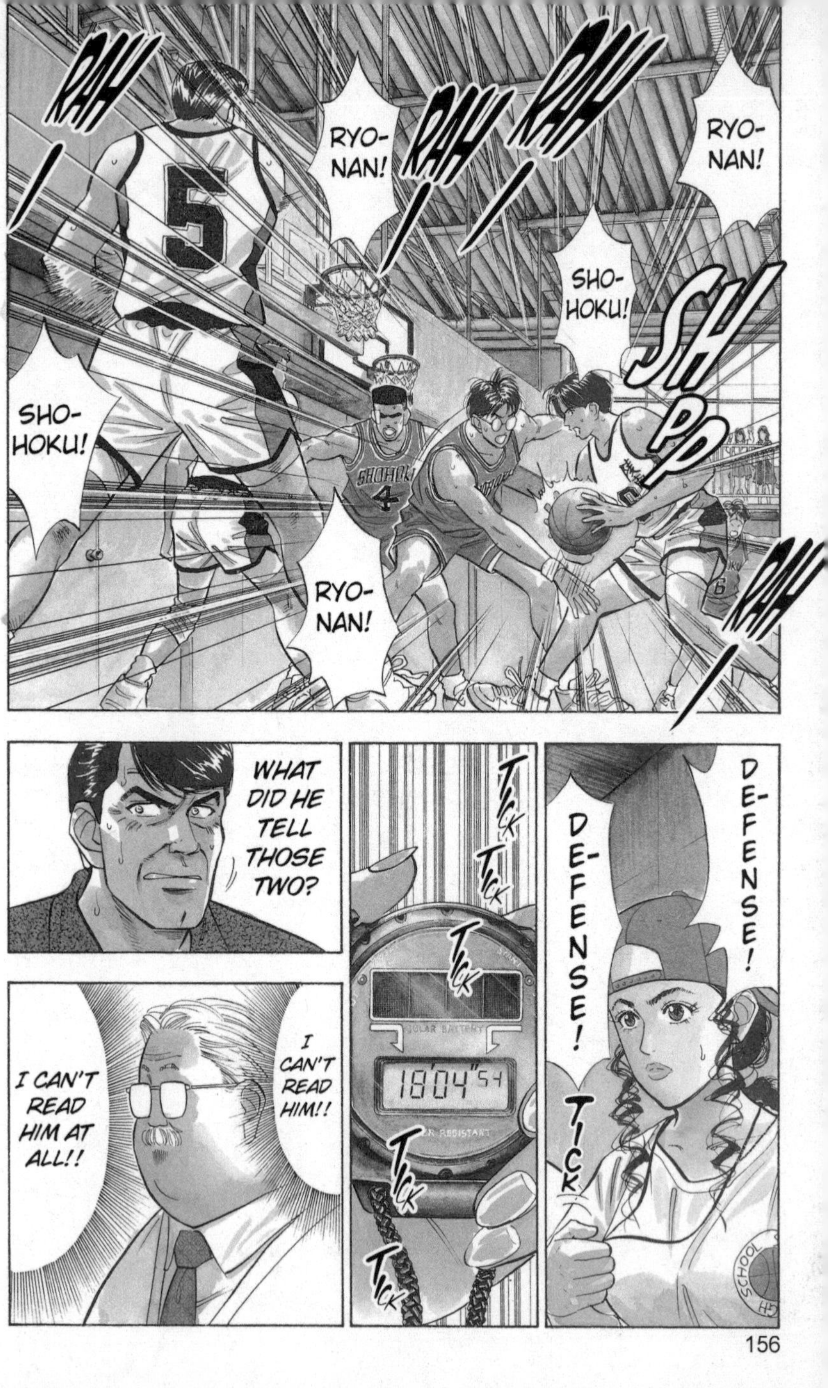
RYO-NAN!
RAH-
RAH-
SHO-HOKU!
SHPP
RAH-
RYO-NAN!
RAH-
RYO-NAN!
SHO-HOKU!
RAH-
DEFENSE!
DEFENSE!
TICK
TICK
TICK
TICK
TICK
TICK
18'04"54
SOLAR BATTERY
WHAT DID HE TELL THOSE TWO?
I CAN'T READ HIM!!
I CAN'T READ HIM AT ALL!!

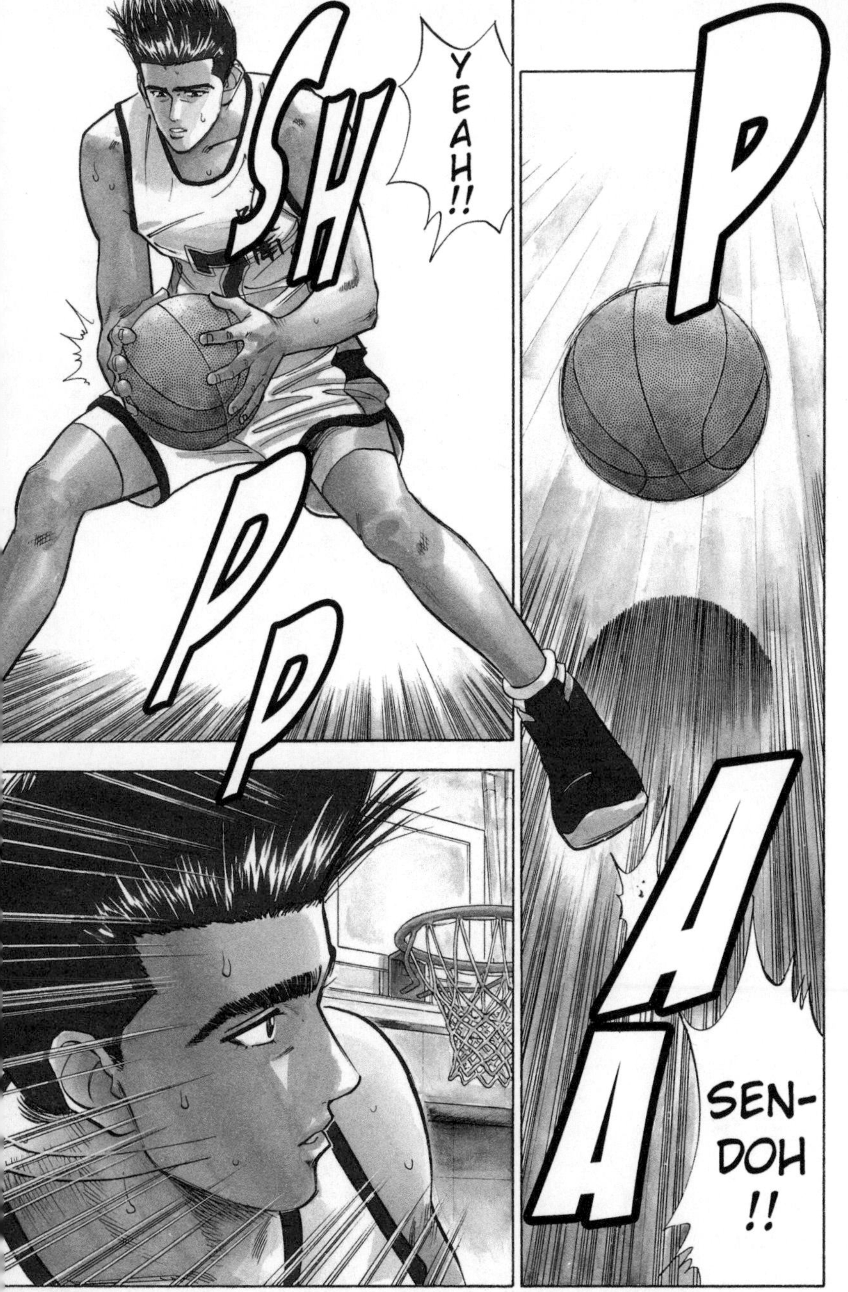
P
AA
SEN-DOH!!
SH
YEAH!!
PP

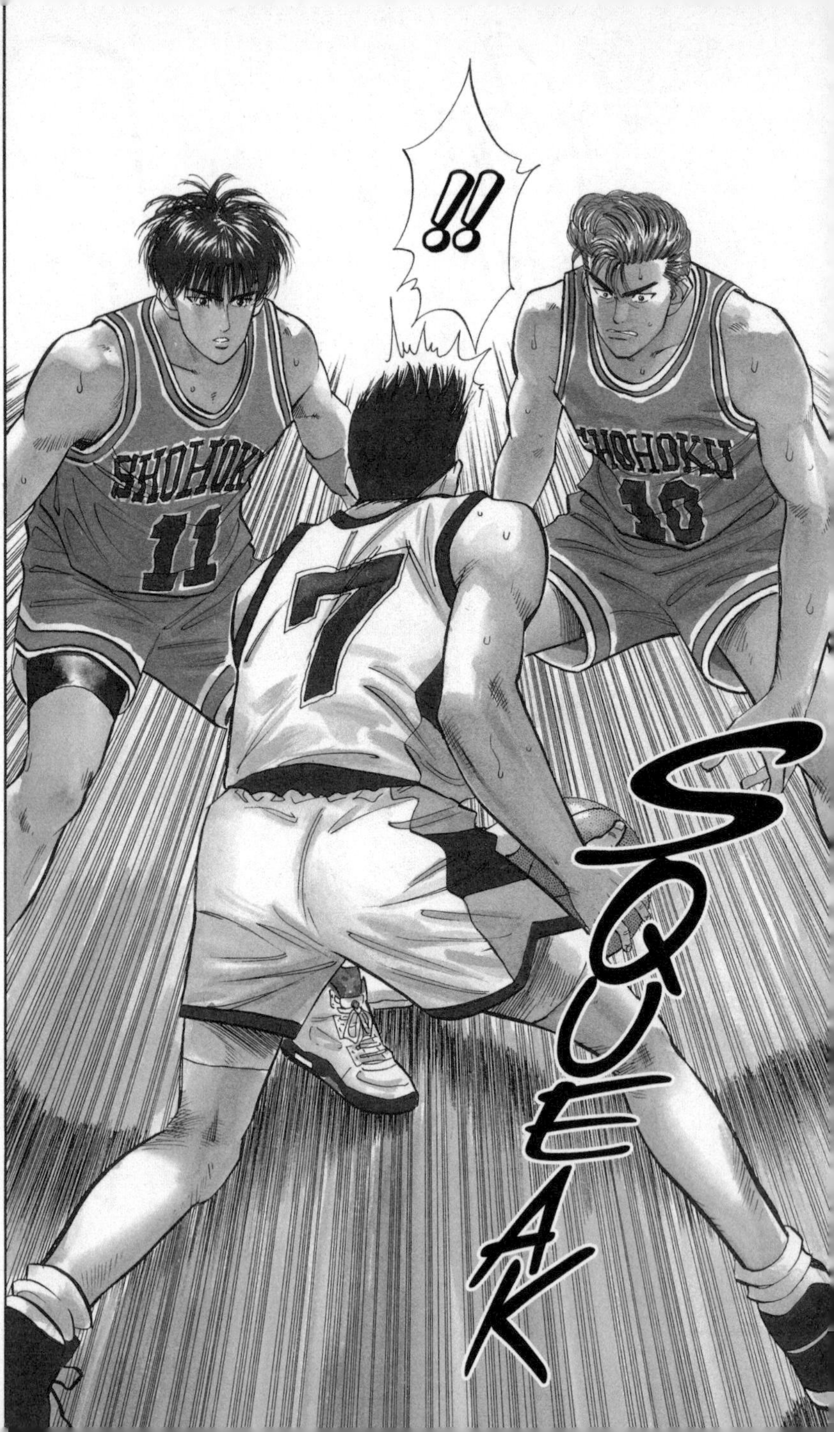
!!
SQUEAK

READ THIS WAY

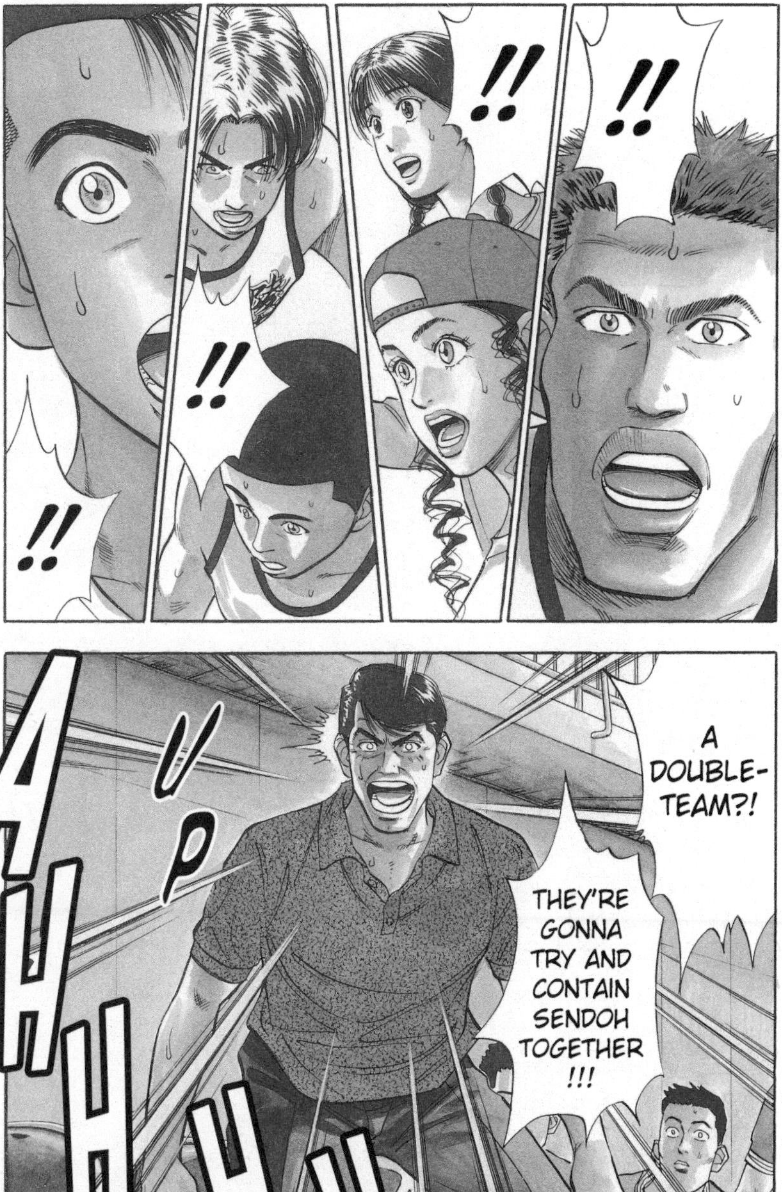
!!
!!
!!
!!
A DOUBLE-TEAM?!
THEY'RE GONNA TRY AND CONTAIN SENDOH TOGETHER!!!

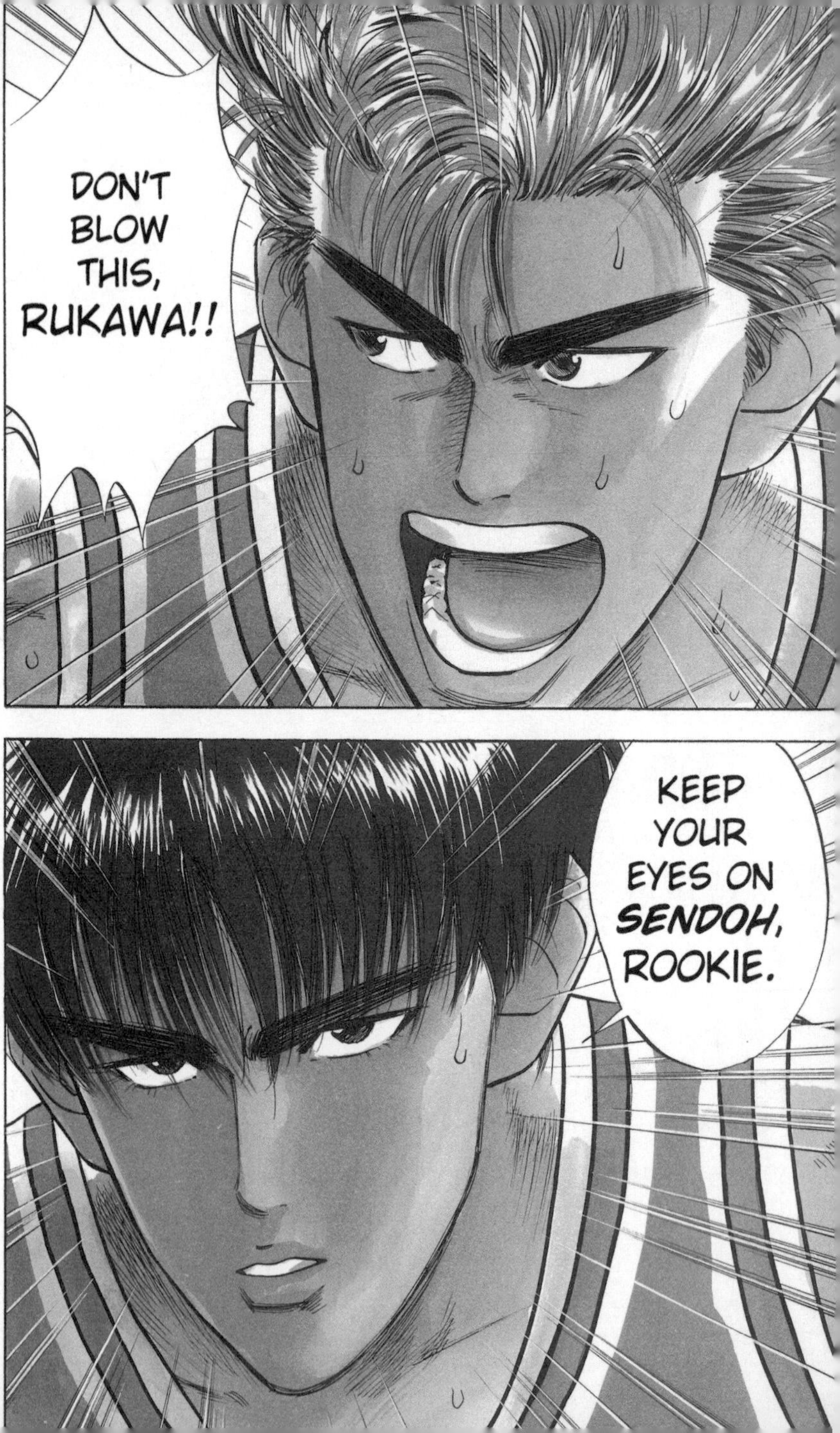
DON'T BLOW THIS, RUKAWA!!
KEEP YOUR EYES ON SENDOH, ROOKIE.

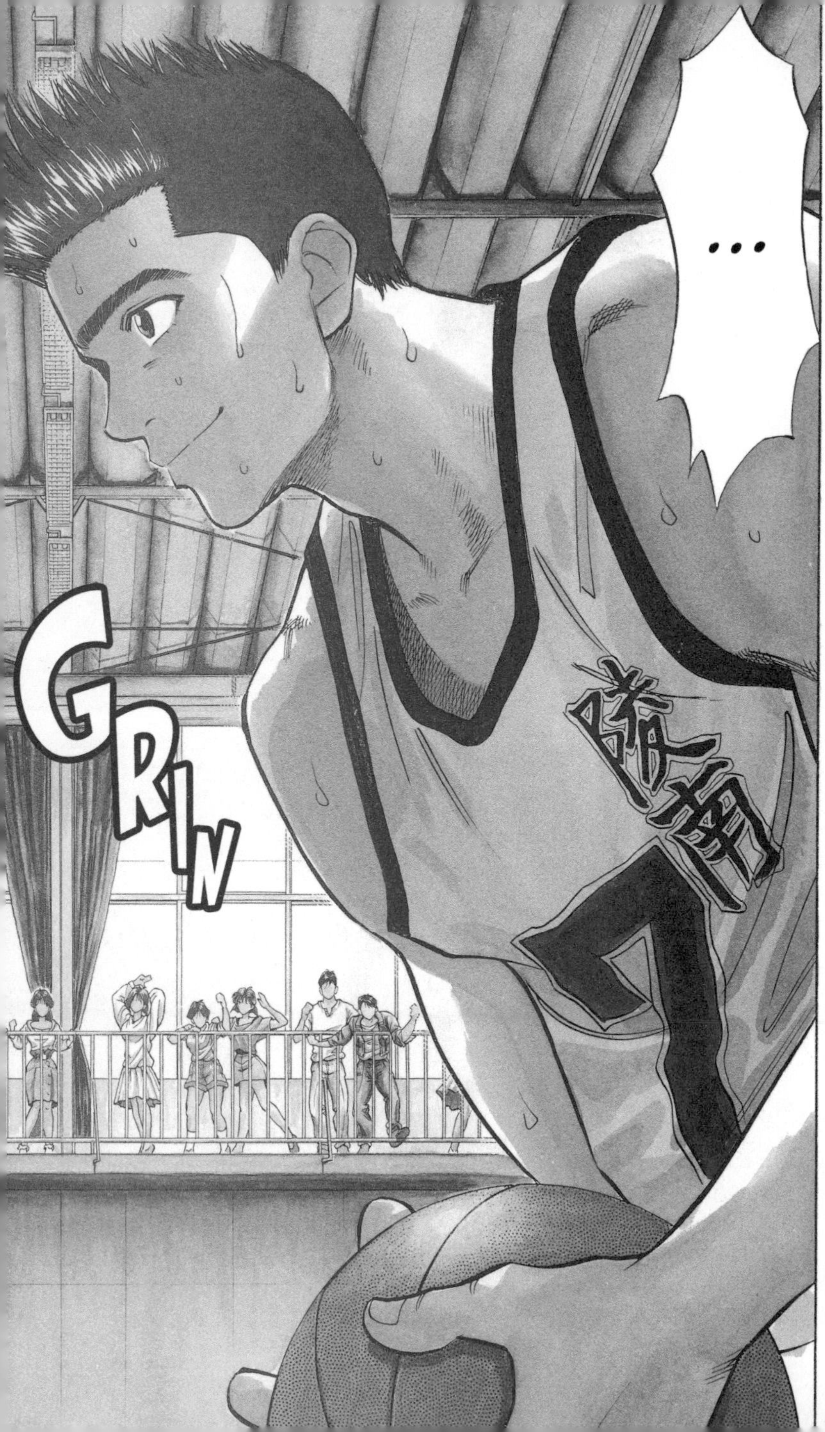
...
GRIN

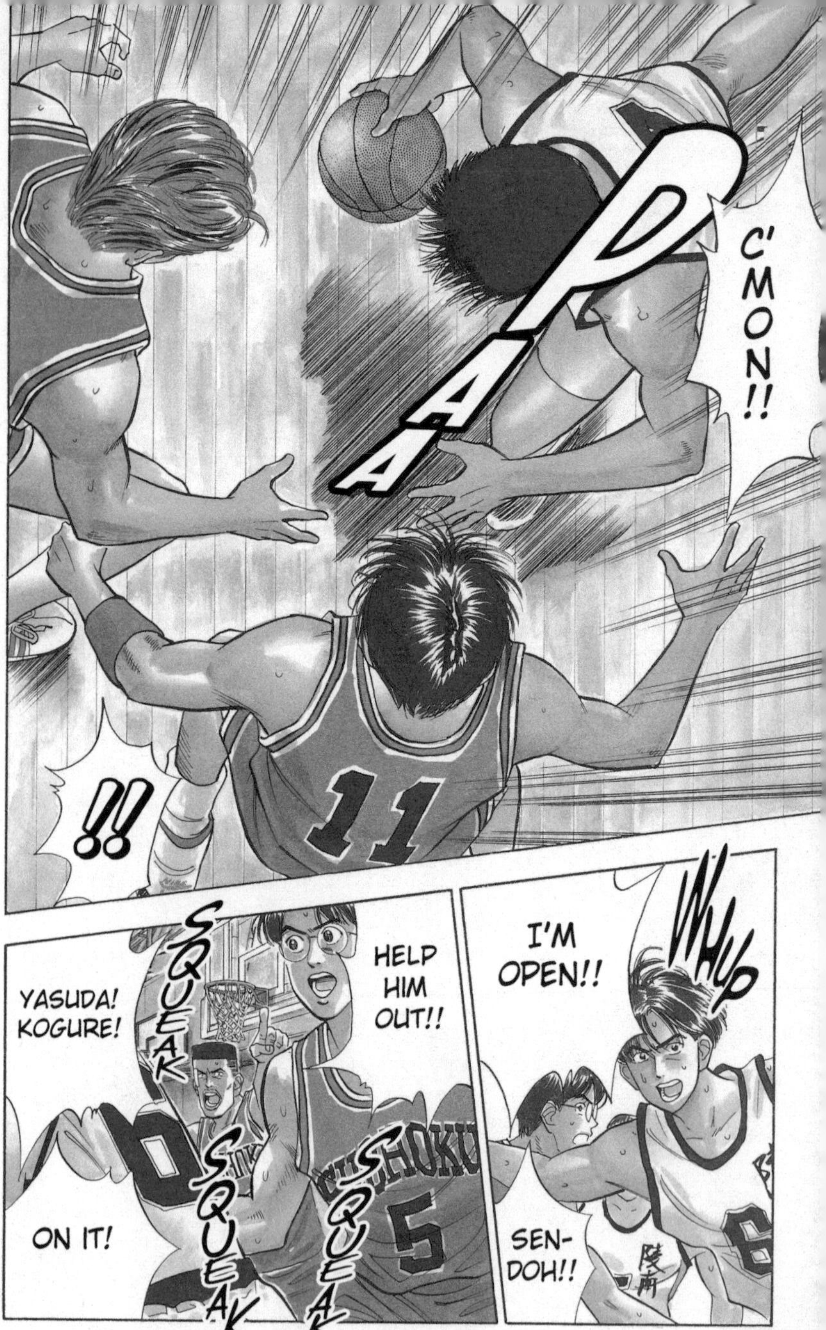
PAAA
C'MON!!
!!
WHUP
I'M OPEN!!
SEN-DOH!!
HELP HIM OUT!!
SQUEAK
YASUDA! KOGURE!
SQUEAK
SQUEAK
ON IT!

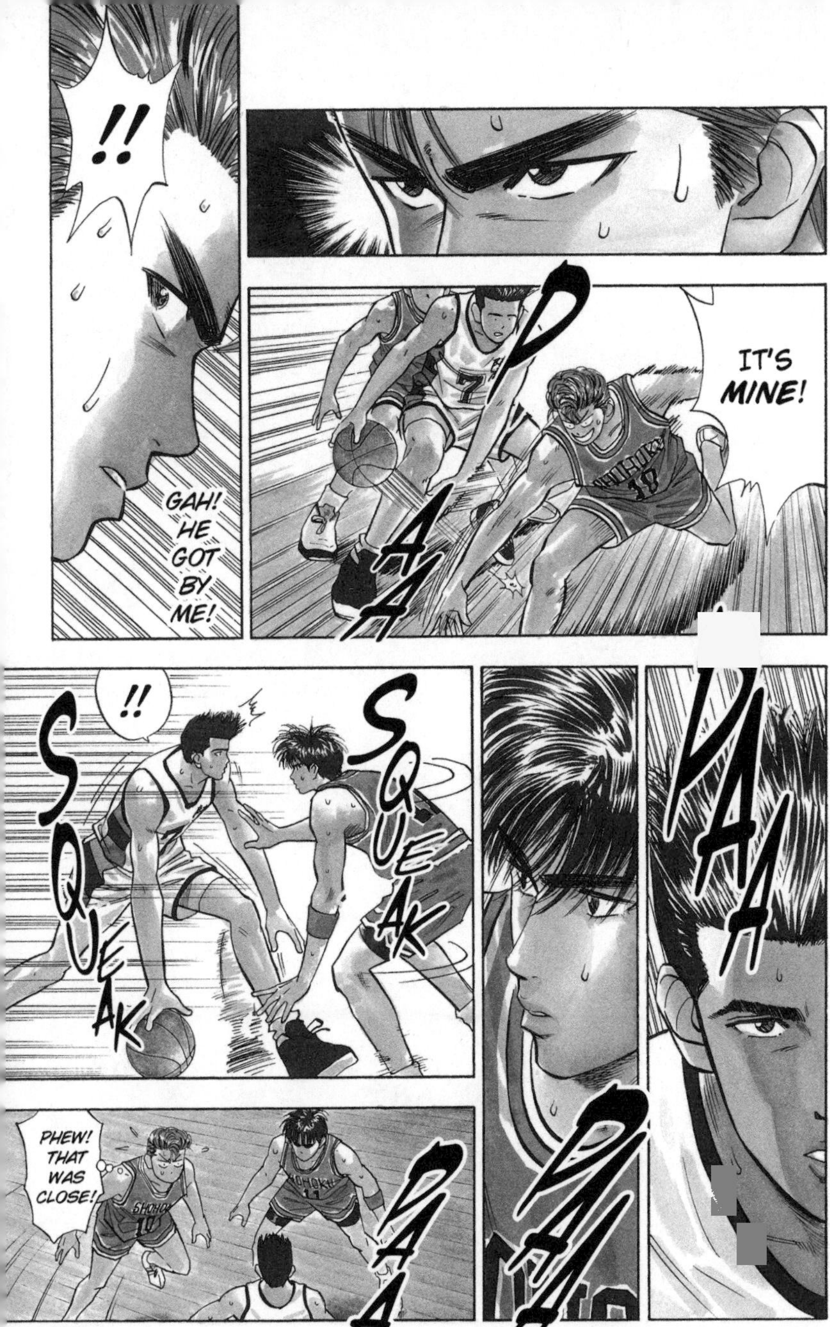
IT'S MINE!
DAAA
!!
GAH! HE GOT BY ME!
DAAA
DAAA
!!
SQUEAK
SQUEAK
PHEW! THAT WAS CLOSE!
DAAA

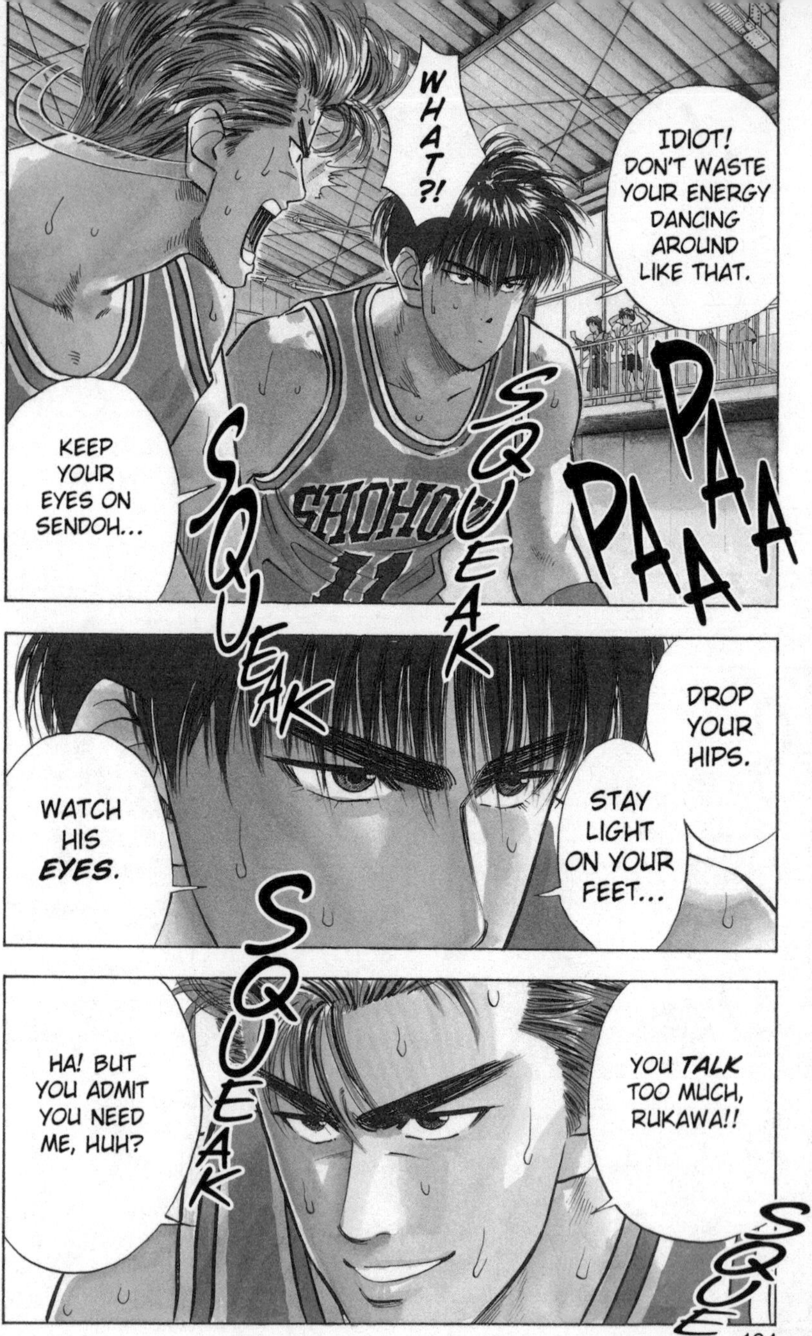
IDIOT! DON'T WASTE YOUR ENERGY DANCING AROUND LIKE THAT.
WHAT?!
PAAA
PAAA
SQUEAK
SQUEAK
KEEP YOUR EYES ON SENDOH...
DROP YOUR HIPS.
STAY LIGHT ON YOUR FEET...
WATCH HIS EYES.
SQUEAK
YOU TALK TOO MUCH, RUKAWA!!
HA! BUT YOU ADMIT YOU NEED ME, HUH?
SQUEAK

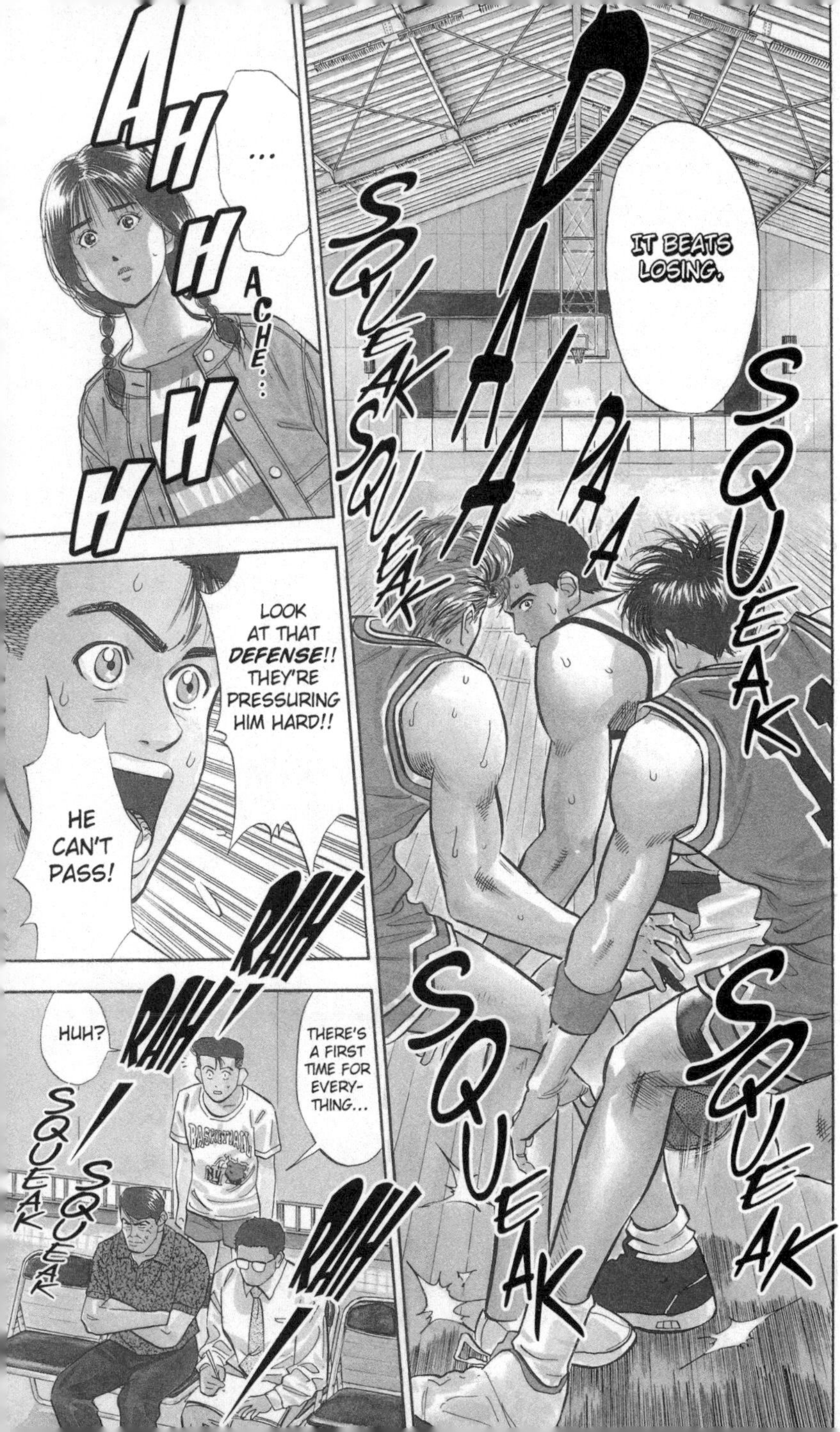
SQUEAK
IT BEATS LOSING.
SQUEAK SQUEAK
SQUEAK
SQUEAK
...
AHHHHH
ACHE...
LOOK AT THAT DEFENSE!! THEY'RE PRESSURING HIM HARD!!
HE CAN'T PASS!
RAH! RAH!
THERE'S A FIRST TIME FOR EVERY-THING...
HUH?
RAH!
SQUEAK SQUEAK

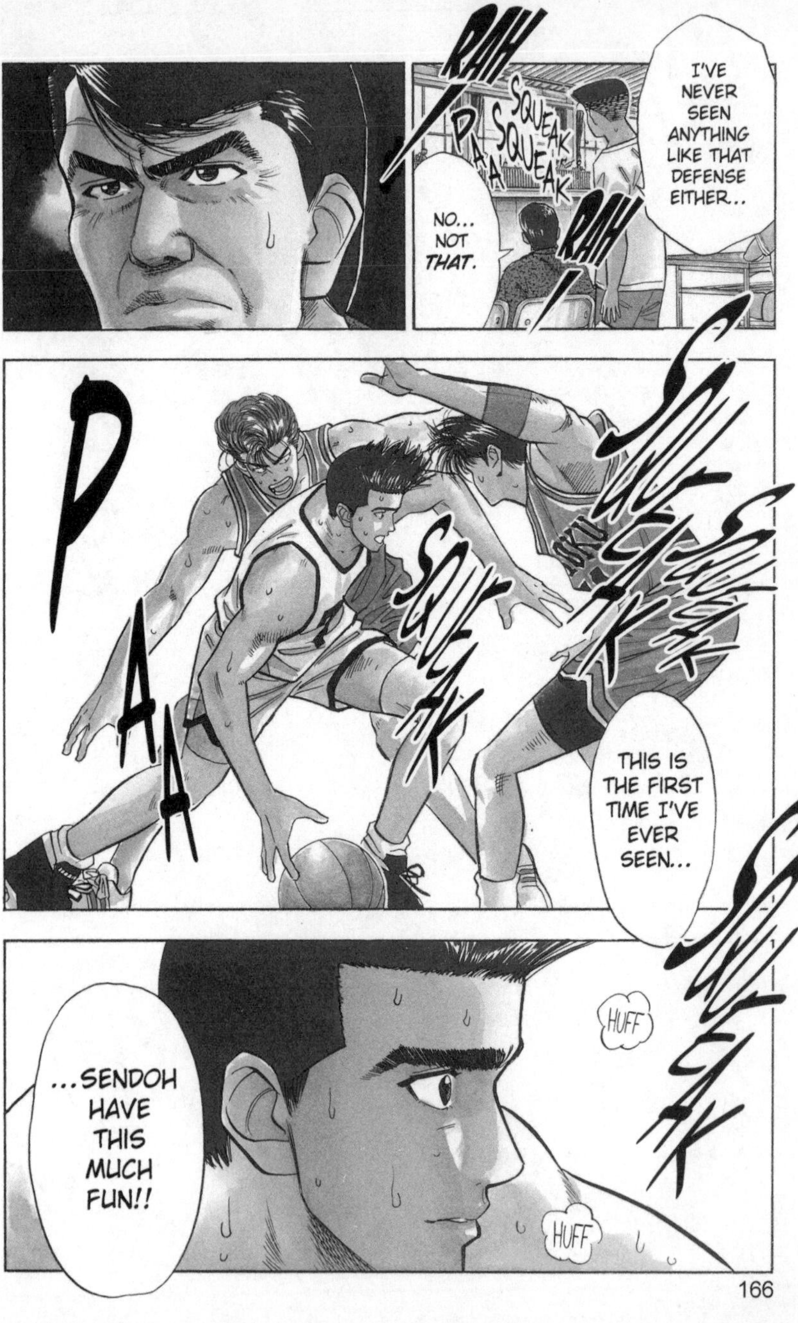
I'VE NEVER SEEN ANYTHING LIKE THAT DEFENSE EITHER...
RAH
SQUEAK SQUEAK
PAA
RAH
NO... NOT THAT.
SQUEAK SQUEAK
SQUEAK
PAA
THIS IS THE FIRST TIME I'VE EVER SEEN...
SQUEAK
HUFF
HUFF
...SENDOH HAVE THIS MUCH FUN!!

#44 SENDOH

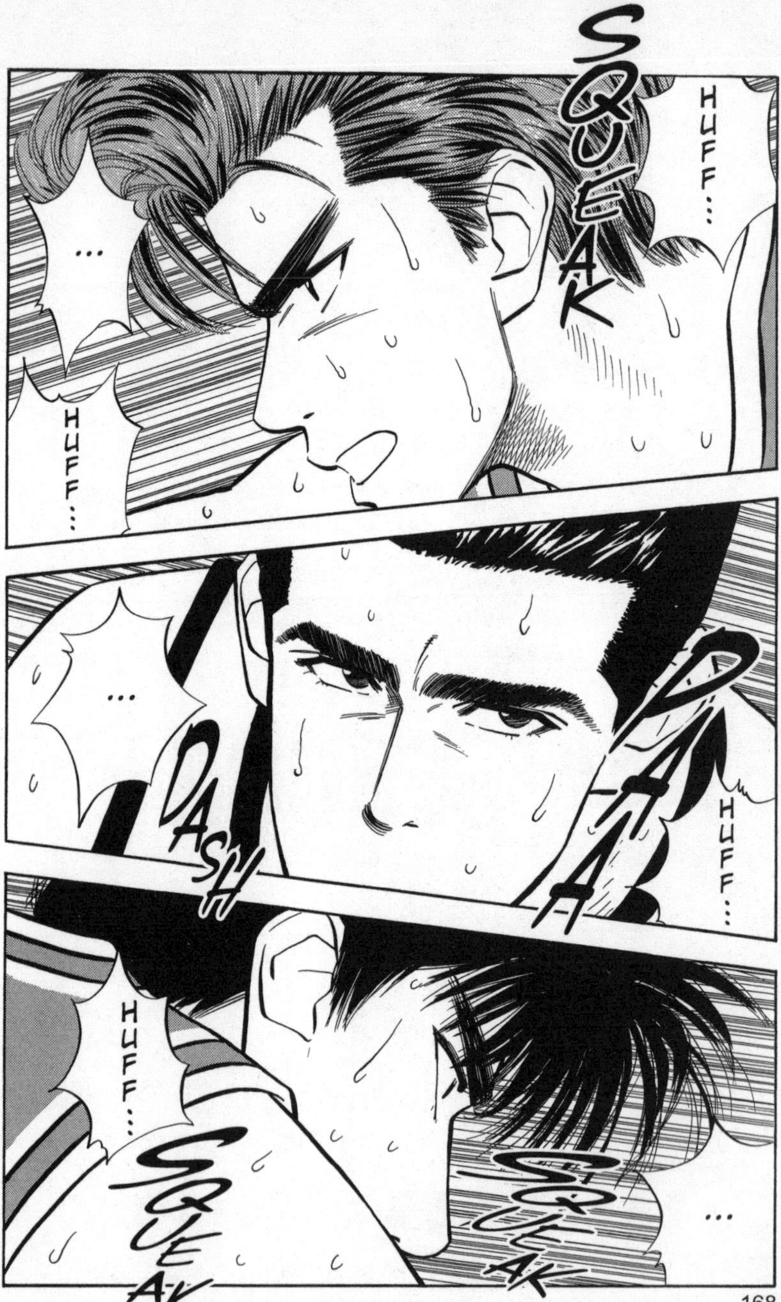
SQUEAK
HUFF...
...
HUFF...
DAAA
HUFF...
DASH
...
...
SQUEAK
HUFF...
SQUEAK

READ THIS WAY

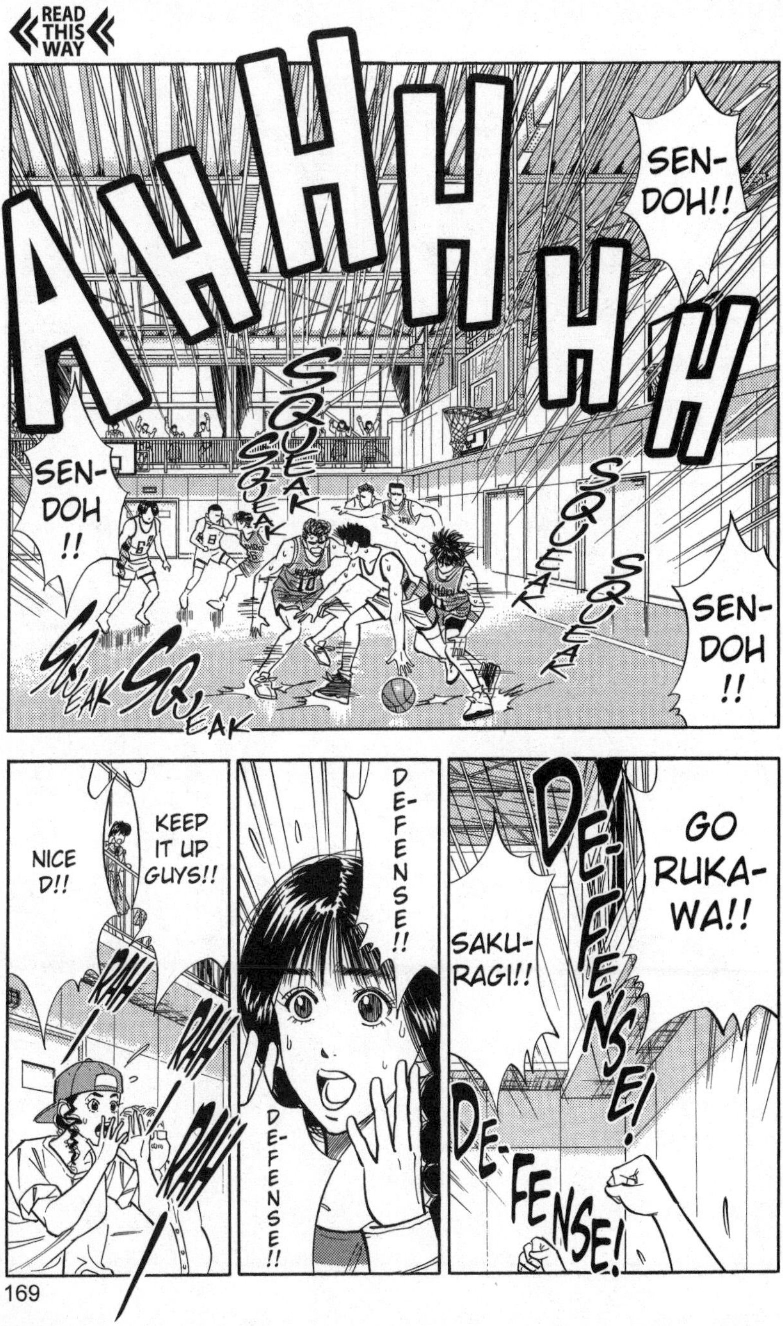
SEN-DOH!!
AHHHHHH
SQUEAK
SQUEAK
SQUEAK
SQUEAK
SEN-DOH!!
SEN-DOH!!
SQUEAK
SQUEAK
GO RUKAWA!!
DE-FENSE!
SAKURAGI!!
DE-FENSE!
DE-FENSE!!
DE-FENSE!!
KEEP IT UP GUYS!!
NICE D!!
RAH
RAH
RAH
RAH

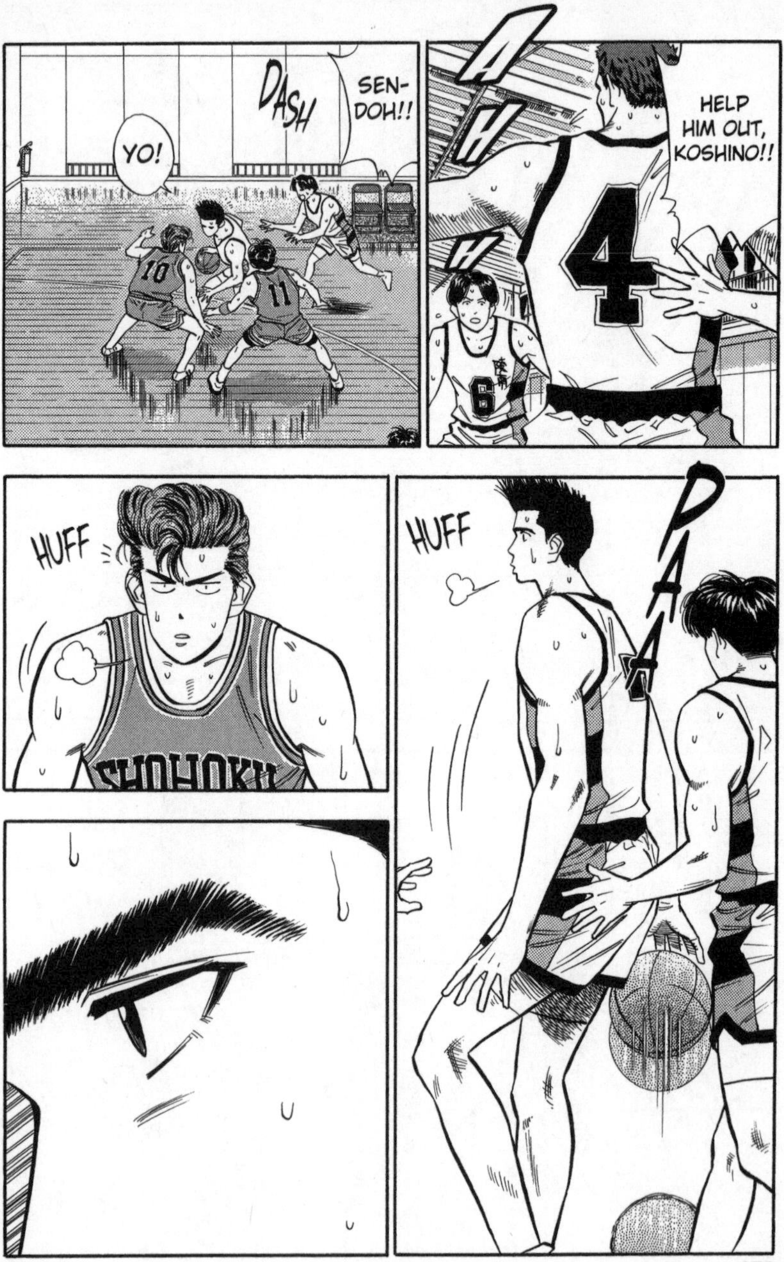
AHH
HELP HIM OUT, KOSHINO!!
SEN-DOH!!
DASH
YO!
PAAA
HUFF
HUFF

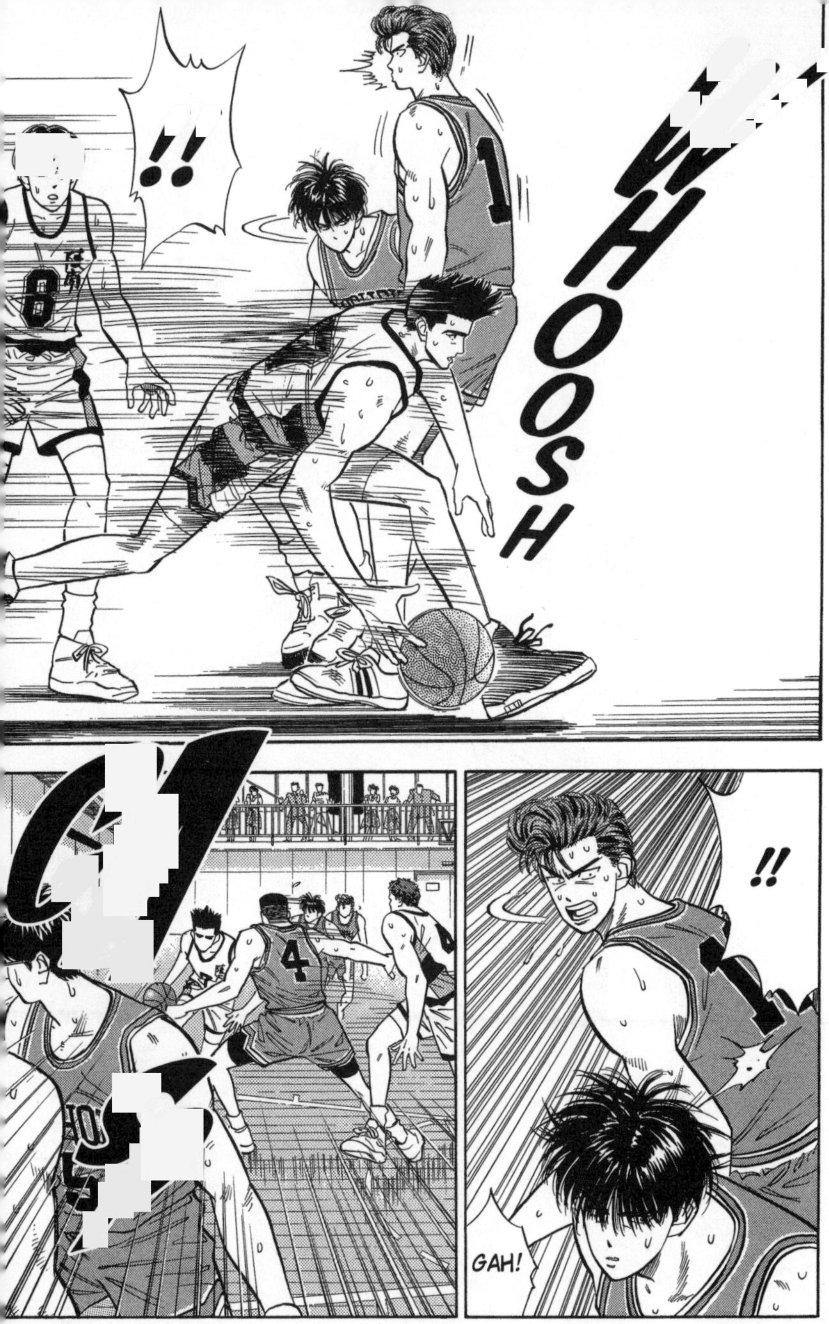
WHOOSH
!!
!!
GAH!

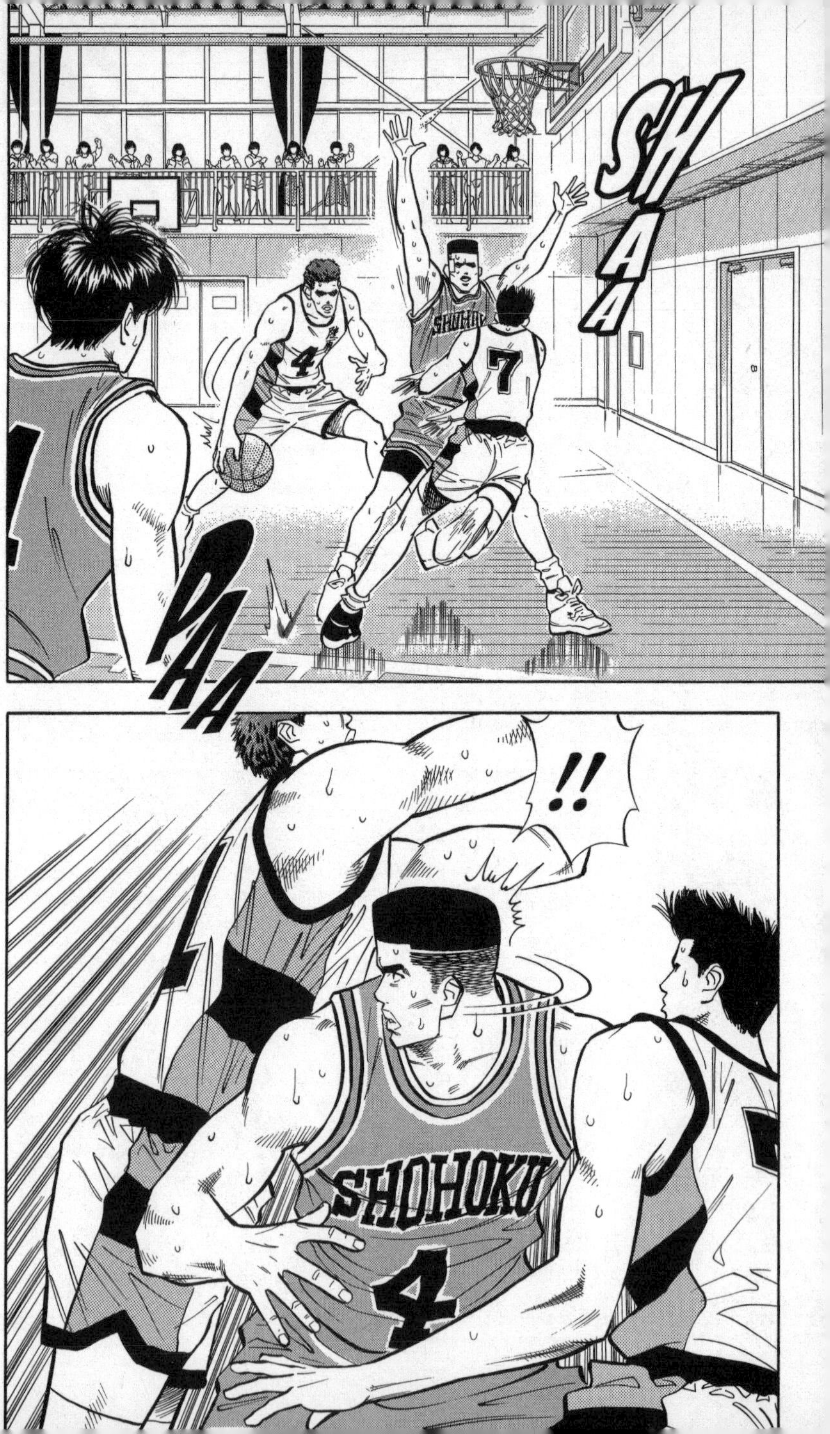
SHAAA
DAA
!!
SHOHOKU

READ THIS WAY

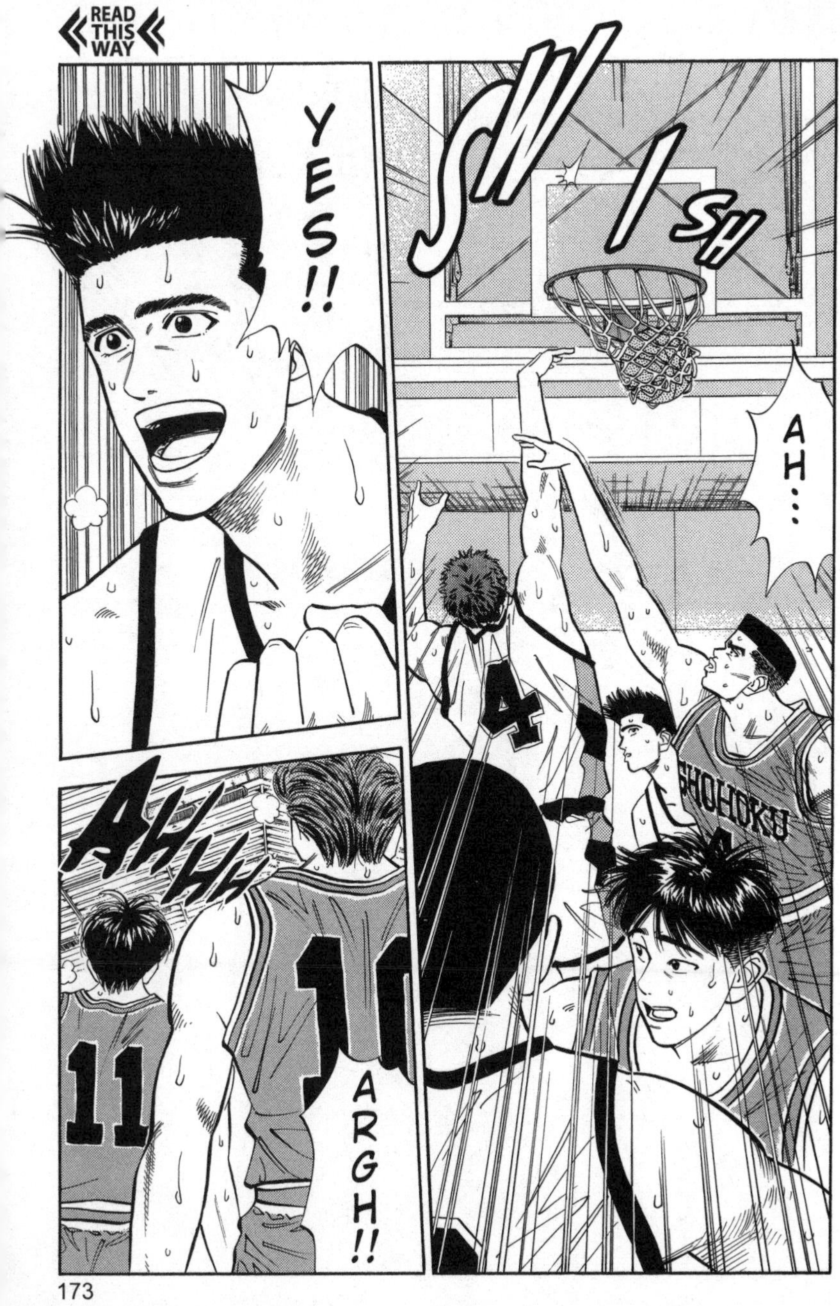
SWISH
AH...
YES!!
AHHH
ARGH!!

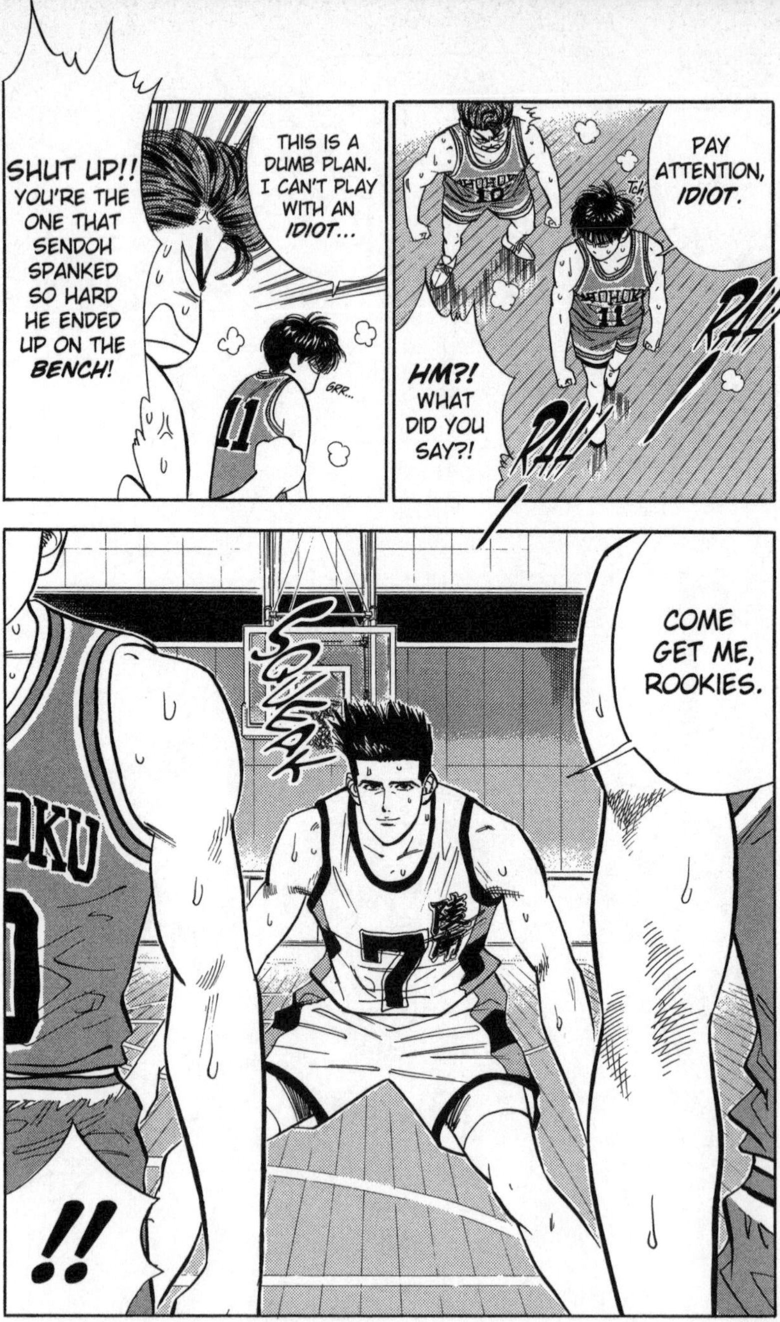
PAY ATTENTION, IDIOT.
TCH
HM?! WHAT DID YOU SAY?!
RAL
RAL
THIS IS A DUMB PLAN. I CAN'T PLAY WITH AN IDIOT...
SHUT UP!! YOU'RE THE ONE THAT SENDOH SPANKED SO HARD HE ENDED UP ON THE BENCH!
GRR...
COME GET ME, ROOKIES.
SQUEAK
!!

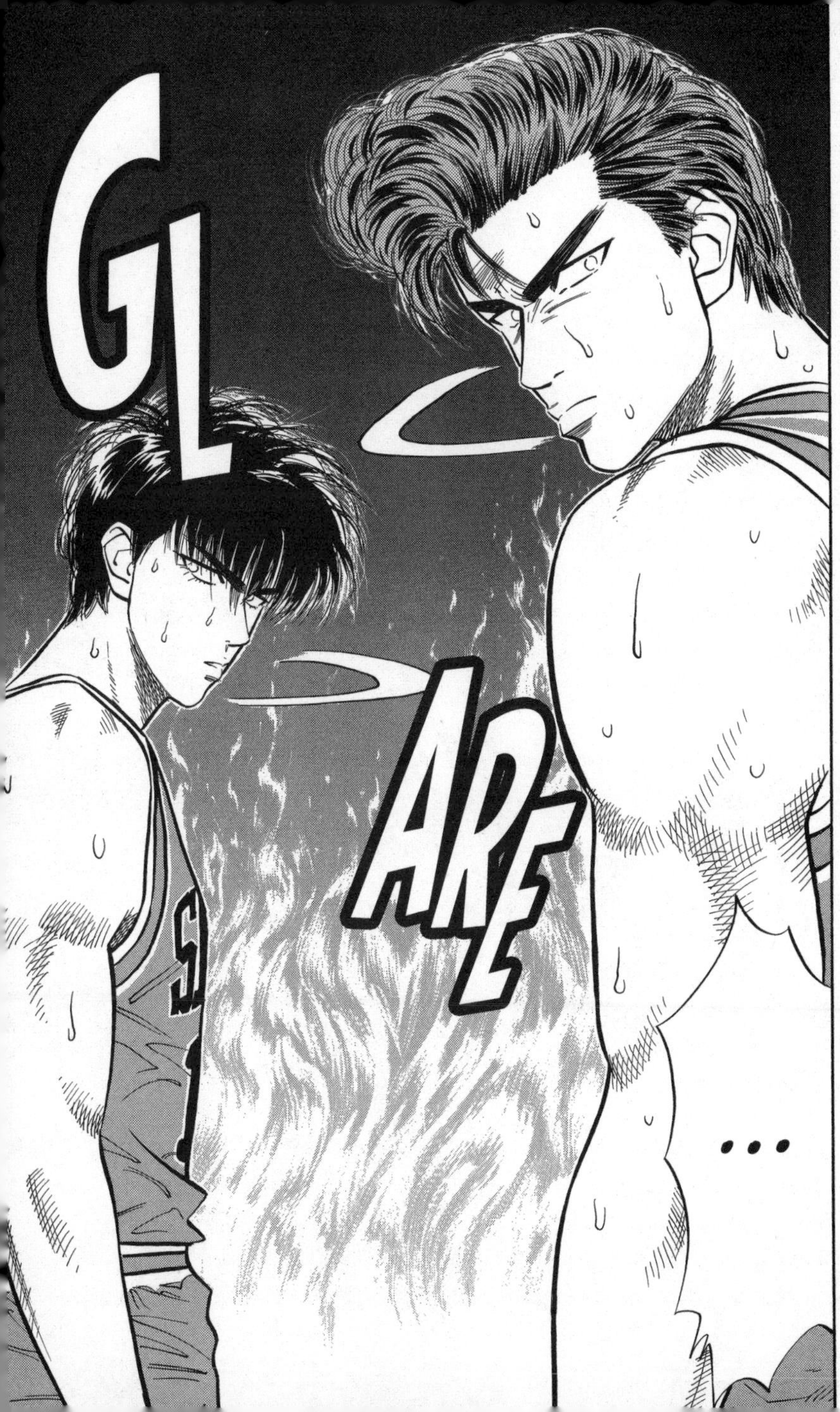
GLARE
...

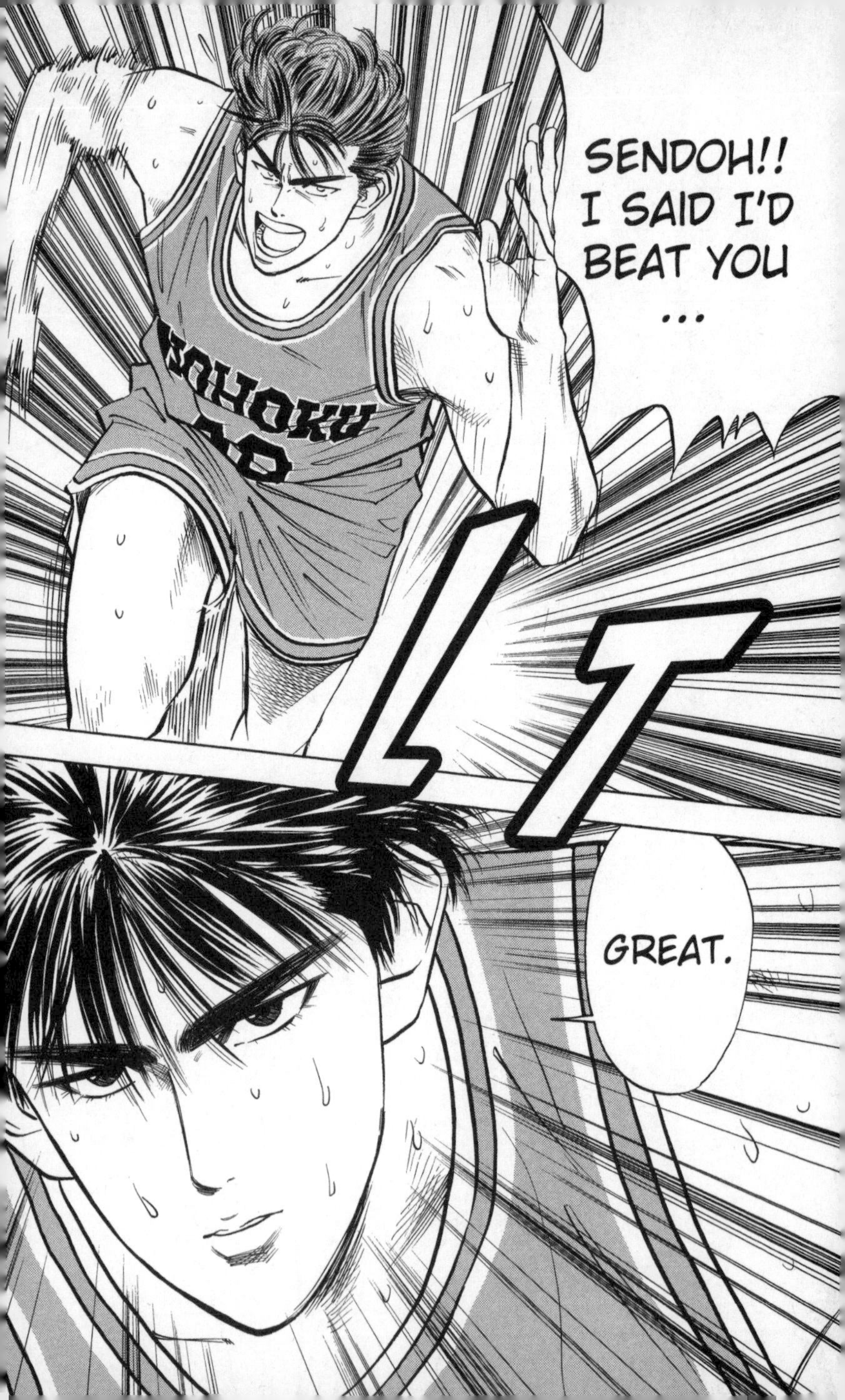
SENDOH!! I SAID I'D BEAT YOU ...
LT
GREAT.

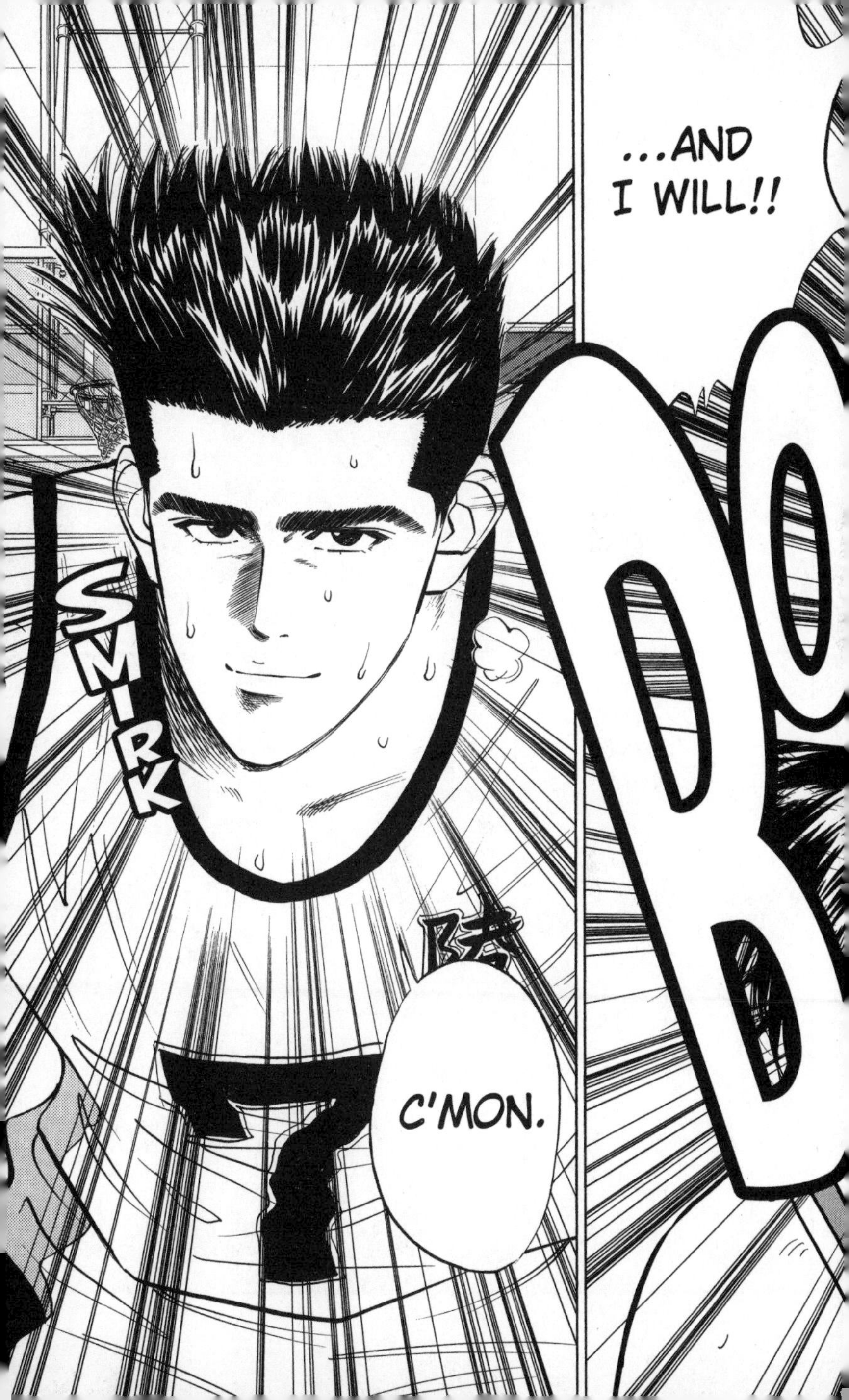
...AND I WILL!!
BO
SMIRK
C'MON.

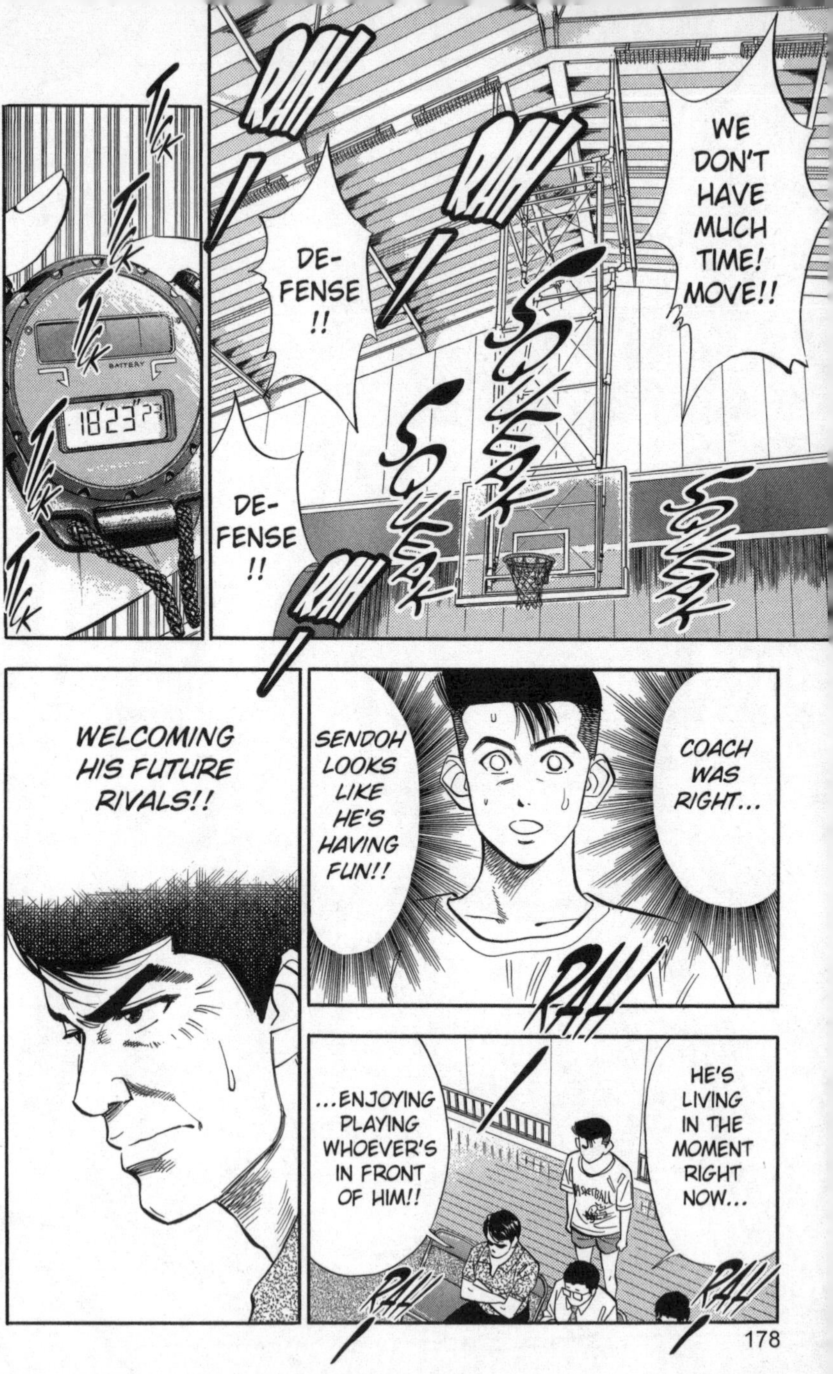
WE DON'T HAVE MUCH TIME! MOVE!!
RAH!
RAH!
SQUEAK
DE-FENSE!!
SQUEAK
DE-FENSE!!
RAH!
SQUEAK
TICK
TICK
TICK
TICK
TICK
BATTERY
COACH WAS RIGHT...
SENDOH LOOKS LIKE HE'S HAVING FUN!!
RAH!
HE'S LIVING IN THE MOMENT RIGHT NOW...
...ENJOYING PLAYING WHOEVER'S IN FRONT OF HIM!!
RAH!
RAH!
WELCOMING HIS FUTURE RIVALS!!

READ THIS WAY

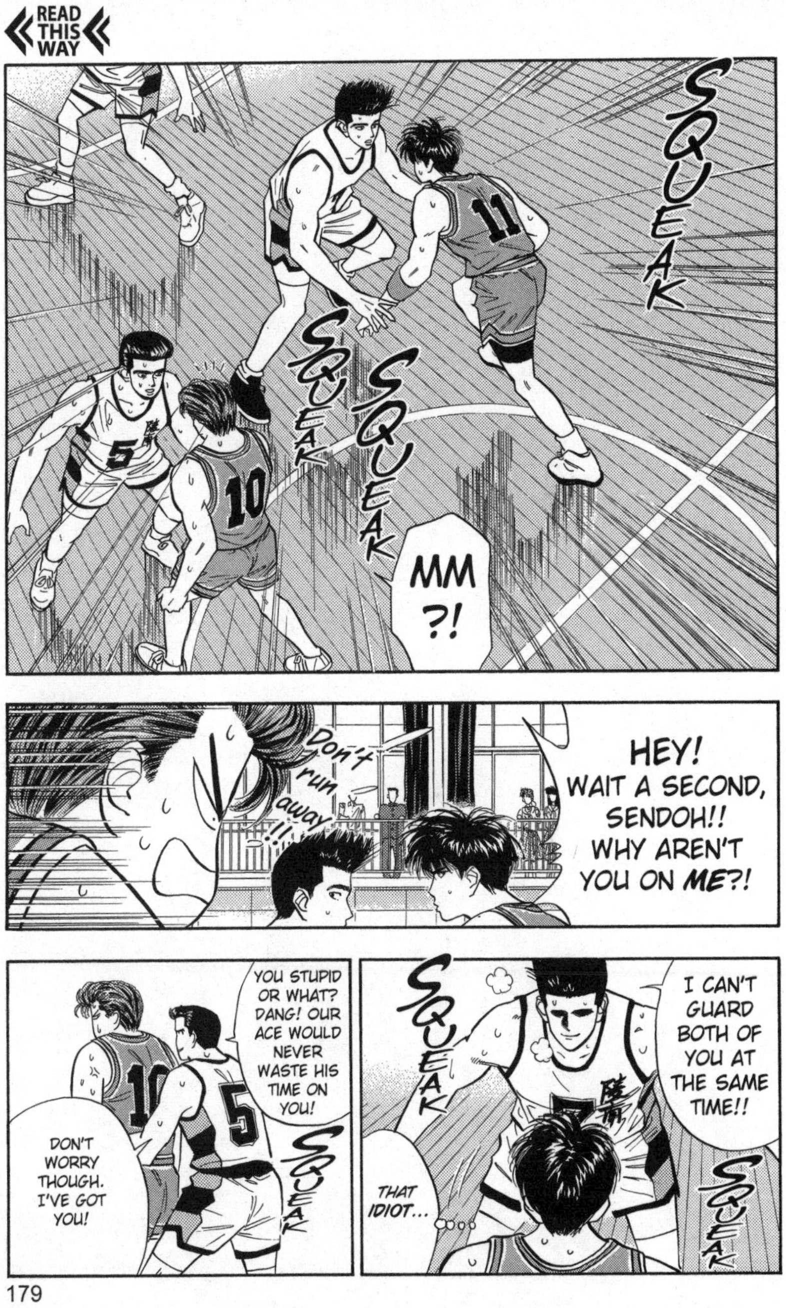
SQUEAK
SQUEAK
SQUEAK
MM ?!
HEY! WAIT A SECOND, SENDOH!! WHY AREN'T YOU ON *ME*?!
Don't run away!!
I CAN'T GUARD BOTH OF YOU AT THE SAME TIME!!
SQUEAK
SQUEAK
THAT IDIOT...
YOU STUPID OR WHAT? DANG! OUR ACE WOULD NEVER WASTE HIS TIME ON YOU!
SQUEAK
DON'T WORRY THOUGH. I'VE GOT YOU!

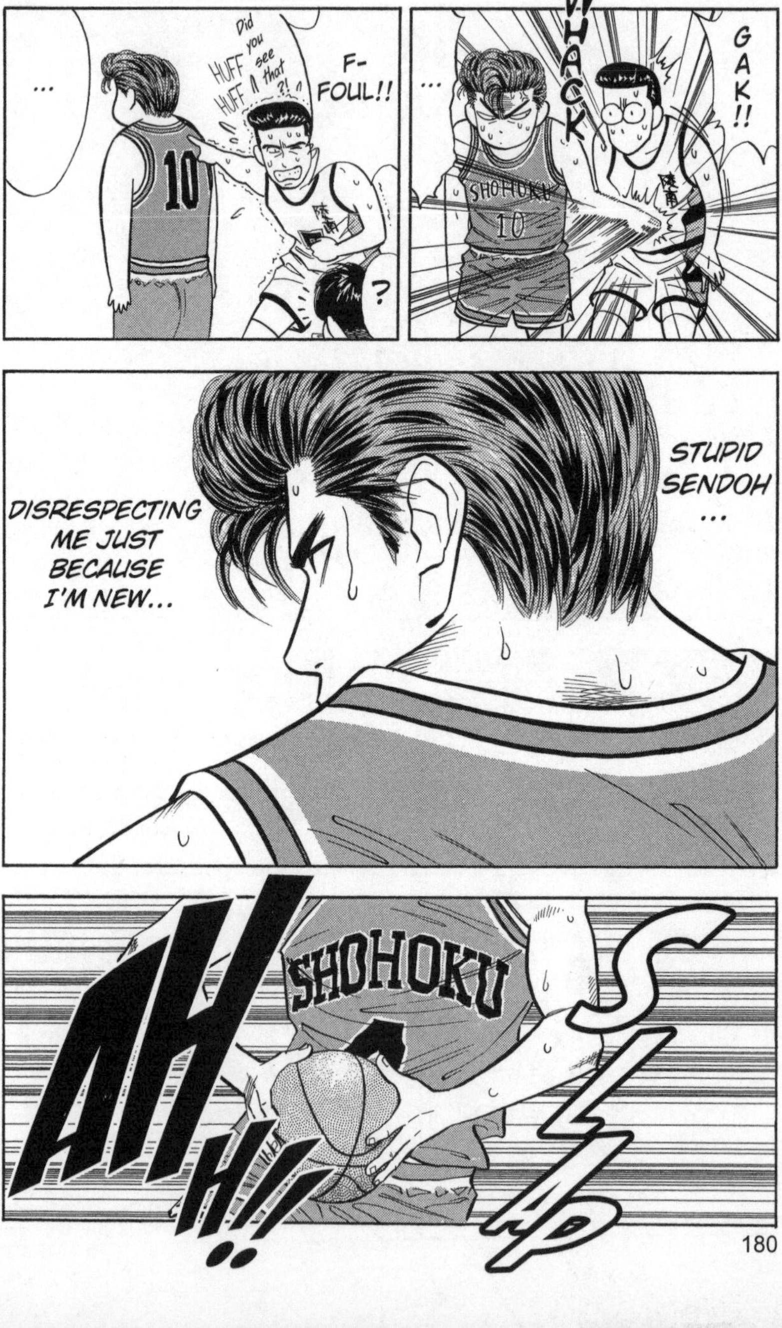
...
WHACK
GAK!!
...
Did you see that?!
HUFF HUFF
F-FOUL!!
?
STUPID SENDOH...
DISRESPECTING ME JUST BECAUSE I'M NEW...
SLIP
AHH!!

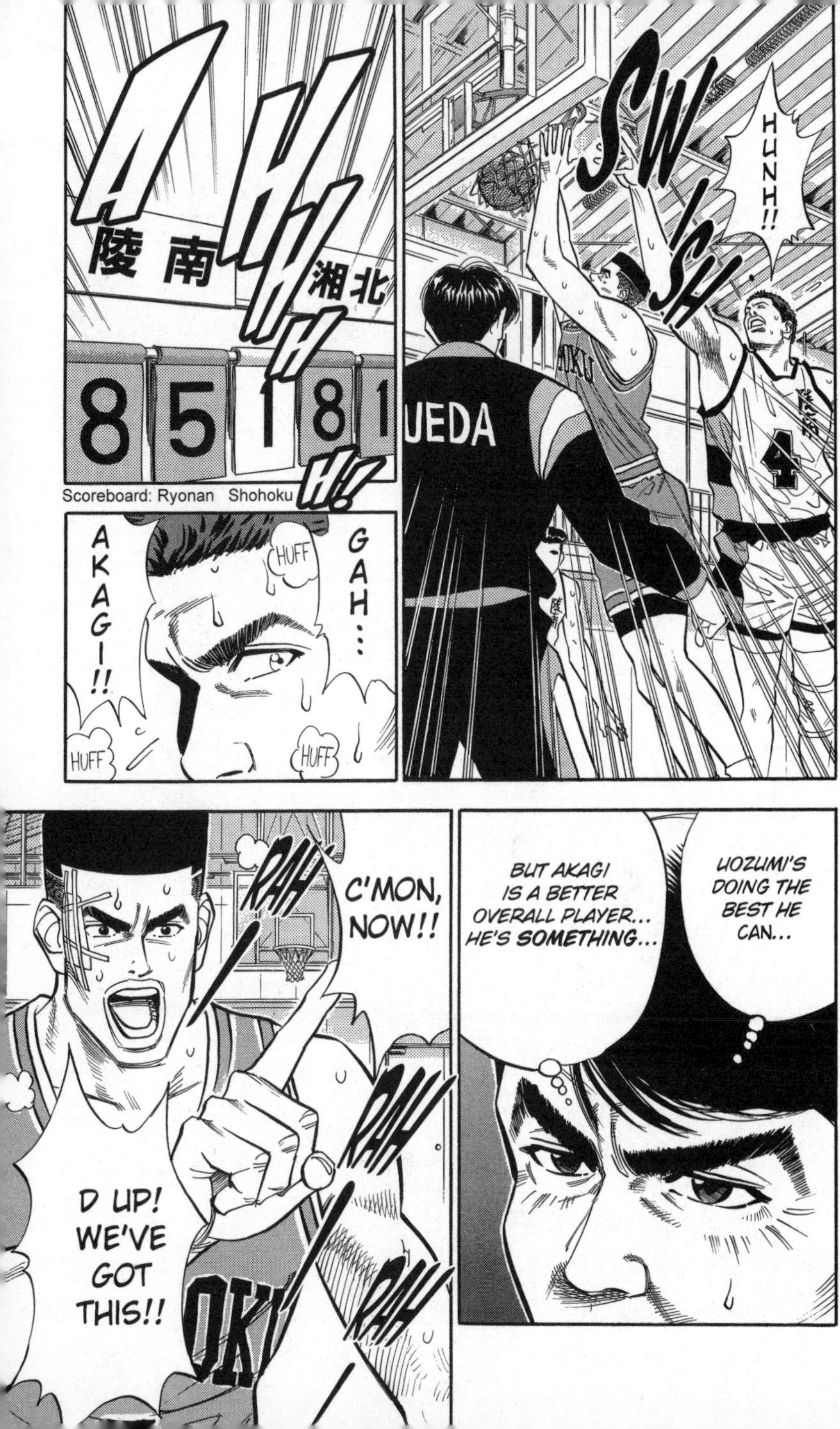
SWISH
HUNH!!
UEDA
AHHHHH!!
陵南
湘北
85
81
Scoreboard: Ryonan Shohoku
GAH...
AKAGI!!
HUFF
HUFF
HUFF
UOZUMI'S DOING THE BEST HE CAN...
BUT AKAGI IS A BETTER OVERALL PLAYER... HE'S **SOMETHING**...
C'MON, NOW!!
RAH
RAH
RAH
D UP! WE'VE GOT THIS!!
OK

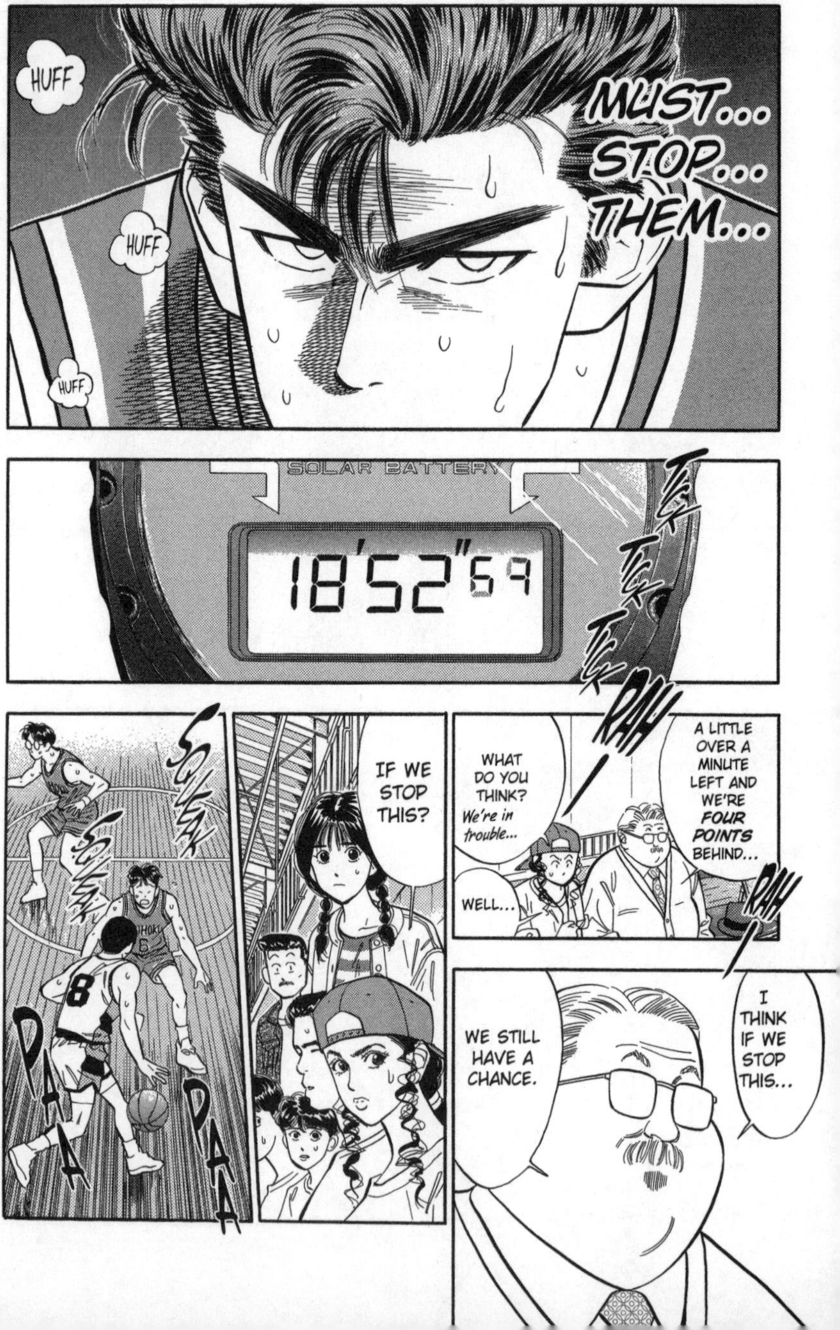

HUFF
HUFF
HUFF
MUST... STOP... THEM...
SOLAR BATTERY
18'52"69
TICK TICK TICK
RAH
A LITTLE OVER A MINUTE LEFT AND WE'RE FOUR POINTS BEHIND...
WHAT DO YOU THINK? We're in trouble...
WELL...
RAH
I THINK IF WE STOP THIS...
WE STILL HAVE A CHANCE.
IF WE STOP THIS?
SQUEAK
SQUEAK
PA PA
PA PA

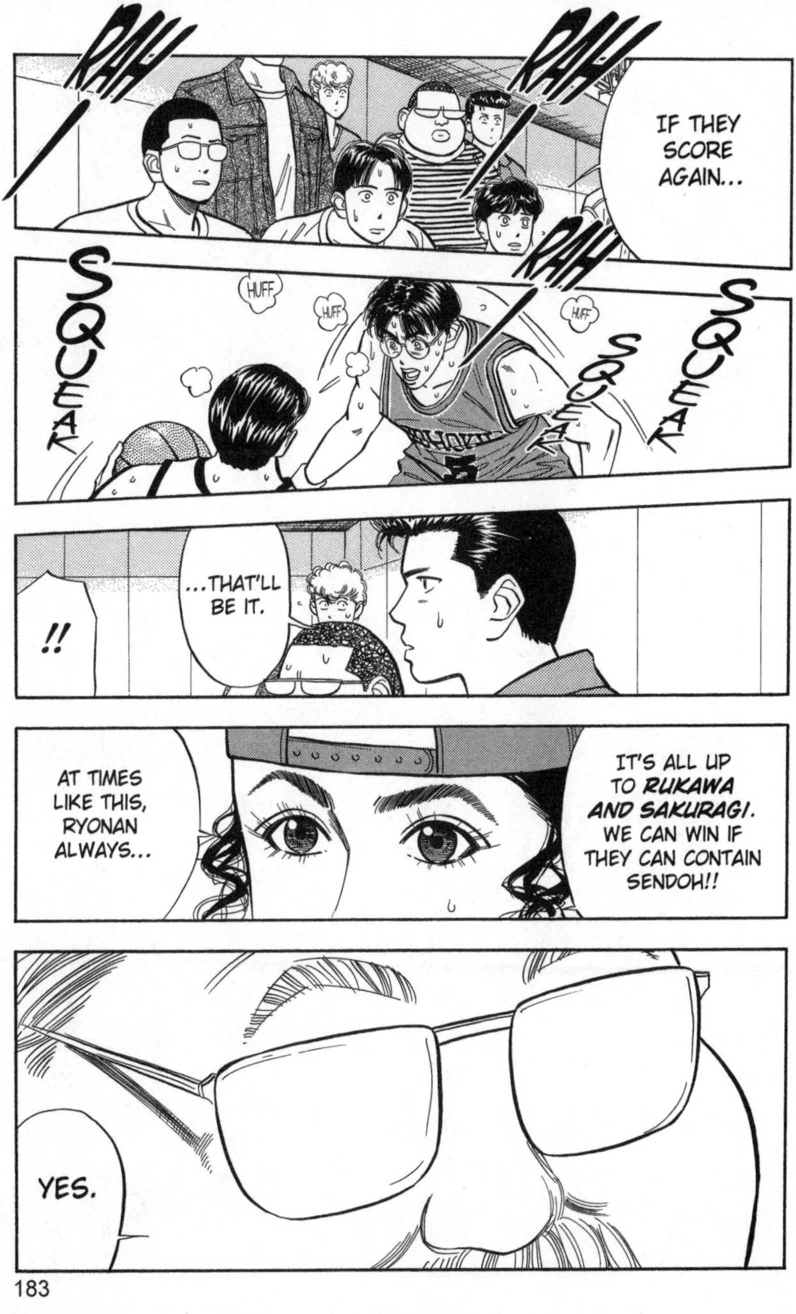
RAH!
IF THEY SCORE AGAIN...
RAH!
RAH!
SQUEAK
SQUEAK
HUFF
HUFF
HUFF
SQUEAK
...THAT'LL BE IT.
!!
IT'S ALL UP TO ***RUKAWA AND SAKURAGI***. WE CAN WIN IF THEY CAN CONTAIN SENDOH!!
AT TIMES LIKE THIS, RYONAN ALWAYS...
YES.

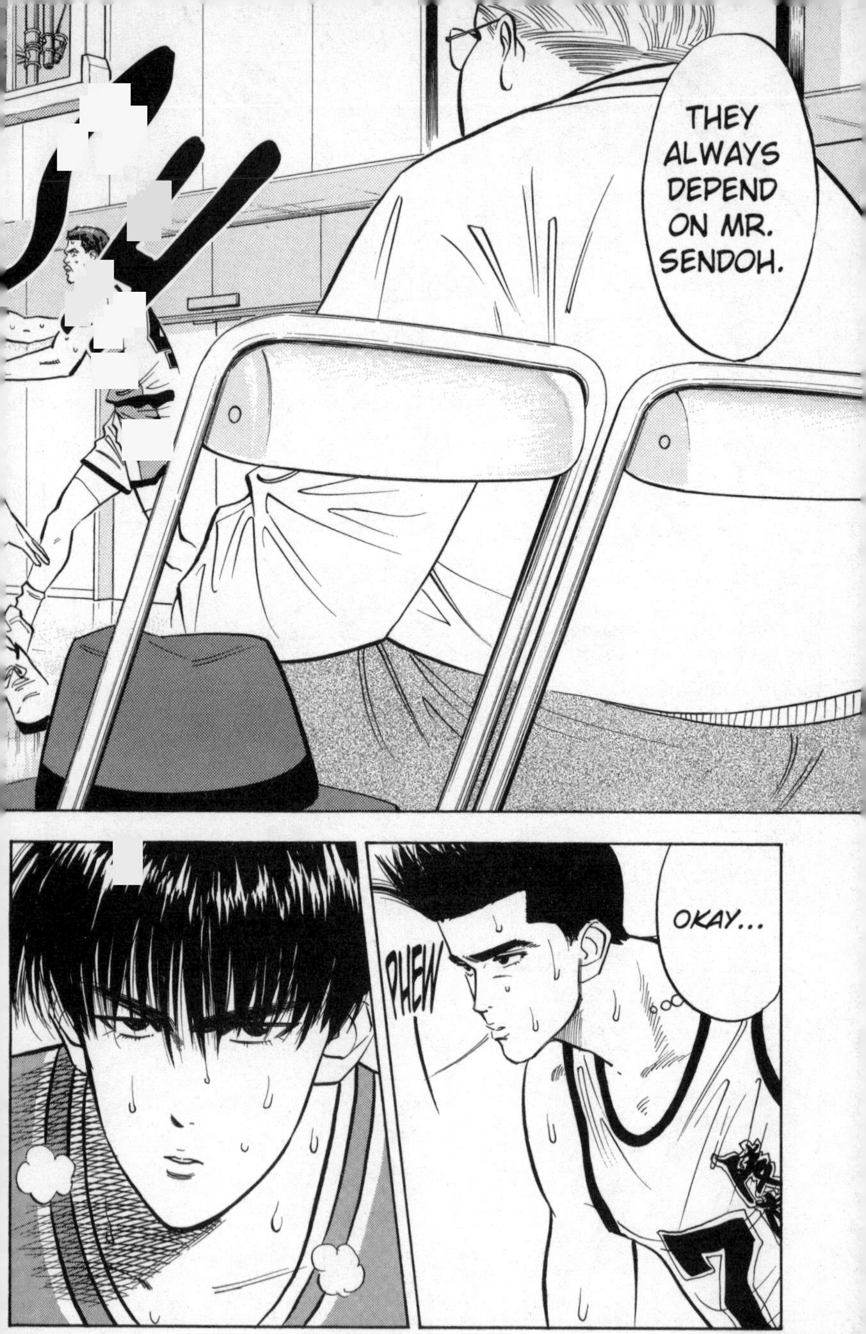
THEY ALWAYS DEPEND ON MR. SENDOH.
OKAY...
PHEW

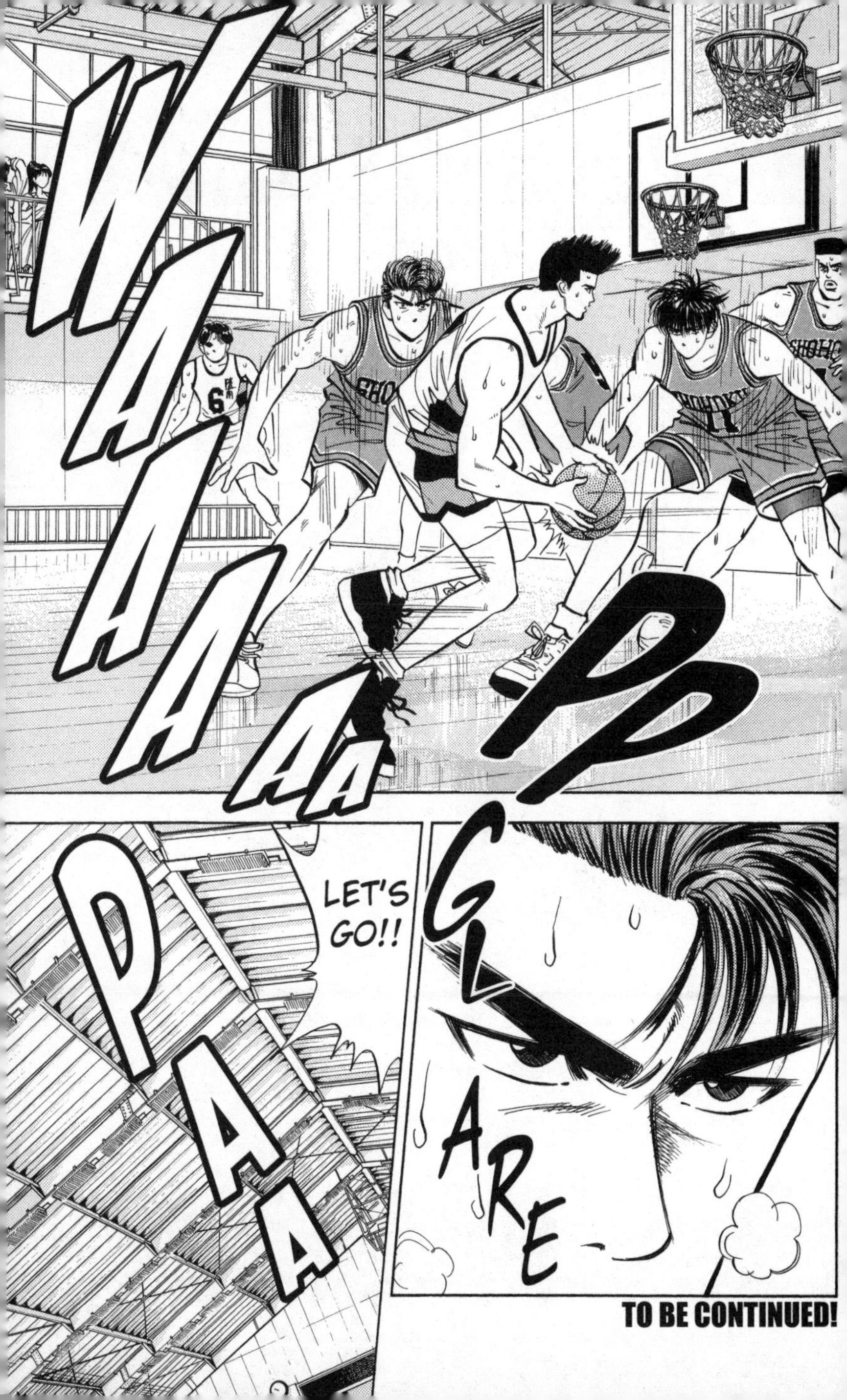
WAAAAA
PP
GLARE
LET'S GO!!
PAAA

TO BE CONTINUED!

Coming Next Volume

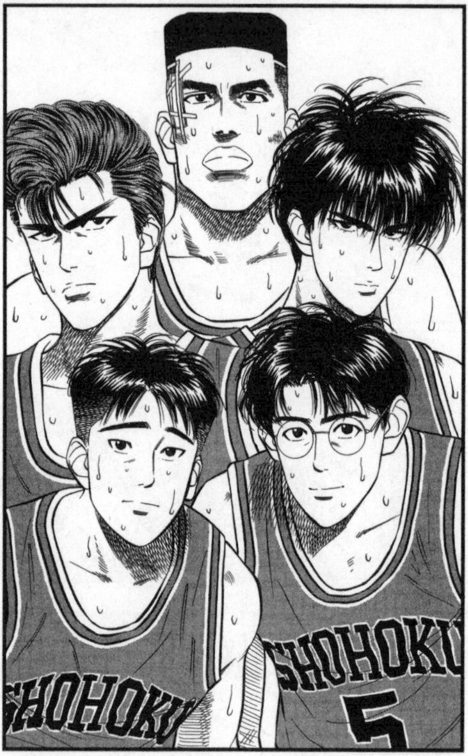
SHOHOKU
SHOHOKU
5

Time is winding down in Shohoku's practice game against Ryonan, and Hanamichi's boys still trail by four points! Ryonan knows that their ace Sendoh is capable of putting the final nail in Shohoku's coffin, but after Hanamichi pulls off a clutch turnover, anything seems possible. He's come a long way in a very short amount of time, but are Hanamichi's natural talents enough to stop a phenom of Sendoh's caliber?

ON SALE NOW

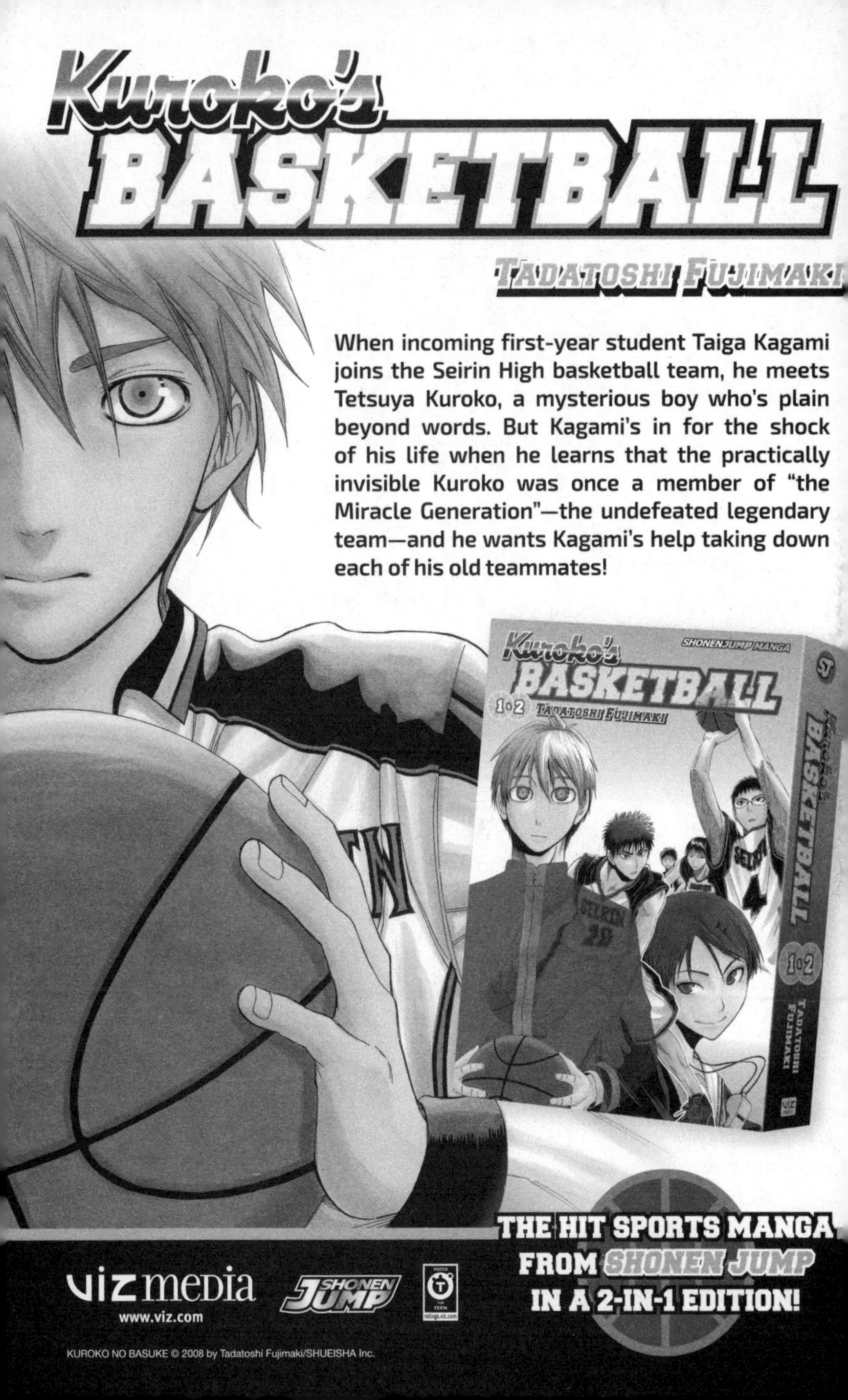
Kuroko's BASKETBALL
TADATOSHI FUJIMAKI
When incoming first-year student Taiga Kagami joins the Seirin High basketball team, he meets Tetsuya Kuroko, a mysterious boy who's plain beyond words. But Kagami's in for the shock of his life when he learns that the practically invisible Kuroko was once a member of "the Miracle Generation"—the undefeated legendary team—and he wants Kagami's help taking down each of his old teammates!
Kuroko's BASKETBALL
SHONEN JUMP MANGA
1•2 TADATOSHI FUJIMAKI
THE HIT SPORTS MANGA FROM SHONEN JUMP IN A 2-IN-1 EDITION!
viz media
www.viz.com
SHONEN JUMP
RATED T TEEN
ratings.viz.com
KUROKO NO BASUKE © 2008 by Tadatoshi Fujimaki/SHUEISHA Inc.

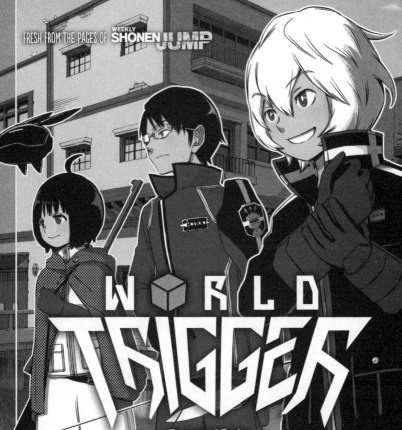

WORLD TRIGGER

Story and Art by
DAISUKE ASHIHARA

DESTROY THY NEIGHBOR!

A gate to another dimension has burst open, and invincible monsters called Neighbors invade Earth. Osamu Mikumo may not be the best among the elite warriors who co-opt other-dimensional technology to fight back, but along with his Neighbor friend Yuma, he'll do whatever it takes to defend life on Earth as we know it.

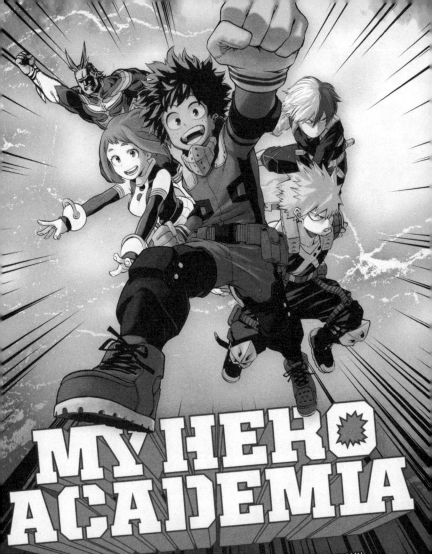

THE BEST SELLING MANGA SERIES IN THE WORLD!

ONE PIECE

Story & Art by EIICHIRO ODA

As a child, **Monkey D. Luffy** was inspired to become a pirate by listening to the tales of the buccaneer "Red-Haired" Shanks. But Luffy's life changed when he accidentally ate the Gum-Gum Devil Fruit and gained the power to stretch like rubber...at the cost of never being able to swim again! Years later, still vowing to become the king of the pirates, Luffy sets out on his adventure in search of the legendary "One Piece," said to be the greatest treasure in the world...

You're Reading in the Wrong Direction!!

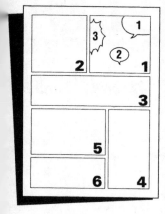

Whoops! Guess what? You're starting at the wrong end of the comic!

...It's true! In keeping with the original Japanese format, **Slam Dunk** is meant to be read from right to left, starting in the upper-right corner.

Unlike English, which is read from left to right, Japanese is read from right to left, meaning that action, sound effects and word-balloon order are completely reversed... something which can make readers unfamiliar with Japanese feel pretty backwards themselves. For this reason, manga or Japanese comics published in the U.S. in English have sometimes been published "flopped"—that is, printed in exact reverse order, as though seen from the other side of a mirror.

By flopping pages, U.S. publishers can avoid confusing readers, but the compromise is not without its downside. For one thing, a character in a flopped manga series who once wore in the original Japanese version a T-shirt emblazoned with "M A Y" (as in "the merry month of") now wears one which reads "Y A M"! Additionally, many manga creators in Japan are themselves unhappy with the process, as some feel the mirror-imaging of their art alters their original intentions.

We are proud to bring you Takehiko Inoue's **Slam Dunk** in the original unflopped format. For now, though, turn to the other side of the book and let the quest begin...!

–Editor

Now available in a 2-in-1 edition!

Maid-sama!

As if being student council president of a predominantly male high school isn't hard enough, Misaki Ayuzawa has a major secret—she works at a maid café after school! How is she supposed to keep her image of being ultrasmart, strong and overachieving intact once school heartthrob Takumi Usui discovers her double life?!

www.viz.com

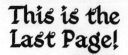

This is the Last Page!

It's true: In keeping with the original Japanese comic format, this book reads from right to left—so action, sound effects and word balloons are completely reversed. This preserves the orientation of the original artwork—plus, it's fun! Check out the diagram shown here to get the hang of things, and then turn to the other side of the book to get started!

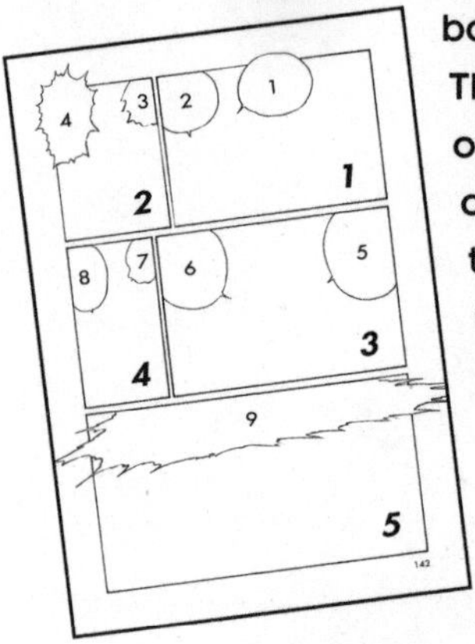
1
2
3
4
1
2
5
6
7
8
3
4
9
5
142

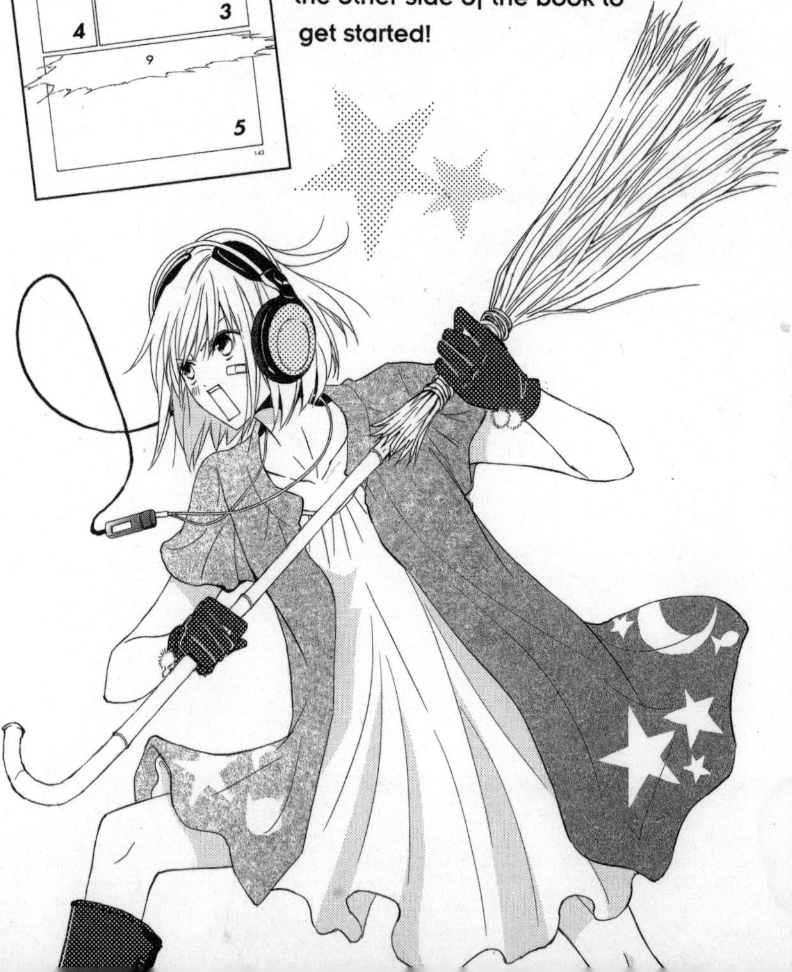